CHINESE AMERICAN TRANSNATIONAL POLITICS

THE ASIAN AMERICAN EXPERIENCE

Series Editor Roger Daniels

*A list of books in the series appears
at the back of this book.*

Chinese American Transnational Politics

HIM MARK LAI

Edited and with an Introduction by
MADELINE Y. HSU

UNIVERSITY OF ILLINOIS PRESS
URBANA, CHICAGO, AND SPRINGFIELD

Frontispiece: Him Mark Lai in a recording studio, 1985

Library of Congress Cataloging-in-Publication Data
Lai, H. Mark.
Chinese American transnational politics / Him Mark Lai ;
edited and with an introduction by Madeline Y. Hsu.
p.   cm. — (The Asian American experience)
Includes bibliographical references and index.
ISBN 978-0-252-03525-8 (cloth : alk. paper)
ISBN 978-0-252-07714-2 (pbk. : alk. paper)
1. Chinese Americans—Politics and government.
2. Chinese Americans—History. 3. United States—Relations—China.
4. China—Relations—United States. 5. Transnationalism. I. Title.
E184.C5L338   2010
973'.04951—dc22   2009041753

CONTENTS

FOREWORD

Roger Daniels

Him Mark Lai, born on Armistice Day, 1925, in San Francisco, is the only major historian of modern America without advanced academic training in history. As he explained to an interviewer in 2000, although many once-closed careers were beginning to open up for talented Chinese Americans in the 1940s, academic positions in the humanities were not. Even if there had been such opportunities, no college or university was interested in Chinese American history, his passion. So he was practical, pleased his parents by earning a degree in mechanical engineering, and went to work for the Bechtel Corporation in San Francisco. He pursued his passion, Chinese American history, in the evenings, on weekends, and during vacations.

The corpus of his previously published work is large and enormously varied. It includes works in both Chinese and English, popular essays in newspapers and local periodicals, bibliographic monographs, learned essays on Chinese American history, teaching materials on Chinese American history, and, toward the close of his career, collections of his essays in book form. Among the more important published volumes are two that demolished the canard that the Chinese immigrants had created no written records: *Chinese Newspapers Published in North America, 1854–1975* (Washington, D.C., 1977) and *A History Reclaimed: An Annotated Bibliography of Chinese Language Materials on the Chinese of America* (Los Angeles, 1986). Other notable works include one of the earliest histories of the American Chinese, *Outlines: History of the Chinese in America* (San Francisco, 1971), and a collection of his scholarly articles, *Becoming Chinese American: A History of Communities and Institutions* (Walnut Creek, Calif., 2004), which deals largely with San Francisco.

The essays in the present collection set forth with impressive detail and trenchant analysis interactions between Chinese America and China since the beginnings of formal relations between China and the United States in the late nineteenth century. A future volume of his essays in this series will be devoted to intellectual and social history.

Him Mark, although he worked assiduously in libraries and with various archives—often archives he himself had rescued—was never a cloistered scholar. He was very much a community historian, steeped in the lore of Chinese America and ready to share his knowledge. In addition, when the initial explosion of ethnic studies occurred at the end of the 1960s, he was invited to teach, at San Francisco State, the first course in Chinese American history ever taught in an American university. Later, when ethnic studies had become more established, he taught a similar course at the University of California, Berkeley.

The essays reprinted here have all been revised and updated for this volume. They show us a senior historian, in full command of his material, making a valedictory summary of a history he was the first to explicate properly.

ACKNOWLEDGMENTS

From the editor: Roger Daniels first approached me at the 2004 Organization of American Historians conference in Boston with the idea of anthologizing Him Mark Lai's articles on politics and the press. This collection has taken longer than any of us anticipated, and I am deeply grateful to Roger and Laurie Matheson for their patience and continuing encouragement and support in seeing it through to completion. Others at the University of Illinois Press include the project editor, Angela Burton, and particularly the copyeditor, Sue Breckenridge, who forged a path through Him Mark's complicated notes and the thicket of personal and organizational names that appear in multiple languages and Romanization systems. Two graduate student assistants undertook with diligence the tedious challenges of data entry and recovery on a number of fronts—my thanks to Dana Nakano at San Francisco State University and Anju Reejhsinghani at the University of Texas at Austin. My appreciation as well for Erika Lee and Mae Ngai who checked and made additions for the bibliography of suggested English-language readings and for Judy Yung, Sue Lee, and Ruthanne Lum McCunn who located the images of Him Mark.

Editor's note: Him Mark Lai passed away on May 21, 2009, leaving an enormous crater at the heart of Chinese American history. The text that follows is as delivered by him to the press, but he did not have the opportunity to address the copyeditor's queries. In particular, Him Mark conducted extensive online research in recent years to take advantage of information newly available from the PRC. Many of these web addresses, unfortunately, are no longer current and I have been unable in most instances to provide updated ones.

CHINESE AMERICAN
TRANSNATIONAL POLITICS

Him Mark Lai and the Politics of Chinese America

Madeline Y. Hsu

When, and if, most people think of a historian, they imagine a stoop-shouldered old man peering nearsightedly at musty, dusty, old tomes. Despite the small kernels of truth engrained in this image, it fails to convey the dedication and occasional bravery required of scholars who use their painstaking research to recover and recount the stories of forgotten peoples and unpopular truths. It requires genuine courage to write about subjects and from perspectives—such as that of women and peoples of color and the poor—that society wishes to overlook. In some instances, state governments have intervened to wield their considerable authority to protect the status quo by silencing such dissenting narratives. In times of war, when even questioning official accounts could be interpreted as enemy action, the risks multiply. Scholars who write about the Chinese in the United States face particular dangers, for their subjects are physically marked with ancestry from a country that figures in the American mind as an impossibly populous, fundamentally different, and largely hostile place. Too often, regardless of their place of birth, citizenship, or cultural affiliations, by virtue of being in America, ethnic Chinese are seen as threats. In this introduction, I explore the difficulties Chinese Americans have faced in trying to reconcile their multiple, seemingly incompatible heritages, and the battles waged by the pioneering scholar Him Mark Lai, who "legitimated" the study of their minority realities.[1]

Despite prevailing images of Chinese Americans as model minorities, such relatively benign perceptions date back only to the mid-1960s, when the sociologist William Petersen first articulated the qualities of this group in "Success Story, Japanese-American Style," which appeared in a 1966 issue of the *New York Times Magazine* and was quickly extended to include Chinese in a *U.S. News and World Report* article that appeared later that same year.[2] Other articles followed and reached a virtual crescendo during the mid-1980s with pieces such as *Fortune*'s "America's Super Minority" that trumpeted the educational and economic success of "Asian immigrants, their children, and their grandchildren" in "crowd[ing] America's top universities" and "tower[ing] above the rest of the population in both dollars and sense."[3] A chorus of national publications such as *Time,* the *New Republic,* and *Newsweek* celebrated the immigrant success stories of a once ostracized group that had become "Those Asian-American Whiz Kids."[4] This celebration of achievements arrived, however, only after more than a century of institutionalized hostility had systematically confined Asians to the margins of American life in terms of employment options, immigration and citizenship, voting rights, residential choices, and marriage options. For the bulk of their history, Asians have been considered and treated as intrinsically un-American.

According to the historian Mae Ngai, "two major elements of twentieth-century American racial ideology evolved from the genealogy of the racial requirement to citizenship: the legal definition of 'white' and the rule of racial inassimilability."[5] In the second year of the American Republic, Congress had already passed legislation that defined Asians as racially incompatible. The Nationality Act of 1790 restricted the right to citizenship by naturalization to free *white* persons. Chinese, Japanese, and Asian Indian people all failed in their court challenges to this racial criterion for citizenship, which would not be lifted until 1943 when America's World War II alliance with China forced Congress to support its claims of friendship by finally permitting members of the Chinese race to gain naturalization rights. This late-eighteenth-century racialization of Asians as unassimilable echoed in the late-nineteenth-century passage of America's earliest immigration laws.

Congress's first decisions to impose controls on the United States' borders were based on widespread beliefs that Chinese people constituted a "yellow peril" that would overwhelm and destroy the civilization of white European Americans unless their numbers were restricted. The Chinese Exclusion Laws (1882–1943) defined Chinese by race and attempted to severely limit their presence in the country. The laws permitted entry to only six strictly defined categories, such as merchants, diplomats, and students. After 1892 the laws also required all Chinese to carry Certificates of Residence or be liable for deportation. Chinese people became the first targets of federal attempts to enforce immigration restrictions and to consistently frustrate these efforts through sophisticated systems of immigration fraud. As such, they confronted constant immigration bureau hostility and harassment as suspected lawbreakers and criminals. The racialization of Chinese as illegal, unassimilable aliens extended to American-born generations, for birthright citizens of Asian ancestry "remained subject to enormous cultural denial by the mainstream of American society, which regarded 'Asian' and 'America' as mutually exclusive concepts."[6]

Systematic discrimination against Chinese Americans extended far beyond such border controls to their daily lives within the United States. By the 1890s, whether they were immigrant or American-born, Chinese could find employment primarily in the dead-end fields of laundries, restaurants, Chinatown stores, and domestic service. Most lived in clearly demarcated urban ghettoes. Finding more permanent purchase on American soil by establishing families was difficult, because laws inhibited the migration of Chinese women and prohibited miscegenation. Through the 1920s and 1930s, America's rejection of Chinese people forced even the growing ranks of American-born Chinese to look toward China for marriage and families, retirement plans, and political involvements. The community that resulted was predominantly male, poorly acculturated, and preoccupied with Chinese affairs, thereby confirming stereotypes of Chinese people as intrinsically foreign. Although second- and third-generation Chinese Americans held American citizenship by birth and were better educated and more acculturated, they were unable to escape the employment and residential ghettoes imposed on their immigrant parents and grandparents. Many felt trapped between the American and Chinese worlds, because they did not really belong in either.[7]

World War II and the cold war complicated this already difficult position. Before World War II, Chinese were primarily a domestic concern for the United States, which focused on purifying the nation of incompatible persons. Over the course of World War II, however, foreign policy concerns gained urgency, as the importance of fostering wartime alliances led the United States to emphasize "America as a racially, religiously, and culturally diverse nation."[8] To bolster this new emphasis on racial integration rather than exclusion, Congress began abolishing more than a century and a half of laws that had segregated employment, residence, voting rights, and marriage. According to Christina Klein, "these legal reforms allow us to see the double meaning of integration in the postwar period: the domestic project of integrating Asian and African Americans within the United States was intimately bound up with the international project of integrating the decolonizing nations into the capitalist 'free world' order."[9] As America turned its attention to a global rather than domestic stage, it sought to enfold more nations and more peoples into its political, economic, and social systems. In this reordering of American political agendas, and thus society and national culture, Asians moved from being unassimilable aliens to become model minorities whose successes exemplified the integrating powers of the American nation.

As a 1947 graduate in engineering from the University of California, Berkeley, and thirty-one-year employee of the Bechtel Corporation, the American-born Him Mark Lai was part of the earliest generation of Asians permitted to embark on what would become known as the model minority path. Although far from being the first Chinese student to graduate from an American university (an honor held by Yung Wing, who graduated from Yale University in 1854), he was among the earliest to gain professional employment commensurate with his educational credentials. In contrast to the experiences of their exclusion-era counterparts, after World War II the diminishing of discriminatory conditions permitted college-educated Chinese Americans of Him Mark Lai's generation to gain white-collar and professional careers and also purchase homes outside of Chinatown. For a community long ostracized as "coolies" and "rat-eaters" and confined to crowded, urban ghettoes, it was a considerable achievement.

Grateful for their new levels of prosperity and acceptance, many Chinese Americans basked in the seeming equality that they had gained and celebrated the advantages of living in a democratic, capitalist nation. Such views were articulated most forcefully by the sociologist Rose Hum Lee, who claimed in her influential 1960 monograph, *The Chinese in the United States of America,* "this is the most auspicious time for the persons of Chinese ancestry to seek integration, because the social climate of the United States has changed since the end of World War II. Racial ancestry is no longer a barrier to full citizenship and social acceptance."[10] This idealistic view of race relations required that Chinese Americans acquiesce to the idea that the United States had indeed become a truly democratic society. In return for their political compliance, they would gain economic prosperity and the secure status of model minorities.[11]

Parallel to the doctrine of integration, however, ran the doctrine of containment. As described by Christina Klein, "containment and integration constituted the two ideological foundations of postwar foreign policy. . . . Containment held that . . . the expansion of communism anywhere in the world posed a direct threat to the U.S. share of world power."[12] In the case of Chinese Americans, the cold war offered not only the opportunity to integrate in unprecedented ways into the American mainstream, but also the considerable danger that they would be contained as potential agents representing the interests of Communist China. America's long history of considering Asians to be inimically foreign was cast into stark relief by the recent incarceration of over 120,000 Japanese Americans during World War II.

The cold war generated its own anxieties and excessive employment of government power in the name of national security. The McCarthy era's persecution of famous writers and intellectuals such as Dashiell Hammett resonate to this day. A lesser known story concerns the even greater vulnerability of Chinese Americans as the Communist threat posed by the immensely populated People's Republic of China (PRC) exacerbated concerns about the already uncomfortably foreign presence of Chinese living in the United States: "Domestic containment policies revived latent 'yellow peril' fears of a combined Chinese threat from both within and outside the nation."[13] While the Chinese could now claim a place in America if they embraced democratic and capitalist ideologies and the idea of America as a truly multiracial society, any divergence from these norms was threatening. Under such conditions, even to suggest that the PRC had legitimate claim to being China's government, or to maintain contact with relatives there was considered politically suspect.

The situation of Chinese Americans was complicated by the reality that many were immigrants who had entered the United States fraudulently in order to circumvent the highly restrictive exclusion laws. Although most pursued highly ordered and law-abiding lives—regularly paying taxes and serving in the U.S. military during World War II—they had only recently gained naturalization rights and the protections of citizenship status. When Chinese Americans fell under government suspicion for leftist activities or sympathies, they could not only be investigated and jailed but also deported for political deviance. As recounted in Renqiu Yu's *To Save China, To Save Ourselves*, the leftist Chinese Hand Laundry Alliance disappeared in the 1950s, as much of its leadership was cast out of the United States only to meet persecution and sometimes death in China. The most notable deportee was the aerodynamicist Qian Xuesun, who had helped to pioneer America's space program as director of the Jet Propulsion Laboratories. Cold war hysteria led to accusations that he was a Communist despite his recent application for American citizenship and the close ties between his wife's family and the Nationalists. After five years of imprisonment and constant FBI surveillance, Qian was deported in 1955 to the PRC, where he pioneered China's first missile institute.[14] Many more Chinese Americans remained in the United States but suffered constant FBI scrutiny and persecution. Tung-pok Chin, a laundry man and occasional writer for the leftist newspaper *China Daily News*, vividly described how even his children received visits from FBI agents while in school, on top of the constant surveillance of his laundry premises.[15]

Chinese Americans faced the scrutiny not only of the American government but of the "free" Chinese one as well. The Kuomintang had been the United States' ally during World War II but had retreated to the island of Taiwan after losing the Chinese mainland to the Communists. This seemingly inexplicable defeat at the hands of Mao Zedong's bedraggled troops exacerbated American fears of communism. The earliest victims of the McCarthy era were members of the Dixie Mission, U.S. government observers who had visited Mao in his wartime headquarters at Yan'an and analyzed accurately the potential of the Chinese Communist Party to lead China. In the hardening lines of wartime confrontation, anybody who was "soft" on communism could be accused of helping the enemy, alleged betrayals for which careers were destroyed.

Cold war exigencies also led the United States to defend Taiwan from Communist attack and to insist that the ousted KMT government on Taiwan hold China's seat in the United Nations. In their common war against communism, the U.S. government permitted the KMT's secret police to extend their reach into Chinese American communities, which were forced to uphold even stricter standards of orthodoxy by supporting the KMT's claim to represent China's legitimate government. Alternative agendas, such as attempts to further develop Chinese American community organizations and consciousness, met with hostility and suspicion. If the KMT held a more narrowly defined conception of correct belief and behavior, it was prepared to wield power more autocratically as in the case of Henry Liu, a journalist assassinated in 1984 in his Daly City, California home for having written an unauthorized biography of Taiwan's president, Chiang Ching-kuo.

And so, the cold war was a time of unprecedented acceptance but also considerable risk for Chinese Americans. Unlike most others of his generation, who relaxed into their educational and economic accomplishments and long-delayed acceptance into the American mainstream, Him Mark Lai chose to go against the grain. He participated in such leftist organizations as the student youth group Mun Ching [Chinese Democratic Youth League] and pursued his interests in Chinese current affairs by writing newspaper articles and hosting a radio show. He also developed his research into Chinese American history. His scholarship not only recovered the stories of a once excluded and vilified group, it also picked at the scab of America's discrimination against Chinese people.

During the 1950s and 1960s, Lai was more protected than other Chinese by the American citizenship he had acquired by birth in the United States in 1925. However, this did not stop the FBI from monitoring his activities and producing a two-and-a-half-inch-thick file. The U.S. government also targeted Lai's foreign-born wife, Laura. For ten years, the Lais as a couple could not travel outside the United States because Laura's passport had been confiscated.

Despite these dangers, and the daunting task of locating information about a group briefly mentioned in only a scattering of historical texts, Lai persevered in researching and writing about such key aspects of Chinese American life as politics, community organizations, the ethnic press, and transnational ties to China. This scholarship laid the foundation for a set of knowledge that was risky on many levels. It criticized American practices of democracy by laying bare the injustices and suffering of the Chinese exclusion era. Lai also underscored the ambiguous place of Chinese people in America, as their marginal status encouraged them to remain invested in Chinese political affairs—particularly during the painfully tumultuous decades leading up to the Communist victory of 1949. His exploration of both extremes of right and left in Chinese American politics acknowledged the existence of active Communists among Chinese Americans but also the occasional unpopularity and repressiveness of the KMT. Such scholarship contradicted cold war agendas of both integration and containment by revealing that Chinese residents had not always been welcome participants in a heterogeneous American nation and that many questioned whether the KMT actually represented the government of China and the Chinese people.

Lai's earliest historical writings appeared in *East/West, The Chinese American Journal* during the late 1960s. He brought together much of this research to teach the first class on Chinese American history at San Francisco State University with another community historian, Phillip Choy. Together with Thomas Chinn, they published this teaching guide as *A History of the Chinese in California: A Syllabus* in 1969.[16] Lai's first scholarly article appeared soon afterward, in a 1972 issue of the *Bulletin of Concerned Asian Scholars* under the title "A Historical Survey of Organizations of the Left Among the Chinese in America."[17] Over the course of more than thirty years, Lai revised and expanded his writing about this subject as changing political climates permitted greater acknowledgment of leftist activities and sensibilities along with access to previously confidential documents. With the official rapprochement of China and the United States during the 1970s and the end of the cold war and fall of the Soviet Union in the 1990s, it has become more possible to describe not only the idealism and shortcomings of Communist and leftist activists but also the persecution and suffering they endured as perceived enemies to the United States and the KMT.

Although a minority of Chinese Americans were actually leftists, their activities highlight the many forms of marginality experienced by their co-ethnics. Chinese American Communists struggled with the conflicted vortex of transnational loyalties and patterns of mobility that demanded their attention, such as the global agenda of the American Communist Party, their own nationalist concerns for China's survival and integrity, and Chinese American community politics and needs. Oftentimes they were not able, or permitted, to fulfill the obligations they felt to implement revolution and social change in so many arenas of Chinese American affairs. Lai's increasingly rich account of this constantly shifting group traces the troubled relationship between historical research and politics in such articles as "Historical Survey of the Chinese Left in America" (1976), "To Bring Forth a New China, to Build a Better America: The Chinese Marxist Left in America to the 1960s" (1992), and "The Chinese Marxist Left, Chinese Students and Scholars in America, and the New China: Mid-1940s to Mid-1950s" (2004).[18] This essay collection includes the most recent updating, "To Bring Forth a New China, to Build a Better America: Historical Notes on the Chinese Left in America." This area of Lai's research demonstrates his painstaking craft as a historian in tracking the activities and various guises of a group that is notoriously difficult to document and describe because of their constant disappearances from historical records—through travels to the Soviet Union and to China—but also through the use of pseudonyms and secret identities. With each revision, Lai gained fuller access to the geographic range of Chinese American Communist networking and publicized once secret identities and affiliations.

Lai illuminates the many risks faced by Chinese American leftists in the overview article that begins this collection, "China and the Chinese American Community: The Political Dimension" which first appeared in the 1999 issue of *Chinese America: History and Perspectives*. The history of the KMT in America underscores the double oppression experienced by Chinese Americans as described by Ling-chi Wang, community activist and professor of Ethnic Studies at the University of California, Berkeley: "The combination of racial oppression in America and the extraterritorial and repressive rule of the homeland government effectively placed the Chinese community in the United States under a structure of dual domination."[19] This article also reveals how Chinese Americans could function politically as both enemies and friends. Lai traces the convoluted course of China's twentieth-century experiments with modern government in the form of constitutional monarchies, fascism, federalism, militarism, regionalism, and communism, and the ways in which many of these political movements sought to enfold the Chinese in America into their causes. By claiming Chinese American energies and resources, at times with great success, these diasporic political organizations confirmed American Yellow Peril suspicions that Chinese were intrinsically foreign, unassimilable, and potential threats. However, when Chinese political agendas confirmed those of America's foreign policy goals, the result was an overlay of both American and Chinese influence over the Chinese American community. This confluence of priorities emerged during the 1930s with the rise of the KMT in an alliance that endured through the 1980s. During this era, American perceptions of the Chinese in their midst became markedly warmer, especially toward the well-connected, well-educated northern Chinese associated with the KMT and as exemplified by the Nobel Prize–winning scientists Chen Ning Yang and Tsung Dao Lee.

The essays offered in this collection demonstrate that the experiences of minorities are central to our understanding of America at large. Although Chinese Americans constituted only about 1 percent of the national population, their cold war experiences highlight how exigencies of global politics and domestic racism afflict the lives of immigrant and American-born populations alike. Him Mark Lai's scholarship also preserves the active and courageous struggle of such minority groups in claiming their share of America's promise. Our knowledge and understanding both of what makes the United States great, but also weak and tyrannical, are revealed in the pages of this book.

CHAPTER 1

China and the Chinese American Community: The Political Dimension

This essay surveys the impact political developments in China had on the Chinese American community and its evolving relationship to China between the nineteenth and twenty-first centuries. When immigrants settle abroad, they generally maintain an interest in homeland affairs and often retain some cultural, economic, social, and even political ties. As immigrants take root in their new homes over time, these ties attenuate and gradually become overshadowed by new interests and priorities. However, if other factors intervene to limit settlement and assimilation, homeland events may continue to play influential roles in the overseas communities for a lengthy period. This pattern can be found in many overseas Chinese communities but were not unique to the Chinese, for roughly analogous behaviors have been exhibited by many other immigrant groups worldwide.

The Tortuous Road toward Modernization

Late Imperial China: The Gold Rush until the 1890s

When Chinese immigrants first arrived and established new homes in the mid–nineteenth century, they brought along their language and customs. Most also continued to maintain close ties with their ancestral villages. In their new homes, Chinese developed institutions for mutual aid and protection. Some of these, such as native-place associations [*huiguan*], clan associations, and umbrella organizations like the Chinese Consolidated Benevolent Association (CCBA), were derived from and congruent with the traditional social organizational structures in China.[1] These groups tried to maintain amicable relations with authorities in China and their representatives in this country. Other organizational forms, such as the Triads and related secret societies, were derived from heterodox groups banned in China. Their ranks were augmented by refugees forced to flee imperial repression of such events as the Triad uprisings in the Pearl River Delta and the Taiping Rebellion of the 1850s and 1860s. These organizations exhibited antagonistic attitudes toward the reigning Qing dynasty (1644–1911) in China.

However, until 1878, for almost three decades after the settling of Chinese in the New World, China stationed no diplomatic representatives in America, nor had Chinese political parties pushing for changes in China been formed, much less begun seeking support from Chinese abroad. At this time, developments in China played only a minor role in New World Chinese communities either on the mainland or in Hawaii.

China's official presence in America began in 1878, when the Qing established a diplomatic mission in Washington, D.C., and a consulate in San Francisco, followed by ones in Honolulu in 1879 and New York in 1883. China had not yet promulgated a nationality law, but traditionally it had operated on the *jus sanguinis* principle that regarded anyone with Chinese blood as being Chinese citizens. Chinese diplomatic missions regarded all Chinese as imperial subjects and believed that it was their prerogative and obligation to provide leadership and guidance to the local Chinese, regardless of their place of nativity. The CCBA and *huiguan* were considered extensions of diplomatic services. Beginning in the 1880s, *huiguan* recruited titled scholars from China as presidents who traveled to America using diplomatic passports. Until the fall of the dynasty in 1911, merchants nominated to serve on the CCBA board of directors also had to be appointed officially by the Chinese consul in San Francisco.[2]

Community leaders also worked with Chinese officials on major community projects. When San Francisco Chinese planned a community-operated school and hospital during the 1880s, they first asked Chinese minister Zhang Yinhuan in Washington, D.C., for approval. It was the Chinese consul general Sun Shiyi who wrote to San Francisco merchants in 1907 to urge the forming of a Chinese Chamber of Commerce, which was finally founded in 1908, the same year Liang Qinggui conducted an official tour of various Chinese communities to encourage the establishment of community-operated Chinese-language schools.[3]

An important function of Chinese diplomatic missions was working with local Chinese residents to further the interests of the Chinese government. When natural disasters struck various parts of China, the consul would encourage merchants and organizations to contribute to relief efforts. For example, in 1882, 1889, 1905, and 1908 the Qing government gave awards to San Francisco traditionist organizations and honorary offices to individuals who contributed the most.[4] The active leadership of Chinese diplomatic officials in overseas community affairs has diminished over the years but continues to the present.

Reform and Revolutionary Movements

By the late nineteenth century, China's status as a sovereign nation had become increasingly precarious. Beginning with the first Opium War (1839–1942) and the Treaty of Nanjing (1842), imperial powers had seized more and more special privileges and concessions from China. They seized and occupied Chinese vassal states and border territories so that by the turn of the twentieth century, dismemberment of the ailing empire seemed a growing reality. Many Chinese, deeply concerned about whether the ancient civilization would survive, sought solutions to restore China's strength, national integrity, and international standing. This growing nationalism fueled activities relating to "national salvation" that spread out to sympathetic Chinese overseas, many of whom believed that a weak China was incapable of protecting their interests abroad. They longed for a strong national homeland that could help to improve their status. This hope would resonate time and again in the succeeding half century of activities among Chinese American and other Chinese communities abroad.

The Chinese in America had responded to threats to China since their first settlement. One of the earliest recorded instances occurred in 1885, when the prefect of Guangzhou (Canton) appealed for donations to the Guangdong defense budget during the war with France over Annam. The CCBAs of San Francisco and Victoria, British Columbia, responded by donating 14,500 and 3,600 yuan, respectively.[5] Although records are unavailable as to whether Guangdong authorities asked for funds during the Sino-Japanese conflict of 1894, China's defeats by France and Japan strengthened demands for change that eventually extended to the Chinese abroad. Newly organized political groups advocating revolution or reform in China were the chief campaigners for change among Chinese overseas.

Even before the Sino-Japanese War, one Sun Yat-sen had petitioned the Qing grand secretary Li Hongzhang that political reforms, not merely purchasing modern weaponry, were necessary to change China into a strong nation. Li ignored Sun's petition, which may have influenced Sun to decide that the corrupt and inept imperial government had to be replaced before China could become a strong nation. This goal was also interwoven with racial overtones, as the ruling Qing were members of an ethnic minority, the Manchus. After an abortive attempt at revolution in Guangdong, Sun left for Hawaii, where he recruited fellow Chinese to found the revolutionary organization Xingzhonghui [Revive China Society] in 1894 in Honolulu. This was succeeded by the Tongmenghui [Revolutionary Alliance], founded in Japan in 1905 by Sun Yat-sen. These revolutionary groups aimed to overthrow the rule of the Manchu Qing and establish a republic.

The rival reform group the Baohuanghui [Protect the Emperor Society], also known as the Chinese Empire Reform Association, had been founded by Kang Youwei in Victoria, British Columbia, in 1899. Kang, a former advisor to the young Emperor Guangxu, had guided him in implementing the Hundred Days Reform. The conservative Empress Dowager quashed this movement and placed Emperor Guangxu under house arrest while Kang fled overseas, where he campaigned for a parliamentary monarchy in which Guangxu would be restored to his throne. In 1906 the Baohuanghui was renamed the Chinese Constitutionalist Party.

These earliest modern political organizations were banned in China. However, taking their cues from the secret societies abroad that successfully defied imperial authorities,[6] they located branches outside the jurisdiction of the Chinese government and made plans for furthering their political programs in China by actively recruiting support from Chinese communities overseas. Both the revolutionary and reform movements established extensive worldwide networks headquartered in Hong Kong and Japan. The Baohuanghui had a total of thirty-seven branches in the United States around 1905, while the Tongmenghui had about twenty-seven branches by the time of the 1911 revolution.[7] The reformers and revolutionaries competed with each other, thereby splitting the community; the Baohuanghui recruited more moderate members, such as established merchants and traditional intellectuals, while the revolutionary movement attracted many small shopkeepers, workers, and younger intellectuals influenced by the West. The Triad Society (Chinese Freemasons), or Chee Kung Tong (CKT), was at first sympathetic to the Baohuanghui but by 1910 had become allies of the Tongmenghui. The reform and revolutionary groups often had tense or antagonistic relations with Qing diplomats, and their activities contributed to undermining the influence of the imperial government in the Chinese American community.

Party leaders often traveled to different branches in this far-flung network to rally support and raise funds. For example, Baohuanghui leader Liang Qichao paid Hawaii a lengthy visit and then traveled to Canada and the United States. The titular head of the Baohuanghui, Kang Youwei, followed soon afterward to visit Canada, the United States, and Mexico. Their rival Sun Yat-sen went to North America and Hawaii four different times between 1894 and 1911, recruiting supporters to overthrow the Qing. These political campaigns enabled the organizations to sink roots into the Chinese community in America. Their appeals to nationalism also conditioned Chinese in America to respond to developments in the Chinese nation as a whole rather than just being interested in specific regions such as Xinning (Taishan), Xiangshan (Zhongshan), or Nanhai counties. This national consciousness manifested in 1908, when Hong Kong Chinese boycotted Japanese shipping over Japanese demands that China apologize for the *Tatsu Maru* affair. In San Francisco the newly founded Chinese Chamber of Commerce cooperated by observing the boycott and passing a resolution levying a fine on any member who violated it.[8] This was the first of numerous occasions through the end of World War II when Chinese in America responded to Japanese threats to China's sovereignty.

Just after the turn of the twentieth century, the Baohuanghui, especially its Honolulu and San Francisco branches, actively gathered support for the 1905 boycott of American goods in China and some Chinese overseas communities to protest the U.S. exclusion laws. During this same period, it sponsored military schools headed by Homer Lea in more than two dozen American cities to train about 2,100 men for a military uprising in China intended to restore the Guangxu emperor to the throne, although the planned uprising never took place. Two clubs with Baohuanghui members left a more lasting legacy when they founded Honolulu's Mun Lun Chinese School in 1911. By 1936 this school had become the largest Chinese school in the United States, with 1,348 students. Not to be outdone, supporters of the rival Tongmenghui opened Wah Mun School a few days later, which became Honolulu's second-largest Chinese school. After 1928 it was known as the Chung Shan School.[9]

Each party also established newspapers in major Chinese communities. In San Francisco the Baohuanghui took over the existing *Chinese World*. Its other organs included Honolulu's *New China Press* (*Sun Chung Kwock Po;* founded 1900) and New York's *Chinese Reform News* (founded 1904). The Tongmenghui had Honolulu's *Liberty Press* (*Chee Yow Sun Bo;* founded 1908), San Francisco's *Young China Morning Post* (founded 1910), and New York's *Mun Hey Weekly* (founded 1915). Chee Kung Tong newspapers included San Francisco's *Chinese Free Press* (founded 1903), and Honolulu's *Kai Chee Sun Bo* (founded 1907), which later became *Hon Mun Po* (1912).[10] The objective of these journals was to propagate political programs and agendas. In so doing, they raised the level of political awareness among the Chinese Americans, starting an era in Chinese American journalism dominated by politics in China.

During the rise of the reform and revolutionary movements, Dick Chun in San Francisco led the formation of Native Sons of the Golden State (NSGS) in 1895 to fight for the civil rights of American-born Chinese. However, as only one-tenth of the entire Chinese population at the turn of the century was American born, their influence on community politics was negligible. Because they were also subject to American racism, many made common cause with the immigrant generation in identifying with China and participating in Chinese political movements. For example, in 1909 the NSGS English secretary Wong Bock You and Chinese secretary Won Hung Fei both became Tongmenghui members and later loyal followers of Sun Yat-sen.[11]

Early Years of the Republic

In 1911 the Qing regime quickly and quietly crumbled, and the Republic of China was established in 1912. The Tongmenghui merged with several small political parties to form the Kuomintang (KMT), or Chinese Nationalist League, later the Nationalist Party of China. The party gained a majority in the Republic's first parliament but soon found itself locked in a power struggle with the authoritarian first president, Yuan Shikai. An abortive attempt to overthrow Yuan in 1913 gave the president a pretext to ban the party. Many party activists fled to Japan to avoid arrest. There, the party regrouped under Sun Yat-sen's leadership.

In America the CCBA led the Chinese community to change the imperial dragon banner of the Qing to the republican flag with five horizontal bars. The Chinese in America who had entertained high expectations for the republican government opposed Yuan's usurpation of power. By this time the Baohuanghui had lost influence among overseas Chinese because of a series of internal scandals. Moreover, after the founding of the Republic it did not establish a party organization in China and played no significant role in China's political landscape. In the meantime, the Chee Kung Tong, erstwhile ally of the Tongmenghui, fell out with Sun Yat-sen when it was unable to register as a political party in China. Since neither the Baohuanghui nor the CKT were willing to rally opposition to the Yuan regime, this responsibility fell to the KMT, which had both the organization and zealous belief in this cause. In 1914 the San Francisco branch of the party founded Minguo Weichihui [Association to Maintain the Republic] with branches on the U.S. mainland and in Hawaii to solicit funds to finance anti-Yuan activities. KMT publications launched a barrage of vitriolic propaganda against Yuan. In 1914 KMT supporters caused a near riot when they invaded and broke up a CCBA meeting that was discussing whether to welcome a soon-to-arrive Yuan envoy to San Francisco. In late 1915 KMT assassins gunned down visiting Chinese journalist Huang Yuanyong, alleged to be a Yuan supporter, at San Francisco's Shanghai Low restaurant.[12]

In China the ambitious Yuan began making plans to become emperor. To secure foreign support, Yuan agreed to Japan's Twenty-one Demands in 1915, granting it concessions and rights in China. When these provisions became known, another round of Chinese American protests against Japanese aggression erupted. San Francisco merchants launched a boycott of Japanese goods and shipping. As no other shipping was available, they pooled resources to found the China Mail Steamship Company. The appearance of this first Chinese American–owned steamship line was a source of pride to the Chinese in America, who had long resented American society's low regard for the weak, nonindustrialized China.

In China, as Yuan made final preparations to claim the emperor's throne, revolts erupted throughout the nation. Yuan was forced to change his plans and died a disappointed old man shortly afterward, in June 1916. A succession of governments dominated by military strongmen came to power in Beijing (Peking). Warlords in other provinces challenged their authority, and China lapsed into civil war. In this time of crisis, the nation was again victimized by the powers. The Versailles Treaty of 1919 that ended World War I rewarded Japan with Germany's former concessions in China's Shandong Peninsula. This outrageous disregard for China's territorial sovereignty led angry students in Beijing to protest in the famous May Fourth Movement.[13] In America the KMT again led in forming the Chinese National Welfare Society to represent Chinese concerns in the Shandong question.

The Kuomintang Unifies China

In 1920 pro-KMT forces succeeded in capturing Guangzhou. The KMT established a military regime there in preparation for a Northern Expedition to unseat the Beijing regime and to unify China. Party headquarters sent agents to America to recruit support using party organs, street meetings, and mass demonstrations to step up attacks on the Beijing regime.[14]

In 1924 Sun Yat-sen's branch of the KMT held a party congress in Guangzhou that passed resolutions to form an alliance with the Soviet Union, accept Communist Party members into the KMT, and support the struggles of workers and peasants. The change encountered resistance from conservative elements within the party, which started separating into left and right factions even as final preparations were being made for the Northern Expedition.

In America a small activist group of leftists, whose key members included Qinghua (Tsinghua) University students attending American schools, joined the American Communist Party and were active in the KMT. By 1925 an open schism occurred in the KMT in America, with the San Francisco party organ *Young China* and important leaders in the General Branch in San Francisco supporting the Right or pro–Hu Hanmin Faction. The Left or pro–Wang Jingwei faction, led by the Seattle branch, convened a party congress in Los Angeles that formed a separate general branch in San Francisco and established another party organ, *Chinese Nationalist Daily of America* (*Kuo Min Yat Po*).

Within the American KMT, the "right" faction struck at the pro–Wang Jingwei faction by secretly contacting the Nanjing government to denounce members of the opposing group. The conflicts could be violent and target the wrong individuals. For example, Hu Shuying, an anti-Communist, pro–Chiang Kai-shek editor of the *Mun Hey* of New York and an officer of the New York sub-branch of the KMT, who had attended the party convention in Los Angeles, unknowingly was listed as a leftist. During a visit to his sick mother in China in June 1927, he was arrested in Shanghai and executed as an antiparty and antigovernment element.[15] In 1931 Wong Buck Hung (Huang Beihong), an officer in the pro–Wang Jingwei Honolulu newspaper *Liberty News*, was detained by the Shanghai police as a suspected Communist on the basis of information from the "right" KMT faction in Honolulu. Being more fortunate than Hu, he was released after seven days.[16] Others were out of reach of the Nanjing regime, but the Kuomintang "right" in the United States threatened the lives of some, while hired hoodlums beat up others.[17] The "right" faction also tried to suppress publication of *Kuo Min Yat Po* through the Chinese envoy in Washington, D.C.[18]

Amid the struggles, the KMT launched the Northern Expedition in 1926. KMT armies advancing northward defeated successive warlords. By fall of that year, KMT armies had captured the middle Yangzi River basin, and the national government at Guangzhou officially moved to Wuhan on January 1, 1927, with Wang Jingwei as the chairman. In April the KMT commander-in-chief, Chiang Kai-shek, ordered a bloody purge of the Left and established a rival government in Nanjing. By August of that year, the Wuhan regime had also expelled Communists and joined with the Nanjing government. The Communist Party in the meantime staged a military uprising at Nanchang against the Nanjing government but were forced to retreat to the Jiangxi Soviet, then embark on the Long March and take refuge in the far north of China around Yan'an.

With the reunification of China within reach, the KMT party branches in the United States tried to assert themselves as representing the ruling party of China. In 1927 an editorial appeared in *Young China,* the rightist KMT party organ in San Francisco, that criticized the traditional procedures and organizational structure of the CCBA. Leaders of the Ning Yung Association, the largest of the traditionist association members in the CCBA, charged that the wording was insulting and demanded a retraction and apology. Instead, *Young China* published yet another editorial that further exacerbated the situation, and the Ning Yung Association leaders, backed by a coalition of the KMT left faction and elements of the Baohuanghui and the Chee Kung Tong, organized a Sanfanshi Ningyang Huyituan [League to Protect the Good Name of County of the Ning Yung Association] that called for a boycott of the paper.[19]

In the midst of this action against *Young China,* the KMT in China launched the second stage of the Northern Expedition in April 1928 and began advancing into Shandong, where Western powers had handed over to Japan Germany's former concessions. On May 3 Japanese troops at Ji'nan opened fire at KMT troops. Five days later a Japanese bombardment inflicted more than eleven thousand casualties. When the Chinese American community received the news, it closed ranks to denounce Japanese aggression in China. The CCBA in San Francisco called an emergency meeting, during which Meizhou Kang-Ri Waijiao Houyuanhui [Association in America to Back Diplomatic Efforts Resisting Japan] was formed. With patriotic fervor permeating the meeting, the assemblage unanimously passed a resolution to replace the Beijing government's flag of five horizontal stripes with the "blue sky, white sun, and the entire ground are red" banner of the Nanjing government. Organizations in San Francisco and other cities soon followed CCBA's lead, although the KMT's political foes refused for several years to raise the new national flag. In 1929 the *Chinese World* continued to fly the old flag on Double Ten National Day, and as late as 1930 the Chee Kong Tong also hoisted the old flag at its convention.[20]

The Ning Yung Association boycott of *Young China,* however, continued a conflict that strained the newspaper's limited financial resources. Several mediation efforts by the CCBA and Frank Ching-Lun Lee, a New York–born deputy minister serving China's Foreign Ministry, all failed. Finally, in 1935 Guangdong governor Lin Yun'gai sent Huang Zicong, a mayor of Shantou who had some contacts among San Francisco Communist leaders from his service as principal at the Morning Bell School. In the meantime, Bing Kung Tong leader Wong Goon Dick, a loyal supporter of the Chiang Kai-shek government, also began discussions with Ning Yung Association leaders Lain Chan (Chen Dunpu) and Lee Shingting (Li Shengting), who were active in the Baohuanghui, and convinced them that the community should unite to deal with the continuing threat of Japanese aggression in China. The boycott was finally called off in August 1935.[21]

By that time, the Ning Yung Association had established thirteen branch associations and twenty-four corresponding sites all over the United States to implement the boycott. The KMT right faction learned from this bitter experience that ideologically the traditionist associations differed from the principles espoused by the KMT and were a force in the community that could not be trifled with. However, during the next few years and particularly the War of Resistance against Japan, the KMT was able to concentrate on recruiting important traditionist organization leaders into its fold.

The Nanjing Government (1928–1937)

The Nanjing regime was soon recognized by the United States and the Western powers as the legitimate government of a unified China. However, it faced opposition within China and among Chinese communities abroad. The regime ruthlessly sought to stamp out opposition through the extensive use of spies and informers to test the loyalty of individual KMT members. In the United States, the KMT right faction unsuccessfully tried to get the Chinese envoy in Washington, D.C., to take steps to suppress *Kuo Min Yat Po.* The existing party newspapers *Chinese Nationalist* in New York and *Liberty Press* in Honolulu remained sympathetic to the left faction, and so the right faction established the rival papers *Zhongguo Ribao* [Chinese Daily] in New York, *United Chinese News* in Honolulu, and the *San Min Morning Post* in Chicago. It also provided intelligence to the Nanjing government that established the basis for banning U.S. publications of political rivals from entering China.[22]

Some members of the KMT left faction worked with Communists who had been expelled from the KMT in America. Together they formed Meizhou Yonghu Zhongguo Gong-Nong Geming Da Tongmeng [Grand Alliance Supporting the Chinese Workers and Peasants Revolution] to express support for the Chinese revolution. In 1929 it reorganized as the All-America Alliance of Chinese Anti-Imperialists (AAACAI) to "lead and organize Chinese in the Americas in the struggle for revolution and against imperialism." The national leader of the group was Y. Y. Hsu, who had been one of the Qinghua University students. The AAACAI worked closely with the American Communist Party and founded the weekly *Chinese Vanguard* in New York around 1930, which became the key voice of opposition from the Left. The KMT Right's response to these published attacks was to encourage police and immigration authorities to harass and deport Communists and other members of the Left.[23]

The KMT government was also attacked from the right by the Baohuanghui and the Chee Kung Tong. Wu Zhuang (Wu Xianzi) was one of the most widely read of these critics as head of the Baohuanghui's overseas organizations. In 1928 Wu became chief editor of the party's most important organ in America, San Francisco's *Chinese World.* During his eight-year term, Wu's sharp commentaries

condemning KMT policies were such an irritant that the KMT tried unsuccessfully to have him deported. Another critic, Cui Tongyue, editor at the Chee Kong
Tong organ *Morning Sun,* was not so fortunate. After Cui published an editorial
critical of the Nationalist government's consul general in San Francisco in 1931,
five men invaded the Chinese school where Cui was a teacher and gave him a
beating.[24] Notwithstanding these acts of resistance and defiance, these foes of the
KMT on the right, with their political allies in China defeated, eventually had to
reconcile themselves to political realities.

With the national government under its control, the KMT looked forward
to reestablishing the leadership role and influence once exerted by the imperial
diplomatic missions in the Chinese community. In 1929 the Nanjing government
requested that Chinese-language schools overseas register with the Ministry of
Education to bring them under party guidance. In 1933 the Overseas Chinese
Affairs Commission (OCAC) also requested that overseas Chinese organizations
register.[25]

The KMT leadership in Nanjing also attempted to bring back under central
party control the dissident factions in overseas communities. In 1933 KMT central
headquarters sent Kalfred Dip Lum to inspect party affairs in the United States.
Upon reaching San Francisco, he organized the Zhongyang Tongzhishe [Society
of Comrades of the Party Central Headquarters], a conservative faction supporting Chiang Kai-shek. The group began recruiting KMT members throughout the
United States and absorbed many members from the right faction, which was
still preoccupied with its feud against the Ning Yung Association.[26]

With the outbreak of the Sino-Japanese War in 1937, all the feuding parties
had to shelve their differences to concentrate on national salvation activities.
Within the KMT, the three factions nominally reunited into a single party. After
the leader of the KMT left faction, Wang Jingwei, defected to the Japanese in
1938, Goon Dick Wong took over the leadership of the remnants of the Left and
its organ *Kuo Min Yat Po.* The western U.S. section of the San Min Chu I Youth
Corps was added to the organizations under Wong's direction.[27]

Visions of a Modern China

Throughout the first quarter of the twentieth century, despite China's turmoil,
the promise of reform, revolution, and a Republic remained beacons of hope for
many Chinese in America. Some were frustrated by the lack of opportunities for
the Chinese and sought to go to China to help in its modernization while seeking suitable careers for themselves. One of the earliest returnees was Fong Foo
Sec who had arrived in America in 1881 at the age of thirteen. He converted to
Christianity and worked his way through school. In 1906 he returned to China
after receiving a masters degree at Columbia University, specializing in English
and education. He became English editor at the Commercial Press in Shanghai,

where he published a number of English textbooks and English-Chinese diction-
aries over a span of more than three decades.[28] Frank Chinglun Lee, the offspring
of a New York Chinese laundryman and his German wife, attended local public
schools, New York University, and the University of Chicago. In 1906 he went to
China to study Chinese, became a follower of Sun Yat-sen, and was exiled with
him during the early years of the Republic. Lee became a deputy minister in the
Ministry of Foreign Affairs after the KMT established the Nanjing government
in 1927.[29] Holt Cheng was born in China in 1878 and arrived in Hawaii in 1892.
In 1900 he migrated to California, where he attended San Francisco's College of
Physicians and Surgeons. After graduating in 1904, he became the first Chinese to
pass the California Medical Board examination. In 1908 he arrived in Guangzhou
where he helped found one of the first schools of western medicine established by
Chinese, Guanghua Medical School.[30] Jun Ke Choy, another example of reverse
migration, was born in Hawaii in 1892. He was inspired by Sun Yat-sen's vision of
a Republican China and departed for China in August 1911. After the founding of
the Republic, the Chinese government granted him a scholarship to return to the
United States to continue his education at Columbia University. After graduating
in 1915, Choy went back to China, where he served in various government posts.
His most notable accomplishment was the reorganizing of the government-owned
China Merchants Steamship Company, of which he was general manager from 1935
to 1941.[31] Yao Guanshun was born George Bow in Grass Valley, California, in 1887.
After completing his studies at Northridge Military Academy, Bow went to China
in 1912. He eventually headed Sun Yat-sen's bodyguards in Guangzhou. His greatest
moment came in 1922, when Chen Jiongming rebelled and attacked Sun Yat-sen's
headquarters in Guangzhou. Yao safely led Madam Sun Yat-sen (Soong Ching
Ling) to escape from the headquarters to a gunboat anchored in the Pearl River.[32]
One of the few overseas Chinese women attracted by the promise of the Chinese
revolution was King G. Won (Wen Zhengde), born in San Francisco in 1900. Her
older brother Hung Fei Won, also San Francisco–born, was an early follower of Sun
Yat-sen and was one of the founders of the first organ of the Tongmenghui. He left
for China soon after the 1911 revolution. King G. Won followed him around the
end of World War I after completing high school. She attended Yenjing University,
and after graduating she married Chen Xiaowei. The couple left for Hong Kong,
where Chen started a newspaper while Won began teaching English at Hong Kong
University. After the founding of the People's Republic of China (PRC), she was
invited to return to Shanghai to teach English.[33] These individuals represent only
a minor portion of the Chinese American population, but an exodus of similar
individuals to China continued steadily up to World War II.

The best known returnees were those in the more glamorous field of military
aviation. As early as 1915 the first licensed Chinese American pilot, Tom Gunn of
San Francisco, had gone to China to head a small air force of two airplanes to be

used in an uprising against Yuan Shikai. However, Yuan died before Gunn could lead his planes into action. The KMT was the most active in raising funds to build up an air force and recruiting aviators among Chinese overseas. Since the United States was the only industrialized nation with a sizable Chinese population that also had an aircraft industry, it is not surprising that many of the KMT's early aviators came from America. One of the earliest recruits was Hawaii-born Sen Yat Young, who went to Guangdong in 1917 to start a military air force for the KMT. He was honored after his death as "Father of the Chinese Air Force." Tom Gunn and Sen Yat Young were two precursors of about two hundred Chinese Americans before World War II who served in the Chinese Air Force.[34]

The promise of China's modernization also attracted capital from Chinese investors overseas. An early instance occurred in 1862, when a Chinese in Peru invested in an export company in Guangzhou. However, the first known instance of investment from a Chinese person in the United States occurred in 1890 when Huang Bingchang invested $100,000 to found the first electric light company in Guangzhou. But the most notable investment was the building of the Sunning Railroad in the Sze Yup [Four Counties] region. Retired Seattle labor contractor Chin Gee Hee advocated building the railroad in 1905 and in 1906 organized the Sunning Railroad Company to raise capital from the Chinese overseas. A great many investors were from Taishan, Chin's native county and the chief intended beneficiary of the railroad. The line ran from Doushan, in south central Taishan near Chin's native village to Beijie, Xinhui County, on the west bank of the West River and was completed in 1913. A branch running from Taicheng, the county seat of Taishan, to Yangjiang was only partially completed when the company ran out of capital. The total length of the completed railroad, including the branch, was 122 kilometers. Although the railroad was unable to connect to China's national railroad network, its existence played an important role in facilitating the economic development of the Four Counties region. During the War of Resistance against Japan, the railroad was dismantled to prevent it being used by the Japanese invaders and was never rebuilt.[35]

The high point of investments by Chinese in America occurred during the first three decades of the twentieth century, but dropped off during the depression of the 1930s and the Japanese invasion of China. These investments included a coal mine (1909) and a gold mine (1915) in Guangdong; a trolley-coach company (1920), a match-manufacturing company (1921), a ceramics factory (1922), and a paper mill (1924) in Guangzhou; a toll highway in Zhongshan (1923); shipping service on the West River (1925); and agricultural enterprises (1913, 1919, 1921, 1923) in Jiangsu and Anhui.[36]

Chinese in America also contributed to build infrastructure to modernize China in the form of hospital facilities, libraries, and schools. According to CCBA records in San Francisco, between 1911 and 1947 sixty delegations from China and Hong Kong visited to solicit donations for various purposes. However, many other charity campaigns did not contact the CCBA. Most solicitations sought contributions to construct schools in Hong Kong and China, usually in the areas in Guangdong from which many Chinese in America had originated.[37] The earliest known donation for school construction occurred in 1871 when Yung Wing, the first Chinese to graduate from an American university (Yale 1854), visited his native village Nanping on his way to Beijing. He proposed to village elders to establish a school and made the first known donation toward a school built with the help of overseas Chinese funding.[38] Overseas Chinese contributions to school construction proliferated only in the first decade of the twentieth century, when the Qing government abolished the imperial examinations and modernized the education system. Many Chinese in America donated generously to build schools, particularly in their native counties. Emigrants from Taishan, who constituted a majority of the Chinese population in America, led the way. According to statistics compiled by the Taishan Office of Overseas Chinese Affairs, Chinese contributions from abroad, including the United States, funded the building of eighty-six primary schools and nine middle schools between 1907 and 1949. Chinese immigrants continued to be solicitous about educational opportunities for their kin and fellow villagers still living in China, and donations for school construction continued after the founding of the PRC.[39]

Self-defense was another cause receiving large donations from Chinese immigrants in America, who sent funds to protect their home villages from bandit raids. These measures were especially common in Kaiping and Taishan counties, where the numerous immigrants and their newly prosperous families were tempting targets for bandits. These donations usually went to purchase firearms, hire night watchmen, and construct watchtowers providing shelter and defense against attacks. Today, many such watchtowers can still be found in Kaiping. The earliest surviving construction was built more than four centuries ago. However, the number of watchtowers only began proliferating during the last years of the Qing era, when 313 were erected. Another 1,490 came into being between 1912 and 1937, with 608 of these dating from the period between 1921 and 1926. On June 28, 2007, the watchtowers in rural Kaiping, representing a unique mishmash of different architectural styles blending east and west, officially gained UNESCO recognition as World Heritage sites.[40]

Watchtowers, however, did not solve the scourge of banditry. Beginning around 1915, many of Sze Yap ancestry, especially those from Taishan, returned from the United States but elected to settle in the relative safety of the Dongshan district in Guangzhou, which developed into a pleasant upscale residential area.[41]

Chinese abroad also responded generously to calls for disaster relief. Some events to which the CCBA of San Francisco donated funds included a flood in Shantou (1922); floods in Guangdong (1912, 1913, 1914, 1915, 1923, 1924, 1931, 1947);

drought in Hebei (1918); drought in nine North China provinces (1925); droughts in Shanxi, Shaanxi, and Henan (1929); and floods in Yangzi River (1931, 1935).[42]

Resistance to Japanese Aggression

During the 1930s, Japan claimed more and more Chinese territory. In 1931 the Japanese military initiated its grandiose scheme to conquer China by seizing Manchuria. It attacked Shanghai in 1932 and invaded the region north of the Great Wall in 1933. The Nanjing government took the position that China was not yet ready to confront the foreign aggressors and first had to suppress its domestic enemies—the Communist armies. However, in the Chinese American community, public opinion and the KMT's political rivals both to the right and the left were overwhelmingly in favor of unified, armed resistance. Despite the Nanjing government's policy of nonresistance, KMT party branches in America went along with public sentiment and joined community campaigns to raise funds to support such resistance leaders as General Ma Zhanshan in Manchuria and General Tsai Ting-kai in Shanghai. In Portland, Oregon, the left faction organized a school to teach basic flying skills to Chinese Americans. The graduates and a few Chinese American pilots from elsewhere were encouraged to join the Chinese Air Force.[43]

Factional differences, however, often marred the community's efforts at national salvation, as various groups had their own political agendas and objectives. In San Francisco the KMT's left and right factions organized different groups competing for public support. In New York the Marxist Left at first worked mainly with mainstream progressives, but after the mid-1930s, it also worked with some success with pro-resistance leaders in Chinatown organizations.[44]

These political differences also emerged when General Tsai Ting-kai visited America in 1934. Tsai was lionized as a hero wherever he went. Chinese Americans, immigrants and American-born alike, were especially proud that Tsai was a fellow Cantonese. Meihong Soohoo, a leader in the CKT and the On Leong Association, escorted Tsai to the West Coast, where the Baohuanghui's Lain Chan and the Bing Kung Tong's He Shaohan served as hosts. Wherever Tsai went, he advocated resistance and attacked Chiang Kai-shek's weak response to Japanese aggression. For this reason, many KMT branches did not send official representation to the welcoming ceremonies, although many members attended.[45]

Despite the increasing public clamor for anti-Japanese resistance, the Nanjing government insisted on continuing its campaigns against the Communists. In 1936 Chiang Kai-shek's ally, the "Young Marshal" Zhang Xueliang, kidnapped the Generalissimo, who had come to Xi'an in Shaanxi where KMT troops were facing the Communists. Zhang convinced Chiang to agree to a truce with the Communists and to prepare to resist Japan. It was none too soon, for Japan attacked at Marco Polo Bridge on July 7, 1937, to begin the Sino-Japanese War.

War of Resistance against Japan

Soon after war officially erupted, the Nanjing government charged the Overseas Chinese Affairs Commission with raising money from the Chinese American community to support the war effort.[46] War relief associations sprang up in many Chinatowns as longtime political foes joined together for the sake of national salvation.

During this time of peril for China, most Chinese in America were willing to sacrifice to contribute to anti-Japanese resistance. But the war relief associations also set obligatory quotas for individual contributors in order to achieve its fund-raising goals. For those choosing not to participate, the war relief associations would try to force compliance using a mix of persuasion and threats. Sometimes such cases escalated to public denunciations of the recalcitrant individuals. The social isolation of the Chinese American community meant that American officials were generally ignorant of or chose to ignore such violations of the law unless they received complaints from the aggrieved parties. Thus, the war relief associations were able to persuade as much as an estimated 70 percent of the Chinese community to contribute to their fund-raising campaigns. During the eight years of the War of Resistance, Chinese in America contributed approximately $25 million to the Nationalist government.[47] Some war relief donations also flowed to Yan'an, to the Communist-led guerrilla areas, especially after the fragile truce between the KMT and the Communists was shattered by the New Fourth Army Incident of January 1941.[48]

The war gave the KMT an excellent opportunity to expand its influence into all areas of the Chinese American community, and its political rivals could do little to stop it. Taking advantage of patriotic feelings, the KMT recruited ambitious and opportunistic people into the party, including many key community leaders from district and clan associations and secret societies. Many rose to lead local party organs and become members of the party's central committee in the United States.[49] Goon Dick Wong, the dominant leader in the U.S. General Branch, passed away in 1940, but by 1944 Yen Doon Wong had inherited his mantle of leadership by being elected to the General Branch's executive committee.

The war also helped the Left reach wider audiences. As ominous war clouds gathered over Europe in 1938, Zhao Jiansheng (Rao Shushi), editor of the Chinese Communist Party organ in Paris *China Salvation Times* (*Giu Guo Sh Bao*), transferred its printing press and type fonts to New York, where it replaced *Chinese Vanguard* as the voice of the Chinese Marxist Left in America. *China Salvation Times* in turn ceased publication in mid-1939, when Rao returned to China to join the war of resistance. In late 1939, a campaign to raise capital for a daily was launched by Tang Mingzhao (Chu Tong) and progressive members of the New York Chinese Hand Laundry Alliance. *China Daily News,* the first progressive daily newspaper, began publication on July 7, 1940, using the printing press and type left by *China Salvation Times*. Tang Mingzhao was the publisher and Ji Gongquan the chief editor. This paper was the earliest Chinese newspaper in the United States to give full coverage to the New Fourth Army Incident. Its more moderate tone compared to its predecessors appealed to readers all over the Americas, and by the mid-1940s its circulation was among the highest of New York Chinese newspapers.[50]

The Chinese Civil War

During World War II, the U.S. Congress repealed the Chinese exclusion acts. Although Chinese immigration was still severely limited, Chinese in America were cautiously optimistic that their status in this country was improving. After the victory over Japan in 1945, China finally was no longer dominated or threatened by foreign imperialism, and could be rebuilt once again into a great nation. The KMT, as the ruling party in a victorious China, politically dominated Chinatowns and consolidated its position by continuously recruiting key leaders of the *huiguan*, clan associations, and secret societies. Its executive committee ballooned from nineteen members in 1946 to twenty-eight in 1948. In 1944 the Overseas Department of the Kuomintang Central Committee and a group of U.S. KMT members gained control of New York's *Chinese Journal* and reorganized it into yet another party organ. The Overseas Chinese Affairs Commission also ensured support for the Nationalist government by subsidizing friendly journals.[51]

The war's end, however, underscored China's exhaustion and the worsening problems of corruption and runaway inflation, and the threat of civil war between the KMT and the Chinese Communists. Many called for an end to one-party rule and fratricidal conflicts, pressuring the Nationalist government and the Communists to agree to a truce. The Chinese government convened a Political Consultative Conference in January 1946, which was attended by delegates from the KMT and the Chinese Communist Party, several small political parties, and nonparty individuals. Distrust between the two major parties soon led to a breakdown of their truce and the onset of civil war. The Communists and their ally, the Democratic League, subsequently boycotted a KMT-dominated National Assembly convened by the Nanjing government in November to pass a new constitution. In the meantime, the KMT's old political rivals in America—the Chee Kung Tong and the Baohuanghui—had stepped up their activities, preparing to play a greater role in China and the Chinese American community during the postwar years.

Chee Kung Tong

The Chee Kung Tong's influence in the Chinese community had waned considerably during the first half of the twentieth century. However, a network of lodges still existed, although greatly shrunken in numbers. In August 1945, a New York convention of delegates from the Americas reorganized the secret society into a political party, the Zhongguo Hongmen [Party of Extreme Fairness]. New York's eighty-year-old patriarch Meihong Soohoo, leader in the CKT and the On Leong Labor and Merchants Association, was elected chair. In July 1946, Chairman Soohoo led a delegation of Hongmen lodges of the Americas to a Shanghai convention attended by Hongmen societies in China and around the world. The decision to change the secret society into a political party, however, was by no means accepted unanimously by the entire Hongmen community in America. Important lodges, such as those of San Francisco and Hawaii, were conspicuously absent from this gathering and did not make the change.

The delegation's leaders were naively ignorant of the byzantine intricacies of the Chinese political situation. The KMT, unwilling to allow the birth of an independent political party that could be a potential threat, had cultivated the support of enough secret society lodges to control the convention. Soohoo and his supporters found themselves outmaneuvered and outvoted at every turn. Despite Soohoo's protests, the convention changed the party name to Chinese Hung Men Democratic Association, and Soohoo was excluded from any significant office. As a consolation, Chiang Kai-shek offered him a seat in the National Assembly, which he rejected. In the meantime, the KMT's Mei Youzhuo had successfully supplanted Soohoo in the On Leong Association. These developments seriously undermined the Chee Kong Tong's potential to challenge the KMT, and the discouraged Soohoo departed for Hong Kong in 1947. There he joined the Zhongguo Zhigongdang [Chinese Chee Kong Tong] organization, which had been reactivated in 1946, and joined the Communist-led People's Democracy United Front in May 1947. With Soohoo gone and the party split, New York's *Chinese Republic News,* the CKT's only remaining organ in the United States, suspended publication around 1949, leaving Vancouver's *Chinese Times* as the only CKT newspaper left in North America.[52]

Chinese Democratic Constitutionalist Party

The Baohuanghui also harbored ambitions of wielding more influence in China and in America. However, by the end of the war, it had branches only in Honolulu, San Francisco, and Montreal in North America. In 1945 Dai Ming Lee, editor of Honolulu's *New China Press* took over management of the ailing *Chinese World* in San Francisco, the political center for Chinese people in the continental United States. Lee's energetic leadership and an infusion of capital by party loyalist Quon Chun of Honolulu's C. Q. Yee Hop enterprises revitalized the party's voice in this important community. In November 1945, the party convened in Montreal and reorganized as the Chinese Democratic Constitutionalist Party (CDCP). Wu Zhuang (Wu Xianzi) and Dai Ming Lee became chairman and vice-chairman respectively. The party's objectives were permanent world peace and establishing a constitutional democracy in China. In August 1946, the CDCP agreed to amalgamate with the Chinese National Socialist Party to form the Chinese Democratic Socialist Party.[53]

Later that year Dai Ming Lee attended the National Constitutional Assembly as a party delegate, while Quon Chun represented Hawaii. Lee was one of the party's representatives who met with KMT and Youth Party delegates to negotiate for reorganization of the national government. However, after Lee reported the results to the party's central committee and departed for Hawaii, the central committee led by Carsun Chang vetoed the plans for reorganization and decided to limit the party's participation. This and other policy disagreements led the CDCP to withdraw from the merger in mid-1947 and to resume its former status. CDCP leaders Wu Zhuang and Dai Ming Lee were given minor posts in the national government but boycotted the offices.[54]

Nationalist Government Politics and the Communist Victory

The Nanjing government held elections in late 1946 and early 1947 for representatives to China's National Assembly, Control Yuan, and Legislative Yuan under the new constitution. KMT dominance of the Chinese American community was indicated by the fact that all American representatives were prominent party members. Competition was fierce, with the different candidates running campaign advertisements in the U.S. Chinese press and otherwise lobbying the electorate. However, their enthusiasm only drew an indifferent response. Only 9,533 ballots were cast in the United States for the Legislative Yuan candidates out of approximately 80,000 Chinese in America of voting age.[55] One probable reason for the poor turnout was that Chinese in America may have regarded these political campaigns as irrelevant to the more substantive challenges facing them in the United States.

China's first National Assembly under the new constitution met in Nanjing in spring 1948 to elect Chiang Kai-shek as president of the Republic of China. KMT control was not complete, however, for General Li Zongren was elected vice-president over Chiang's objections. Li Zongren had rallied around himself most of the liberal and other elements in the assembly seeking reform and changes in the government and received the position despite all the pressure that Chiang brought to bear on assembly members to vote for his candidate.

Activities of the Left

The Nanjing government's major opposition in China was the Chinese Communist Party (CCP). Like the KMT, the CCP also sent party members to the United States, although in much smaller numbers, to guide implementation of its political objectives. Unlike the KMT, the Communist Party did not form a party organization in the United States: it acted chiefly through progressive organizations, such as the Chinese Hand Laundry Alliance and the closely affiliated Chinese Youth League in New York and San Francisco's Chinese Workers Mutual Aid Association and Chinese American Democratic Youth League. The lone news organ was New York's *China Daily News*. What this group lacked in numbers, however, it made up for in its close working relationship with the U.S. Communist Party and mainstream progressive organizations.

Just before the war ended in 1945, high-ranking Communist leader Dong Biwu arrived in San Francisco to participate in the United Nations Conference on International Organization. Afterward, he traveled in the United States for four months, making speeches and giving press interviews criticizing the corruption of the Nationalists and calling for an end to the civil war and formation of a democratic coalition government. For the next few years, these were the main points of attack used by progressives against the Nationalist regime.

In 1946 KMT general Feng Yuxiang arrived in America, ostensibly heading a delegation to investigate irrigation and water conservation projects. Feng soon dropped all pretenses and began attacking the Chiang regime and its American supporters in the civil war. He soon became allied with other KMT dissidents and Chinese Communists and their supporters in the United States; he founded the Overseas Chinese League for Peace and Democracy in China in New York in November 1947 with himself at the head. The organization advocated democracy in China and opposed American interference in the Chinese civil war.[56]

During 1948, the People's Liberation Army captured large parts of northeastern and northern China, followed by the annihilation of Nationalist armies in east central China. President Chiang resigned on January 21, 1949, ostensibly handing over the reins of power to Li Zongren, who became acting president. But with Chiang continuing to maintain independent political and military authority, Li had only limited powers.[57] The rout of Nationalist forces continued as the People's Liberation Army easily crossed the Yangzi River barrier on April 21 and captured the Nationalist capital of Nanjing and Shanghai in short order. On October 1, 1949, the victors and their allies declared the founding of the People's Republic of China with its capital at Beijing. By then, Communist armies were already approaching the southern metropolis of Guangzhou.

As the Nationalist defeat became a rout in 1949, a Chinese American population weary of civil war, corruption, and inflation anticipated an imminent end to their agony. Some community leaders were ready to show open support for the pending regime. Progressive students were active on campuses, with organizations and publications urging Chinese students to prepare themselves to return to help reconstruct their ancestral homeland. On May 4, 1949, Henry Tsoi began publishing *China Weekly,* the first newspaper supporting the Chinese Communists in San Francisco's large Chinese community. After the founding of the PRC, businessmen Joe Yuey and Sam Wah You led another progressive group to outbid the KMT to purchase *Chung Sai Yat Po,* the oldest daily newspaper in the community. The new owners changed the editorial policy to support the PRC. During this same period, Situ Huimin, then studying filmmaking, also met with community progressives to found the World Theater in San Francisco in late 1949. It was the first theater to show progressive films from China to the

Chinese American community.[58] The following year, many students from China and some idealistic Chinese Americans hastened to China to contribute to the construction of a new nation.

Despite the apparent growing support for the PRC, developments in international and domestic events soon applied brakes to its further progress. In 1948 the cold war had begun with the Soviet Union's Berlin blockade. The same year anti-Communist hysteria in the United States ramped up with the Alger Hiss investigation by the House Un-American Activities Committee. These developments created an atmosphere favorable to the continued survival of the KMT, despite their imminent defeat on the Chinese mainland. Thus on October 9, 1949, when San Francisco's Chinese Workers Mutual-Aid Association celebrated the founding of the People's Republic of China in Chinatown, the local KMT leadership was bold enough to hire hoodlums to break up the meeting and seize the five-starred flag of the new government. The next evening, on the Double Ten National Day, KMT partisans passed out leaflets calling for the eradication of fifteen progressives from the Chinese community.[59]

A Divided China and the Cold War

As the defeated Nationalist regime crumbled around him, acting president Li Zongren flew to the United States in December 1949 for medical treatment. Afterward, bitter about his experience with Chiang's manipulations of the recent past, Li refused to join the remnants of the Nationalist regime in their refuge on Taiwan, although in March 1950 Chiang arbitrarily resumed the presidency. In the Chinese American community KMT agents worked feverishly to organize support for the hard-pressed regime. As early as March 1950, party central committee member Huang Wenshan, who had arrived in the United States in 1949, proposed formation of the Anti-Communist National Salvation League with headquarters in New York City or San Francisco and branches in other major Chinese American communities. In September Zheng Yanfen, director of the Overseas Party Affairs Section of the KMT, also came from Taiwan to organize further anti-Communist activities.[60]

Initially Chinese Americans failed to respond to these initiatives. However, political developments soon changed the situation. In May 1950 Albert Chow, KMT General Branch executive committee member and an activist in Democratic Party politics in America, visited with Chiang Kai-shek in Taiwan. Afterward, he met with President Harry Truman on June 26, 1950, to report on his visit and to urge more support for the Nationalist government to fight the Communists.[61] It so happened that fighting had broken out in the Korean Peninsula with North Korean troops thrusting into South Korea just a day earlier. On June 27, Truman ordered U.S. troops to aid the retreating South Korean armies and also deployed the Seventh Fleet to the Taiwan Straits to block the PRC from attacking Taiwan.

It is not known whether Chow's discussion with Truman had any bearing on this decision, but it came in the nick of time for the beleaguered KMT regime.

In November, after General Douglas MacArthur had ordered his troops to cross the thirty-eighth parallel and approach the Chinese border, Chinese armies entered the conflict to support North Korea. The U.S. government then issued orders to freeze Chinese government assets in this country, embargo trade, and restrain Chinese students in the United States from leaving for mainland China. It also resumed military aid to the Nationalist regime. After cessation of the Korean War in 1953, the departure of a number of Chinese scientists became the subject of high-level negotiations between the United States and the PRC. Among those returning to China was rocket scientist Qian Xuesun, who become the father of the PRC's missile program.[62]

After the PRC entered the Korean War, scattered anti-Chinese incidents occurred in the United States. Many Chinese Americans became apprehensive that they would suffer the fate of Japanese Americans during World War II and be incarcerated in concentration camps. The time was ripe for the KMT to act on these fears. On December 28, 1950, Yen Doon Wong, central committeeman of the KMT General Branch in the United States, and director of the Chinese Consolidated Benevolent Association and the Ning Yung Association, led the formation of the first Anti-Communist League in the United States. Wong became its first president. There was little open opposition to its formation. Other Chinese communities soon followed with local leagues. Wong became the chief liaison between the KMT in America and in Taiwan, and he made frequent trips to Taipei for consultations on strategies and policies for political work among the Chinese in America. In the 1960s, the Taiwan regime gave him the title of Advisor on National Affairs.[63]

While war ravaged the Korean peninsula, the shattered KMT regrouped in Taiwan. In November 1953, the third plenary session of the seventh central committee passed a "Plan to Strengthen Overseas Work." The central task of overseas work was in "uniting and organizing the overseas Chinese to support the anti-Communist national salvation struggle" and "to strengthen our side, win over the neutrals, and to disintegrate the enemy." The United States became one of the principal centers for KMT party activity. Party work was to be supervised by the Cell for Direction of Overseas Activities.[64]

Some of the major tasks for overseas party work were to gather intelligence in overseas Chinese communities; win over anti-Communist elements in the community and establish a united front for anti-Communist national salvation activities; eliminate pro-Communists from Chinese organizations and use various means to break up or gain control in pro-Communist organizations; strengthen cultural propaganda and provide support and guidance for Chinese newspapers and Chinese schools; support loyalist enterprises and encourage investment in Taiwan; assist party branches and loyal Chinese organizations to establish enterprises for trading with Taiwan, with the profits to finance local anti-Communist "national salvation" activities; and train local cadres in Taiwan by specialists sent from central headquarters.[65]

The Overseas Chinese Affairs Commission became an important medium for carrying out these policies. Major party leaders and conservative leaders in traditionist organizations were appointed as commissioners or as advisors to the commission to buy their loyalty; they also functioned as the eyes and ears of the Taiwan regime. This practice had begun before World War II, but the number of appointees increased greatly after World War II, particularly after the KMT regime fled to Taiwan.

After the KMT regime's debacle on the Chinese mainland, many party members did not go to Taiwan but emigrated abroad. Some entered the Chinese American community and reinforced overseas party branches. Many of these new immigrants were better educated than earlier Chinese immigrants. Some newcomers had political experience as minor officials or KMT party workers. These individuals came at a time when Chinese American society was entering a new era, changing from a bachelor-oriented society to a family-oriented one. As discriminatory laws and practices were gradually being repealed, Chinese Americans found their horizons widening as they increasingly entered the American mainstream. Chinatown traditionist institutions confronted declining memberships as Chinese Americans moved away from Chinatown and increasingly found association activities irrelevant to their lives. The associations themselves were also drifting as they sought to define their roles in a changing community. Under these circumstances the leadership in many associations fell into the hands of a few. Pro-Taiwan partisans among the newcomers became active in these organizations and a number easily entered leadership circles. Many pro-KMT intellectuals also became principals and teachers in Chinese-language schools or editors of Chinese-language newspapers. Given the prevailing anti-Communist atmosphere in the United States and the adverse effects of the PRC's land reform programs, political movements, and socialist economic reforms of the 1950s among Chinese Americans and their families and relatives, many in the community acquiesced to the conversion of community institutions to KMT-controlled tools used in Taiwan's struggle with the PRC.

Some newcomers who were formerly high- and middle-ranked officials were able to do even more to help the Taiwan regime. When Chen Lifu, formerly a powerful figure in the KMT, settled in the United States, he and seven other loyalists purchased New York's *Chinese Tribune*. Former KMT official Pan Gongzhan (Pan Kung-chan) became the paper's chief editor in April 1951. Others who were academics found positions in universities and think tanks, which helped them to shape America's China policy. One example was the former diplomat Paul K. T. Sih, who arrived in New York in 1949. In 1959 he became founding director of the Institute of Asian Studies (changed to Center of Asian Studies in 1964) at

St. John's University in New York. Sih continued to have close relations with the Taiwan government and became an apologist for its policies.[66]

Chiang Kai-shek's brothers-in-law, H. H. Kung and T. V. Soong, were even more influential. They had fled China in 1947 and 1949 respectively to take up residence in New York, where they became active backers of the China Lobby. The foundation for this group was laid around 1940, when the Nationalist government began establishing agencies and missions in Washington to publish pro-Nationalist propaganda and to lobby for more military aid to China. After World War II, when defeat was looming, Madame Chiang Kai-shek arrived in December 1948 to guide the reorganization and expansion of lobbying efforts to shore up the sinking regime. Soong and Kung became key players cultivating and financially backing a group of pro-KMT lobbyists and politicians, such as Senator William Knowland of California and Congressman Walter H. Judd of Minnesota, that eventually became known collectively as the China Lobby. This group was extremely influential in U.S. politics and maintained U.S. support of the Nationalist regime to prevent normal diplomatic relations with the PRC for over two decades.[67]

Toward the end of the 1950s, as the protective shield provided by the U.S. Seventh Fleet and massive doses of American aid enabled Taiwan to attain some stability, the KMT regime initiated a variety of low-key tactics to win over the uncommitted majority in U.S. Chinese communities. In early 1957, New York CCBA president and KMT member Shing Tai Leung discussed with western U.S. KMT leaders convening a national conference to discuss anti-Communist actions and support for Taiwan. They reached the conclusion that, in view of the ongoing U.S. government investigation of Chinese immigration fraud in which many Chinatown leaders were implicated, such a conference would have broader support if it focused on immigration and refugee issues. Accordingly, the National Conference of Chinese Communities in America was convened in Washington, D.C., and gave birth to the National Chinese Welfare Council. At first there were high hopes and expectations among Chinese Americans for this organization; however, by the second convention of the council in 1959, KMT supporters were in firm control, with the organization parroting the Taiwan propaganda line.[68]

Taiwan's propaganda was directed primarily toward showing the world that it was the defender of freedom and traditional Chinese culture. But it also aimed to show that the regime enjoyed overwhelming overseas Chinese support. In San Francisco and other major Chinatowns, it became the annual practice for the Chinese Consolidated Benevolent Association and the Anti-Communist League to issue proclamations on Double Ten affirming the resolve of "all Chinese to support the fight against communism and restore the nation." Later, the Anti-Communist League in San Francisco also held public "memorial services for victims of Communist barbarities on the mainland." A symbolic act in some of these ceremonies was the public burning of Chairman Mao Zedong's portrait.

In conventions convened by various traditionist organizations, KMT members would propose resolutions pledging "undying loyalty to President Chiang and everlasting allegiance to the Republic of China."

Destruction of the Left

During this critical period of the 1950s, the anti-Communist hysteria and the delicate political situation of Chinese people in the United States discouraged any display of support for the PRC. U.S. government agents increased surveillance and harassment of PRC supporters. The situation was favorable for the KMT to eliminate their rivals. In New York, the KMT masterminded a boycott against the *China Daily News,* the major pro-PRC Chinese newspaper in the United States. News vendors were threatened. Cooperating government investigators lent a helping hand by harassing subscribers and advertisers. In 1952 the Justice Department indicted *China Daily News* managing editor Eugene Moy, business manager Albert Wong, three Chinese Hand Laundry Alliance members who were on the newspaper's board of directors, and several others. All were convicted for violating the Trading with the Enemy Act, a law passed by Congress in 1917 that had never been enforced until then. By 1962 the paper had to go to semiweekly publication.[69]

During this period, the Immigration and Naturalization Service was investigating Chinese communities for immigration fraud, which was widespread among Chinese who entered during the exclusion era. They particularly targeted pro-PRC individuals, and a number were stripped of their citizenship status and threatened with deportation, another situation that discouraged participation in progressive activities.[70]

Failure of the Third Force

During the cold war era, the CDCP organ *Chinese World* under Dai Ming Lee's leadership became a major focal point for non-Communists and anti-Communists disenchanted with the KMT regime, and the paper's circulation increased throughout the 1950s. Lee was joined on staff by J. K. Choy, who had returned to the United States in 1945 after serving the KMT government in China for almost three decades. Possessing an astute political sense honed by decades of experience in office in Republican China, he advised the CDCP. In 1949 he helped organize an English edition of *Chinese World* to reach a wider audience. He also served as a director of the paper from 1953 to 1955. In 1954 Choy founded the anti–Chiang Kai-shek, anti-Communist Crusade for Free Democratic China, Inc., with himself as executive director.[71]

In 1954 former Nationalist official Wu Shangying urged former acting president Li Zongren to organize an anti-Communist anti-Chiang third force that could court favor in the United States. Wu and Li flew to San Francisco to confer with Dai Ming Lee. On their arrival, KMT supporters distributed handbills in Chinatown signed by a Quanqiao Chujiantuan [All-Overseas Chinese Kill-Traitor Corps] warning Li not to organize an opposition party. Disregarding the warnings, the Free China Political Organizations (FCPO) was formed and included the Committee for Revival of the KMT, the CDCP, and the CKT, together with the Freedom Front of Hong Kong and the Chinese Democratic Alliance. Li became the chairman. The group's objectives were to overthrow the Communist regime and to force Chiang Kai-shek from power. However, the group fell apart the following year when Li disclosed at a June 11, 1955, New York press conference that he had proposed to the governments of the United States, Great Britain, and India that Formosa, the Pescadores, Quemoy, and Matsu be demilitarized and that the status of these territories be guaranteed by the Big Four Powers during negotiations between the Chinese Nationalists and the Chinese Communists. In the event that such negotiations should fail, an internationally supervised plebiscite would be called on the question of whether Taiwan should remain autonomous or become part of the PRC. The Nationalist representative at the United Nations, Tingfu F. Tsiang, immediately denounced the proposal, which he attributed to the "leftist press." Not wishing to be associated with a move that could be interpreted as overthrowing the Republic of China, the CDCP and the CKT jointly announced their withdrawal from the FCPO.[72] By that time Chiang Kai-shek appeared to be in firm control in Taiwan, and the United States quickly lost interest in Li as head of an alternative force.

Still ambitious to extend the CDCP's influence, Dai Ming Lee launched an East Coast edition of *Chinese World* in 1957. The effort failed in two years and incurred heavy financial losses. It proved to be the CDCP's last major initiative. In 1961 Dai Ming Lee passed away and with him went the principal driving force behind the CDCP. The party rapidly declined. *Chinese World* closed down in 1969, and the party headquarters building was sold in 1975. Honolulu's *New China Press* managed to struggle along until 1978.[73]

Changing Winds

As the KMT regime's situation in Taiwan improved, it continued to work through diplomats and party branches to consolidate control of the Chinese American traditionist organizations. However, despite the lack of dissident voices, the community did not exhibit enthusiastic support for the Taiwan regime. The party organs faced increasing financial deficits as circulation and advertising revenues dropped, and they ceased publication one by one.

The Taiwan government, however, found Chinese Americans to be more receptive in the less political realm of arts and culture. It began to send teachers for music, drama, dance, and Chinese-language classes and encouraged the organization of cultural and social groups. Their primary function was to propagate Chinese culture substantially in consonance with Taiwan's ideological guidelines.

In 1960 the Overseas Chinese Affairs Commission also began supplying textbooks to Chinese-language schools. These books used the traditional Chinese characters in contrast to the simplified characters introduced in the PRC in 1956. They also included political propaganda.[74] KMT control of the Chinese schools and key Chinatown institutions and the U.S. trade embargo ensured the exclusion of cultural imports from the PRC.

Challenges from the New Middle Class

By the 1960s, the old political rivals of the KMT could no longer effectively challenge its domination. Other challengers, however, soon emerged. During America's postwar era of prosperity, Chinese people had been entering many fields closed to them during the exclusion era. Many became professionals or were employed in clerical, technical, and engineering positions. These conditions fostered the growth of a Chinese American middle class rooted in American society and also accelerated their Americanization. Many Chinese found their horizons expanding beyond the bounds of Chinatown. However, the KMT-imposed, pro-Taiwan, anti-Communist orthodoxy encouraged in the traditionist organizations an ultraconservative community leadership that was more interested in politically supporting Taiwan than in providing effective leadership to a changing community. Others would attempt to fill this void.

The spark was provided by the civil rights movement, which heightened political and social awareness among the new Chinese American middle class. The push for equality in American society inspired a renewed interest in Chinese American issues and a push for greater participation in mainstream politics. Because of their connections to mainstream politicians, these middle-class Chinese Americans were seen as potential threats to the hegemony of the conservative traditionist organizations. In most communities, these antagonistic relations led to tension, but direct conflicts were usually avoided. In San Francisco, however, the antagonisms over community domestic issues became confrontations intertwined with politics in China.

One of the first challengers to the established traditionist order was J. K. Choy, who in 1957 had founded and become manager of the highly successful Chinatown branch of San Francisco Federal Savings and Loan Association. In 1960 Choy established a Chinese Community Center at the business as a launching pad for social and political action in Chinatown.[75] He began to make and publish statements attacking ineptitude and corruption in Chinatown's traditionist associations. In 1962, as a member of the Chinese Hospital's board of directors, he invited the Presbyterian Medical Center to study the workings of the institution. The report was very critical of the hospital, but the traditionist organizations that dominated the hospital board managed to shelve the report. Such actions led conservative Chinatown circles to regard Choy as a threat to their vested interests in the status quo.

In 1963, inspired by the promise of the Kennedy presidency, Choy teamed up with Joe Yuey and others concerned with improving the Chinese community to found the San Francisco Greater Chinatown Community Service Association (SFGCCSA) "to keep pace with the times by providing the maximum amount of social and other community services to help the underprivileged in communities throughout the country." Among the SFGCCSA's founders were activists connected with churches and community groups and prominent businesspersons, professionals, and enlightened community leaders. The SFGCCSA became a platform independent of the CCBA and traditionist associations that could advocate and launch community projects. Choy and Joe Yuey became respectively the founding president and executive vice-president.[76]

Using the SFGCCSA as a platform, J. K. Choy, Joe Yuey, and a diverse group of interested parties founded the Chinese Culture Foundation (CCF) of San Francisco in 1965. This new institution tried to steer a middle-of-the-road course in the PRC-Taiwan struggle. KMT partisans, however, perceived it as an attempt to evade KMT control in the field of culture and to provide an entry point for PRC cultural activities. They seized every available opportunity to discredit the organization's leaders or to attack it. In 1966 they struck at the outspoken founder Choy. On October 12, 1966, rumors circulated in Chinatown that the Chinatown branch of San Francisco Savings and Loan Association was about to fail and that Choy, the manager, had fled to Mexico. A run started on the Chinatown branch as anxious Chinese Americans flocked to withdraw their hard-earned savings. More than $3 million in funds was disbursed in three days before the panic subsided. Later, in 1969, the Chinese community buzzed with talk alleging that one of the CCF founders, Alan Wong, was affiliated with Communist and radical groups. Wong was a community activist who was also a member of the SFGCCSA board. He was active in the War on Poverty program, where he had often clashed with conservative board members from the CCBA. He had also openly advocated better understanding between the United States and the PRC. Wong finally had to run a personal advertisement in the Chinese newspapers to refute the groundless allegations.[77]

KMT partisans also attacked the Chinese Culture Foundation. A pretext was provided by Joe Yuey, who was quoted in an interview in the February 23, 1970, issue of *Newsweek* as saying: "It's a question of what a government can do for the people. The Nationalists were in power for forty years and nothing happened. Look at China now, after only twenty years. No matter how you look at it, the Communists are helping the people."[78] Pro-Taiwan directors on the CCBA board thereupon pushed through a resolution withdrawing CCBA support from the CCF and instigated a boycott by the traditionist organizations against the foundation's facilities and events that lasted into the 1980s. In 1971 the San Francisco KMT leaders Yen Doon Wong and C. T. Shew also wrote to President Chiang Kai-shek to halt shipment of cultural objects and decorations that had been promised to the CCF by Taiwan authorities in 1970.[79]

The CCF was not the only new group in the Chinese community. Congressional passage of President Lyndon Johnson's War on Poverty program led to the proliferation of Chinatown social agencies funded by non-community sources. By the decade's end, ethnic minority struggles for equal rights had inspired the appearance of many activist groups in the community. These organizations, based on American models, forged numerous ties to mainstream politicians and groups and to other ethnic community organizations. They reflected changing political and social currents among the new Chinese American middle class that often brought them to loggerheads over community issues with the traditionist associations led by the CCBA. In San Francisco conflicts over community issues became open confrontations. In 1971 the two sides were pitted against each other over desegregation in public schools and in the board election for the Chinatown–North Beach Economic Opportunity Council. In both cases the conservatives, who had more resources, beat off liberal challenges.[80] Despite these setbacks in the face of entrenched KMT control, the new groups succeeded in claiming a part of the Chinese American power structure by avoiding further direct confrontations with the old guard and cultivating the support of members of the new Chinese American middle class, opponents of the KMT, and liberal mainstream politicians.

Since their primary focus was the American political scene, these liberals professed an open-minded attitude on China politics. In 1972, just before President Richard Nixon made his historic visit to the PRC, Joe Yuey, attorney Gordon Lau, and CCBA director Ernest Wong headed a Chinese Americans for Better U.S.-China Relations Committee to gather signatures petitioning Nixon to improve foreign relations. All three were at the time directors on the CCF board. KMT ideologues naturally objected to this action, and the KMT organ *Young China* attacked the group in an editorial.[81]

The end of the 1960s also saw the rise of militant Asian American groups, including the Red Guards Party (RGP; founded 1969 in San Francisco), I Wor Kuen (IWK; founded 1969 in New York; established a branch in San Francisco in 1971 and combined with the RGP; spawned the Chinese Progressive Association in 1972), the Asian Community Center (ACC; founded 1970 in San Francisco as an activities center; Wei Min She [WMS] was formed in 1971 to lead and coordinate activities associated with the ACC, including a bookstore and a garment cooperative), and Asian Studies Group (founded 1972 in New York; changed to Workers Viewpoint Organization [WVO] in 1973; spawned Asian Americans for Equal Employment [AAFEE] in 1974).[82] During the same period, groups influenced by the WVO also emerged in the smaller Chinese American communities, such as Yellow Seeds in Philadelphia and the New Youth Center in Chicago;[83] in Honolulu there was the Third Arm. The membership of these groups comprised mostly college-age Chinese Americans who had been influenced by the U.S. civil rights and anti–Vietnam War movements and, from the PRC, the teachings of Mao Zedong and the idealized image of egalitarian Marxist rhetoric and the Cultural

Revolution that they represented. Among their supporters were pro-PRC elements surviving from the early cold war period.

Possessing the impetuous spirit of the proverbial newborn calf who is not yet worldly wise enough to fear the tiger, these militants did not hesitate in confronting the traditionist organizational structure. What these groups lacked in numbers and resources they made up for with messianic zeal. Although their foci were mainly on community issues, these militants also openly espoused the PRC revolution. In 1970 the RGP was first to stage a public celebration of the PRC's National Day, October 1st. Around the same period, the IWK and WMS started showing PRC-produced feature films. Also in 1970, members of the ACC opened Everybody's Bookshop to sell publications from the PRC and other radical literature. Although these groups lacked a broad base of community support and remained only annoying gadflies to the KMT, they successfully breached the KMT's ideological blockade. Their activities declined during the mid-1970s with the rising tides of conservatism in America. Some were also disillusioned by the turn of events in the PRC, with the death of Mao and fall of the Gang of Four revealing some of the problems of the Cultural Revolution.[84]

The Diaoyutai Movement and Chinese Nationalism

The 1970s brought a changing domestic and international situation that affected Chinese international students and immigrant intellectuals. The seminal event was a sovereignty dispute between Japan and China over the Diaoyutai Islands, which set off a wave of protests and demonstrations involving Chinese from many countries.

In 1969 the United States and Japan issued a joint communiqué establishing Japanese sovereignty over the Ryukyu Islands (Okinawa), including the Diaoyutai Islands, known to the Japanese as the Senkaku Islands. The cluster of uninhabited Diaoyutai islets were located between Okinawa and Taiwan but had long been used as a base by Chinese fishermen. In 1969 a report of the United Nations Economic Commission for Asia and the Far East had suggested the possibility of large hydrocarbon deposits in the waters off the islands, greatly adding to their value. The PRC and Taiwan governments disputed Japanese claims, inspiring Chinese students and intellectuals overseas who had been influenced by the social unrest of the times to protest against this perceived infringement on Chinese sovereignty. A political movement developed, involving students and intellectuals from Taiwan, who were originally from mainland China, plus some students from Hong Kong and community activists.[85]

Toward the end of 1970, students at Princeton University issued a pamphlet, *Diaoyutai xu zhi* [What One Should Know about Diaoyutai], that circulated widely among Chinese students in the United States. On January 19, 1971, University of California students led five hundred students and scholars from nine northern California universities and colleges in a demonstration asking the Taiwanese government to protect Chinese interests in Diaoyutai. Another demonstration occurred in Washington, D.C., on April 10, 1971, with the participation of more than four thousand community activists, students, and scholars from thirty American institutions. These actions failed to provoke action on the part of the Taiwanese government, leading the students and scholars to convene a series of conferences discussing issues of national concern to China. An increasing majority became critical of the Taiwan regime's inaction and came to recognize that resolution of the Diaoyutai issue required a strong unified China. At a conference at Ann Arbor in September 1971, a hundred movement activists decided to shift the objective of the movement from a narrow patriotic focus on preserving China's territorial integrity toward the broader objective of promoting reunification of the mainland and Taiwan. That fall, a first group of five students accepted invitations to visit the PRC. Others followed during this period of relaxing tensions between the United States and the PRC.[86] However, the movement collapsed when the United States turned over control of the islands to Japan in May 1972 leading some of the idealistic participants to join pro-PRC militant activists in the Chinese community. Others continued to actively promote U.S.-China friendships.[87]

Toward Normalizing Relations between the United States and the PRC

These developments encouraged a coalition of activists and pro-PRC elements to establish the weekly *Chinese Voice* under the editorship of John Ong in 1969. It became the first openly pro-PRC newspaper in San Francisco in two decades. The newspaper became a daily in 1971; however, financial difficulties exacerbated by internal power struggles led to its demise in 1972. Before the paper's demise, Maurice Chuck, one of its editors, founded the weekly *San Francisco Journal* with a similar political slant.

As the tense relations between the United States and the PRC continued to ease, political winds in the Chinese communities began to shift. In New York activists from the Diaoyutai movement joined the struggling *China Daily News*. After the PRC displaced Taiwan from the United Nations in 1971, Tang Mingzhao (Chu Tong) from the PRC, former publisher of *China Daily News,* became Under-Secretary General for Political Affairs and Decolonization at the United Nations in 1972. His office urged the formation of a committee headed by Kenneth T. C. Moy, Henry Chin of the Chinese Hand Laundry Alliance, and Chen Tianxuan of the *China Daily News* to raise additional capital for the newspaper. Daily publication resumed January 1, 1977.[88]

After President Nixon's visit to China in 1972, many restrictions formerly imposed on U.S.-China relations were removed. Chinese Americans could once again visit their relatives in mainland China. The trade embargo was lifted. Cultural and educational exchanges were initiated. Chinese Americans began to be less wary about expressing their opinions about Chinese politics. In 1977 a coalition of professionals, academics, and community members founded the National

Association of Chinese Americans (NACA), with a number of chapters all over the United States, with a key objective of promoting U.S.-China friendship. The first president was Nobel Prize–winner Chen-ning Yang, who also had supported the Protect Diaoyutai Movement.[89] The same year, Honolulu witnessed the emergence of the Chinese Community Service Association of Hawaii, which held similar objectives.[90] Despite the political goals shared by the NACA membership, the gulf in understanding between the Chinese immigrant community and western-ized middle-class professionals and academics spurred Kenneth Moy to form a separate NACA chapter in the New York Chinatown community in 1981.[91]

Meanwhile, the KMT continued to exert power in the Chinatown traditionist organizational structure through adroit manipulation and maneuvers. In 1973 KMT elements on the Sue Hing Association board of directors revised the bylaws to block Joe Yuey from serving as president of San Francisco's chapter of the association and eventually gaining the position of CCBA president. Yuey was the first nominee to be rejected by the Sue Hing Association board in its century-old history.[92]

After the United States resumed normal diplomatic relations with the PRC in 1979, PRC diplomats acted similarly to their Taiwan counterparts by courting the traditionist associations with visits and invitations to functions at the consulate and to junkets in China. The competition with Taiwan sometimes generated tension and conflict within the organizations. For example, a power struggle in San Francisco's Tsung Tsin Association during the early 1980s resulted in several court cases that ended with victory for the KMT supporters and secession of the pro-PRC faction to form the Sanfanshi Keshu Lianyihui [San Francisco Hakka Friendship Association].[93] Similar confrontations and polarization in other or-ganizations continued to surface from time to time.

On other occasions, China's diplomatic representatives encouraged community supporters to form new organizations friendly to the PRC that paralleled existing ones in function. Some examples from the early 1980s include San Francisco's Chinese American Association of Commerce (founded 1980) and similar busi-ness groups in New York City, Philadelphia, and Los Angeles.[94] There were also associations such as Zhongshan Quanxian Zhongxue Tongxuehui [Association of Alumni of Zhongshan County Middle Schools] (Chung Chung Alumni As-sociation; founded 1982) and Wuyi Tongxiang Lianyihui [Friendship Association of Fellow Villagers from the Five Counties] (founded 1988) in the San Francisco Bay area.[95]

Taiwanese Dissidents

The anti-KMT government movement among native Taiwanese can be traced to February 28, 1947, when their protest against KMT corruption and its treat-ment of them as a conquered people was brutally suppressed by the Nationalist Army.[96] As the KMT imposed martial law, leaders of the protests fled abroad rather than remain and be imprisoned or killed. One group joined the People's

Consultative Conference headed by the Chinese Communists. In 1950 another group fled to Japan. Headed by Liao Wenyi, it was the first to advocate independence for Taiwan. Fifty or so Taiwanese students who had come to study in the United States also advocated Taiwanese independence. Five University of Pennsylvania students—John Lin (Lin Rongxun), Edward Chen (Chen Yide), Tom Yang (Yang Dongjie), Jay Loo (Lu Zhuyi), and Echo Lin (Lin Xihu) organized the underground Committee for Formosans' Free Formosa (3F) in the East Coast at the end of 1955. Jay Loo, writing under the nom de plume Li Tianfu, published essays that laid out the theoretical basis for Taiwan independence. These early independence movement activists were later joined by Kenny Yang (Yang Jikun) from the University of North Carolina, George Lu (Lu Jianhe) in Minnesota, and Larry Kuo (Guo Hanqing) from Washington, D.C.

Despite its underground nature, the KMT soon learned of 3F's existence and requested that the FBI investigate. In late 1957, 3F was dissolved, and United Formosans for Independence (UFI) was formed to take its place in early 1958. UFI came into the open in 1961, when it called a press conference on the anniversary of the February 28 repression. In August, seven to eight people participated in a demonstration, the first organized by UFI, against the Taiwanese government's Vice-President Chen Cheng, who was then visiting the United Nations in New York. Later that year in the fall the first Formosan Students Club was secretly formed at Kansas State University.[97] Many students from Taiwan in the United States at this time were affected by the currents of civil rights upheaval in American society, and many were critical of the lack of democracy in Taiwan. Increasing numbers became interested in exploring the independence issue and a number of Taiwan Yanjiuhui [Taiwan Study Societies] were formed.

Repression in Taiwan increased, while independence groups in the United States met in Philadelphia in 1966 to found United Formosans in America for Independence (UFAI) and published "Taiwan zijiu xuanyan" [Declaration of Taiwan's Own Salvation] in the *New York Times*.[98] On January 1, 1970, UFAI and independence groups from other countries formed World United Formosans for Independence (WUFI) headquartered in New York. In April that year, UFAI members demonstrated against Chiang Ching-kuo, Chiang Kai-shek's son and heir apparent, when he visited Los Angeles, Washington, D.C., and New York. In the last city, two members tried unsuccessfully to assassinate Chiang. In August 1979, a bomb destroyed the telecommunications system of the KMT government's New York office. The Kaohsiung Incident of December 10, 1979, was a response to the Taiwan government's crackdown on the opposition periodical *Formosa Weekly* and touched off a rash of terrorist acts in the United States. A week later, an unknown gunman sprayed bullets at the Washington office of the KMT government. A bomb explosion followed two days later. Other bombings occurred in New York, Los Angeles, and Chicago in January 1980. In July 1980, a bomb blast at Torrance, California, killed the brother-in-law of the mayor of Kaohsiung. These incidents led the FBI to treat UFAI as a terrorist organization.[99]

After 1979 immigration from Taiwan, especially of nonstudents, increased greatly. Many of these new immigrants were prominent dissidents who joined the emerging Taiwanese community of former students who had remained in the United States by acquiring permanent status and citizenship. They had begun to establish families and careers as professionals and entrepreneurs. A growing number of these pro-independence activists opposed the use of terrorism and advocated employing legal democratic action to gain independence. Others simply advocated self-determination for Taiwan. Various publications reflected the different philosophies. In 1980 Xu Xinliang revived *Formosa Weekly* in Los Angeles, after which UFAI started publishing *Taiwan Tribune* in New York at the end of 1981.

In 1982 independence movement leaders lobbied Congress successfully for a separate immigration quota of twenty thousand for Taiwan. The same year, Taiwanese leaders met to form the Formosan Association for Public Affairs (FAPA).[100] FAPA became very active in lobbying such politicians as U.S. Representative Stephen J. Solarz of New York to pressure the KMT regime to democratize. Another key FAPA accomplishment was to convince the U.S. Bureau of the Census to add "Taiwanese" as a reporting category in the 1990 Federal Census separate from "Chinese." In the 1990s, it also encouraged Taiwanese to list Taiwan as their country of birth rather than China, an act that sometimes caused bearers of such passports to be barred from entry into the PRC.

After Taiwan lifted martial law in the late 1980s, Taiwanese were allowed to resume contacts with the Chinese mainland and to organize political opposition parties. Many pro-independence dissidents returned to the island, where they became active in the Democratic Progressive Party (DPP).

Taiwan authorities responded to the political activities among Taiwanese students and academics in the United States by developing an extensive network of informants to gather intelligence on KMT critics. Informers were mostly KMT members and were usually paid for their services. The information was funneled through the various consulates to the Taiwan government. Such intelligence led to the arrest of Huang Qiming, a University of Wisconsin PhD candidate, when he visited Taipei in 1966. He was accused of leading a Taiwan Study Society and also of attending a UFI meeting in Chicago. He was sentenced to five years imprisonment. The United States exerted pressure to secure his release, but he was forbidden to leave Taiwan.[101]

Chen Yuxi was another political activist who had participated in anti–Vietnam War demonstrations and also allegedly read Communist materials in the library of the East-West Center in Hawaii. When he sought to renew his Taiwanese passport to continue his graduate studies, his application was rejected, and he had to leave the United States. He stopped over in Japan on his way to Taiwan and applied for admission at Hosei University in Tokyo. Two weeks after being accepted, Japanese immigration officers turned him over to Taiwan agents, who forcibly returned him to Taiwan. A military court tried and convicted Chen in 1967 for sedition and sentenced him to death. After protests from concerned people in Japan and the United States, Chen's sentence was reduced to seven years' imprisonment. Continued international pressure finally led to his release in 1971.[102]

Taiwan government surveillance intensified after the Diaoyutai movement of the early 1970s. In 1978 Rita Yeh, a graduate student at the University of Minnesota, returned to Taiwan after four years of study. She was arrested on her arrival and accused of plotting to overthrow the government and spreading Communist propaganda. In 1980 a military court convicted her of sedition and sentenced her to fourteen years in thought-reform prison. An even more tragic fate awaited Professor Chen Wencheng of Carnegie-Mellon University, who returned to Taiwan with his child for a visit in 1981. Chen died under mysterious circumstances after being detained by the police for interrogations.[103]

Each of these cases was followed by a brief flurry of exposé articles, usually in university newspapers. Although Taiwanese officials routinely denied the accusations, during the 1970s bad publicity caused by overzealous implementation of the surveillance system resulted in the transfer of several government officials stationed in New York back to Taiwan.[104] However, the system continued until martial law ended during the late 1980s. The spying cowed many students and intellectuals but also fueled demands for democratization and, in some cases, for the independence of Taiwan.

Taiwanese authorities also cracked down on intellectuals. The most notorious case was the assassination of journalist Henry Liu, an immigrant from Taiwan and a frequent critic of the Chiang government, who wrote an unauthorized biography of Chiang Ching-kuo. In 1984 Vice-Admiral Wang Xiling, head of military intelligence in Taiwan, sent members of Taiwan's Bamboo Gang to kill Liu at his home in South San Francisco, allegedly because he was a double agent working for the PRC. The next year Lee Ya-ping, publisher of *International Daily News,* was arrested when she visited Taiwan for allegedly publishing articles supporting PRC overtures for the reunification with Taiwan. The U.S. State Department exerted strong pressure on the Taiwanese government leading to her release after nine days.[105]

The KMT also blacklisted dissidents and critics and issued orders for their arrest. Most were associated with the Taiwan Independence and Taiwan Democratization movements. However, according to one source, the list also included such individuals as Fu Chaoshu, the publisher of the liberal *Centre Daily News,* and tai-chi master Guo Lianyin (Lien-ying Kuo), who had been elected to the National Assembly and then became a PRC supporter. None of these lists was ever made public, but their existence was confirmed by the fact that certain individuals were banned from entering Taiwan. Supposedly, the blacklists were abolished in 1991 after the lifting of martial law in 1987.[106]

Changing Relations: Taiwan and the PRC

Normal diplomatic relations resumed between the United States and the PRC in 1979. Taiwan's diplomatic mission was downgraded to become the Coordinating Council for North American Affairs (CCNAA; renamed Headquarters for Taipei Economic and Cultural Representative Office in the United States in 1994). The influence of Chinese politics on the Chinese American community also changed accordingly.

The PRC replaced Taiwan in the United Nations in 1971. In order to overcome Taiwan's international isolation, the KMT government greatly increased its lobbying efforts, especially in America. The effectiveness of the China Lobby's successor efforts was so great that *U.S. News and World Report* judged it to be second only to that of the state of Israel.[107]

The Taiwanese regime continued to cultivate and nurture political, economic, and cultural connections in the Chinese American community. In 1972 it established a Guojia Jianshe Yanjiuhui [National Construction Research Association; also referred to as Guojianhui] that annually invited one to two hundred Chinese scholars and professionals active in various fields overseas to meet in Taipei to give their views on political, economic, cultural, and diplomatic issues regarding Taiwan. In 1974 participants from the eastern United States formed the Meidong Guojian Lianyihui [National Construction Friendship Association of the Eastern United States]. In 1977 membership was opened to all Chinese scholars and professionals, and the organization changed its name to Meidong Huaren Xueshu Lianyihui [Chinese American Association of Professionals and Scientists of the Eastern United States]. Related associations sprang up in the Midwest, the South, and the West during the same period. Each of these associations had up to several hundred members and periodically organized conferences.[108]

In 1989 the CCNAA's Science Group worked with individuals and corporations in San Francisco Bay area high technology industries to form the Monte Jade Science and Technology Association. The group's objective is to promote cooperation and the mutual flow of technology and investment between Taiwan and the United States, in part echoing Taiwan's need for advanced technology transfers. In 1993 it became a national organization with branches in the West, East, Southeast, Midwest, Washington, D.C., New England, Pittsburgh, and Philadelphia. In the 1980s and 1990s the CCNAA also encouraged and assisted in the formation of such organizations as Zhonghua Guang-Dian Xuehui [Chinese Society of Light and Electricity; founded 1989], Xigu Hua-Mei Bandaoti Xiehui [Silicon Valley Chinese American Association of Semiconductor Industries; founded 1991], and Beijiazhou Hua-Mei Hangtai Xuehui [Chinese American Aerospace Society of

North America; founded 1991]. The CCNAA also maintained ties with numerous other organizations of Chinese scholars, professionals, and scientists that were predominantly supporters of Taiwan. In the 1990s, as the PRC's developing economy flourished, some of these organizations began dialogues with specialists in corresponding fields in the PRC.[109]

After the United States recognized the PRC and severed diplomatic ties to Taiwan on January 1, 1979, KMT activists in America initiated the annual practice of performing a flag-raising ceremony on Double Ten National Day to demonstrate continued support for the Republic of China. It used other means to attract Chinese American followers. In 1985 the OCAC established and staffed a Chinese Culture Center (which shared the name of the Chinese Culture Center operated by the Chinese Culture Foundation) in San Francisco. Since then it has founded nineteen such centers worldwide, ten in the United States and another three taken over from the KMT and operated as community activity centers. In 1987 the OCAC announced a plan to act as guarantor to help overseas Chinese secure capital for businesses. The NT$1 billion Overseas Chinese Credit Guarantee Fund for Loans [about US$ 2.5 trillion] was announced in 1988 and began accepting applicants in 1989. After ten years, thirty loan-service offices worldwide, of which twenty are in the United States, had granted loans totaling $408 million. About 85 percent of the recipients were immigrants from Taiwan, with the rest coming from Vietnam, Cambodia, and Laos. Immigrants from the PRC are excluded from consideration. After 1993 the Taiwanese government also encouraged supporters to lobby for Taiwan to be admitted to the United Nations as the Republic of China on Taiwan. Although these efforts have thus far failed, they contributed to the efforts of Taiwanese lobbyists in Washington to generate enough political pressure to force the U.S. State Department to grant a visa to Taiwanese president Li Teng-hui to speak at Cornell University in 1995.[110]

Taiwan's two largest opposition parties, the DPP and the New Party, both established party branches and support groups in the United States to compete with KMT groups. Several groups opposed to the KMT founded the DPP in 1986 in Taipei. In 1991 it branched out to the eastern and western United States. Most of the DPP's support derived from existing organizations of native Taiwanese that had long been active in opposition to the KMT and sympathetic toward independence for Taiwan.[111]

The New Party was a splinter group of the KMT formed in Taipei in 1993 by KMT members who disagreed with Taiwanese president Li Teng-hui's policy favoring native Taiwanese, but included many who favored eventual reunification with the China mainland. In 1994 the party established its first overseas branch in the San Francisco Bay area in 1990, Haiwai Xingzhonghui [Revive China Society Overseas]. New Party members were troubled by political trends accompanying the rise to power of Li Teng-hui. The party had begun as a group within the KMT in 1990, with the aim of supporting party reform to promote prosperity and stability in Taiwan and eventually to reunite the Chinese nation. Because of the similarity in political philosophy of the two groups, many in the Haiwai Xingzhonghui became active members of the San Francisco branch of the New Party. In 1994 Dai Qi (Tai Chi), who headed the branch and was also a Haiwai Xingzhonghui member, began publishing the semimonthly *Taipei Report*, with articles highly critical of Li Teng-hui's administration. Cecilia Yen, another former KMT member, was editorial writer for the publication. The branch also formed Friends of the New Party in North American Chinese communities, which raised $70,000 for the party's 1995 election campaign. By 1996 forty such support groups were said to exist in the United States. In 1994 Friends of the New Party founded the New Association of Chinese Americans to promote Chinese culture, to influence Taiwan and mainland China, and to support U.S. candidates.[112] Many of the New Party's followers in the United States were immigrants who had accompanied the Nationalist government to Taiwan after 1945. By the late 1990s, the party was running a weak third after the KMT and the DPP.

When the opposition, especially the New Party, began to make inroads into KMT support in the Chinese American community, supporters of President Li Teng-hui organized Bei Meizhou Li Denghui Zongtong zhi You Lianyihui [Friendship Association in North America of Friends of President Li Teng-hui] in August 1996. Its mission was to support Li's policies and to bolster his image. The association was headquartered in Los Angeles and had seven regional branches in other parts of the United States and one each in Mexico and Canada. By early 1997, the number of U.S. branches had grown to seventeen, as other areas vied for recognition of their efforts by the Li administration.[113]

Democracy Movement in the PRC

During the 1980s, large numbers of students and scholars from the PRC came to study in the United States. Among them were dissidents, including Wang Bingzhang. Wang was among the first group of government-sponsored students sent to Canada. After receiving his MD degree from McGill University in Montreal in 1982, Wang announced that he was "leaving the medical field to join the democratic movement to strive for spring in the ancestral land." He relocated to New York, where he and other PRC dissidents began publishing *China Spring* in December 1982. The magazine attacked "feudal despotism" and "bureaucratic special privileges" and called for "real democracy and rule of law, freedom and human rights" in China. In December 1983 the China Spring Democratic Movement convened in New York and formally assumed the name Chinese Alliance for Democracy (CAD). CAD lobbied successfully for the support of some American politicians. However, during the next few years a series of power struggles beset the organization and many founders left. Wang was expelled in March 1989 by an anti-Wang group led by Hu Ping. His supporters then held a convention and founded the Zhongguo Minzhudang [Democratic Party of China]. Although

CAD and the Democratic Party of China recombined in June 1991, Wang did not return.[114]

Another early democracy movement organization was the Chinese Democratic Education Foundation, founded in 1985 in San Francisco. Its primary driving force was Huang Yuchuan, a former PRC labor camp inmate who immigrated to the United States in the 1970s and became a successful businessman. Huang was one of the first in the Chinese American community to support the China Spring movement. Beginning in 1986 the foundation annually awarded a plaque and $2,000 to "outstanding fighters for democracy" in the PRC, Taiwan, and Hong Kong.[115]

Dissidents within the PRC made the headlines again in spring 1989, when a mass of demonstrators led by university students occupied Tian'anmen Square in Beijing to protest government corruption and demand democracy. The government responded by imposing martial law and on June 4 initiated a military crackdown that led to many deaths, injuries, arrests, and destruction of property. Extensive on-the-spot coverage by international news services, and well-publicized accounts by dissidents and their supporters of the bloody carnage and atrocities, gained considerable sympathy worldwide for the demonstrators, although many of these initial descriptions proved to be highly exaggerated or of debatable veracity. The first democracy movement newspaper in the United States, *Press Freedom Herald,* began publishing on June 9 under the sponsorship of the Chinese Overseas Journalists Association. The chief editor was Cao Changqing, a dissident who had been a journalist in Shenzhen.

Pro-PRC ranks fell into disarray as supporters differed in their evaluation of the June 4 crackdowns. On one hand, *Centre Daily News,* a national newspaper that had tried to be evenhanded in its coverage of Taiwan and the PRC, defended the PRC government's position, leading democracy movement supporters to organize a campaign pressuring advertisers to withdraw. On July 5, Fu Chaoshu resigned as publisher and head of the newspaper's board of directors. On September 18, the paper ceased publication. On the other hand, *China Daily News* condemned the military repression in Beijing and was in turn denounced by the Chinese Hand Laundry Association, including some members who had been founders of the newspaper. Businesses connected with the PRC also pulled their advertising. Since the management could not find alternative sources to make up for this critical revenue, *China Daily News* had no choice but to close down on July 29. At that time it was the oldest Chinese newspaper in New York. On January 5, 1990, the newspaper resumed weekly publication as *China Press,* funded by PRC interests. By August 31, it had resumed daily publication. The newspaper also began editions in San Francisco in 1992 and Los Angeles in 1994. This paper can now be considered the semiofficial voice of the PRC. The first managing publisher was Xiong Feiwen, formerly of the PRC's China News Service.[116]

Immediately after the Tian'anmen Incident, pro–democracy movement organizations in the United States mushroomed. Membership included a range of political colorations from conservative to liberal. Most were ad hoc groups organized principally to raise funds. Others had a more defined mission. In San Francisco a group that included former PRC supporters founded the Foundation for Chinese Democracy (FCD), which organized the first North American conference of community-based prodemocracy organizations in December 1989. Afterward, the Federation of Overseas Hong Kong Chinese of Washington, D.C., the Southern California Foundation for Chinese Democracy of Los Angeles, the Tian'anmen Memorial Foundation of New York/New Jersey, the Toronto Association for Democracy in China, and the Vancouver Society in Support of the Democratic movement formed the North American Coalition for Chinese Democracy (NACCD) as an informal network. The NACCD's mission was to provide coordination and support to North American community-based organizations to further the cause of human rights and democracy in China. In January 1991, the NACCD began publication of the English-language quarterly *A Changing China*. A group consisting of computer manufacturer Lester Lee, attorney Edward Lau, and others led the formation of Silicon Valley for Democracy in China (SVDC) on July 15, 1989. SVDC frequently broadcasts to the PRC over Voice of America. It also operates a Web site with news of its activities and of dissidents.[117]

After the Tian'anmen Incident, a number of the demonstration's leaders and other dissident intellectuals escaped from China. On September 22, 1989, they met with other dissidents in Paris to found the Federation for a Democratic China (FDC). Yan Jiaqi was elected chairman and Wan Runnan secretary-general. In February seventy delegates from twenty branches and twenty-three liaison offices in the United States met in San Francisco to establish the U.S. chapter of the FDC.[118]

Factionalism and political infighting were already evident during the FDC's first convention in Paris. Questions arose regarding the mishandling of $561,681 donated to the FDC up to November 1989. Charges began to float that some leaders had squandered funds on extravagant office and living expenses. There were also complaints regarding arrogant, elitist attitudes on the part of some leaders.[119] As publicity concerning their tarnished images spread, donations to the dissidents from the disappointed Chinese American community fell off dramatically.

In early 1990 the FDC began exploratory talks with CAD leaders about a possible merger. The two entities held a joint convention in Washington, D.C., in January 1993 and formed Alliance for a Democratic China (ADC); however, FDC and CAD each maintained their own organizations. Xu Bangtai became chairperson of the joint group.[120]

By the late 1990s, time had greatly softened the initial shock and horror regarding the events of 1989. The democracy movement had an ever-narrowing circle of supporters, mostly among students and intellectuals. It has reentered the consciousness of the Chinese American community occasionally when there is a protest about an alleged human rights abuse in the PRC or during memorial services commemorating the Tian'anmen Incident. Occasionally, the news media reports about dissidents exiled from the PRC, some of whom have joined the

ADC while others have pursued individual agendas.[121] One particularly active but controversial figure was Wu Hongda (Harry Wu), who established the Laogai Research Foundation to expose forced labor camps in the PRC.

The democracy movement has remained an irritant in U.S.-PRC relations. Periodically, dissidents testify before congressional committees regarding alleged abuses of human rights in the PRC. The human rights issue is used by the United States as leverage in negotiations with the PRC. In domestic politics, politicians such as Representative Nancy Pelosi of California also criticize human rights abuses in China to generate political capital. Within the Chinese American community, however, even though there may be sympathy for efforts to improve conditions in China, there is only limited interaction between the population and the Democracy movement.

During the early twenty-first century, the Falun Gong cult has emerged as an aggressive dissident group. Li Hongzhi introduced Falun Dafa [Practice of the Wheel of Law] in the PRC in 1992. It attracted numerous practitioners and was banned on July 20, 1999, by the PRC government as "jeopardizing social stability." Falun Gong members who succeeded in leaving China resurfaced to reestablish the group abroad in many western countries, including the United States, and mounted attacks on the Chinese Communists, using the news media, radio, television, and the internet.[122]

Changing Attitudes toward the PRC

A side effect of the Tian'anmen Incident was that it persuaded Congress to pass the Chinese Students Protection Act in 1992, enabling approximately fifty thousand students and visiting scholars to receive permanent-resident status so that they could avoid returning to the PRC and facing possible persecution.[123] This act contributed to the growth of a community of PRC immigrants.

Although the PRC continued to deal severely with dissidents and barred the return of most members of the democratic movement to China, the government continued economic policies that led to rapid development and significantly improved living standards in many parts of China. Along with the rest of the international community, many Chinese Americans who had initially denounced the PRC government's handling of the Tian'anmen Incident began viewing it more pragmatically as a nation striving hard to modernize and realize its vast potential while avoiding being overcome by numerous difficult and deep-rooted social, economic, and political problems. Many Chinese Americans began to contribute to China's development by investing capital and expertise or by working to achieve better understanding between the two countries. In 1990 a group of concerned Chinese American leaders in business and industry formed the Committee of 100 to encourage constructive relations between the peoples of the United States and greater China and to encourage the full participation of Chinese Americans in all fields of American life.[124]

In the meantime a great number of new immigrants, students, visiting scholars, and personnel and families connected with PRC enterprises continued to arrive in America. By the last decade of the twentieth century, recent immigrants from the PRC formed a sizable community. Publications appeared expressing their viewpoints and concerns. In general, these publications were not anti-PRC, but they often published items critical of events in China. Two of the earliest such newspapers were the *China Journal* weekly in Los Angeles County (founded 1992) and the monthly *New Continent* in the San Francisco Bay area. A daily, *Zhong Guo Daily News,* also began publishing in Los Angeles in 1997.

Newcomers from the merchant and working classes founded new native-place organizations and chambers of commerce. Such organizations were especially numerous among immigrants from the Fuzhou area who settled in New York City. The changed conditions produced immigration from more diverse regions of China, which required different social, professional, and business networks, including such native-place associations as the Beijing USA Association in Flushing, New York (founded 1991), and the Beijing Association of the USA in Sunnyvale, California (founded 1993), Los Angeles (founded 1995), Washington, D.C. (founded 1996), and Houston (founded 1997). New immigrants also formed alumni associations, such as San Francisco's Northern America Guangzhou High School Alumni Association, founded in 1996 by graduates of more than 120 high schools in Guangzhou. New scholarly and professional associations proliferated. A major one was the Chinese Association for Science and Technology (founded in 1992 in New York), which by the mid-1990s had more than 1,500 members and five regional branches and specialty branches, such as Zhongguo Lü-Mei Dianzi ji Xinxi Jishu Xiehui [Chinese Electronics and Telecommunications Technology Society in America; founded 1993] and Zhongguo Lü-Mei Gongcheng Xuehui [Chinese Engineering Society in America; founded 1995]. One of the association's objectives is to promote technological cooperation and trade between the United States and the PRC. Other professional organizations with similar objectives include Chicago's Association of Chinese Scientists and Engineers (USA) (founded 1992), New York's Zhong-Mei Jinrongjia Xiehui [Chinese American Society of Financiers in America; founded 1994], and others.[125] Owing to the comparatively recent arrival of these immigrants, their professional organizations were fewer and had much shorter histories than the ones founded by Taiwanese immigrants. As tensions between the Taiwan and PRC governments eased, there has been increased dialogue between these professional groups.

Some of these new groups, together with existing pro-PRC groups, formed new umbrella organizations that paralleled the existing CCBA organizational structure. One of the earliest was Huashengdun Huaren Gejie Lianhehui [Federation of Chinese Organizations of Washington, D.C.], established in 1984. The fact that the PRC embassy was in the city may have facilitated its early debut. In 1986 the United Federation of Chinese Associations in New York was founded in the city where the PRC United Nations delegation was located. By the late 1990s, the number of member organizations in this group had expanded from the founding fifteen to about sixty. In the Midwest, Zhijiage Huaren Gejie Lianxihui [Chinese American Associations of Chicago] was founded in 1998. Thus far, no corresponding group has appeared in San Francisco. Most of the activities of these umbrella groups are of a social and political nature, such as organizing spring festival banquets, celebrating October 1st National Day and the return of Hong Kong to China, and welcoming delegations from the PRC.[126]

In the area of education, the growth of the PRC immigrant community led to the rise of two rival school systems. When immigration from Taiwan began to increase in the 1970s, parents became concerned about their offspring preserving their Chinese heritage. Parents united to establish Chinese-language schools. In the 1990s, there were more than four hundred such schools in the United States, belonging to ten regional Chinese school associations, some of which had existed since the mid-1970s. These associations in turn formed the National Council of Associations of Chinese Language Schools (NCACLS) in 1994. This entire organizational structure enjoyed a close relationship with Taiwan's Overseas Chinese Affairs Commission, which offers free textbooks with traditional characters and using the Chinese phonetic alphabet as a pronunciation aid. The commission also helped to organize annual teacher training sessions.[127]

The growing numbers of new immigrants from the PRC and their families also organized Chinese-language schools by the end of the 1980s. By 1995 the number had increased to about a hundred, approximately a sixth of the total number of Chinese schools in the United States. These schools formed the Chinese School Association in the United States (CSAUS) in 1994 and worked actively with Beijing's Overseas Chinese Affairs Office to develop textbooks using simplified characters and pinyin transliteration.[128] The competition between the two systems of written Chinese gave birth in the 1990s to a continuing polemic in Chinese-language newspapers debating the merits and shortcomings of traditional and simplified characters.[129]

Changes in the demography of the Chinese American community and improvements in the PRC economy have caused the number of PRC supporters to increase significantly. For example, when Taiwanese president Li Teng-hui spoke at Cornell University during his controversial 1994 visit, pro-PRC students protesting his visit shared the limelight with pro-Li and pro-Taiwan independence demonstrators, a phenomenon that would not have occurred a decade earlier. PRC supporters now emulate the flag-raising ceremonies first introduced by pro-Taiwan partisans. In San Francisco Chinatown, long a KMT bastion, the five-starred flag of the PRC was raised in public in September 1994 at the pro-PRC Chinese American Association of Commerce. A few weeks later the flag was also hoisted over the venerable Suey Sing Labor and Merchant Association.

Suey Sing elder Joe Yuey had pressed the association to pass such a resolution as early as 1972, but heavy pressure from the Chinatown traditionist organizational structure forced the group to back down.[130] Conditions had indeed changed during the two decades that had elapsed!

By the mid-1990s, October 1st National Day celebrations had become larger in scale and more patriotic in theme. The 1997 celebration in Alhambra, Los Angeles County, included a parade and flag-raising ceremony and attracted a crowd of ten thousand.[131] However, many traditionist associations still flew the flag of the Republic of China; others flew the organization's own flag or no flag at all. This development had been evolving since the early 1970s; the traditionist community organizational structure is no longer monolithic in its attitudes toward the PRC and Taiwan.

Changing Picture in Taiwan

After Chiang Ching-kuo's death in 1988 and the lifting of martial law, the Taiwanese political scene changed dramatically, as the native Taiwanese Lee Teng-hui served as president for two terms. Internal power struggles and divisions in the ruling KMT party coupled with corruption facilitated the ascension to power of the opposition DPP in the late 1990s. In 2000 the DPP presidential candidate, Chen Shui-bian, won against a divided opposition. In 2004 he won again, but only by a narrow margin.

The Taiwanese government lost some support among Chinese Americans due to perceptions that the DDP favored Taiwanese—descendants of pre–World War II settlers on Taiwan—over the later arriving mainlanders and other Chinese overseas, their perceived intention to eventually permanently separate Taiwan from China, and the continued economic growth and prosperity in the PRC. A number of conservative traditionist organizations distanced themselves from the DPP-government and made common cause with pro-PRC pro-unification groups. A number of traditionist clan and native place associations began hoisting the PRC national flag. In San Francisco, the Nam Hoy Fook Yum Association was the first to do so on May 11, 2002.[132] In New York, the local Gee How Oak Tin Association raised the five-starred flag in October, 2002.[133] On the other hand, a number in the Taiwanese community became active supporters of the DPP, and some even returned to the island.

By the early years of the twenty-first century, Chinese politics as reflected in the contemporary Chinese American community are more complex than ever before. Beyond the basic issue of supporting the PRC or Taiwan are added the additional complications of democracy movement demands regarding human rights in the PRC, reunification versus independence for Taiwan, and competition between the KMT, the DPP, and other political parties for support.

Concluding Words

The Chinese American community has been predominantly foreign-born ever since coming into existence in the mid–nineteenth century. It should not be surprising that many Chinese Americans maintain many ties to their ancestral homeland and retain strong interests in developments there. However, the relationship between China and the Chinese in America has been in a constant state of dynamic change, resulting in many shifts in attitudes. Thus, the responses of Chinese Americans to events in China have varied during different periods in the community's history.

The Chinese in America encountered white racism soon after they first arrived in California in large numbers. Local, state, and federal governments also demonstrated unwillingness to accept Chinese people as equal partners in American society through the passage of discriminatory laws. In 1882 this hostility culminated in the passage of the first Chinese Exclusion Act. For the next sixty-one years, Chinese faced highly restrictive entry conditions and, regardless of social class and place of birth, were often subjected to prejudice and discrimination in America. Alienated by their sustained rejection from mainstream American society, many Chinese continued to regard China as their home. During the exclusion period, many willingly made heavy financial commitments to support modernization efforts in China, and a significant number also actively participated in furthering China's political objectives.

These loyalties began to change during World War II. The Chinese Exclusion Acts were repealed, and the social and economic status of Chinese Americans began to improve as they gained greater rights to participate more equally in American mainstream society. In the meantime, the Chinese civil war resulted in the founding of the Communist People's Republic of China and a refugee Kuomintang regime in Taiwan. Soon afterward, the cold war led the United States to impose an embargo on the PRC, cutting off Chinese American communications with their native villages. Supporters of the Taiwan regime exploited the tense Sino-American relations to muzzle dissident opinions in the Chinese American community and to claim its support in its struggle with the PRC. Chinese Americans were relegated to passive and impotent roles in this conflict.

With the opening of China, the democratization of Taiwan, and the influx of a large immigrant population starting in the 1970s, Chinese American activism concerning Chinese politics reemerged and became more diverse and complex. Besides the main protagonists, the PRC and Taiwan, many other voices advocated Taiwan independence or demanded greater democracy in China. The Chinese in America in the meantime had also changed. Activists supporting these causes are now a very small minority. Although the rest of the community retains a sense of connection to China, and probably will for some time to come, most individuals view events there with the perspective that America, rather than China, is their permanent home. This is the fundamental changing of attitudes from only a half century before.

CHAPTER 2

Anarchism, Communism, and China's Nationalist Revolution

The different Chinese left movements from the late nineteenth through the greater part of the twentieth century were offshoots of important political and social movements of the West. Probably because the Chinese population constituted only a small minority in the United States, little scholarly attention has focused on the historical development of these movements among them. This essay strives to piece together information scattered among many publications and oral sources to reconstruct this history and the varying roles of the individuals involved. This essay emphasizes activities concerning Chinese people in America rather than interpreting the inner workings, conflicts, or ideological leanings of global left movements.

Two factors stimulated the emergence and rise of left-wing activities among Chinese in America: the desire to improve their status in America, where they faced exploitation and racial oppression and the hope of modernizing China into an internationally respected nation. These developments began with the reform and revolutionary movements at the turn of the twentieth century, continued during the Republican era of Kuomintang (KMT) party rule, and culminated with the Chinese Communist Party (CCP) and the establishment of the People's Republic of China (PRC). As we shall see, in the history of the Chinese Left in America, these two goals were the main influences shaping the development of the Left among the Chinese in America with one or the other predominating during different periods.

Introduction of Socialist Philosophies

During the late nineteenth century, preaching about labor solidarity and utopian doctrines was widespread in American society. At the same time, most organized American labor groups and their political allies spearheaded the anti-Chinese movement as part of their struggle against capitalism. Even the Socialist Party, despite its emphasis on the common interests of the proletariat regardless of race or nationality, was hostile toward Chinese labor.[1] Thus, it is doubtful whether the

American socialist movement ever attracted more than a handful of Chinese in America during this period. Only the anarcho-syndicalist Industrial Workers of the World (IWW), which steadfastly practiced the belief that fraternity bound all wage earners regardless of race, advocated enrolling Japanese and Chinese members as equals into unions. However, the IWW represented only a small percentage of workers in America.

Writings about leftist philosophies that originated in East Asia were much more effective in influencing some segments of the Chinese population in America. The latter half of the nineteenth century was a time of multifaceted travail for China, which was beset by internal turmoil and foreign aggression. Many concerned Chinese sought solutions that would save their nation from imperialist subjugation—including the promises of socialism.

The socialist movement had gained importance in Western nations since the mid–nineteenth century. During these early years, few Chinese were aware of the movement, but they gained greater exposure to it gradually through Western traders and missionaries at the treaty ports and increasing visits to Western countries. In 1871 the missionary-run *Church News,* which was founded in 1868 in Shanghai, reprinted extremely hostile Western press reports about the Paris commune. Zhang Deyi, English interpreter to the special Chinese envoy to France, also published a more objective eyewitness account in 1873 but did not describe much of its ideological foundations.[2]

In subsequent years, the *Church News'* successor publications, *Chinese Globe Magazine* and the *Review of the Times,* reprinted western press items about socialism, anarchism, and nihilism; however, terminology was not unified and standardized. In 1898 the *Review of the Times* published the first systematic exposition applying various utopian socialistic philosophies to proposals for China's reform but without referencing Marxist socialism. Karl Marx and other prominent socialists were not mentioned by name until 1899, when an abridged translation of Benjamin Kidd's "Social Evolution" was published as "Datongxue" [Utopian Philosophies] in *Review of the Times.*[3]

The early 1900s witnessed publication of an increasing number of essays and books on socialism, many translated from Japanese. *Shehuizhuyi,* the modern Chinese term for socialism, first appeared in print in 1901 in a Chinese translation from Ariga Nagao's *History of Modern Politics.*[4]

During this period, Chinese Marxists and anarchists were chiefly intellectuals and students who had gone abroad to study and become politically active reformers and revolutionaries. Through Japanese and European writings, they learned about the ideas of Bakunin, Kropotkin, Marx, Engels, and others. Many articles touching on these doctrines appeared in newspapers and periodicals established by reform and revolutionary organizations in Hong Kong and Japan.[5]

Early reformist Chinese writers generally favored the socialist-democratic doctrines of the Second International. Among younger revolutionaries, growing interests in anarchism and nihilism paralleled this phenomenon.[6] By the middle of the first decade of the twentieth century, advocates of anarchism as the guide for revolution began to predominate in Chinese socialist writings.

During this time, both the reform and revolutionary movements established footholds among Chinese communities abroad. At different periods, the Hongmen (secret societies or fraternal orders also known as Triads) allied with the reformers and then the revolutionaries. Around the turn of the twentieth century, first the reformers, then the Hongmen, followed by the revolutionaries, founded newspapers in major New World Chinese communities such as San Francisco, Honolulu, Vancouver, and New York City. These newspaper offices disseminated such publications as the reformist *Xinmin Congbao* [New People's News Miscellany] and the Sun Yat-sen–led Tongmenghui's [Revolutionary Alliance] *Min Bao* [People's News] that not only propagated each movement's political agendas but also explored socialist concepts and developments and their potential applications for the Chinese situation. In 1904 the reformer Liang Qichao, whose writings appeared in *Xinmin Congbao,* reported favorably on his four meetings with socialist party members during his 1903 trip to America. In 1905 Sun Yat-sen visited the secretariat of the Second International in Brussels and identified his revolutionary movement with the world socialist movement. In his forward to the first issue of *Min Bao* that appeared November 26, 1905, Sun remarked on the rising tides of anarchism and socialism in Europe and America and predicted that the socialist revolution was approaching.[7]

The Russian Revolution of 1905 fueled the growing popularity of anarchism among some members of the Tongmenghui and its successor organization, the Kuomintang. By 1907 Chinese students in Japan and France had formed anarchist organizations, with the French group publishing *Xin Shiji* [*La Novaj Tempoj;* New Era], which attracted readers in China and overseas.[8] The teachings of Proudhon, Bakunin, and Kropotkin gained in popularity as petty bourgeois Chinese intellectuals embraced the concept of committing acts of terrorism to help destroy the old order. Liu Sifu, also known as Shifu, was an influential convert as a Cantonese scholar from a well-to-do family in present-day Zhongshan, an area with numerous emigrants. Liu was arrested and jailed after a failed bombing attempt against a Qing official in Guangdong in 1907. After his release from prison in 1909 he became a firm believer in nihilism. In 1910, together with Xie Yingbo, Gao Jianfu, Chen Jiongming, and others, he organized Zhina Anshatuan [Assassins Society of China] in Hong Kong to attack Qing officials. Others joined the group, including Zheng Anfu (also known as Zheng Bi'an), who later joined the Chinese anarchist movement in America.[9]

Chinese in America were also learning about the anarchist movement during this period. Around 1907–8 the IWW recruited two Chinese sympathizers in San Francisco to translate some of their literature.[10] In 1909 a Honolulu book club was already in existence and met periodically to discuss such works as "A Critique of

Socialism," "Scientific Socialism," and "Marx."[11] In 1910 news of Wang Jingwei's attempted assassination of the Qing prince regent in Beijing was probably an inspiration for George Fong and Zhu Zhuowen to make a similar attempt in November on the visiting Qing Prince Zai Xun at the Oakland train station.[12]

Kiang Kang Hu and the Chinese Socialist Club

After the 1912 inauguration of the Republic of China, the first Chinese president, Yuan Shikai, inadvertently contributed to the further development of the Left among Chinese abroad when his autocratic regime forced the exodus of numerous political activists, including Jiang Kanghu (Kiang Kang Hu), who had been a member of the Tongmenghui. Kiang had led the founding of a socialist study society, which became the Chinese Socialist Party in early 1912. In October 1913, President Yuan proscribed this party, and Kiang fled to the United States where he founded the Chinese Socialist Club in San Francisco's Chinatown on January 17, 1914, with the call for "sympathizers to gather together to study the doctrine." The group was open to "all compatriots in America, male and female regardless of party or school of thought, who believe in Socialism."[13]

The club soon published Kiang's *China and the Social Revolution*, which was one of the earliest Chinese socialist writings published in America.[14] After teaching Mandarin Chinese in Chinatown and at the University of California, Berkeley, and helping to build and catalog the Chinese library collections of both Berkeley and the Library of Congress, Kiang returned to China in 1920.[15] He probably regarded the Chinese Socialist Club as only a minor incident in his career. Nonetheless, the seed that he planted germinated among the Chinese in San Francisco.

Kuomintang Members and Socialist Philosophies

Immediately after Kiang's flight from China in November 1913, President Yuan ordered the dissolution of the KMT, his principal opposition. Led by Sun Yat-sen, Kuomintang leaders had already started fleeing abroad after the failure of a July 1913 anti-Yuan insurrection. In 1914 San Francisco KMT supporters founded the Pingmin Shubaoshe [Book and Newspaper Reading Room for Common People], which provided a meeting place and mailing address for the Chinese Socialist Club. During the 1910s, such KMT party members as Xie Yingbo and Feng Ziyou participated actively in the Chinese Socialist Club and other socialist organizations.[16]

For example, Xie Yingbo, who had been linked to the anarchist Liu Sifu in Hong Kong, reputedly joined the Socialist Party and attended classes on socialist doctrines in New York. When a Beijing warlord government sought a loan in the United States in May 1918, New York KMT member Zhao Gongbi (Chu Su Gunn) allegedly persuaded the Socialist Party headquarters in Chicago to distribute leaflets and contact President Woodrow Wilson in an attempt to scuttle the negotiations. After the World War I armistice, Xie Yingbo also allegedly contacted the Socialist Party to ask for help convincing delegates to the Versailles Peace Conference that the warlord government in Beijing was illegal and that its delegate should not be seated.[17] Although these were only gestures by the relatively powerless Socialists and KMT, they demonstrate the timbre of much of the Chinese Left's activities during this period. Although concerned with the lot of workers, the predominance of émigrés ensured that most of their activities targeted developments in China. This mix of domestic and international priorities remained dominant influences on the development of the Chinese American Left in succeeding decades.

The political climate in the United States during the 1910s and 1920s was rabidly hostile toward radicalism.[18] The primary targets were white radicals, especially European immigrants, but the KMT also encountered great suspicion. When the KMT sent Wu Tiecheng to Honolulu in late 1914 to serve as editor for the *Liberty Press*, China's envoy to America sought unsuccessfully to have him deported as an anarchist.[19] Confirming the negative perceptions of American authorities, KMT member Liu Beihai assassinated the suspected Yuan supporter, journalist Huang Yuanyong, at the Shanghai Low restaurant in San Francisco Chinatown in December 1915. In Victoria, British Columbia, in September 1918 another KMT member, Wang Chang, shot and killed Tang Hualong, an ex-official of the warlord government that had succeeded the Yuan regime.[20]

The transnational reach of Chinese American radicalism also flowed from west to east, as Chinese throughout the world learned about American union organizing and strike methods.

Labor and Politics

Workers returning to China around the turn of the twentieth century brought with them knowledge of these concepts and practices. Some joined the revolutionary movement, such as Ma Chaojun (Ma Chao Chun), who emigrated from Hong Kong to San Francisco in 1902 and became a dockyard worker. He joined Sun Yat-sen's revolutionary movement and in 1906 helped to organize workers in Hong Kong supporting the revolutionary cause. In order to avoid interference by the British authorities, Sun's group masqueraded as a workers' club for self-education and recreation and was one of the earliest labor organizations to be formed in Hong Kong and China.[21]

Subsequently, Chinese labor organizations formed among industrial workers in larger cities in China. Xu Qiwen, a member of Kiang Kang Hu's socialist party, founded Zhonghua Minguo Gongdang [Labor Party of the Republic of China] in Shanghai in January 1912. The party recruited foremen from different trades and crafts as members, and thereby automatically enrolled all workers in their respective jurisdictions. The party advocated developing Chinese-owned industries, educating workers, improving workers' welfare, and instilling a military spirit among workers. However, the party did not involve itself in labor-management disputes except as a third-party mediator. The party regarded Sun Yat-sen as its honorary leader and actively campaigned against Yuan Shikai, efforts that proved to be short-lived when Xu Qiwen was captured and executed after a failed attack on the Shanghai Arsenal on May 26, 1913. Although brief, the party's example inspired similar activities among other Chinese.[22] The New World emergence of such organizations indicates that the goal did not die with Xu but continued with the arrival of other exiled activists, many of whom were sympathetic to the KMT.

Labor Organizing in North America

Immigrants from China, many influenced by anarcho-syndicalist philosophies, were active in labor issues among the Chinese population on the North America mainland. The widespread labor unrest in the United States and Canada that peaked during the years following World War I probably contributed to such developments.

One of the first major labor organizing efforts occurred in Vancouver, with the founding of the Zhonghua Gongdang [Chinese Labour Association] in 1916 and that group's efforts to organize sawmill workers in the area. In 1918 and 1919, the association led successful strikes that won on such issues as shortening the workday from ten to eight hours. The activist Chen Shuyao and political exile Zheng Bi'an, a fellow townsman and associate of anarchist Liu Sifu, were actively supporting the group. Their labor organizing activities led the Canadian government around 1919 to adopt repressive measures pressuring them to leave the dominion and immigrate to San Francisco.[23]

In the United States, Chinese spearheaded a major labor organizing effort in 1918, when Chicago waiters organized the Mon Sang Association to demand better working conditions.[24] However, the largest group of Chinese organized workers was the Sanfanshi Gongyi Tongmeng Zonghui [Workers' League of San Francisco, or Unionist Guild], founded in 1919 in San Francisco, which at the time had the largest population of Chinese shirt-factory workers.[25]

The Unionist Guild first targeted factories in San Francisco and Oakland. On May 18, 1919, it presented a list of nine demands to factory owners. After strike threats and several negotiating sessions at the Yeong Wo Association in San Francisco, they finally signed agreements with thirty-two factories.[26] Following this initial success, the Unionist Guild attempted to expand its influence, with mixed results. In September 1919, the Unionist Guild announced the creation of two additional departments: one for agriculture and one for miscellaneous occupations. However, these recruiting attempts could not be sustained.

The organization was one of the earliest Chinese labor groups to reach out to seek the fraternal support of American labor unions. After the "May 30 Massacre," during which British police fired on and killed numerous Chinese demonstrators in Shanghai, General Executive Secretary Alice Sum of the guild contacted mainstream American labor unions futilely seeking support for the strikers and their families.[27]

The guild's initial successes also led factory owners to organize countermeasures. By uniting against the workers, the employers frustrated several guild-led strikes during the next few years. Unable to rally broad workers' support and basically isolated from mainstream organized labor, the guild's fortunes declined, and it faded from the Chinatown scene during the late 1920s.

At its peak, the Unionist Guild claimed a nominal membership of about a thousand, although there were far fewer active members. This represented the high point of anarcho-syndicalist activity among Chinese workers in America. The demise of the guild demonstrated the difficulty faced by Chinese workers striving for lasting gains without much fraternal support from workers in the larger society.

Hawaii

Kuomintang supporters founded a workers' club in Honolulu in 1915 and formally registered it at the Chinese Consulate the next year as Zhongguo Gongdang Tan-xiangshan Zhibu [Hawaii Branch of the Chinese Labor Party].[28] The group strove to unite Chinese workers, improve their livelihood, promote public welfare, and further China's national salvation. Membership was open to all. It functioned as a social center for workers and as a branch of the Kuomintang.[29]

In 1920 Xie Yingbo led another effort in Guangzhou to launch the Huzhu Zongshe [Mutual Aid Society], which included members from several dozen handicraft unions, many of whom were influenced by anarcho-syndicalist philosophies. This move inspired a group of young, China-educated intellectuals to found a Honolulu Huzhu She [Hoo Cho Society] in 1923. This society established a public reading room with more than a thousand volumes and began publishing *Hoo Cho Monthly* in 1925 to spread the philosophy of mutual aid. They ran out of funds after publishing thirteen issues in 1926 and refocused on education to found the Hoo Cho Chinese School.[30]

These Hawaiian organizations did not further develop into labor movements. A possible reason is that during this period many Chinese were becoming middle class and the working class was too small to sustain a labor movement.

On the Mainland

During this period, immigrant labor activist Chen Shuyao founded *Mingxing Xunkan* [Bright Star 10-Day Publication] in Vancouver in 1919 to propagate anarcho-socialist ideas among Chinese workers. Workers' clubs also emerged in the smaller Boston and New York Chinese communities. In 1919 Zhao Taimou and others began publishing the periodical *Laodong Chao* [Labor Tide], which ran for four issues. However, with the anti-radical hysteria of the times, these organizations faced an ever-present threat of police harassment and arrests, forcing Chen Shuyao to depart Vancouver for San Francisco. The *Chinese World* on January 18, 1919, reported a police raid on New York's Chinese Workers Club that resulted in the confiscation of allegedly IWW literature and the arrest of four persons who claimed to be students.

In San Francisco in March 1924, the Unionist Guild founded the monthly *Kung Sing*, which included news and essays on the labor and anarcho-syndicalist movements and selected literary works. By this time, however, the guild was already in decline. Ping Sheh [Equality Society] would assume the banner of the Chinese American anarchist movement in San Francisco. Founded around 1921, its active members included such immigrants as Zheng Bi'an, Chen Shuyao, and Cai Xian (better known as Liu Zhongshi, Red Jones, or Ray Jones). This group published a monthly magazine, *Pingdeng* [Equality], from 1927 until 1941, featuring numerous pieces by anarchists in America and abroad.[31] During 1927 and 1928, it included several articles by the famous writer Bajin, under the name Li Feigan and others; since some issues included several of his articles, Bajin used different pennames for each.[32]

Ping Sheh also infrequently published and distributed other pamphlets and leaflets in support of radical causes. The anarchist movement was on the decline, and the climate was still implacably hostile, particularly among law enforcement officers. For example, in March 1928 San Francisco police arrested Cai Xian as he distributed English-language leaflets supporting the anarchists Sacco and Vanzetti. Although he was released after a week without any criminal charges, the police confiscated *Pingdeng* and other publications found in Ping Sheh's headquarters. Ping Sheh and *Pingdeng* managed to survive until the eve of World War II.[33] In the late 1920s, only a handful of other anarchist groups existed in the Americas, such as Hei She [Black Society] in Mexico, Jue She [Awareness Society] in New York City, and Ren She [Benevolence Society] in Los Angeles.[34]

In 1934 Liu Zhongshi helped found Wuzhengfu Gongchanzhuyizhe Lianmeng [Alliance of anarcho-communists], which published the *Wuzhengfu Gongchan Yuekan* [Anarcho-communist Monthly].[35] However, this group apparently attracted few adherents. The decentralization and anti-leadership principles of anarcho-syndicalists were ill-suited to large-scale organizations with the resources necessary to confront wealthy and complex industries. Size called for disciplined mass action, which ran counter to syndicalist concepts of spontaneity. Their ultra-left attitudes, such as standing aloof from relatively conservative trade unions, also isolated them from the mass of workers. Thus during the 1920s and the 1930s, the better-organized Marxist Communists continued to make headway in the labor movement and sounded the death knell of the syndicalist groups by absorbing their members.[36] After the 1920s, Communist Party organizers dominated the Chinese American Left.

Early Interests in Marxism among Chinese in America

Around the turn of the twentieth century, Marxism was only one of several competing forms of socialism among Chinese at home and abroad, but it gained ascendance with the successful Russian Revolution of 1917. The success of the Communist movement attracted numerous idealists and activists. In China an increasing number of intellectuals and university students took to Marxist philosophy during and after the May Fourth Movement of 1919 and the CCP was founded in 1921.

Chinese in America showed interest in Marxism as early as December 1919, when Oi-won Jung, a KMT party member who had also been active in the Chinese Socialist Club, helped organize Xin Shehui [New Society] in San Jose, California, "to study capitalism and communism and the radical politics of the New Russia."[37]

Jung was among the generation of Chinese going in increasing numbers to study in Japan and Western nations after 1911. Some had already learned of Marxist tenets while in China; others gained exposure while abroad. Chinese work-study students in France had already formed a clandestine Communist cell in the spring of 1921, even before the founding of the CCP in Shanghai that July.[38] However, conditions were not yet ripe for similar developments among Chinese in the United States.

Two leaders of the CCP studied in America during the early 1920s. Zhang Wentian, who would become a member of the CCP political bureau in 1931, had little opportunity to show his Marxist leanings while working as an editor at San Francisco's *Chinese Republican Journal* in 1922 and 1923. However, while in China, Zhang had already pioneered using Marxist analysis to interpret Chinese society and the revolution. During his fourteen months in the United States, he audited classes at the University of California, Berkeley, and wrote essays for publications in China, including a translation of "Developments in Policy in Soviet Russia: An Explanation of the Planned Economy of the Soviet Republic," which was the earliest essay introducing the New Economic Plan in Chinese. However, he did not formally join the CCP until 1925, after leaving the United States.[39]

Chen Gongbo, one of the fifteen delegates attending the CCP's first congress in 1921, had also arrived in the United States for graduate studies in 1923 and in 1924 completed an MA thesis entitled "The Communist Movement in China," in which he described for the first time in English the background and early history of the party and included English translations of six documents from the first Congress. By this time, however, Chen had withdrawn from further participation in CCP activities.[40]

University Students and Marxism

Despite the presence of these Chinese Communists in the United States, until 1925 there was hardly any contact between the Communist Party of America (later the Communist Party of the United States of America, or CPUSA) and the Chinese immigrant community.[41] However, shifts in the KMT in China during the early 1920s encouraged the emergence of a more active left wing. In January 1924, after a series of secret meetings between Sun Yat-sen, the CCP, and representatives from the Communist International (Comintern), a national congress of the KMT convened in Guangzhou to reorganize the party into a more tightly focused, militant, revolutionary entity modeled after the Communist Party of the USSR. The gathering approved three policies to further national revolution: (1) to forge an alliance with the USSR, (2) to admit Communists as individual members into the Kuomintang, and (3) to give active support to Chinese workers and peasants. Shortly afterward, Chinese Marxists began wielding their influence among Chinese in China and the United States. This wing of the KMT enjoyed a measure of support among Chinese who longed for a modern and strong nation, although they were still only contenders for power in China.

A number of Chinese Marxists in the United States were university students. Their status as temporary residents influenced their choice to focus more on political developments in China. Qinghua (Tsinghua) University students were particularly prominent among the early leaders of Chinese Communists in America.[42] Their careers illustrate how Chinese evolved from militant nationalists to Marxist revolutionaries.

Intellectuals and students have always been among the vanguard Chinese nationalist, reform, and revolutionary movements. Tsinghua University students actively protested in the May Fourth Movement against the Versailles Peace Treaty and the transfer of the Shandong peninsula from Germany to Japan. This violation of China's territorial integrity inspired Tsinghua students in other struggles against imperialism and other issues in the university and in Chinese society.

In 1920 Shi Huang led a group of students in forming Weizhen Xuehui [Truth-Only Learned Society]. They had three main objectives: (1) to seek truth to improve society, (2) to value physical labor and understand the living conditions of the impoverished masses, and (3) to stress moral behavior among their members to match words to actions. Weizhen Xuehui members became active among Beijing workers and attempted to raise their political consciousness. In spring 1923, seven male students from Tsinghua—Shi Huang, Ji Chaoding (C. T. Chi), Xu Yongying (Y. Y. Hsu), Hu Dunyuan (Thomas T. Y. Hu), Zhang Youjiang (Y. C. Chang), Luo Zongzhen, and Mei Ru'ao (Ju-Ao Mei)—and Luo Jingyi (S. S. Lo), the lone female student from the middle school attached to Beijing Normal University, formed Chaotao [Surpassing the Peach Garden], a secret policy-making core group within Weizhen Xuehui.[43] Chaotao's members sought to effect national salvation through political action and advocated learning from the revolutionary spirit of Sun Yat-sen and V. I. Lenin.

In the summer of 1924, the leader Shi Huang traveled south to Guangzhou with fellow Chaotao member Y. Y. Hsu. They spoke with Li Dazhao, one of the founders of the CCP, and Sun Yat-sen. The two idealistic youths were deeply impressed by the advice of these senior revolutionaries. After returning north, Shi Huang arranged a retreat of the Chaotao group to discuss Li and Sun's advice at length. The student group expressed its unanimous desire to work toward the liberation of all humankind and, according to S. S. Lo, favored joining the Communist movement. However, even though the Chinese Communist Party had been in existence since 1921, the group members did not join, probably because they were soon to depart for study in America.

Shi Huang and C. T. Chi left in fall 1924. Shi enrolled in Stanford University to study Asian history, while Chi went to the University of Chicago, also to study history.[44] The year after they settled down to their courses, the bloody labor crackdowns by Western policemen in Shanghai and Guangzhou inflamed nationalist anti-imperialist sentiments in China and among Chinese abroad.[45]

In America the Communist Party formed the All-American Anti-Imperialist League (AAAIL) at a Mexican Communist Party convention in April 1925 after being criticized by the Comintern for not carrying out "a sufficiently energetic campaign against imperialism." The league was headquartered in Chicago, and Manuel Gomez (Charles Shipman) of the Communist Party of America served as secretary of the United States section. Also known as Liga Anti-Imperialista de las Américas, the league focused on Latin America. However, like the Communist International, it supported China's anti-imperialist struggles. In response to western aggression in China, party workers organized "Hands off China" meetings in a number of American cities. They often worked with the local KMT and invited Chinese speakers to these meetings. In turn, non-Chinese sent by the Communists spoke at meetings organized by the KMT.[46]

By the fall of 1925, the remaining Chaotao members, some of whom had just been demonstrating in China, also arrived in the United States. In a reunion of the group called by Shi Huang in Berkeley, California, the participants unanimously resolved that while seeking an education in America they would actively work to further the revolution in China.

Even as they committed to the nationalist cause while overseas, in China Sun Yat-sen's leftward shift had increased stresses and strains in the fragile KMT coalition. Conservative members of the party felt threatened by the more militant left-wing factions allied with the aggressive Communists. The polarization and antagonism between left and right grew, and after Sun Yat-sen died in Beijing in March 1925, the right-wing faction engineered the assassination of Liao Zhongkai, the leader of the left-wing faction. In November 1925, conservative party leaders met at the Western Hills in Beijing and pronounced themselves the party's central committee. They passed resolutions expelling Communist Party members from the KMT and called for a party congress to be held in Shanghai in March 1926. The revolutionary government in Guangzhou, in an attempt to keep the coalition together, called for a rival congress to be held in January.

Conservative KMT members in America, who had became alarmed at the increasingly radical policies of the Guangzhou regime, approved the actions of the Western Hills faction. Over the years, many KMT party members had become financially established in America. While they firmly supported the fight against feudalism and foreign imperialism to facilitate the development of modern enterprise, the militancy of the Chinese workers and peasants seemed threatening to their economic interests and political position in China. When the American KMT delegates, Tan Zan (Chan Tom) and Chen Yaoyuan (You Foon Chan), arrived in China, they chose to participate in the Western Hills–sponsored congress. Although the KMT in Guangzhou finally regained the upper hand and reiterated support for Sun's three policies of allying with the Soviet Union, cooperating with the Communists, and helping workers and peasants, tensions remained between the left- and right-wing factions.

Radical students, such as the Chaotao group, also supported Sun Yat-sen's three policies and opposed foreign imperialism. C. T. Chi, an early student leader, participated in Hu'an Houyuanhui [Association Supporting (China in) the Shanghai Incidents] in Chicago to oppose imperialist aggression in China. He lectured to non-Chinese audiences, thereby launching a career as an eloquent spokesperson about the Chinese revolution to mainstream American society. He also helped edit *Zhicheng Qiao Sheng* [Voice of Chicago Chinese].[47]

In the summer of 1926, Shi Huang and Y. Y. Hsu met with Communist Party district secretary Levin at an anti-imperialist convention in San Francisco. That fall they had joined the KMT and became active in the party's left-wing faction. Levin recruited them to join the AAAIL.[48] Through league activities, they would establish a working relationship with the Communist Party in San Francisco.

As Chinese nationalists, Chi and other Chaotao leaders became involved in internationalist, anti-imperialist, labor coalitions. Upon returning to Chicago after the Berkeley meeting with his Tsinghua classmates, Chi also joined the AAAIL. He was already becoming well known as a speaker, and in late October 1925 he spoke at the American Negro Labor Congress. His description of bloody events of May 30, 1925, "moved the listeners to impressive silence." That winter he and Shi Huang attended a convention of Chinese students in Chicago, where they engaged in a spirited debate with right-wing nationalists who questioned the suitability of Sun Yat-sen's three policies for the national revolution. The assemblage then overwhelmingly elected Chi to head the local Chinese Students Association, thus affording him a convenient platform for anti-imperialist activities.[49]

In May 1926, radical students, spearheaded by members of the Chaotao group, followed the lead of the AAAIL to express anti-imperialist sentiments when meeting in San Francisco and forming the Students' Society for the Advancement of Sun Yat-senism in America (SASYS). SASYS branches soon appeared in Chicago, New York, Philadelphia, and Madison, Wisconsin. In September a five-member executive committee was elected, three of whom were from the Chaotao group— Shi Huang, C. T. Chi, and Y. C. Chang (Zhang Yucang).[50]

Although SASYS membership remained relatively small, the group actively joined leftist members of the KMT in attacking the views of the Right. The first issue of its publication *Geming* [Revolution] appeared in 1926, edited by Y. Y. Hsu, and included articles critical of Chiang Kai-shek and KMT party affairs in America. These criticisms immediately incurred the wrath of the KMT right-wing faction, and before the year was out, SASYS was embroiled in polemics with the San Francisco branch of the KMT and the party organ *Young China*. On university campuses, SASYS also battled nationalistic students of the Dajiang She [Great River Society], led by Luo Longji and others in debates and publications.[51]

In 1926 Manuel Gomez recruited C. T. Chi to become one of the first Chinese to join the Communist Party. Chi was immediately selected as a delegate to represent SASYS and the AAAIL at the World Anti-Imperialist Congress and then the International Congress of Oppressed Peoples, both held in Brussels in February 1927. During his voyage to Europe, he met the American progressive Harriet Levine, whom he later married in the summer of that year. While in Europe, Chi contacted the European branch of the CCP and joined the organization with inspiration from news of revolutionary progress in China. Shortly after he became a CCP member, however, the KMT purged Communists from its ranks.[52]

In the meanwhile, in March 1927, Shi Huang and S. S. Lo joined the CPUSA. Y. Y. Hsu also left the KMT to join the CPUSA soon after Chiang Kai-shek's bloody anti-leftist purge in China. All but one member of the rest of the Chaotao eight also became party members and dissolved the Chaotao group, its mission accomplished.[53] S. S. Lo, the lone female Chaotao member, spoke fluent Cantonese and made frequent speeches in San Francisco's Chinatown publicizing the atrocities committed by imperialist aggressors. She also taught Mandarin to the Cantonese population and thereby helped her left-wing fellow Mandarin-speaking students interact with the local Chinese American population.[54]

Left-wing activism among students also emerged in other parts of the United States. In June 1925, three Chinese students participated in a conference on the Chinese situation organized by the League for Industrial Democracy in New York City. Sometime in 1926, ten Chinese immigrant workers formed a Chinese Workers Alliance and were recruited into the CPUSA. Subsequently, radical students also joined. Li Daoxuan (Li Tao Hsuan) was one of the most prominent and had apparently first joined the party in San Francisco in 1927 but had gone east to enroll at Columbia University.[55]

Other students in places like San Francisco, Chicago, Philadelphia, Boston, and Madison also joined the CPUSA, including Xie Qitai, Huang Gongshou, Li Fahuan, Wu Zhaofa, Hu Dunyuan (Thomas T. Y. Hu), Zhang Bao (Mo Guoshi, Mo Zhendan), He Zhifen, Su Kaiming (Frank K. M. Su), Yu Zhipei (T. P. Yu), Wei Minghua, Chen Kemei, Yu Guangsheng (Yu Rixin), Zhang Hongmei, and others.[56]

Most of these radical students, like the great majority of Chinese students in America, spoke Mandarin, while the bulk of Chinese Americans spoke Cantonese. Significant barriers of language, culture, and class posed daunting challenges for those students seeking to organize as outsiders to the Chinese American community. Such difficulties may have contributed to the choice of many Chinese radicals not to stay in America but to work for revolution in China.

Intra-Party Struggles and Parting of Ways

While Chinese leftists were increasing their American organizing during the mid-1920s, the course of political developments in China and the rest of the world significantly shaped their efforts. Some members of the Chinese Left, along with sympathetic Western journalists and social workers, intermittently participated in the unfolding events in several of these arenas. Their visibility in the United States influenced public opinion in Western countries.

Even while the conflict between the Chinese Left and Right festered, the KMT's new leader, Chiang Kai-Shek, launched the long-planned Northern Expedition from Guangzhou in mid-1926 to unify the nation. By year's end, KMT armies had reached the Yangzi River and established a central government at Wuhan. Meanwhile, in the United States, the conflicts between left and right led the Guangzhou faction of the KMT overseas department to suspend officers of the U.S. General Branch who supported the Western Hills faction. The left-wing Seattle branch led a move to convene a party convention in Los Angeles to elect another slate of General Branch officers. However, the existing General Branch defied the orders and continued operations supported by those party branches that had not attended the Los Angeles convention.

The left-wing faction was apparently on the rise in America when Shi Huang, Shi Zuo, and Y. Y. Hsu became part of the General Branch's five-member Committee on the Abolition of Unequal Treaties. The trio wrote jointly to the Communist Party leadership in San Francisco on March 29, 1927, claiming that co-operation between the Workers Party and KMT would advance Communist Party objectives while enhancing the influence of the Kuomintang in America.[57] However, the left-wing students' interpretation of political developments proved wildly over optimistic, for scarcely two weeks later, on April 12, 1927, Chiang Kai-shek ordered a bloody purge of Communists from the KMT and proclaimed a rival national government in Nanjing (Nanking) on April 18. Ironically, the district Workers Party executive committee, in response to the apparently improving working relationship between the KMT left-wing faction and Workers Party, had passed a resolution on April 13, 1927, calling for the formation of a Chinese faction.

At this point, the pro-CCP Left still hoped that the Wuhan regime would continue supporting the KMT-Communist alliance. However, the situation in China soon turned against the Communists. Under Wang Jingwei's leadership, most KMT members of the weakening Wuhan regime were more interested in reaching an accommodation with the Chiang Kai-shek regime in Nanjing, despite the opposition of left-wing leaders such as Madam Sun Yat-sen (Song Qingling or

Soong Ching Ling), He Xiangning (Madam Liao Zhongkai), the foreign minister Eugene Chen, and Deng Yanda, head of the general political department.

In June the executive committee of the KMT central committee of Wuhan officially abrogated the KMT's agreement with the Soviet advisors led by Mikhail Borodin. In mid-July the Wuhan government decided to split with the Communists. On July 14, Madam Sun published "Statement Issued in Protest against the Violation of Sun Yat-sen's Revolutionary Principles and Policies" in the English-language *People's Tribune*. The KMT confiscated this issue, but the American editor William Prohme managed to telegraph the entire text for publication in New York. The Chinese version was later distributed in leaflet form.[58]

Fearing for the Soviet advisors' safety, Eugene Chen hastened to arrange their departure from China. On July 27, a group of some thirty people took the train from Wuhan to Zhengzhou to begin an arduous overland trek of 1,800 miles across Mongolia and the Gobi Desert to Moscow in a caravan consisting of five passenger automobiles and three trucks. The group included Borodin and other Soviet advisors; Chen's two sons, Percy and Jack; interpreter Zhang Ke; and the influential American socialist and journalist Anna Louise Strong.[59] In the meanwhile, Deng Yanda and He Xiangning resigned from the Wuhan government, and Deng made his way to Moscow, while He retreated to Hong Kong.[60]

Disguised as the servant of Rayna Prohme, Madam Sun boarded a passenger vessel to Shanghai. Eugene Chen sent his daughters, Sylvia (Si-lan) and Yolanda (Yu-lan), under assumed names to Shanghai accompanied by an interpreter, while he also went there separately disguised as a Japanese businessman. Soon after Madam Sun arrived in Shanghai, Rayna Prohme went to the Soviet consulate to arrange passage for the group to the USSR. In the dead of night in mid-August, the group and a Russian interpreter quietly slipped aboard a Soviet tramp steamer bound for Vladivostok, whence the group traveled overland by rail to reach Moscow in September.[61]

In China the Communists also abandoned hope of working within the KMT and organized an armed uprising at Nanchang on August 1, 1927, followed by uprisings during the autumn harvest in Hunan beginning on September 8, 1927, and an uprising in Guangzhou on December 11, 1927, led by Zhang Tailei. These largely uncoordinated insurrections resulted in heavy losses for the Communists at the hands of the better organized and armed KMT armies. In April 1928, Zhu De led the remnants of the Nanchang Uprising to combine forces with the worker and peasant armies led by Mao Zedong from his revolutionary base at Jinggang Shan in Jiangxi. In the meantime, representatives from the three KMT factions—the Western Hills group in Shanghai, the Chiang Kai-shek–led faction in Nanjing, and the Wang Jingwei–led faction in Wuhan—formed a coalition government in Nanjing on September 20, 1927. However, during the next few months a power struggle between the left faction led by Wang Jingwei and the right-wing factions resulted in the latter gaining the upper hand by the end of the year. Wang Jingwei was forced to relinquish his power and on December 16, 1927, departed for France.

On November 1, 1927, the three leaders of the Kuomintang left in Moscow— Deng Yanda, Eugene Chen, and Madam Sun—announced the formation of a "Provisional Action Committee of the Kuomintang of China." By this time, ultra-left ideology was gaining ascendancy in the CCP. However, Stalin's government was no longer interested in working with the Kuomintang Left, and so Deng Yanda left for Berlin in December; Madam Sun followed in March 1928, accompanied by Zhang Ke, while Eugene Chen traveled alone to Paris in May, leaving his children enrolled in Soviet schools.[62]

In Berlin, Deng Yanda and Madam Sun met routinely to discuss why the revolution had failed.[63] Madam Sun returned to China briefly in 1929 for the official entombment of Sun Yat-sen in a mausoleum in Nanjing. Back in Germany, she received visits from He Xiangning and her children Liao Mengxing (Cynthia Liao) and Liao Chengzhi. The Liaos introduced her to Hu Lanqi, who was then studying in Germany and had joined the German Communist Party. Hu accompanied Madam Sun to China when the latter decided to end her exile to continue her advocacy in China for the Chinese revolution. Madam Sun settled in Shanghai's French Settlement in August 1931.[64] Since the KMT could not arrest or interfere excessively with the activities of the widow of the revered founder of the Republic, Madam Sun played a key role during the 1930s rallying support for progressive activities in defiance of KMT repression.

In Shanghai Madam Sun resumed old acquaintants and made new contacts among the Chinese Left and sympathetic expatriates living in the International Settlement who used their special status in China to advance the revolutionary cause.

Agnes Smedley was a prominent supporter. She arrived in Northeast China in December 1928 as a correspondent for the *Frankfurter Zeitung* but had met Madam Sun earlier, in Moscow in November. By May 1929, she had settled in Shanghai, where she renewed her acquaintance with Madam Sun. She also befriended the social scientist and political activist Chen Hansheng (Chen Han-seng, Geoffrey Chen) and New Zealander Rewi Alley, who had arrived in Shanghai in April 1927, just as Chiang Kai-shek's henchmen were arresting and executing Communists and suspected leftists.

These two helped Smedley better understand the great inequities in Chinese society. By 1930 Smedley had befriended Edgar Snow, still a young unknown journalist working for *China Weekly Review*. She also met the novelist Mao Dun, and the two began working together to translate modern Chinese literary works. Through Mao Dun, Smedley met the renowned writer Lu Xun and other members of the newly organized League of Left-Wing Writers. In May 1931, she also befriended Harold Isaacs, a wealthy young New Yorker who had come to China in search of adventure. Smedley introduced Isaacs to Frank Glass, a Trotskyite journalist and founding member of the Communist Party of South Africa. Glass soon radicalized the young man, who began to view critically the KMT-CCP struggle and China's situation.[65]

In June 1931, just as Madam Sun was preparing to return to China after a visit to Europe, the Shanghai Municipal Police arrested Paul and Gertrude Noulens, members of the Pan-Pacific Trade Union Secretariat and secret representatives of the Communist International, and turned them over to the Nanjing government. This incident became a cause célèbre among the European Left and its sympathizers. In August KMT authorities arrested Madam Sun's close associate Deng Yanda, who had returned from Germany in May 1930 to organize opposition to Chiang Kai-shek. Even as Madam Sun tried desperately to negotiate for Deng's release, the KMT executed him, leading her to issue a blistering condemnation of the Chiang government.

By late 1931, Madam Sun had met Harold Isaacs through Agnes Smedley, and together with Glass the three started a newspaper to publicize the struggle against KMT authoritarian rule. The *China Forum,* with Isaacs as editor and financially backed by the CCP underground, began publication in January 1932. The paper claimed to provide "News and Views of the Chinese scene now ignored, distorted, or suppressed!!" and reported on the "murky facts of Shanghai life and political concerns." A column in the newspaper, "Observer," was written alternately by Chen Han-seng and Garfield Huang, a leading critic of Chiang Kai-shek's drug policy. Underground Communists and their sympathizers regularly supplied news items. The *China Forum* ran until early 1934, when CCP leaders halted funding due to Isaacs's perceived anti-Stalinist and pro-Trotskyist views.[66]

On July 12, 1932, Madam Sun joined with Agnes Smedley, Chen Han-seng, and others to form the Paul and Gertrude Ruegg Defense Committee to attract international attention pressing for their release. Signatories of the committee appeals included the likes of Edgar Snow. Such tactics helped reduce the Rueggs' death sentences to life imprisonment in Nanjing.[67]

In December 1932, Madam Sun and a coalition of liberals and progressives furthered their struggle against the KMT by founding the China League for the Protection of Civil Rights to advocate for all political prisoners. Most of the league's members were in Shanghai, but there was also an active branch in Beiping (Beijing). The principals included such staunch Communist supporters as Madam Sun, the writer Lu Xun, the publisher Zou Taofen, journalist Hu Yuzhi, and such liberals as Hu Shi, journalist Cheng Shewo, writer Lin Yutang, and Academia Sinica director Cai Yuanpei. Agnes Smedley and Harold Isaacs also regularly attended meetings in Shanghai. As a loose federation of liberals and leftists concerned with civil rights, they differed greatly in their attitudes toward the KMT regime, with some bitterly opposed, others supportive of rivals to Chiang Kai-shek within the KMT, and some even voicing critical support for the KMT. The league publicized the plight of political prisoners but was not markedly successful in securing releases. The aggressive efforts of some league leaders to expose alleged human rights abuses and torture of prisoners and to free all political prisoners soon fostered disputes that led to the expulsion of Hu Shi in March 1933. Soon afterward, Lin Yutang and others resigned. After KMT agents assassinated its executive director Yang Xingfo in June 1933, league activities effectively ceased.[68]

Kuo Min Yat Po and the Grand Alliance Supporting the Chinese Workers and Peasants Revolution

The ascendance of Chiang Kai-shek's KMT during the 1920s forced the Chinese Marxist Left in America to redefine its direction. Because of the crisis in the KMT-CCP alliance in China, the KMT-left-wing faction in America faced an uncertain future. Radical Chinese in America at first sought to remain in the KMT, especially through the Kuo Min Yat Po [Chinese Nationalist Daily of America], the party organ established by the Los Angeles party convention in San Francisco that began publication on June 30, 1927, as an attempt to supplant Young China. The newspaper began publication in June with Y. Y. Hsu as one of the editors.

The tremendous uncertainties about Chinese politics imposed great pressure on the left-wing faction in America and destabilized the Kuo Min Yat Po staff. The founding chief editor, Huang Lingshuang (L. S. Wong, Huang Wenshan), resigned toward the end of July. His successor, Huang Shijun, lasted only until October 10, and Y. Y. Hsu ascended to the top post. Hsu proceeded to recruit such left-wing students as Xie Qitai (better known in later life as Zhang Hanfu) to the paper's editorial staff. The same year Hsu also sponsored Xie to join the Workers Party. Hsu and the other leftists on staff in their turn only lasted a few months, as adverse political developments in China eroded their positions at the newspaper. By early 1928, Hsu and the students had been forced out, with Ma Dianru (Din Yee Ma) from the executive committee of the KMT General Branch succeeding him as chief editor.[69]

The break between the KMT and the CCP ended cooperation between the two groups in the United States as well. SASYS and its publication Geming could no longer operate within the KMT to work toward national revolution. Leftists transitioned from being largely part of a student movement toward organizing more in the Chinese American community, particularly the working class. In 1927 Shi Huang led progressive KMT members and the Chinese Marxist Left to found Meizhou Yonghu Zhongguo Gong-Nong Geming Datongmeng [Grand Alliance Supporting the Chinese Workers and Peasants Revolution, or ACWP] to express their continuing support for the Chinese revolution. As a media outlet, the ACWP considered taking control of a new left-wing weekly founded by Jiang Xizeng (Hsi-Tseng Tsiang, better known as H. T. Tsiang), a former editor at Young China, whose political differences with the conservative Western Hills faction led to his physical ejection from the newspaper office and expulsion from the KMT. Toward the end of 1926, Jiang and some friends began publishing a mimeographed Chinese-language weekly, *Meizhou Pinglun,* that criticized the Chiang Kai-shek regime. An English supplement, the *Chinese Guide in America,* was added with the eleventh issue published February 12, 1927.

In April, the district Workers Party leadership attempted to cultivate a Chinese faction by formalizing a relationship with the *Chinese Guide in America.* It passed a resolution to form a Guide Publishing Company under the direction of a Communist Party committee. However, such Chinese party members as Shi Huang, Y. Y. Hsu, and Y. C. Chang, who had constant interaction with Jiang, complained that Jiang was a right-winger whose move to the left was an opportunistic response to the diminishing of right-wing power in America. Shi considered Jiang politically untrustworthy and charged that he had hidden agendas against the Communist Party. The Communist Party soon found that Jiang had his own ideas regarding his publication and was unwilling to relinquish editorial control. With these strained relations and mutual suspicions, the Communist Party unsurprisingly rejected Jiang's application for membership. Before long, immigration authorities detained Jiang, and publication of the *Guide* halted abruptly. However, Jiang's contacts and conflicts with the Communist Party still did not end. After his release on bail, Jiang went to New York, where he became a creative writer under the name H. T. Tsiang. Even though his literary works were published in the Marxist Left's *Daily Worker* and *New Masses,* his reputation for noncooperation with the party line soon caught up with him. In 1935 *New Masses* accused him of being an opportunistic individualist and dismissed his works as exhibitionism. That some of his Chinese critics such as Y. Y. Hsu had also relocated to New York might have contributed to the negative criticisms.[70] However, despite his dismissal by this CPUSA organ, Tsiang produced some of the earliest English-language writings by the Chinese Left.

National Chinese Bureau

Just one month before Tsiang's incarceration, in June 1927, a provisional National Executive Committee of the Communist Party's Chinese Faction formed, and it held its First National Conference in Chicago in September, at which it drafted a constitution. In November the committee chose San Francisco as headquarters for the National Bureau of the Chinese National Fraction (Chinese Bureau) at the Communist Party's central office.[71] Operating clandestinely, the bureau formulated policies to guide Chinese party members operating in the United States. Shi Huang became its first secretary in 1927. Eventually, the Chinese Bureau set up sub-bureaus in such areas as New York City, Philadelphia, Boston, Chicago, and Madison that had a critical mass of Chinese party members.

To replace *The Chinese Guide in America,* the Chinese Bureau gave approval for publication of a mimeographed Chinese language weekly *Xianfeng Zhoukan*

[Vanguard] at the end of 1927. In April 1928, the ACWP began publishing *Chinese Vanguard* once a month, although this schedule was difficult for the nine-person publishing team. That summer Y. Y. Hsu also became editor of a Chinese-language CPUSA publication—the monthly mimeographed magazine *Gongchan* [The Communist], sponsored by the Communist Party.[72]

In early 1928, the CPUSA moved its national office from Chicago to New York, and the Chinese Bureau and ACWP soon followed. New York became the center of Marxist organizing even for Chinese members and despite the size of San Francisco's Chinatown.

The newly recruited Chinese soon became active CPUSA members. Shi Huang, who had just received his MA degree from Stanford University, went to Cuba to organize Chinese workers in the sugar industry. At the time, the Machado government had banned the Communist Party and targeted suspected Communist activists for assassination, imprisonment, or deportation. The Chinese consul soon learned of Shi's presence and demanded that he leave within twenty-four hours. But Shi managed to delay long enough to found a party organization. After returning to America, he organized Chinese workers in Canada, before going to Moscow in 1929 to enter the International Workers School.[73]

The many Chinese student members of the Communist Party were understandably eager to return home to participate in their national revolutionary struggles. The CCP delegation to the Communist International, acting through the CPUSA, sent a number of these students to Moscow to train to become party cadres in China. Xie Qitai arrived in Moscow in 1928 before Shi Huang.[74] Former Chaotao member Luo Jingyi, along with Li Fahuan, and Huang Gongshou, attended the Soviet Chinese Labor University in the USSR in 1927 and 1928.[75]

In 1927 the Chinese Bureau sent C. T. Chi and Y. C. Chang to China to participate in the August First uprising at Nanchang.[76] They journeyed to Berlin where they joined a group that attended the tenth anniversary celebration of the October Revolution in Moscow. There they met up with the Chinese delegation. By this time, the KMT had split with the CCP in China, and the party organization decided that Chi and Chang should not return to China. Instead, they studied at Moscow's Sun Yat-sen University and interpreted for Chinese Communists who had fled to Moscow with Borodin, attended the Sixth Congresses of the Communist International and the CCP, and acted as secretaries to the Chinese delegate Deng Zhongxia. In 1928 the American Communist leader William Z. Foster, who was in Moscow to attend a meeting of the Communist International, suggested that if they could not proceed to China, they should go to the United States to publish a newspaper. Chi decided to return to and join the *Daily Worker*. Chang stayed but was later dismissed by Wang Ming from the Communist Party.[77]

On July 20, 1929, Chi served as the ACWP delegate to the Second Congress of the League against Imperialism.[78] Back in the United States, he joined the central committee of the Chinese Bureau, and under the pseudonym R. Doonping, he wrote a series of articles about China in the *Daily Worker* in November and December of 1929.[79]

In 1929 the ACWP gained a more global perspective by participating in the Second Anti-Imperialist World Congress held in Frankfurt, Germany, and joined the World Anti-Imperialist League. Soon afterward, it reorganized as the All-America Alliance of Chinese Anti-Imperialists (AAACAI) to match this new international scope. The AAACAI's objective was to "lead and organize Chinese in the Americas in the struggle for revolution and against imperialism."[80] It was the chief subsidiary organization connected with the American Chinese Marxist Left before World War II and was a proving ground for Communist sympathizers, some of whom were eventually invited to join the party. In Philadelphia Frank K. M. Su, a former Tsinghua student who joined the American Communist party in 1929, became editor and translator for *Chinese Vanguard*.[81]

During the late 1920s, the AAACAI frequently voiced its opposition to the KMT regime in the *Chinese Vanguard*'s pamphlets and leaflets. Members spoke on street corners and occasionally organized demonstrations. Despite their relatively small numbers, the Marxist Left influenced the Chinese American community. For example, in July 1929, AAACAI and progressive members of the Chinese Students Alliance, the CPUSA, and the Anti-Imperialist League organized simultaneous anti-KMT protests in New York, San Francisco, and Los Angeles that led to near riots and arrests by the police.[82] Despite such efforts, however, the Chiang regime was already successfully consolidating power in China, and such demonstrations petered out.

Around this time, *Chinese Vanguard* was able to purchase a set of lead type and moved its offices to New York to become the official organ of the Su Zhaozheng chapter of the AAACAI. The first typeset issue of *Chinese Vanguard* rolled off the press on April 3, 1930. Until 1938 this paper remained the national voice of the Chinese Marxist Left. It was closely associated with the CPUSA, and initially both organizations' offices were in the same building as the *Daily Worker*. The CPUSA provided office space and printing facilities. With few financial resources and low circulation, the paper was chronically short of operating funds and annually called for reader donations to continue publishing.[83] Despite such constraints, it served as a conduit for Chinese people across North America to learn of progressive activities outside their otherwise isolated communities. The paper also often published short creative works by Chinese in America that should be considered early examples of progressive Chinese American literature. By spring 1930, circulation reached an estimated five hundred to a thousand.[84]

San Francisco Chinese Students Association

China's revolution also inspired political activism within the Chinese American community. The Chinese American population had been predominantly male, consisting mostly of laborers and merchants. But by the 1920s, the numbers of families slowly increased. A growing population of young Chinese chafed under the discriminatory conditions in America, and some looked to the success of China's revolution for hope of a better future. This was especially evident in San Francisco, which had the largest Chinese population and many businesses, associations, newspapers, and language schools that made it the de facto economic, cultural, and political capital of Chinese America. Thus, the community had a general branch of the Kuomintang that actively supported the Chinese revolution and stimulated political activism among the population, especially idealistic youth. By 1924 the evolution of the Chinese revolution inspired seven or eight Chinatown students at St. Mary's School to establish Sanminzhuyi Yanjiu She [Society for Study of the Three Principles of the People, or SSTPP], with objectives similar to those of SASYS, which had been established by university students.

Xavier Dea (Xie Chuang), an immigrant who had arrived in 1923 at age eighteen to join his father's fruit and candy stand business, helped to establish this group. Before coming to America, Dea had already supported the revolutionary cause. In America he soon found that the SSTPP lacked the contacts and experience to accomplish much. Unlike the Chinese university students, who had easier entree to American mainstream society, the isolated working-class Chinatown Chinese had sharply limited interactions with the larger society.

In mid-1925, Dea began attending high school but dropped out a year later. It was probably at this time, in August 1926, that he came into contact with Y. Y. Hsu and Li Gan, members of the Kuomintang left wing with ties to the local Workers (Communist) Party. The two soon established ties with Dea and other members of the SSTPP.[85]

The Young Communist League in San Francisco was seeking to establish a youth group to funnel anti-imperialist propaganda activities in Chinatown. In spring 1927, Dea and several others, including his junior high school classmate Benjamin Fee (H. T. Chang), Olden Lee, and Guo Huangsheng, founded the San Francisco Chinese Students Association (SFCSA). A more ambitious undertaking than the SSTTP, the group targeted the recruitment of the three thousand Chinese students in San Francisco schools.[86] Under the leadership of Dea and Fee, the SFCSA coordinated the ideological content of its activities with that of SASYS. Chaotao members, especially Cantonese speaker S. S. Lo, were particularly useful liaisons linking the Cantonese-speaking community progressives with the radical Mandarin-speaking Chinese students.

The SFCSA attracted members of the student organization at the Nam Kue Chinese School, who used the school's facilities to publish *Qunsheng* [Voice of the Masses], a mimeographed monthly with an anti-imperialist perspective and circulation of about three hundred. When the shocked conservative school administration discovered the publication, it expelled the students and banished the paper from its premises. The SFCSA, which had been borrowing the facilities of Nam Kue and Yeong Wo schools for meetings and activities, had to move its meetings to the clubrooms of the more sympathetic Unionist Guild.[87]

The SFCSA became affiliated with the national Chinese Students Alliance. Ostensibly founded for social and educational purposes, the active membership was limited in number; however, their zeal and organized actions made up for their limited numbers, as they reached out to form coalitions with Chinese students from various San Francisco schools. SFCSA-led activities became highly politicized under the guidance of Xavier Dea, Benjamin Fee, and others. As among other Chinese leftist student groups, the SFCSA leadership was mostly male. The lone female was Fort Bragg–born Chen Junqi (Eva Chan), who joined the group's executive committee in June 1928.[88]

In 1928 the SFCSA and Chinese-language school students organized protests condemning the massacre of demonstrators by warlord Duan Qirui's troops on March 18, 1926. On May 7 later that year, students from eight student groups made speeches at the corner of Washington Street and Waverly Place in Chinatown to criticize Yuan Shikai's acquiescence to Japanese imperialist demands. According to Benjamin Fee, the SFCSA mobilized a thousand students to demonstrate in commemoration of the May 30 massacre.[89]

The association supported the KMT left-wing faction and the AAACAI through Chinatown street corner rallies and mass meetings, with members making political speeches and putting on topical skits. Despite their zeal, however, the students lacked political power and did not greatly threaten conservative control in the community. Nonetheless, the SFCSA was a constant irritant to the KMT right wing. Possibly at the latter's instigation, two detectives from the Chinatown Squad of the San Francisco Police Department raided the association's headquarters on January 9, 1929, and closed it for alleged Communist activities.[90] Although of questionable legality, this heavy-handed suppression of freedom of expression cowed many of the students, and the organization's activities waned. The publication *Qunsheng* seems to have continued publication until 1931, when the claimed circulation numbered five hundred.

University Students, Exiles, and the Chinese Community

The conflict between the right and left in Chinatown was soon mirrored in the struggles among Chinese university students in America. Although only a small minority, left-wing students had the advantage of better organization and a clear agenda. In late 1927, they gained control of the national student organization, the Chinese Students Alliance (CSA). Chaotao members Mei Ru'ao (Mei Ju-ao) and CPUSA member Hu Dunyuan (Thomas T. Y. Hu), served as two of the next three chief editors of the alliance's publication, *Chinese Students' Monthly.* Articles sympathetic to the Marxist Left began to predominate. In 1930 Yu Zhipei (T. P. Yu), another party member, became president of the alliance. But the Marxist Left found it difficult to maintain control over a constituency of students that, by the very nature of their elite and privileged family backgrounds, tended to be politically moderate or conservative. By this time, many students were also coming to terms with the ascendance of the KMT right wing in China, and they often rejected the tactics used by the Left. In 1930 the conservatives and moderates worked together to oust T. P. Yu from the presidency and Thomas T. Y. Hu from the editorship on charges of using the CSA for "red propaganda" purposes.[91] This internal struggle so exhausted and demoralized the organization that *Chinese Students' Monthly* suspended publication in 1931. However, the continued deterioration of the political situation in China would nurture progressive ideals among university students and scholars until the appropriate spark could reignite the flames of their patriotism.

The end of the 1920s marks the closing of the formative period of the Chinese Marxist Left in America. In these early years the Left moved from a close identification with the Kuomintang to become an active opposition. During this era, the Communist International led Communist parties all over the world. Under this arrangement, a member of a Communist party in one country could move to another and participate fully as a member of that nation's Communist party.[92] Through these international networks, the CCP transmitted its political directives concerning Chinese issues to the CPUSA as guidelines for action. These transnational contexts would greatly influence how the Chinese Marxist Left in the United States responded to China's struggles in the face of Japanese aggression.

CHAPTER 3

Organizing the Community:
Communists during the Great Depression

After the Kuomintang (KMT) purged leftists from its ranks in 1927, Chinese na-tionalist politics grew increasingly complicated in both China and America. In China the Marxist leftists were forced to go underground or flee abroad, while in America Communists and their sympathizers constantly faced police repression, and noncitizens confronted the additional threat of deportation.

During the Great Depression of the 1930s, the Chinese Marxist Left tried to take root firmly in American soil, particularly by organizing workers among the Chinese communities of New York and San Francisco. It followed the political line delineated by the Communist International to combat imperialism, which by mid-decade was modified to be the struggle against fascism.

Many early leading party members in the United States had been university students, often Mandarin speaking, who as dedicated patriots often left or hoped to return to China. In the meantime, however, the KMT crackdowns had forced many leftists to take shelter in the extraterritorial protection offered by the foreign concessions while others went abroad. Restrictive American immigration laws permitted few to enter the United States.

One of this select group was Chen Qiyuan (Chi-yuen Chen, C. Y. Chen), a scholar and native of Guangzhou who had been elected an alternate member of the Kuomintang central executive committee in 1926. However, after opposing the anti-Communist purge, he was expelled and fled an arrest order. Chen went first to Hong Kong and eventually wound up in New York during the Great De-pression. He worked variously as a Chinese school teacher, newspaper editor, an interpreter, before finally ending up as a shipyard laborer. He eventually joined the Communist Party of the United States of America (CPUSA) and became a member of its Chinese Bureau. As a Cantonese intellectual, he bridged the Cantonese-speaking Chinatown community and the Mandarin-speaking leftist intellectuals.[1]

Occasionally radical seamen working on transoceanic vessels also stayed and participated in leftist activities in America. For example, Zhuang Jingmin from

Bao'an County jumped ship at Los Angeles in late 1928 and made his way to New York, where he participated in the Tung On Association along with many fellow seamen. He also joined the Grand Alliance Supporting the Chinese Workers and Peasants Revolution (ACWP) and helped publish the *Chinese Vanguard*. In 1930 the ACWP sent him to organize Chinese seamen when it petitioned the New York Chinese Consolidated Benevolent Association (CCBA) to protest a proposed law to deport aliens without legal residency rights.[2] The CCBA together with the Chinese Consulate both rejected this request. The KMT organ *Mun Hey* accused Zhuang of being a CPUSA lackey, thereby greatly compromising his ability to organize. In 1930 he followed the ACWP leadership's suggestion that he relocate to Europe.[3] Even though such landings of radical seamen on American soil were not rare, they were only transients and remained on the periphery of the Chinese Marxist Left movement in the United States.

During this period, Chinese leftists made progress in bridging the wide gulf between intellectual activists from China and the Cantonese workers who comprised the majority of Chinese in America. During the late 1920s, the Communist Party was able to recruit working-class Chinese from the local community, most prominently Xavier Dea (Xie Chuang). His impressive organizational abilities, demonstrated through the San Francisco Chinese Students Association (SFCSA) impressed Y. Y. Hsu, who sponsored the young radical to join the Young Communist League in December 1927. In August 1928, the league supported him for full party membership. By this time, Dea had become active in the Kung Yu Club.[4] Chinese American Benjamin Fee also joined the party a year later. Other working-class Chinese American Communists included Liu Kemian (Hartmann Liu), Zhao Yue, Lin Tang (Thomas Lem Tong), Ouyang Ji, Cen Huijian (Alice Sum), Zeng Dingyuan, Chen Houfu (Chan Hau Fu in Cantonese), He Huiliang, Feng Hanping, Zhou Binghun, and Xu Jiyuan.[5]

The Chinese Left functioned as part of the CPUSA under the leadership of Earl Browder. Browder had considerable experience in China, having led an international labor delegation expressing support for the Chinese revolution at the behest of the Soviet Union in 1926. Browder's delegation had arrived in Guangzhou on February 17 and continued to other parts of Guangdong, Jiangxi, Hubei, Hunan, and Hankou, accompanied by Tan Pingshan of the Chinese Communist Party (CCP). Browder later reported to the Communist International (Comintern) concerning Chiang Kai-shek's bloody purge of the Communists. That same year he also wrote "Nationalism and the Chinese Civil War," describing what his delegation had witnessed in Shanghai. While admitting the setback to the revolution, he nonetheless expressed confidence that it was only temporary. In May 1927, the Red International of Labor Unions (RILU) met in Hankou to form the Pan-Pacific Trade Union Secretariat. Protected by the extraterritoriality of the foreign concessions, Browder was able to serve as its general secretary in Shanghai in 1927–28, and he also edited the *Pan Pacific Monthly*. He also submitted the article "Wages and Working Conditions in China," to the *Chinese Students' Monthly,* a publication of the Chinese Students' Alliance in the United States. While in Shanghai, Browder had close contacts with such prominent figures as Mikhail Borodin, Madam Sun Yat-sen (Soong Ching Ling), Madam Liao Zhong-kai (He Xiangning), Zhou Enlai, Zhu De, and Liu Shaoqi. He gained considerable insights into the Chinese revolution and global perspectives on the Communist movement, which later influenced CPUSA policies toward Asian developments and the recruitment of Asian American members. He also continued to submit articles to the *Chinese Students' Monthly* after returning to America.[6]

Browder returned to find a party divided by the struggle to remove Trotskyist James Cannon and Bukharin supporter Jay Lovestone. He ascended to the post of general secretary when the influence of the CPUSA reached its peak in American society.

Chinese party members seem to have sided with Browder's prevailing faction and thus were minimally affected by the factional struggles. The party began to establish itself in the Chinese community. However, although the number of Chinese party members grew rapidly, the absolute number of party members overall remained quite small. In September 1927, shortly before the First National Conference of the Chinese Faction, there were eighteen members, including ten "workers" and eight "students." This number grew to twenty-four nationwide by May 1928, to thirty-three in August 1928, and to fifty-one in February 1929.[7] These numbers remained low probably because the students most inclined to join stayed only temporarily in America, while many Chinese immigrants had used false documents to gain entry. Both situations tended to discourage open support of leftist causes for fear of attracting police or immigration authority attention. CPUSA maintenance of strict party discipline also limited participation. However, what Communist Party members lacked in numbers, they made up with zeal, discipline, and dedication to their cause.

San Francisco: From the Kung Yu Club to the Chinese Workers Mutual-Aid Association

After the collapse of the KMT-CCP alliance and the temporary ebbing of revolutionary tides in China, the Chinese Marxist Left in the San Francisco Bay area focused more on organizing workers locally. Earlier, Xavier Dea had organized the Society for the Study of the Three Principles of the People (SSTPP) to support Sun Yat-sen's policies. Before Y. Y. Hsu left for New York in 1928, he had concluded that SSTPP propaganda activities were too abstract to be easily understood or accepted by the general Chinatown population and reorganized the group into the Geming Gongyu Julebu (Kung Yu Club) to focus on organizing Chinatown workers. Xavier Dea was a key leader of this group as well, and he edited the club's mimeographed newsletter, *Kung Yu,* featuring articles exposing capitalist exploitation of workers, advocating class struggle, and attacking imperialism and feudalism. The publication claimed a circulation of five hundred in February 1931.[8] Benjamin Fee was also a member and attended the Western Regional Conference of the All-American Anti-Imperialist League (AAAIL) in San Francisco in June 1929 to speak about the Chinese situation. At the conference's close, he was elected to the executive committee of AAAIL's California Section.[9] Many of the group's dozen or so activist members had been San Francisco Chinese Students Association activists, while others were newly recruited workers from Chinatown.

These young activists were eager to implement Marxist-Leninist theory and demonstrate that they could improve the lot of workers. The Cantonese-speaking activists were more successful than their Mandarin-speaking predecessors in recruiting disaffected Chinatown workers. Key recruits included a general merchandise store worker named Lei (Louie in Cantonese) and Feng Mian (Fung Min in Cantonese), a deliveryman for a Chinatown restaurant.

During 1928 Chinatown food workers had many complaints concerning low wages, fourteen-to-sixteen-hour workdays, and no vacations. The club's leaders dogmatically pushed the workers to demand an eight-hour day. Workers were not confident that they could win on such an issue, and the employers rejected it as leading to unacceptably high economic losses. The radicals group also tried to organize workers in the printing and other small industries, but despite their zeal, failed due to inexperience. They did not consider the fact that many Chinese had immigrated with help from relatives in America who were also their employers. In many businesses, management-worker relationships were complicated by kinship ties and debt obligations. Thus, the club's early efforts had limited appeal.[10]

The Kung Yu Club was more successful in assisting with the Chinese Laundry Workers Union (Sai Fook Tong) strike in early 1929. Xavier Dea represented the club in working with the union to devise strike strategies. In this early cooperative effort between Chinese and non-Chinese progressives in the labor movement, members of mainstream labor unions helped to picket in front of the struck laundries. After a weeklong work stoppage, the laundry workers won. After the strike ended, the San Francisco Labor Council invited Billy Chan and Alice Sum from the Chinese Laundry Workers Union to give a report on the strike. Xavier Dea's prominent role, however, made him a marked man in conservative circles.[11]

Later that same year the United States stock market crashed, and the Great Depression began in earnest. Communist Party members in the left-wing Trade Union Unity League led the formation of a National Unemployed Council (NUC) in 1930, as national struggles for "work or bread," "unemployment insurance," and other relief measures escalated. Branches of the NUC formed in different communities and among various ethnic groups.

Within San Francisco's Chinatown, the Kung Yu Club actively supported this movement. Members braved police harassment and arrest for blocking traffic and disturbing the peace to make speeches on the street and distribute literature.

Police conducted intimidating home searches for radical literature. In April 1930, police actually arrested Xavier Dea and Xie Jue as they and other Kung Yu members made speeches at a Chinatown street corner, and brutally assaulted them at the police station before turning them over to immigration authorities at Angel Island Immigration Detention Station in San Francisco Bay to be deported as subversive aliens. Some weeks later, the International Labor Defense posted bail for their release.[12] At the end of that year, Benjamin Fee departed for the USSR to study at the Lenin School for training in leadership.[13]

In January 1931, the Kung Yu Club established the San Francisco Chinese Unemployed Alliance.[14] One of its most publicized acts was a march on the CCBA involving about a hundred unemployed Chinese workers. Yu Pengcheng (Pang Ching Yee in Cantonese), Xavier Dea, Luo Liang (Law Leung in Cantonese), and American-born Chen Junqi (Eva Chan) presented demands for immediate relief efforts.[15] Many of these marchers later joined a massive demonstration of the unemployed in San Francisco's business district in one of the earliest instances of American Chinese participating in a labor protest outside Chinatown. Soon thereafter, in May 1931, immigration authorities arrested Xavier Dea again as a subversive alien and incarcerated him on Angel Island. While there, Dea won the trust of other detainees and became head of the Angel Island Liberty Association. He aroused their patriotic feelings with news of Japan's recent aggression in China, organized a protest against the substandard food, and served as head negotiator with the authorities.[16] In May 1932, faced with deportation to China and an uncertain fate, Dea chose to go to the Soviet Union.[17]

Toward the end of 1931, Benjamin Fee returned from the Soviet Union and married fellow activist Eva Chan. He also organized the Resonance Association as "an organization of Chinese youth for the struggle against imperialism" in San Francisco. The group claimed an initial membership of fifteen. An important move was to take over the publication *Resonance,* which had been issued by the now defunct Chinese Students Association to serve as the West Coast version of the East Coast's *Chinese Vanguard.* Benjamin Fee became the editor. The four-page, mimeographed publication struggled, because conservative Chinatown leaders had excluded *Resonance* staff from using Chinatown printing facilities, forcing them to typeset and print at the Japanese American Golden Gate Printing Company, which was sympathetic to the Left. Despite their zeal, it was difficult for the young Marxists to sustain this journalistic effort, which claimed a circulation of five hundred in 1931. It stopped publication for good in the mid-1930s.[18] Marxist efforts to cultivate a youth movement would not succeed until the end of the 1930s, when increased immigration from China and support for China's anti-Japanese war efforts stimulated the flowering of a diversity of youth activities.

In the meantime, despite the arrest and deportation of its leader, Xavier Dea, the Unemployed Alliance remained active. In early 1933, it sent seven representatives to a hunger march at the state capital of Sacramento, demanding "cash payments for relief of unemployed workers, opposition to the arrest and deportation of unemployed aliens, and passage of a workers' unemployed insurance law."[19]

With the ongoing depression and growing unemployment, the San Francisco government finally undertook some relief measures in early 1933 to avoid the boiling over of discontent. In Chinatown the CCBA worked with the municipal government to establish a soup kitchen and rooming house for the unemployed and homeless.[20] That year, Congress passed the Federal Emergency Relief Act to aid the unemployed, the National Industrial Recovery Act to regulate business conditions, and other laws to create jobs. As a result, the Unemployed Alliance declined as the labor movement shifted to emphasize increased job security and higher wages.

The Chinese Marxist Left also established a Chinese Workers Center to help Chinese workers find employment and to provide social and education services. The center claimed a membership of about a hundred; however, some key members had belonged to the Kung Yu Club. The Chinese Workers Center had not been in existence long when the San Francisco police raided and closed its office as an alleged Communist stronghold during the general strike of 1934.[21]

Despite such setbacks, a small group of dedicated Chinese Marxists continued to try to organize Chinese workers. They turned their attention to the Chinatown garment industry, which employed the most factory workers in the community, people who worked long hours under notoriously poor conditions. During the early 1930s, such militants as Karl Fung, Margaret Young, and George Bun Low linked up with the Communist-led Trade Union Unity League (TUUL) to form a Chinese branch of TUUL's Needle Trade Workers Industrial Union, which led a series of strikes and work stoppages in Chinatown factories in early 1934, with mixed results.[22] An anecdote about Cai Cangming (Joe Git Choy, Quai Bun Lowe, Lawrence Lowe) recounted how he tried to foment a strike in his older brother's factory and was temporarily expelled from the family for his efforts. Although his older brother, Choy Sut Chew, was a veteran member of the KMT, these political differences did not seem to permanently affect the two brothers' fraternal regard for each other.[23]

The young activists ultimately failed in their labor organizing efforts due to their inexperience and dogmatic application of American labor movement tactics to Chinatown conditions, as described in chapter 4. They were not even able to persuade workers belonging to the existing Chinese Garment Workers Guild, Jinyi Hang [Gam Yee Hong], to support their actions.[24] But the Marxist Left kept trying and learned from each failure.

Members of the Chinese Marxist Left were among the first Chinese to break through the color line and be admitted to mainstream labor unions in San Francisco, which had a long history of anti-Chinese sentiments. During the early 1930s, Benjamin Fee had led a failed attempt to pressure the Dollar Steamship Line to hire American citizens of Chinese descent as seamen. However, the Chinese Marxists continued in their efforts to persuade American unions to accept Chinese members and worked with progressives from all groups on labor issues. About twenty members of the Chinese Left were active in the San Francisco waterfront strike that culminated in a general strike in 1934. Afterward, with the assistance of progressive union members, some Asians, including a few Chinese, were admitted to the International Longshoremen and Warehousemen Union.[25]

In November 1934, the International Ladies Garment Workers Union (ILGWU) began organizing in San Francisco's Chinatown. Benjamin Fee, working as an ILGWU organizer, formed a Chinatown local but had little impact recruiting members, possibly because he was already widely known as a leftist. The ILGWU's Jennie Matyas, an anti-Communist, then forced him out around 1936 and took over his recruiting efforts.[26] She was no more successful than Fee, until worker dissatisfaction at the National Dollar Store factory, the largest in Chinatown, offered a window of opportunity. In 1938, after a 105-day strike, the ILGWU was finally able to gain employer recognition of a Chinatown union local.

Through these struggles, Chinese militants grew increasingly aware that they needed to cooperate with progressive elements in the mainstream American labor movement to improve working conditions of the Chinese in America. A key opportunity arose when the Alaska Cannery Workers Union (ACWU) attacked the exploitative and oppressive Chinese contract system used by the Alaskan Packers Association (APA) salmon canneries to recruit Chinese workers, among others. In 1936 picket lines of multiethnic workers struck at the dock to halt the loading of supplies onto APA ships. The APA finally capitulated to this pressure and recognized the union. The union agreement improved working conditions, abolished the contract system, and established hiring halls for recruiting workers.[27] In these efforts, the Chinese leftists worked behind the scenes to avoid discovery by and reprisals from the Chinese contractors, who had gang connections.

In 1937 Benjamin Fee became third vice-president of the multiethnic ACWU, which dispatched Sam Young and Willie Fong to organize in Alaskan canneries. During their return trip, they listened to Chinese workers' requests for an organization that served social purposes and promoted their welfare.[28] After reaching San Francisco, they established the Chinese Workers Mutual-Aid Association (CWMAA) in October 1937, with Sam Young, Zhao Tianzuo, Benjamin Fee, and Peng Fei as founding officers.

At this point, the Marxist Left organization received a setback when Benjamin Fee had marital problems and an extramarital affair that undermined his leadership among his fellow progressives. In August 1937, Lawrence Lowe married Fee's former wife, Eva, in San Francisco and the two left for Hong Kong with Fee's infant son.[29] In October 1938, the Communist Party ordered Fee to resign his position at the CWMAA and move to New York, where he became a translator at *China Salvation Times,* under the editorship of Zhao Jiansheng. He disagreed frequently with Zhao and soon left. Fee either quit or was dropped from the party, and he no longer played any significant role in CPUSA activities. Happy Lim succeeded Fee as CWMAA secretary.[30]

The CWMAA represented a more mature stage in the development of the Chinese Marxist Left in the United States. It strove to unite Chinese workers to improve their status and to better their working conditions. The officers promoted the philosophy of shared working-class identity regardless of ethnic background—a concept that was grounds for much of the association's strength and success.

From its original roles of providing employment information about the canneries and bringing together returned cannery workers, the CWMAA expanded to include workers from other occupations. Through their extensive links to mainstream unions, the CWMAA was able to channel Chinese workers to jobs in broader sectors of the economy. It encouraged Chinese workers to join labor unions and to value working collectively. The CWMAA evoked a responsive chord among Chinese workers and quickly enrolled four to five hundred members soon after its founding. Membership seems to have peaked around six hundred.[31]

The CWMAA was most effective in helping Chinese find employment in the mainstream labor markets and movement. Around the time of the CWMAA's founding, progressives also established a Chinatown branch of the International Workers' Order, enabling many Chinese workers to benefit from this early form of health insurance.[32] Despite these successes, the CWMAA and the Marxist Left were much too small in size and resources to be able to exert much influence in a Chinese community dominated by a complex network of conservative interests.

New York City: From Sojourning Students to the Chinese Hand Laundry Alliance

On the East Coast, economic conditions and the pull of homeland patriotism leeched many potential leftist leaders from the United States. During the late 1920s and early 1930s, many Chinese CPUSA members, especially university students, departed for the Soviet Union or China. They sought, in part, to participate actively in the Chinese revolution. This patriotism toward China was compounded by the difficulty of making a living in Depression-era America, and the relentless harassment of Chinese residents by immigration authorities further fueled the exodus.

Immigration laws had long been used by the federal government to expel "undesirable" aliens. The stringent Chinese exclusion laws rendered members of the Chinese Marxist Left, especially those in the country on student visas, especially vulnerable to deportation proceedings. Under this constant threat, many members of the CPUSA operated under assumed names. For example, Shi Huang was known in the party as Dongsheng and Tontien, C. T. Chi as Dongping, Y. Y. Hsu as Huafa, Li Daoxuan (Li Tao Hsuan) as H. Linson and Toddy, Zhang Bao as Xuehan, Benjamin Fee as H. T. Chang and Suarez.[33]

Despite these attempts at secrecy, immigration authorities obtained enough information from informers and other sources to harass Chinese Communists constantly. And so, the post of secretary of the China Bureau central committee changed often from the late 1920s through the early 1930s. Like Xavier Dea in San Francisco, Li Tao Hsuan, secretary of the Chinese Bureau central committee, was detained at Ellis Island in late 1930 and deported to the USSR around 1932. In the summer of 1932, Zhang Bao (Mo Zhengdan) took over the position and avoided being arrested at New York's Worker Center only because the school receptionist delayed the federal agents long enough to enable him to escape by a side entrance. Zhang later surfaced in Moscow around September 1932.[34] His successors until the Sino-Japanese War were He Zhifen (Henry Hahn, Chee Fun Ho), Y. Y. Hsu, Yu Guangsheng (Yu Rixin), and Tang Mingzhao (Chu Tong, Chew Sih Tong). When Congress passed the Voorhis Act in 1940, which would have compelled the CPUSA to register as an agent of a foreign power, the CPUSA withdrew from the Comintern and also canceled the party membership of four thousand noncitizens. The party leadership also ordered Chu Tong, who was a U.S. citizen, to head the Chinese Bureau. Y. Y. Hsu, however, served the longest on the Chinese Bureau, from its origin in 1927 until his departure for China in 1946. For most of the period up to the late 1930s, he headed the ACWP and also edited the *Chinese Vanguard*. He was Chinese Bureau secretary from 1933 to 1935 and again from 1945 to 1946.[35]

As in San Francisco, New York's Chinese Marxist Left tried to organize China-town workers, particularly through the All-America Alliance of Chinese Anti-Imperialists (AAACAI). They also attained only limited success due to inexperience and a doctrinaire approach. The Chinese Marxist Left was not able to organize the Chinese Unemployed Alliance of Greater New York until 1933, two years later than their counterparts on the West Coast.[36] The Chinese Unemployed Alliance tried to petition for relief from the New York CCBA but was rebuffed.[37] The alliance was somewhat more successful in soliciting donations from local businesses and also gained the assistance of other New York unemployed councils to prevent the illegal eviction of a Chinese tenant. However, the alliance's leadership grew increasingly concerned with the problem of unemployment at the national level and paid diminishing attention to helping the local unemployed population. When the national movement faded after Congress passed various relief measures, membership in the alliance dropped from a high of several hundred to a low of forty in 1934. That same year, the Chinese Marxist Left established a Chinese Workers Center with goals similar to the one in San Francisco.[38]

Organizing Chinese workers in New York continued to be difficult, as the Left sought a revolutionary Chinese industrial proletariat in accordance with classic Marxist doctrines. But the occupations available to Chinese on the East Coast were very limited. Most worked in small restaurants and laundries, and there were hardly any garment workers. In small businesses, the proprietors often worked alongside their employees, and class divisions were blurred. Moreover, employers and employees often had personal relationships, which were often reinforced by kinship or regional and clan ties. These factors made it extremely difficult for unions to convince workers to make demands on employers.

The maritime industry was a more promising area for labor organizing. Chinese crewmen on the numerous oceangoing vessels docking at New York endured extremely exploitative conditions. Through the *Chinese Vanguard,* the AAA-CAI often expressed sympathy and support for their struggles, and the Chinese Marxist Left was probably very eager to mobilize them. However, many seamen had already joined the pro-KMT Chinese Seamen's Union (CSU). The KMT regarded the CSU as a political arm of its party apparatus and maintained control by purging any radical elements from leadership roles. Thus, it was the CSU that took the lead in the 1936–37 National Maritime Union strike in which Chinese seamen successfully won better working conditions. The Chinese Marxist Left did manage to recruit supporters among seamen, however, and even used them as international couriers.[39]

Chinese unions, however, did not exist in Chinese-owned business establishments. Instead guild-like organizations in such industries as restaurants and laundries provided some protection for group economic interests. These guilds consisted of employers, independent operators, and workers and did not concentrate solely on promoting the interests of workers. One of these guilds, however, the Chinese Hand Laundry Alliance (CHLA), gave the Chinese Marxist Left an unprecedented opportunity to develop a friendly base in New York's Chinatown.

New York City had the highest number of Chinese laundries in the United States—around three thousand in 1930. During the Depression, these businesses competed fiercely with white-operated establishments, which lobbied the New York Board of Aldermen to pass an ordinance imposing a high licensing fee and security bond on Chinese-run laundries. This tactic most affected small establishments, which operated with only marginal profits.

The laundrymen were dissatisfied with the inept way the New York CCBA handled their problem.[40] With support from the liberal Chinatown paper, *Chinese Journal,* activist laundryman Lei Zhuofeng (Louis Wing) and other laundry operators organized the CHLA in 1933 to agitate successfully for modification of the onerous ordinance. After this initial victory, the CHLA won over most of the laundrymen in New York to become the first Chinese American organization to flourish outside the framework of the CCBA-led Chinatown traditionist association system.[41]

The CCBA, however, would not let the CHLA defy its authority without challenge. Late in 1933, the CCBA sued Y. K. Chu, editor of the *Chinese Journal,* for slander because he had published criticisms of the traditionist power structure. A pro-CCBA minority faction also challenged the CHLA leadership. They were expelled in early 1934 and founded a rival organization, but the bulk of the members remained with the CHLA.

The Marxist Left was at first ambivalent about the CHLA and regarded it as an organization of petit bourgeois proprietors. However, after establishing itself in New York and becoming active among Chinese workers, it soon became evident that both the China Bureau and the ACWP emphasized support of the Chinese revolution rather than struggling for improvements in the livelihood of the working class. Thus, they became easy targets for right-wing attacks labeling them as extremist agitators not interested in the welfare of the workers. Y. Y. Hsu responded on February 15, 1933, in an editorial appearing in *Chinese Vanguard* summarizing ACWP experiences and asserting the need to be more involved with the daily struggles of the masses in order to gain their confidence.

Thus, the ACWP became more actively involved with the CHLA. By early 1934, they began to see it could be a potentially valuable ally in the struggle against the traditionist Chinatown hierarchy and the KMT. The Marxist Left began to mobilize its Chinatown supporters and mainstream progressives to support the CHLA and Y. K. Chu against the CCBA's attacks.

CHLA leaders were wary of the Marxist Left, but in the face of CCBA hostility, they had little choice. The Left quickly demonstrated its clout by mustering allies in progressive circles and in the labor movement to help defeat a New York City License Bureau requirement that all laundry license holders must show proper immigration status—a matter of critical concern because many Chinese laundrymen were illegal immigrants.[42]

Soon, the Chinese Marxist Left and the radical faction of the CHLA formed an alliance. They founded the Quon Shar [Masses Society] in 1935 so that the progressive group could independently express its opinions about China and Chinese American issues without implicating the less politicized members of the CHLA. This politically active group, which included some CPUSA members, guided the CHLA while maintaining a close relationship with the Chinese Marxist Left. Under the influence of the Left, the CHLA publicly opposed what it described as outmoded ideas and feudal customs in Chinese society. Many of its members had little to do with traditionist Chinese organizations.[43]

The Marxist Left and the CHLA leadership tightened their bonds even more when Communist Party member Chu Tong assumed the post of English secretary for the CHLA in 1937. This was a significant development because Tong was a Cantonese who had spent his youth in San Francisco's Chinatown, unlike many of the earlier East Coast Marxist leaders who were sojourning Mandarin-speaking students from northern China. Tong's ancestral county was Enping, in the area of Guangdong from which most Chinese on the United States mainland had originated.[44]

Through the CHLA, the Chinese Marxist Left acquired a base within the largest Chinese community in the eastern United States. The CHLA was never more than a guild-type organization of small proprietors and workers, but its importance lay in its collective strength. CHLA members and the Chinese Marxist Left found common ground in their fight against racial discrimination and the dominance of the traditionist Chinatown power structure. The many immigrant CHLA members shared the Left's concerns about events in China and also thought that the civil war should cease and that the KMT and Communists should unite against Japanese aggression.

However, the laundrymen were, by the very nature of their business, individualistic and opposed to unionization that threatened their low operating costs. The Chinese Marxist Left faced the dilemma of protecting and developing its ties to the CHLA without assuming antilabor positions. For example, when the American Federation of Labor (AFL) entered New York's Chinatown in 1939, intending to unionize restaurant and eventually laundry workers, the Chinese Left attacked the move. Zhao Jiansheng (Rao Shushi) of the progressive weekly *China Salvation Times* and Chu Tong, the CHLA English secretary, wrote editorials pointing out that the laundry business was a nonmechanized industry of mostly small individual proprietors or partners with few employees. Tong stated that little antagonism existed between employers and employees, calling for a guild-like organization rather than unionization.[45] The AFL's efforts eventually failed, and the Chinese Left was able to further consolidate its base in the CHLA.

Chinese Marxist leftists were also active in other cities. For example, in Los Angeles Wei Minghua, a Chinese student, organized branches of the Anti-Imperialist League and Unemployed Alliance and gave speeches on the Chinese revolution and the Chinese soviets. In late 1932, he was arrested by the Los Angeles Police Department's "Red Squad" and turned over to immigration authorities, who deported him to the Soviet Union.[46] However, most other Chinese communities were often too small or too dispersed to be effectively organized, and San Francisco and New York remained the principal centers for Chinese Left activities.

New York leftists focused on building a base to present a united front against the KMT in Chinatown, while their counterparts in San Francisco worked to organize workers together with progressive union members. These different approaches would converge with the Sino-Japanese War and the onset of World War II, when the anti-Fascist struggle fused the priorities of the Marxist Left.

The Anti-Fascist Struggle

The 1920s and 1930s witnessed the rise of Fascist regimes in Italy, Japan, and Germany. In 1922 Benito Mussolini seized power in Italy and established his dictatorship. Hitler and the Nazis gained official office in 1933. Japanese aggressions against China began soon after its 1895 victory in the Sino-Japanese War. After annexing Taiwan and Korea, Japan began its territorial designs on mainland China. In 1931 the Japanese Kwantung Army occupied China's three northeastern provinces and established the puppet state Manchukuo. In the face of these expansionary, militaristic, and openly racist governments, the Comintern led a coalition of progressives, liberals, and pacifists to form the International League against

War and Fascism in Amsterdam in August 1932. The American branch, founded in 1933, was known as the American League against War and Fascism.[47]

At their 1935 Seventh Congress in Moscow, the Communist International directed Marxist leftists in capitalist countries to form people's fronts to fight fascism. Following this order, the CCP also issued a manifesto calling for Chinese people to form a united front to resist Japanese aggression. This text first appeared in Chinese in *Giu Guo Bao* [National Salvation News] in Paris and in English in *Newsletter of the Communist International* in Moscow. Copies found their way to China.[48]

Giu Guo Bao had started publication in May as the organ of the CCP delegation to the Comintern, with the editing and typesetting being done at Moscow. The French government closed the newspaper in November 1938 at the behest of the KMT government, but it resumed publication on December 9 as *Giu Guo Sh Bao* (*Au Sécours de la Patrie*) to communicate the spirit of the CCP's August 1 Manifesto, first as a semimonthly but later as a weekly publication.

Giu Guo Sh Bao continued publication until war clouds began gathering in Europe in 1938 and Stalin's ruthless purges devastated its editorial ranks. So many fell victim that the CCP had to suspend publication on February 19, 1938, with the excuse that the staff had returned to China to participate in the War of Resistance. Less than two weeks later, even the chief editor, Li Lisan, was arrested and would not see China again until after World War II. Soon afterward, the editors Zhao Jiansheng and Loh Tsei moved the printing press and type fonts to New York City, with the ultimate objective of starting a daily newspaper there.[49]

The Chinese Marxist Left participated in the anti-Fascist resistance in Spain as well. From the outset, Mussolini and Hitler had poured in men and munitions to support Francisco Franco, who was trying to overthrow the Republican regime. The Soviet Union countered by aiding the beleaguered Republicans, and the Comintern called on progressive people around the world to lend support. About a hundred Chinese volunteered, including some from *Giu Guo Sh Bao* and a few from the United States by way of the AAACAI's *Chinese Vanguard*.[50]

CPUSA member Zhang Ji (Chi Chang) was one of the first American volunteers. He was a mining engineering graduate who had attended the University of California and University of Minnesota. He arrived in Spain in April 1937 and served as a driver in a transportation team but was kept from the front due to a bad back and chronic illness. He left Spain for Paris in late 1938. By that time, the Sino-Japanese War had already started, and Chang departed for Hong Kong.[51]

Eight of the nine known surviving Chinese volunteers withdrew with the International Brigade to France in early 1939. Six were detained at the camp at Gurs but managed to contact Zhao Jiansheng (Rao Shushi) of *China Salvation Times* in New York City. Zhao published an appeal for readers to help them return to China to participate in the war effort there. Soon afterward, delegates to the Third World Youth Congress at Nice visited three of the detainees, and in October 1939, the Chinese consulate finally issued passports for the six to return to China.[52] At least twenty-two non-Chinese medical volunteers who volunteered in Spain also continued to China, including Dr. Norman Bethune, who was later canonized in CCP history as a symbol of selfless heroic internationalism.[53]

Such courage contrasted starkly with China's nonresisting leadership, which facilitated the Japanese invasion. Chiang Kai-shek headed the central government in Nanjing but faced challenges from various KMT factions, local warlords, and Communist insurgents. When Japanese forces occupied Manchuria in 1931, Chiang's first priority was to pacify and unify the rest of China before attempting to repel the foreign invaders. Rather than combating the Japanese, Chiang's secret police worked assiduously to ferret out and eradicate Chinese dissidents in areas that remained under government control.

As Japanese aggression and KMT internal political repression continued, the ranks of those opposed to KMT policies grew. Liberals and the left wing, with the backing of the underground CCP, eventually formed a coalition around these issues. In major Chinese cities such as Wuhan, Beijing, Shanghai, and Hong Kong, the anti-Japanese cause brought together both Chinese and non-Chinese destined to play significant roles in the left movement not only in China but throughout the world through the 1940s.

Japanese aggression increased with an attack on Shanghai in 1932 that met with stiff resistance by the Nineteenth Route Army. That same year, the Japanese government set up a puppet Manchukuo regime and continued to invade the provinces just north of the Great Wall.

With Japan occupying more Chinese territory, concerned Chinese and non-Chinese alike worried about the lack of central government commitment to protecting Chinese sovereignty. The CCP quickly detected the changing popular mood and positioned itself as the party advocating resistance in stark contrast to the KMT's appeasement. Leftist sectarianism dominated the thinking of the CCP leadership. Patriotic or progressive roles were ascribed to workers and peasants only, thus denying such roles for other strata of society. Middle-of-the-road "centrists" were considered untrustworthy when serving the progressive cause. Thus, at one point, the CCP discouraged all contacts with Madam Sun and anti–Chiang Kai-shek military men. However, by 1933 this separatist thinking was beginning to change. When the CCP underground organized a secret Far Eastern Conference of the World Committee against Imperialist War in Shanghai's International Settlement on September 30, 1933, Madam Sun was elected chair, which reaffirmed the CCP's acknowledgement of the importance of Madam Sun to China's national salvation and the revolutionary movement.[54]

In 1934 Madam Sun, together with He Xiangning, Zhang Naiqi, and others pushed for the formation of a Chinese National Committee for Armed Self-Defense (CNCASD). In April the CNCASD preparatory committee publicized the Basic Chinese National Program for Fighting Japan that had just been issued by the CCP Central Committee with signatures from 1,779 prominent Chinese supporters, including Madam Sun. A CNCASD declaration on fighting Japan followed in June. Both documents called on the Chinese people to arm themselves and to organize into a united front to resist Japanese aggression.[55] Under KMT repression, the populace could not really arm themselves, but the proclamations served to greatly heighten popular awareness of the threat to China.

As Japan extended its occupation toward the Great Wall, the northern cities of Beijing and Tianjin became the next targets. The CCP underground had been active in this region but by 1934 had ceased to function effectively after constant hounding and arrests by the KMT secret police. For example, Tang Mingzhao (Chu Tong) from San Francisco was one of those jailed. He had become caught up in nationalistic fervor and joined the CCP. He soon became head of the organizational department of the Beijing party committee; however, the KMT secret police soon discovered and arrested him. Since he was an American citizen, the U.S. embassy was able to secure his release, but he had to leave China. He transferred to Berkeley, California, in 1933 where he became active in the CPUSA branch at the university.[56]

In early 1935, Japan began using Chinese puppets to agitate for "autonomous rule" in Hebei province around Beijing and Tianjin. As China's historical capital, Beijing inspired particularly powerful patriotic sentiments. The May Fourth Movement had occurred there in 1919, and the Chinese Marxists had first organized at Beijing University. The presence of the two-hundred-thousand-strong Northeast Army together with numerous refugees that had retreated to Hebei from the occupied northeastern provinces further fueled nationalist sentiments. The CCP had reestablished a provisional Beijing party committee around June 1935; however, only about twenty members were able to maintain contact with the main party organization.[57] Augmented by popular dissatisfaction with the KMT government's appeasement policies, the CCP's image as the chief defender of Chinese sovereignty grew with Japanese aggression in North China. On August 1, 1935, the CCP delegation to the Communist International in Moscow called for national unity against Japan. The party intensified its organizing efforts among students and intellectuals to form a united front to force the KMT government to begin active resistance. A large-scale demonstration in Beijing on December 9, 1935, signaled the turn in the public mood toward active protection of Chinese territory.

Some foreign faculty and journalists in Beijing played active roles in these developments. Two of the best known were the American journalists Edgar and Helen Foster Snow. In fall 1933, Snow joined the Yenching University journalism department as a lecturer. The couple also launched a project translating Chinese contemporary literature by eminent writers such as Lu Xun and Mao Dun into English with the help of students Xiao Qian and Yang Gang, both of whom later became well-known journalists.[58] The Snows were not Marxist revolutionaries but were strongly humanitarian. Their observations and personal experiences of China led them to form views critical of the KMT regime and to sympathize with the Chinese revolutionary movement. At their Beijing home, they hosted student activists and shared information that they had picked up as journalists. One of these activists, Wang Rumei (Huang Hua), recalled that Agnes Smedley became a courier for the students' requests to Madam Sun for advice. Edgar Snow claimed to have urged the students to use demonstrations to pressure authorities. On December 9, four to five thousand students and faculty from Beijing middle schools and universities protested in calling for national unity to resist Japanese aggression, for an end to the selling out of China's interests, and for the government to respect civil rights. On December 12, the student association's officers, Gong Pusheng and Gong Weihang (Gong Peng), co-chaired a press conference attended by foreign correspondents to make their case known to the world. On December 16, ten thousand students staged another mass demonstration.[59]

After December 11, university and high school students in other major cities staged mass meetings or demonstrations. With Snow's support, the foreign press corps was on hand to witness these events and report to the world about police use of violence and arrests to suppress the demonstrators. Some of the activists, such as Gong Pusheng and Lu Cui (Loh Tsei) later journeyed to Europe and America and contributed to leftist activities there.[60] Some Chinese American students also participated, such as Zhang Xixian (Constance Chang) from Los Angeles. She later returned to America in 1937 to study for an MA at Columbia University, and in 1938 married her former Nankai classmate and then CHLA English secretary Chu Tong. Arthur Chung (Zhang Weixun), a half brother of Constance's father, was another American-born activist. He had attended Nankai Middle School, Yenching University, and the National Medical College of Shanghai. At Yenching, Chung met Liang Siyi (Sylvia Liang), the fifth daughter of Liang Qichao. They both participated in the December student demonstrations and joined the underground CCP. After graduation, they married and returned to the United States, and Chung served his medical internship in Los Angeles. Peking University's Liang Faye (Francis Leong) was a participant from San Francisco who moved with the University to Yunnan during the War of Resistance. After returning to America when the war ended, he became a leading member in the Overseas Chinese Federation for Peace and Democracy in China.[61]

Through the momentum generated by these demonstrations, national salvation associations emerged in Beijing, Shanghai, and other cities and coalesced into an All-China National Salvation Association in June 1936. Representing the association, the educators Tao Xingzhi, Qian Junrui, and Loh Tsei of the All-China Students Federation attended the World Youth Conference in Geneva and the World Peace Conference in Brussels that August. They visited Chinese communities elsewhere in Europe to encourage the formation of other national salvation advocacy groups. Tao and Loh continued to North America in early 1937 to spread the message. The KMT government responded with further repression of the organizing. In late 1936, it arrested leading National Salvation Association activists in Shanghai and other cities and issued a warrant for Tao Xingzhi's arrest.[62]

Teams comprised mostly of students fanned out in the cities and the country-side to raise general awareness of the crisis facing China. Shanghai became the center for writers, composers, and film directors creating works with patriotic and anti-imperialist themes that targeted Chinese audiences at home and abroad. Many films featured songs that became popular standards, such as the stirring "March of the Volunteers," which later became the national anthem of the People's Republic of China. There were also widely performed propaganda skits, of which one of the best known was *Fangxia ni de bianzi* [*Lay Down Your Whip*].[63]

Choruses that performed songs advocating resistance proved to be very effective in attracting the participation of workers, commoners, and students. In February 1935, Liu Liangmo of the Shanghai YMCA organized the Minzhong Geyonghui [People's Choral Society] to form choruses in Shanghai and Chinese communities throughout the world to cultivate patriotic sentiments and awareness of China's crisis. The growing popularity of Liu's group attracted crackdowns by the authorities. After open hostilities began in 1937, Liu left Shanghai to continue these choral activities in his native Zhejiang. When KMT authorities sought to arrest him in 1940, Liu left China for the United States under the auspices of the YMCA.[64]

The YWCA also participated in the national salvation movement. Cora Deng, director of the women workers night school program, was a founder of the first organization in Shanghai to advocate resistance to Japanese aggression.[65] A number of Chinese and American staff members also identified with anti-imperialist activities and sympathized with the Chinese revolutionary movement. Talitha Gerlach (Xie Lishu), who began working for the YWCA in China in 1926, became a supporter of the Left movement.[66] In 1934, while heading the Students Department of the Shanghai YWCA, she joined a Marxist study group initiated by the German Hans Shippe that included her colleagues Cora Deng, Maud Russell, Lillian K. Haass, Rewi Alley, George Hatem, and several other Chinese and Western progressives. Maud Russell, who had begun working for the YWCA in China in 1917, was persuaded by her experiences and observations in China to become anti-imperialist and dedicated herself to Marxist theory and the Soviet Union.[67]

Since 1927 the YWCA had also been active in workers issues and directed considerable efforts toward educating workers. Although membership included only a percentage of all female workers, many were politicized and became activists fighting for better wages and workers rights. A disproportionate number joined the Communist movement. During the 1930s, Lillian Haass hired members of the Chinese Left to work as YWCA staff, arguing that they were the "people of the future." The Chinese YWCA Industrial Department established informal relations with the CCP through women employees rotated between the organizations. For example, Gong Pusheng, a Yenching University student leader, joined the Shanghai YWCA staff after graduating in 1936. She joined the Communist Party in 1938 while still working with the YWCA.[68]

Although such institutions as Beijing and Yenching universities and the YMCA and YWCA espoused Western liberal political philosophies, during the Republican-era they existed in a China under authoritarian rule with an entrenched feudalistic society that allowed scant room for ideals such as theirs. Under such conditions, many concerned Chinese, especially the younger generation, felt compelled to move leftward or to ally themselves with the Left. This shift on the part of the political center significantly changed the dynamics between the CCP and the KMT so that despite the latter's dominance of Chinese politics, the influence of the CCP could no longer be ignored.

During these momentous transformations, Madam Sun established a publication to succeed *China Forum* to publicize the struggle against repression and foreign aggression. Agnes Smedley contacted CPUSA secretary-general Earl Browder in 1935 for assistance. Browder dispatched his secretary, Grace Granich, and her husband, Max, to Shanghai to help start publishing the semimonthly *Voice of China* in March 1936. *Voice of China* attained a wide readership that peaked at 7,500 with distribution in China, the United States, Southeast Asia, and even Japan. It advocated unity in resistance to Japanese aggression and publicized leftist activities and policies in China and the antifascism policy of the Comintern. The publication ran until November 1937, when the Japanese occupied Shanghai and the Granichs returned to the United States, where Max Granich became managing editor of the influential *China Today*.[69]

Agnes Smedley left Shanghai soon after the Granichs arrived. In September 1936, she reached Xi'an, the headquarters for the warlord generals Zhang Xueliang and Yang Hucheng, who were under orders from Chiang Kai-shek to attack the Communist base in Shaanxi.[70]

By that time, the Red Army had broken out from the KMT encirclement of their Jiangxi base, completed the epic six-thousand-mile-long Long March, and just reached the Communist base in northern Shaanxi. Upon learning of their arrival from the underground, Edgar and Helen Snow sought permission to visit Yan'an. They sent feelers to the CCP organization through the student activist leader David Yu (Yu Qiwei; Huang Jing) and Madam Sun. Edgar Snow received an invitation to visit Yan'an with the Lebanese American physician George Hatem (Ma Haide). Hatem had arrived in Shanghai in 1933 and become sympathetic to the objectives of the Chinese Revolution. He had met Agnes Smedley, Rewi Alley, and Madam Sun, who arranged for him to travel to Shaanxi with Snow in June 1936.[71]

Snow and Hatem rendezvoused in Xi'an, where they met with the Rev. Wang Fushi (Dong Jianwu), who acted as their guide.[72] Wang Rumei interpreted for Snow during his four-month stay in the CCP area. Afterward, Hatem remained in the Communist area to serve as a physician, while Snow returned to Beijing to author *Red Star over China,* perhaps the most effective publicity supporting the Chinese Communists to reach international audiences.

Red Star over China described Snow's visit and was first published in October 1937 in London and in January 1938 in New York. It provided the first detailed report about the Communist base in Shaanxi and introduced the Chinese Communists to Western readers. Snow was considered an objective and non-ideological reporter whose largely affirming views received enthusiastic responses. Ironically, CPUSA reviewers were quite critical, because they regarded Snow's remarks about the Soviet Union and the Comintern to be disparaging. The Workers' Book Shop banned the work from its shelves, and *New Masses* refused to advertise it.[73]

Even before the publication of *Red Star over China,* the *China Weekly Review* had published Snow's interviews with Mao Zedong, and the *Shanghai Evening Post and Mercury* had printed a detailed account of a speech he delivered at a Beijing church. Readers eagerly devoured every word. Translations appeared in Paris's *Giu Guo Sh Bao* and New York's *Chinese Vanguard.* Wang Fushi, a student refugee from the Japanese-occupied Northeast translated and published an abridged Chinese edition *Waiguo jizhe xibei yinxiangji* [Report of a Foreign Journalist's Impressions of the Northwest] around April 1937 at Snow's request. In May 1937, Wang Fushi also interpreted for Helen Foster Snow during another five-month trip to the Communist area that produced the book *Red Dust.*[74]

Snow had met Smedley in Xi'an in late October on his way back to Beijing. Despite her disappointment at Snow's scoop, she soon reaped the international rewards of being the only Western journalist on site when the generals Zhang Xueliang and Yang Hucheng kidnapped their commanding officer Chiang Kai-shek on December 12, 1936, thereby changing the course of China's history. They forced the generalissimo to agree to end the civil war and unify the country in resistance to Japan. After Chiang's release, New Zealander James Bertram, who had originally come to Beijing on a Rhodes Scholarship to study Mandarin, arrived to join Smedley. His book *Crisis in China* was probably one of the best contemporary accounts of the Xi'an Incident by a Westerner. Shortly afterward, in January 1937, the CCP officially invited Smedley to visit Yan'an. She was still there when the Marco Polo Bridge Incident finally ignited China's open War of Resistance against Japan.[75]

Most Chinese people in America were deeply concerned with their homeland's struggles against Japanese aggression. Their patriotism manifested itself both in the larger society and within the Chinese community. The international movement included the fight against Japanese militarism as one part of the general antiwar, anti-Fascist campaigns. The American Marxist Left, in alliance with liberals and pacifists, initiated most of the anti-Japanese activities, because the small Chinese population in America was too isolated from the larger society. C. T. Chi, however, was one of the few Chinese able to play a key role in activities targeting mainstream Americans. After returning from Europe in the late 1920s,

Chi already had a reputation as an able Marxist theoretician and an exceptionally capable propagandist for the cause of Chinese Communism. Upon assuming duties as a member of the Chinese Bureau of the American Communist Party, he became a leader in policy implementation. Under the pen name R. Doonping, Chi published articles about China in the *Daily Worker*. Using this pseudonym, Chi also co-authored an English language pamphlet, *Soviet China,* with Zhang Bao, writing under the name M. James. The pamphlet traced the development of the Communist movement in China and provided one of the earliest descriptions of the soviet republic in Jiangxi.[76]

Chi had long been familiar to the Marxist Left in America and the international community of Communists. He was well acculturated, knew a wide circle of non-Chinese, and had married fellow Communist Harriet Levine in 1928. After returning from Europe in 1929, he entered graduate school at Columbia University. His doctoral dissertation, a pioneering work examining China's economic history from a Marxist perspective with influences by Wittfogel, impressed intellectual circles when it was published in England in 1936 as *Key Economic Areas in Chinese History.*[77]

During these years, Japan's intensifying assault on China made clear its goal of absorbing the entire nation. As the Communist International began focusing on an antiwar, anti-Fascist policy at the beginning of 1933, Chi met with a few other American Communist party members and his wife's cousin Philip J. Jaffe to found Friends of the Chinese People (which later became American Friends of the Chinese People, or AFCP) in New York. The Left also led the formation of similar groups in Canada, England, France, Belgium, and other countries.[78]

The AFCP quickly established branches all over the United States and attracted support among liberals and members of the Left, including progressive Japanese in this country. It sponsored lectures on China that emphasized the Chinese revolution and organized mass meetings and demonstrations supporting China's struggle against Japanese imperialism. Its 1935 activities included a February protest in New York that drew over a thousand people; an April 29 waterfront demonstration protesting the sale of scrap iron to Japan; a May 14 debate between J. W. Philips, editor of the AFCP magazine *China Today* and a Japanese apologist; and a June 20 demonstration of more than two hundred people before the Japanese consulate on June 20.[79]

The AFCP organ *China Today* published articles denouncing Japanese aggression and essays sympathetic to the Chinese Communists and critical of the KMT government. As one of the editors, Chi politically guided the publication. To hide his identity and protect his student immigrant status, he wrote under a variety of pseudonyms—C. T. Chan, Hansu Chan, Huang Lowe, or Futien Wang. Chi was also a persuasive speaker who, under the auspices of the AFCP, lectured frequently on the situation in China from CCP perspectives.

The effect of these activities and the writings of such sympathetic journalists as Anna Louise Strong, Edgar Snow, and Agnes Smedley did much to make the American public more aware of the situation in China. However, since the China issue was only one of many facing a society mired in the Great Depression, the effect on national policy was limited. Even though a number of public figures paid lip service in support of China, the U.S. government maintained its "neutrality," while continuing to allow corporate interests to ship scrap iron to China's invader and otherwise continuing to profit from trade with Japan. In contrast, due to the numerous ties, personal, business, and otherwise, of Chinese overseas to their ancestral homeland, Japanese designs on China became issues of great concern, and many Chinese American activities focused on the anti-Japanese movement.

Japan's growing aggression inspired Chinese university students to mobilize again after the hiatus that followed their exhausting political struggles of the late 1920s. Qing Ruji and other progressive students responded quickly to the CCP's call for nationalist resistance to Japanese imperialism. Representatives from universities and colleges throughout the United States and Canada convened in Chicago from August 30 to September 4, 1935, and founded the Chinese Students Association of North America (CSANA), which passed a resolution calling on the KMT government to end the civil war and concentrate on fighting Japan. Qing Ruji became executive director with Ma Zusheng and Han Maolin as deputies. They soon learned that their limited funds and dispersed population of fewer than two thousand did not allow for many activities other than publication. Moreover, the mostly Mandarin-speaking students still found it difficult to communicate with the largely Cantonese-speaking Chinese American population. Their non-immigrant status also put them at risk for deportation. Qing soon attracted the attention of immigration authorities, who arrested him and forced him to return to China in 1938. To gain effectiveness, the students would have to coordinate more with local communities, as suggested in an essay titled "Meiguo laogong yundong yu Huaqiao zhi qiantu" [The American Labor Movement and the Future of the Chinese in America] by Chu Tong, then in his final year at University of California at Berkeley, in the CSANA publication of January 1937.[80]

As would be expected, China's troubles generated tremendous concern in the Chinese American community. Japan's occupation of Manchuria prompted an outpouring of patriotic sentiment that only intensified with the Japanese attack on Shanghai in 1932. The Nineteenth Route Army, which consisted mostly of recruits from Guangdong, offered heroic resistance. Chiang Kai-shek's KMT government, however, was more interested in suppressing the Communist insurgency than in fighting the Japan invasion. For the next few years, the Chinese Marxist Left in America was able to present itself as a leader of the resistance and formed coalitions with different non-KMT Chinese groups to attack the KMT's greatest weakness—its apparent passivity in the face of Japanese aggression in order to chip away at the KMT's political influence.

The Chinese Marxists in the two principal centers of San Francisco and New York often coordinated their activities. The New York Left benefited from a firm base of supporters in the CHLA, the strength of the CPUSA, and an extensive mainstream progressive movement. As early as 1934, the Chinese Unemployment Alliance of Greater New York, the CHLA, the AAACAI, the Chinese section of the International Labor Defense, and the Seamen's Union organized a Niuyue Huaqiao Kang-Ri Jiuguo Lianhehui [Overseas Chinese Resistance to Japan and National Salvation Federation of New York, or RJNSF-NY] to work with such allies as the AFCP to turn American public opinion against Japanese aggression. In May that same year, Madam Sun and others organized the CNCASD in Shanghai. The Chinese American Left quickly committed its support.[81] Later that year, the Chinese Left participated in a "Hands off China" conference in New York, organized by the AFCP and attended by 108 delegates from 54 organizations.[82] Although the participants were primarily progressives and their supporters, the conferences did attract wider attention.

On August 1, 1935, a CCP manifesto calling for all Chinese to form a united front galvanized Chinese in China and abroad after years of KMT insistence on wiping out internal dissent before resisting the foreign invaders. For example, in New York, the KMT and the KMT-dominated CCBA had been reluctant to cooperate with the Left. In early 1935, the CCBA rejected an application from the RJNSF-NY to use the auditorium of the CCBA-operated Chinese school to commemorate the 1932 Japanese attack on Shanghai.[83] But after the August First manifesto, community feelings began to change. When progressives proposed the formation of a Kang-Ri Jiuguo Xiehui [Chinese Association for Resistance to Japan and National Salvation Association, or RJNSA], key traditionist associations responded favorably. Under such pressure, the CCBA reluctantly convened a meeting of community organizations, including those on the Left. A broad-based umbrella organization was formed that included leaders from the left and right in its executive ranks, such as Situ Meitang (Maytong Seto) of the powerful On Leong Tong; C. Y. Chen of RJNSF-NY and former central committee member of the KMT; Wu Xianzi, editor of the *Chinese Republic News* and leader in the Chinese Constitutionalist Party; Y. K. Chu of the *Chinese Journal,* and other prominent leaders from the Chinese Chamber of Commerce and other traditionist organizations.[84]

The Marxist Left in San Francisco also actively participated in the anti-Fascist struggle but with less success. As early as 1933, Benjamin Fee, with the Japanese American Communist Karl Yoneda, spoke against Japanese aggression in China. In 1934 Fee again spoke on "Manchukuo, Japan's Puppet" at a "Japan Night" program chaired by Yoneda.[85] But San Francisco's Chinese Left was less successful in working with general Chinese population, because San Francisco had long been a KMT stronghold and the Left lacked a solid base of support similar to that of New York's CHLA. Although the San Francisco branch of the CNCASD and the CCBA both advocated resistance to Japan, the latter barred the CNCASD from participating in the Double Ten National Day parade in 1935.[86] Similarly, the Left was shut out of the coalition of community groups who formed the Guomin Kang-Ri Jiuguo Hui [Chinese National Salvation League] under the leadership of General Fang Zhenwu, a famous resistance advocate who toured the United States and Canada advocating national unity against Japan.[87]

The Chinese Marxist Left in San Francisco also attempted to use the press to reach the public but found it difficult to raise enough money to sustain a progressive publication. In 1935 the San Francisco branch of the CNCASD established the short-lived *Ziwei Yuekan* [Self-Defense Monthly]. In 1936 the San Francisco branch of the AFCP launched *Mon Kow*, a bilingual monthly, but the effort was again brief.

In mid-November 1936, Tao Xingzhi, a founder and member of the board of directors of the All-China Federation for National Salvation (ACFNS), accompanied by Loh Tsei, an ACFNS delegate, arrived in New York from Europe, where they had been in Paris attending the founding of the Quan-Ou Huaqiao Kang-Ri Jiuguo Lianhehui [Federation of Chinese in All Europe for Resisting Japan and the Salvation of China] in Paris. The two toured the United States, Canada, and Mexico to publicize China's struggles against Japan. In New York, C. Y. Chen introduced them to community leader Situ Meitang and gained his support. The two joined the Chee Kung Tong. Tao also spoke several times at the CHLA. They were still in the United States when Sino-Japanese hostilities began on July 7, 1937.[88] Such efforts would soon bear fruit as China's desperate plight forced into alignment Chinese throughout the world regardless of their political or philosophical differences.

CHAPTER 4

The War of Resistance against Japan

The Sino-Japanese Conflict

The advancing Japanese invasion generated an upsurge of Chinese patriotism that forced the Kuomintang (KMT) to agree to work with the Communist Party of China (CCP). After successfully purging Communists and their supporters from the government and driving them underground, KMT repression temporarily ceased in 1937 as it formed a coalition, at least in name, with the CCP in order to resist the Japanese. The immediate cause for this about-face occurred in December 1936, when the "Young Marshal" Zhang Xueliang kidnapped the KMT leader Chiang Kai-shek in Xi'an and forced him to agree to the truce for the sake of national survival. It would be the Japanese Army, however, that struck first by attacking the Marco Polo Bridge near Beijing on July 7, 1937. Slightly more than a month later, they attacked Shanghai and captured the city on November 12 after fierce fighting. The former KMT capital of Nanjing fell soon after on December 13.

By October 1938, the Japanese had run down the coast and seized Guangzhou, effectively occupying most of China's major coastal ports and most industrialized regions. By this time, the KMT had abandoned even Hankou on its retreat inland and established its wartime capital at Chongqing in the far western province of Sichuan. As the war settled down to a territorial stalemate, the Japanese established a rival puppet regime in Nanjing, headed by Wang Jingwei.

During the first years of the war, the KMT and CCP forces maintained a wary truce in the face of a common enemy. The CCP's Workers and Peasants Red Army reorganized as the Eighth Route Army in September 1937. This was followed in October 1937 by the formation of the New Fourth Army, composed of guerilla forces in the Yangzi River Basin and South China. In December the CCP established the Changjiang Ju [Yangzi River Bureau] in Wuhan to supervise and coordinate party and New Fourth Army activities in thirteen provinces in the Yangzi River basin and South China, headed by Wang Ming with Zhou Enlai as deputy. One of the bureau's early tasks was to establish an Eighth Route Army liaison office in Hong Kong in December 1937.[1]

As the situation in China deteriorated in 1938 with the Japanese capture of Wuhan, the CCP replaced the Yangzi Bureau with the Nanfang Ju [Southern Bureau] headed by Zhou Enlai, which established an office in Chongqing in January 1939. One of its missions was to strengthen the CCP's influence in the KMT-controlled areas and to cultivate the support of various groups opposed to the ruling regime.

After the fall of Wuhan, the Communist guerilla forces expanded their operations in territory formerly controlled by the KMT. Friction between KMT and Communist forces increased and boiled over in the New Fourth Army Incident in southern Anhui. In January 1941, KMT troops ambushed and nearly annihilated the CCP's New Fourth Army units as they marched northward to new positions in Jiangsu. From that time forward, KMT forces blockaded CCP-controlled areas, and sharp lines of demarcation resumed between the Right and Left in China and abroad; however, the two sides still strove to maintain a superficial façade of unity against Japan.[2]

In the meantime, runaway inflation afflicted China's wartime economy, accompanied by increasing corruption and repression on the part of the Nationalists. As more Chinese began to turn away from the KMT, the CCP's Southern Bureau seized the opportunity to cultivate support by forming united fronts with various disaffected groups in society to push for democratic reforms. Many idealistic university students, including even the children of leading KMT cadres, became radicalized while attending college in China and joined the CCP or participated in activities led by the CCP and its affiliated groups.

Active Roles of Sympathetic Foreign Nationals

When the war broke out, the journalists Agnes Smedley and Helen Foster Snow (Nym Wales) were in the Communist base in northern Shaanxi. In September they left for Xi'an. While Snow remained behind, Smedley joined the Eighth Route Army in the field for several months before leaving for Hankou in early 1938. She covered the war from there until the city fell to Japanese forces. She spent the next eighteen months until April 1940 roaming the hills of the Yangzi River Valley east of Wuhan, visiting KMT and CCP resistance units. Smedley returned to the United States in 1941. Her book about China's war, *Battle Hymn of China* (1943), was considered by some to be one of the best examples of reporting from World War II.[3]

Edgar Snow, who was in Beijing, remained for a few months after the war's outbreak. He provided cover for many blacklisted students whom he helped to escape in disguise, including Deng Yingchao, Zhou Enlai's wife, who had been recuperating from tuberculosis. Snow finally left when the *London Daily Herald* sent him to cover the fighting in Shanghai. In company with James Bertram, Edgar Snow journeyed to Xi'an, where he reunited with his wife. James Bertram decided to travel onward to Yan'an in October 1937 and became the first British journalist to interview Mao Zedong. Bertram then joined the Eighth Route Army for five months in North China and wrote the book *North China Front* (1938) based on these experiences.[4]

In the meantime, the Snows arrived in Shanghai in October, two months after the first Japanese attacks. As witnesses to the destructiveness of the war, Chinese and Western sympathizers met to discuss ways of maintaining industrial production to support resistance efforts. Helen Foster Snow suggested organizing a nationwide movement of rural industrial cooperatives. New Zealander Rewi Alley, a factory inspector in Shanghai, supported this plan, and after considerable discussion and planning, the first Committee for the Promotion of Industrial Cooperatives (CPIC) began in April 1938. After lobbying government officials for support, it launched the Association of Chinese Industrial Cooperatives (ACIC) in Wuhan in August, with Rewi Alley as technical advisor to what became known as the Gung Ho Movement. Soon afterward, the association established offices in Hong Kong, Shanghai, and Chongqing.[5]

Hong Kong as China's Liaison with the Outside World

When the war began, Hong Kong already supported a small underground CCP organization. The CCP leadership in China realized that for the time being, the British colony could provide useful access to overseas contacts. Zhou Enlai notified Hong Kong authorities through the British ambassador Clark-Kerr of the CCP's intention to establish a liaison office in Hong Kong.[6]

Soon after Shanghai fell to the Japanese, the CCP Central Committee advised Madam Sun Yat-sen (Soong Ching Ling) to leave. On December 23, 1937, with the help of Rewi Alley, she slipped on board a foreign-flag coastal ship bound for Hong Kong. Liao Chengzhi joined her to establish, and with Pan Hannian to lead, an Eighth Route Army office to raise funds for the CCP armies, to cultivate the support of the Chinese overseas, and to recruit volunteers to participate in the War of Resistance. Located on the second floor of 18 Queen's Road Central, the office was known to the general public as Yuehua Company, a tea dealer.[7]

As if to emphasize Hong Kong's importance as an entrepôt, while Madam Sun and Liao were still settling down, C. Y. Chen of the Chinese Bureau of the Communist Party of the United States of America (CPUSA) in New York cabled CCP member Xuan Quanguang in Hong Kong to notify him of the scheduled arrival of the *Empress of Japan* on January 20, 1938, with medical supplies and an American and Canadian medical team that included Dr. Norman Bethune, nurse Jean Ewen, and Dr. Charles Parsons bound for the Communist-controlled areas. Xuan and Lawrence Lowe, who had arrived from the United States in 1937, arranged accommodations in Hong Kong and made travel arrangements to send the group into China. Three days later, the team flew to Hankou, where Zhou Enlai arranged land transportation to Yan'an. In the end, only Bethune, Ewen, and the medical supplies completed the journey, arriving at their destination on March 23.[8]

In the meantime, through such journalists as James Bertram, who arrived in Hong Kong after months in the war zone, the Eighth Route Army office learned of the acute shortage of medical services and supplies on the front lines. Liao Chengzhi, his older sister Liao Mengxing (Cynthia Liao), and his cousin Deng Wenzhao (M. C. Tang) tried to organize another Canadian medical team to go to China. The plan came to naught, however, since the Eighth Route Army office did not have the necessary contacts. The Liaos then approached Madam Sun, believing that her international fame made her the ideal person to head an organization that could effectively appeal for support worldwide. Madam Sun readily agreed to lend her name to their efforts, and on June 14, 1938, the China Defense League (CDL) came into being with an office at 21 Seymour Road. Shortly afterward, a Shanghai branch was established with YWCA worker Talitha Gerlach as secretary. Gerlach, as the only non-Chinese participant, used her status as a nonbelligerent foreign national to smuggle funds and supplies to the resistance. Every week she would also board an American liner anchored in Shanghai to leave letters and other material in the ship's mailbox for the CDL in Hong Kong. Gerlach continued these efforts until her return to the United States in 1940. En route, she stopped by Hong Kong to meet Madam Sun for the first time.[9]

Soon after the founding of the CDL, Madam Sun personally visited Guangzhou to help form a local branch. There she met Israel Epstein, a journalist who had contributed articles to *Voice of China*. When Epstein had to leave Guangzhou for Hong Kong after the city's fall to the Japanese, he joined the league. He became a close associate of Madam Sun and spent a year enlisting worldwide support for China.[10]

The Eighth Route Army office and the China Defense League remained separate entities until they ceased operation altogether with the outbreak of the Pacific war; however, they cooperated closely in many efforts. The two groups cooperated to translate into English Mao Zedong's essays "Shijian lun" ["On Practice"], "Maodun lun" ["On Contradictions"], "Lun chijiuzhan" ["On Protracted War"], and "Lun xin jieduan" ["On the New Phase"], which were published by the Eighth Army Office in 1939 and 1940.[11]

The leadership of the CDL reflected a united-front type organization. Madam Sun chaired the central committee; T. V. Soong was the president; Hilda Selwyn-Clarke, wife of the Hong Kong Director of Medical Services in Hong Kong, was the honorary secretary; Hong Kong University history lecturer Norman France was the honorary treasurer; banker M. C. Tang was the treasurer; and journalists James Bertram and Israel Epstein handled international outreach. The central committee also included Liao Chengzhi and Cynthia Liao. Cynthia Liao also was Madam Sun's secretary and office manager. The CDL published a biweekly English-language newsletter reporting on news of the War of Resistance. It solicited funds and medical and other supplies to support the guerillas and for war relief. It also helped to establish and supply international peace hospitals for war casualties in the guerilla areas.[12]

Over four years, the Eighth Route Army office periodically published the mimeographed *Huaqiao Tongxun* [Overseas Chinese Newsletter], which it distributed to the overseas Chinese press and organizations. The newsletter featured articles about Communist Party policies, the situation in the Communist areas, and Eighth Route and New Fourth Army military campaigns. After the New Fourth Army Incident, Zhou Enlai ordered the office to establish a daily newspaper, and *Hwa Shang Pao* began publication on February 10, 1941. The office also recruited volunteers from the large Chinese populations in Hong Kong, Macao, and southeast Asia to serve in various capacities, mostly in the Communist-held guerrilla areas.[13]

In the winter of 1937, Lawrence Lowe recruited his older brother Cai Xingzhou (Joe Fook Tsoi, Henry Tsoi) to join the CCP. Tsoi had graduated from Meiji University in 1935 and had been active in the National Salvation Movement. The two brothers reported directly to Liao Chengzhi. In April 1940, Liao sent Henry Tsoi to immigrate to the United States to establish a courier system using Communist Party–member seamen on trans-Pacific ships. Tsoi also assumed responsibility for coordinating CCP party affairs on the West Coast.[14]

This move was part of the CCP's effort to strengthen liaisons abroad to encourage continuing support for the War of Resistance and to gather intelligence. Also, it created other possible alternative sites in case British colonial authorities in Hong Kong began yielding to Japanese pressure to police and limit anti-Japanese activities.

Liao Chengzhi had already sent a dozen party members to the Philippines to lay the groundwork to publish a newspaper in the Chinese community there to drum up support for the War of Resistance. Lawrence Lowe was sent to Manila in early 1938 as a teacher at the Hongguang Primary School, operated by the Chee Kung Tong [Chinese Freemasons, or Triad Society]. By the end of 1939, he began planning and organizing for the publishing of the underground mimeographed periodical *China Report*. Liao's brother-in-law Li Shaoshi arrived to launch the publication, which was printed and distributed through the Manila postal system. During this period, other CCP members sent from Hong Kong established Meifan Printing and Jian'guo Publishing companies, which began publishing *Jian'guo Bao* [National Construction News] on May 1, 1940. Around this time, police became suspicious and placed Lowe under surveillance and raided his residence. Rendered ineffective for further underground activities in the Philippines, Lowe returned with his family to Hong Kong, where he continued his work with Liao Chengzhi, while his wife Eva helped with typing at the CDL. The growing threat of war in the Pacific forced Lowe and his family to return to America in July 1941.[15]

Hong Kong also provided a base for international outreach for the Chinese Industrial Cooperatives Movement (CICM). Madam Sun suggested to Edgar Snow that it was better to organize an International Committee for the Promotion of Chinese Industrial Cooperatives from abroad. Snow accepted her advice and help to win the support of the colonial governor to make Hong Kong the center of this committee. Better known as the Gung Ho International Committee, it was founded in January 1939, with Madam Sun as the honorary chair and Hong Kong Anglican Bishop R. O. Hall as official chair. Social worker Ida Pruitt, who had arrived in January from China, helped organize the committee and served as the interim executive secretary. When Chen Han-seng arrived in Hong Kong in June after completing a three-year stint with the Institute of Pacific Relations in the United States, he replaced Ida Pruitt as executive secretary when she left for America to set up a CICM support group. Around this time, the New China News Agency (NCNA) sent Hu Yuzhi to start an English-language propaganda publication in Hong Kong for distribution abroad. Hu consulted with Chen, who agreed to edit the monthly *Far Eastern Bulletin* with the help of English progressive Elsie Fairfax-Cholmeley (Qiu Moli). Besides regular news sources, the *Far Eastern Bulletin* sometimes included items based on communications sent by Talitha Gerlach from Japanese-occupied Shanghai. It was said to be the first newspaper to make public the news of the New Fourth Army Incident. Hu Yuzhi went on to Singapore in 1940 to be editor of *Nanyang Siang Pau* as part of the CCP strategy to strengthen liaison with supporters abroad.[16]

The Gung Ho International Committee operated for two and a half years before the outbreak of the Pacific war shut it down. During that time, it handled about twenty million U.S. dollars in foreign donations. The United States, the Philippines, and England established committees in its support.[17]

The CICM recruited Chinese and non-Chinese with professional and managerial expertise, including University of Chicago chemistry PhD Huang Wenwei, Canadian Chinese mechanical engineer Lang Wang, and others. Honolulu-born Chee Kwon Chun, a graduate student in agricultural economy at the University of California, Berkeley, arrived at the Hong Kong Eighth Route Army office in July 1939 bearing an introductory letter to CCP leader Zhou Enlai from Sha Zhipei, Zhou's former classmate at Tianjin's Nankai Middle School. After Liao Chengzhi arranged for Chun to meet Zhou, Chun went on to Yan'an. Upon his return to Chongqing, his brother-in-law Sun Fo introduced him to Rewi Alley, who recruited him into the Gung Ho movement. In late 1939, he became director of the CICM office in Qujiang, northern Guangdong.[18]

John Jan of Sacramento, a 1933 graduate in mining engineering from the University of California, sailed for Hong Kong in August 1940, expecting to serve with the KMT government's Mining Ministry at Chongqing. While he waited in Hong Kong, Rewi Alley recruited him to travel to the Ganzhou office in Jiangxi. Jan spent the rest of the war years with the Gung Ho Movement in Southeast China.[19]

With the approach of the Pacific war, the offices of the Eighth Route Army, CDL, the Indusco International Committee, and connected principals relocated to safe havens on the Chinese mainland. Madam Sun flew from Hong Kong in December, just hours before the Japanese entered the city. Indusco executive secretary Chen Han-seng and his wife and two nieces disguised themselves as refugees and escaped to Guilin in February 1941, but Elsie Fairfax-Cholmeley was interned by the Japanese.[20]

The supporting journalists moved with the shifting tides of war to the various war theaters. Edgar Snow was in Wuhan but left for Hong Kong and the Philippines. In all these places, he raised money for the CDL and New Fourth Army. In Manila he started a Philippine Association for Industrial Cooperatives. He later visited Chongqing and then Yan'an, which was blockaded soon afterward by Nationalist troops. With the imminent collapse of the United Front, Snow would be the last Western correspondent to visit Yan'an for five years. Soon after his return to the Philippines, the New Fourth Army Incident occurred. The KMT government was displeased by Snow's dispatch on the event and canceled his press privileges. Israel Epstein returned to Hong Kong in 1941 after covering the war in Wuhan and Chongqing. When the colony fell, Yang Gang, earlier associated with the Snows in Beijing and now an editor at the newspaper *Ta Kung Pao,* disguised Epstein as a wounded civilian before she and other progressive cultural workers slipped through Japanese lines to northern Guangdong. The Japanese, however, saw through Epstein's disguise and threw him into a civilian internment camp but Epstein managed to escape, accompanied by Elsie Fairfax-Cholmeley, who later became his wife. Epstein then covered the war in China and was part of a journalistic team that broke through the Nationalist blockade to visit Yan'an in 1944.[21]

Influencing American Policy Makers and the Public

In the West the Marxist Left had raised alarms early regarding the Fascist threat. The Sino-Japanese War introduced a new stage in the anti-Fascist struggle. The war forced Max Granich, editor of Shanghai's *Voice of China,* to return to America, where he became managing editor of *China Today,* published by the American Friends of the Chinese People (AFCP). He continued to sound the alarm about the Fascist menace, while the AFCP and other progressive groups stepped up efforts to rally support for China. For example, on October 1, 1937, the AFCP, the American League against War and Fascism (ALWF), and members of the Chinese community sponsored a meeting attended by twelve thousand in Madison Square Garden to voice support for China. Soon afterward, when Japan sent "envoys of good will" to visit the United States, the Northern California chapter of the ALWF organized a Peace and Democracy Conference attended by representatives from progressive unions and organizations including such Chinese groups as the Chinese Workers Mutual-Aid Association (CWMAA), International Workers'

Order (IWO), United China War Relief (UCWR), and the Chinese consulate to discuss boycotting Japanese goods. When the Japanese delegation disembarked at San Francisco on October 27, more than one thousand hostile demonstrators, including two hundred Chinese, met it. When the envoys reached New York on November 6, the AFCP and ALWF massed two hundred picketers at their hotel, the Waldorf-Astoria. On the same day, the Chinatown section of the IWO mobilized two hundred protesters at the Japanese consulate in San Francisco.[22]

As events moved inexorably toward war in China, leading members of the Marxist left decided that to be more effective, their message had to reach mainstream Americans beyond progressives. In 1936 C. T. Chi joined the Chinese delegation to an international conference held by the Institute of Pacific Relations (IPR) at Yosemite, California. At the conference Philip J. Jaffe, T. A. Bisson, and Chi, all from *China Today,* met with Frederick Vanderbilt Field, secretary of the American Council of the IPR and also a CPUSA member. They jointly decided that it was time to start a magazine of greater academic stature than *China Today* that would target policy makers.

In 1937 *Amerasia* made its debut. Its politically diverse editorial board included a number of well-known scholars in East Asian studies. Chi was a founding board member and for a while wrote a feature column titled "Far Eastern Economic Notes." *Amerasia* had a small but influential circulation that peaked at around two thousand, approximately a third of which were government agencies all over the world. Libraries, teachers, and the news media comprised another third of the subscribers.[23]

In 1936 Owen Lattimore, chief editor of *Pacific Affairs,* the quarterly journal of the IPR, had asked for recommendations for the position of deputy editor from member councils and decided to hire Chen Han-seng at the suggestion of the USSR Council. The council, however, did not mention that Chen and his wife were fugitives from China who had taken refuge in the USSR to avoid being arrested as communists. To avoid questions concerning their presence in the Soviet Union, the Chens traveled to Paris to give the appearance that they were coming to America from that city. They were accompanied by Wu Kejian, who was going to Paris to become editor of the *Giu Guo Sh Bao.* They then set sail from London on the same vessel with IPR secretary general Edward C. Carter and his secretary, Elsie Fairfax-Cholmeley. After reaching New York, Fairfax-Cholmeley became secretary for *Pacific Affairs* and befriended the Chens.[24]

At the beginning of 1938, the Canadian branch of the IPR invited Chen to spend more than two months traversing Canada from coast to coast to speak on the significance of the Xi'an Incident and the Chinese people's resolve to resist Japanese aggression. When he was in New York, Chen Han-seng published articles under assumed names in *Chinese Vanguard* and its successor, *China Salvation Times,* to present the views of the CCP to Chinese in America. He was in frequent contact with key CCP members in the area, particularly C. T. Chi and Y. Y. Hsu.

He was active as well among Chinese students, and, with Loh Tsei, represented the Chinese Section of the International Peace Campaign in New York. After three years at *Pacific Affairs,* the Chens received CCP orders to proceed to Hong Kong to help the war effort there. In May 1939, the Chens set sail, accompanied by Elsie Fairfax-Cholmeley, who had obtained a commission from the IPR to study traditional agricultural tools and methods in China's interior.[25]

In early 1937, the International Secretariat of the IPR appointed C. T. Chi to its research staff. Financed by a ninety-thousand-dollar grant from the Rockefeller Foundation, Chi was to study China's contemporary economic situation and went to China in 1938 to collect field data. En route, he visited Hankou, where his father, Ji Gongquan (Chi Kung-ch'uan), and family were refugees from the war from their native Shanxi. Chi discussed with Zhou Enlai in Chongqing the possibility of his family moving to Yan'an. Instead, Zhou suggested that Chi take them to New York, where they could be useful in United Front activities during the upcoming Pacific war. Chi accepted this advice and returned to New York on February 2, 1939, with his father, stepmother, two stepbrothers, and stepsister. His father joined him in editing *National Salvation Times* and helped prepare the founding of *China Daily News.*[26]

During their service at the IPR, Chi and Chen wrote many scholarly essays for *Pacific Affairs* and *Far Eastern Survey.* After their departure, Y. Y. Hsu continued their work and published twelve essays in *Pacific Affairs* and *Far Eastern Survey* between 1941 and 1944. His association with the Dong Biwu delegation finally led the KMT to exert pressure on the IPR to discharge Hsu in 1946.[27] The articles by Chen, Chi, and Hsu offered Marxist interpretations of China's social, political, and economic issues and influenced current thinking concerning China in American academic and policy-making circles. However, to put their roles in the proper perspective, they were only 3 out of a total of 1,394 contributors, including about a hundred other Chinese-authored articles representing a wide political spectrum.[28]

China War Relief Activities

After the outbreak of the Sino-Japanese War, China received great sympathy as a victim of aggression. Groups varying widely in ideological and political orientations merged in their response to the urgent need for materials and funding for war relief and support for China's war effort. The progressive American League for Peace and Democracy (ALPD) and others formed the China Aid Council (CAC) to raise funds for medical supplies for refugees and war victims. One of the CAC's early accomplishments was to recruit a Canadian and American medical team, including the renowned Dr. Norman Bethune, to bring urgently needed medical services and supplies to Communist-held territory in Shanxi.[29]

Upon her return to New York City in 1939, Ida Pruitt helped to organize the American Committee in Aid of the CIC, better known as Indusco, to raise funds for the CICM. She served as executive secretary from 1939 to 1951. With such prominent individuals as Eleanor Roosevelt as honorary chair, Indusco raised much of the international funding for the Industrial Cooperatives movement between 1938 and 1945. Talitha Gerlach, who returned to America in 1940, also maintained ties with the CDL and Indusco and frequently spoke and raised funds for them.[30]

Other groups with their own areas of humanitarian concerns and agendas also lent support; however, their separate efforts were overwhelmed by the enormity of China's needs. After considerable discussions to centralize and coordinate fundraising activities, representatives from the American Bureau for Medical Aid to China (ABMAC), the China Emergency Relief Committee, the China Aid Council, the American Committee for Chinese War Orphans, the Church Committee for China Relief, China Famine Relief, Indusco, and the Associated Boards for Christian Colleges in China (ABCCC) formed United China Relief (UCR) in February 1941 to act as an umbrella organization while disbursements of funds remained under control of each individual organization. The author Pearl Buck became the chairperson, and the board included such well-connected individuals as Henry Luce, John D. Rockefeller, David O. Selznick, and Wendell Willkie. This influential board facilitated access to funding from corporate America, but politically, the board tended to be conservative. China Aid Council and Indusco were the only organizations in UCR that channeled their funds exclusively through the China Defense League and were excluded from the UCR decision-making circle.[31]

Anti-Japanese Propaganda and Cultural Politics

An important activity of all these groups was to issue propaganda to promote public awareness of the importance of China's War of Resistance. In places with concentrations of Chinese, they usually played some role as participants and even as speakers or cultural performers in such activities targeting mainstream society. Reflecting the temper of the times, the Chinese Left played important, although not necessarily dominant, roles, especially in communities where it was well organized, such as New York or San Francisco.

Chinese from abroad, including a number who had opposed the KMT government, also contributed their talents. Among these was Si-lan Chen, Eugene Chen's oldest daughter, who had just arrived from England in spring 1937. She performed in a "dance recital of modern China and the USSR" in New York in January 1938 to raise money on behalf of the AFCP for medical aid to China. The same year, her brother, Jack Chen, arrived from England to exhibit modern revolutionary Chinese art and woodcuts in New York as part of a world tour to rally support for the Chinese people.[32]

In summer 1940, Liu Liangmo, formerly of China's YMCA and a pioneer in the use of choral music to arouse Chinese patriotic feelings, arrived in the United

States with his family. Ostensibly, he came to study under the sponsorship of the YMCA, but in reality he was escaping from KMT harassment. Liu organized a chorus at New York's Chinese Youth Club that performed at many war rallies. In 1941 the chorus recorded War of Resistance songs in Chinese, featuring Paul Robeson as soloist. The selections included the "Yiyongjun jinxingqu" [March of the Volunteers], now the national anthem of the PRC, sung in Chinese and English. Liu was alleged to have brought along a score of the *Yellow River Cantata,* a stirring composition expressing the spirited resistance of Chinese people toward their Japanese invaders, which had just been completed by Xian Xinghai in 1939 in Yan'an. However, the Westminster Choir first performed this work in America in Trenton, New Jersey, on October 9, 1945, at a concert arranged by the CAC under the patronage of New Jersey governor Charles Edison and Claire Booth Luce. This performance was based on a hand-copied score given to Israel Epstein in Yan'an in 1944.[33]

Another performer arrived in New York in mid-July 1942 to study writing, drama, and dance. The film actress Wang Ying (Wang Yung, Wang Yong), accompanied by her good friend Xie Hegeng, was chosen by the China Institute to represent China in an international youth congress in Washington, D.C. Afterward she joined counterparts from the Soviet Union, Great Britain, and the Netherlands on a national round of wartime rallies. Author Lin Yutang introduced Wang to Pearl Buck's East and West Association which arranged for her to perform folksongs, war songs, and the famous Chinese wartime skit *Fangxia ni de bianzi* [*Lay Down Your Whip*] at the White House on March 15, 1943. In 1945 she headed the East and West Association–funded China Theater Group, which toured the country for a year presenting modern Chinese plays and other performances in English on college campuses.[34]

During this period, there was a great demand for speakers on China issues. Organizations such as the China Institute often maintained a speakers list to meet such needs. The interpretations presented by speakers varied over a wide political spectrum. From the Left, Gong Pusheng was a frequent speaker. She had begun working for a master's degree in religion at Columbia University in September 1941, which she completed in 1942. During her two-year stay, Gong was active among youth and liberal circles. She worked with Eleanor Roosevelt and knew Paul Robeson and Pearl Buck well. She traveled to more than half of the forty-eight states, making anti-Fascist speeches at more than a hundred universities and colleges and other organizations. She returned to China in 1943 to support the war effort and reached Chongqing only after a three-month journey by way of the Cape of Good Hope, Calcutta, and Kunming.[35] Zhang Shuyi was another Yenjing University student who joined the CCP during the December 1935 demonstrations in Beijing. After graduation she worked for the YWCA in Shanghai. In 1941 she came to the United States to enroll as a graduate student in sociology at Columbia University. She married Y. Y. Hsu around 1943. In 1943 and 1944, she was part of a U.S. YWCA delegation that visited YWCAs all over America. In 1945 she participated in United China Relief fund-raising campaigns.[36] The activist Pu Shouchang was another popular speaker who traveled to many places in America on behalf of the East and West Association.[37]

Relations of the Left and Right in Chinese America

With the outbreak of the Sino-Japanese War in 1937, the CCP and the KMT had effected a truce to fight their common foe. In America, the Marxist Left, the KMT, and traditionist organizations also temporarily halted their quarrels. In New York the Chinese Hand Laundry Alliance (CHLA) gave whole-hearted support to the Niuyue Huaqiao Kang-Ri Jiuguo Chouxiang Zhonghui [New York Overseas Chinese Association to Raise Military Funds for Resisting Japan and National Salvation], which formed in late October 1937. However, CHLA also acted independently of the association. In 1938 it collected funds to purchase four ambulances, two for the KMT Army, and two for the Eighth Route Army.[38]

On the West Coast, the CWMAA was also very active in the United China War Relief Society (UCWRS), the San Francisco umbrella organization that co-ordinated fund drives and activities west of the Mississippi and in several Latin American countries. The CWMAA also helped to educate the public by inviting speakers on subjects ranging from support for the war effort to union organizing. However, the KMT Party in America, together with leaders of conservative traditionist organizations in the Chinatowns, many of whom were also KMT party members, tended to set the political tone for coalition activities due to their affiliation with China's ruling political party.

The CWMAA contributed to the important protest against the loading of scrap iron bound for Japan in December 1938. The CWMAA received news of the intended shipment from contacts in the American labor movement. While its own members hastily gathered at the pier, the CWMAA called on the Chinese community to join them. Within a few days, Chinatown students, workers, merchants, housewives, and many sympathizers converged on the waterfront to express their opposition. The longshoremen refused to cross the picket lines. Even though the freighter finally did load the scrap metal, this dramatic display of unity by the Chinese community impressed many Americans. It was not the only such demonstration in this country, nor was it the earliest. But because more than three thousand Chinese people participated, this action attracted considerable media attention and boosted the campaign for an embargo against Japan.

Cooperation between the Marxist Left and the KMT did not last long. The New Fourth Army Incident of 1941 fractured the CCP-KMT alliance in China, and the Marxist Left withdrew from active support for the KMT-dominated

UCWRS. Instead, they routed much of their contributions to such groups as the China Aid Council, which supported Madam Sun's China Defense League and the Communist-led guerrillas.[39]

China Daily News

In the mid-1930s, the CCP appeared to have decided to try to establish a friendly Chinese-language organ in the Chinese community in America, the largest in the Western world. When Chen Han-seng left Moscow in 1936 to become editor of *Pacific Affairs,* Kang Sheng, the CCP representative to the Communist International (Comintern) asked him to help found *Huaqiao Ribao* [Overseas Chinese Daily] in the Chinese American community. Chen recalled being told by the editor Wu Yuzhang in Paris that *Giu Guo Sh Bao* might cease publication and have its equipment moved to the United States to be used by the intended *Huaqiao Ribao.*[40]

The outbreak of Sino-Japanese hostilities made more urgent the need for the Chinese American Left to establish its own newspaper voice. The impending European war provided the opening for editors Zhao Jiansheng (Rao Shushi) and Loh Tsei to suspend publication of *Giu Guo Sh Bao* and move the printing press and type fonts to New York. Shortly afterward, *Giu Guo Sh Bao* merged with the *Chinese Vanguard* and resumed publication as *China Salvation Times* in 1938. Chen Han-seng published some articles in *Chinese Vanguard* and *China Salvation Times* under a nom de plume, but he left for Hong Kong before the plans for a *Huaqiao Ribao* could be realized.[41]

During the 1950s, Zhao Jiansheng (Rao Shushi) was purged in China. Party historians have largely ignored his history, and since Zhao did not publish any memoirs, not many details are known of his American experiences. However, we do know that after arriving in New York, Zhao exercised his power as a representative for the Communist International to order the reorganization of the Chinese Bureau. Meizhou Yonghu Zhongguo Gong-Nong Geming Datongmeng [Grand Alliance Supporting the Chinese Workers and Peasants Revolution] was dissolved to match the Comintern's switch to United Front tactics. Some members, such as C. Y. Chen, were dropped from the party; Yu Guangsheng became the secretary replacing Y. Y. Hsu, who was sent to the West Coast to organize maritime workers. Zhao's moves left the Chinese East Coast party organization in disarray and vulnerable to infiltration by opportunistic KMT elements. This may explain Zhao's decision to cease publication of *China Salvation Times* on October 13, 1939, and depart for China, ostensibly to participate in the War of Resistance but without founding a Chinese American daily newspaper.[42]

By 1939 the War of Resistance had entered a new phase, as Japanese forces occupied major coastal cities and the KMT government retreated far inland to Chongqing. The CCP decided that it was the right time to implement its long cherished plan of establishing a daily newspaper that could appeal to wider audiences. Its alliance with CHLA proved to be invaluable in launching this enterprise.

At that time, newspapers in New York's Chinatown supported the New York CCBA and routinely rejected articles submitted by CHLA members. Even *Chinese Journal,* which earlier had championed CHLA's cause, had become cautious in the face of pressure from community conservatives and often rejected articles submitted by CHLA activists as too radical. Thus, the CHLA leadership felt the need for a friendly publication of its own. When the Chinese Marxist Left, led by Y. Y. Hsu, initiated moves to raise capital to establish a daily newspaper, the CHLA instantly declared its support, and a committee led by CHLA English secretary Chu Tong began to raise capital to launch the new newspaper.[43]

The committee received contributions from progressives all over the country, but the bulk came from more than 270 investors, mostly CHLA members, who bought shares at ten dollars each to raise slightly more than eight thousand dollars. About five to six thousand dollars went toward buying a suitable printing press and additional lead type to supplement those left by *China Salvation Times.* The first issue of *Meizhou Huaqiao Ribao,* or *China Daily News,* appeared on July 8, 1940. C. T. Chi's father, Chi Kung-ch'uan, became chief editor, and Eugene Moy edited the literary section. Chu Tong was the general manager, and his wife, Constance, managed the financial records and circulation. Unlike *Chinese Vanguard* and *China Salvation Times,* which were openly party organs and whose readership consisted basically of progressives, the new newspaper assumed a more moderate stance to appeal to a wider audience that included not only leftists but also liberals and more moderate segments of the Chinese community. Chi Kung-ch'uan left after a year, but under his successors Chu Tong, Thomas Lem Tong, and Eugene Moy the newspaper continued its successful courtship of new readers.[44]

Trans-Pacific Communications Network

On the West Coast the Marxist Left had a different task. Henry Tsoi arrived in San Francisco in April 1940, entrusted with establishing a network using Communist Party members working as seamen on trans-Pacific ships as couriers. Tsoi also delivered a letter from Zhou Enlai to Earl Browder, then head of the CPUSA, with two suggestions: that CCP members living in the United States be considered members of the CPUSA but act independently of the CPUSA while their activities and names of CCP members not be made public; and that the CPUSA help set up the maritime couriers network. Browder agreed to both of these points.[45]

In the Chinese Bureau, Tsoi assumed Lawrence Lowe's former responsibilities of coordinating and leading CCP activities on the West Coast, while Chu Tong, who also was party secretary of the Chinese Bureau, supervised party affairs on the East Coast.[46] The courier network quickly took shape to deliver printed documents, publications, and much-needed medical supplies. In the meantime, Lawrence Lowe returned with his family from Asia in July 1941.[47] America's entry into the Pacific war disrupted the courier system, as all major East Asian ports fell into Japanese hands. Henry Tsoi himself was drafted into the army and was unable to rebuild the network until 1947 after his discharge in late 1946.[48]

Cultural Activities

With the outbreak of open war, Chinese cultural performances and exhibitions were much in demand to serve the war effort. An earlier section has described the extensive programs featuring Chinese performers in mainstream American venues, but in Chinese American communities, particularly such major ones as San Francisco, New York, and Honolulu, cultural activities flowered to an unprecedented extent through the efforts of a variety of groups with diverse political and social backgrounds that drew mostly on youths or young adults.

The Left in China, which had long used literature and the performing arts effectively to communicate to broad audiences, was particularly influential in such cultural activities as choral singing and staging of vernacular dramas. Students in many Chinese-language schools sang songs of the War of Resistance, and many memorized the lyrics of *March of the Volunteers,* which became a popular piece sung or performed at Chinese war rallies. Organizations and schools also frequently staged vernacular dramas such as the poignant skit *Lay Down Your Whip.* There was even an ambitious production in Cantonese of left-wing playwright Cao Yu's classic *Thunder Storm* in San Francisco.[49]

Two factors encouraged the development of cultural activities: changing demographics in the Chinese American community with the influx of new immigrants from China, and the need for propaganda to support and sustain the war effort.

In 1938 the Japanese had captured Guangzhou, the economic, cultural, and political center of the Pearl River Delta and the region from which most Chinese in America had emigrated. Many anxious parents sought to bring their children from China to safety in the United States. By the end of the 1930s, some 11.1 percent of Chinese people in America were between the ages of fifteen and nineteen as a result of this immigration and natural growth. On the mainland, San Francisco had the most youths with 4,500, second only to Honolulu's 5,400. However, the proportion of immigrants was probably higher in San Francisco. New York and Los Angeles had approximately 1,100 and 800 Chinese youth respectively.

These new arrivals included many young adults and intellectuals who had been exposed to two decades of new ideas and changes in China and whose political thinking embraced a mixture of political ideologies—nationalism, liberalism, and socialism. Some had been organizers or active participants in the *jiuwang* [salvation from annihilation (of China)] movement organized by the Communist-led United Front. These newcomers arrived in a Chinese America that had been little affected by the latest developments in China's cultural scene and which was greatly lacking in youth-oriented activities. It was natural that young people and young intellectuals with kindred interests sought each other out to establish social clubs. In many cases, schools and institutions provided convenient venues for the emergence of such gatherings, which later developed into independent groups. Activities often included social functions, sports, literary writings, vernacular dramas, choral singing, and instrumental music. Often young intellectuals teaching at the various schools encouraged such activities. That many of these activities would also support war propaganda campaigns further fostered their growth.

From 1937 until 1945, the KMT-CCP truce allowed the Left and Right to coexist in the community. The Left had quickly realized that the cessation of the KMT-CCP civil war and unification of Chinese resistance efforts offered an opportunity to expand its influence within the Chinese American community. In March 1938, New York City's Chinese Youth National Salvation Club, more familiarly known as the Chinese Youth Club (CYC), became one of the earliest progressive Chinese youth groups in the United States. The group was closely tied to the CHLA. Many CYC members were laundry workers employed all over the city, and the CYC clubroom was in the same building as the CHLA. The club actively supported the Chinese war effort by organizing lectures on current events, photo exhibitions, film showings, and choral performances, as well as participating in fundraising campaigns. The CYC also participated in the flourishing progressive youth movement by joining the American Youth Congress and events such as the May First Labor Day parades, demonstrations urging boycott of Japanese silk goods, and other protests on the Brooklyn waterfront protesting the shipping of scrap iron to Japan. In 1938 the CYC published the bilingual *The China Youth,* which included news on the youth movement in the United States and Canada.[50]

Conditions for youth club activities were most favorable in the San Francisco Bay area. San Francisco not only had the largest number of Chinese in America, most Chinese also had to live within the Chinatown area due to racial discrimination. This housing discrimination, which was an obstacle preventing Chinese from assimilating into the larger society, ironically facilitated the retention of Chinese culture and language and the development of a great diversity of Chinese American cultural and recreational activities within the community. During the Sino-Japanese conflict, the Bay Area supported the largest number of Chinese independent youth clubs. Most groups established clubrooms in one of the basements that abounded in Chinatown. The members were usually young immigrants and overwhelmingly male, although there were also a few American-born female members as well. Such youth groups' war relief efforts began in 1937 and peaked between 1939 and 1942. After America entered the war, many Chinese Americans joined the armed forces or the merchant marines, thereby draining participants from club activities.

The outbreak of the Sino-Japanese War had inspired the founding of Chick Char Musical Club in December 1937, a few months before the founding of New

York's CYC. The club's name derived from the phrase *chizha fengyun* [commanding the wind and clouds]. Chick Char began with a mixture of intellectuals and youth with liberal and Left sympathies who met to perform the folksong "Fengyang huagu" [Flower Drum Song of Fengyang], with lyrics revised by Tao Xingzhi. Tao was then touring the United States to urge resistance to Japanese aggression. Upon arriving in San Francisco, he allegedly encouraged the group to perform the song to rally support for national salvation. Chick Char often performed at pro-China functions and rallies such as Bowl of Rice events and anti-Japanese demonstrations. The club's performances later expanded to include Cantonese operatic arias and music, and vernacular dramas.[51]

The emergence of the CYC in New York City had not immediately inspired similar developments in the San Francisco Bay Area. One reason was that San Francisco was the headquarters of the KMT General Branch, which had great influence in Chinatown affairs. Another possible factor was the uncertainties about the leadership within the Marxist Left due to the departure of Benjamin Fee. In the meantime, the KMT tried to harness San Francisco's intellectuals in forming the Minduo [People's Bell] Drama Society in September 1938. The membership included a mix of older intellectuals and young adults, while party faithful dominated the leadership.[52] However, this party-controlled organization did not make many inroads among new arrivals. Instead, the Lufeng Drama Society emerged from the growing young immigrant population and debuted its first dramatic performance in June 1940.[53]

By then, the Left in San Francisco was ready for a new direction. The CWMAA under new leadership had developed sufficiently to play a role similar to that of the CHLA in New York. In San Francisco's Chinatown, anti-leftist sentiments had eased with the KMT-CCP truce. Although the Left still lacked the resources to establish a news organ, conditions were favorable enough for a youth group similar to New York's CYC.[54]

On July 21, 1940, Li Yuan, a progressive Chinese school teacher and the CWMAA's Happy Lim convened the first meeting of the newly formed Xin Wenz Yanjiuhui [New Chinese Alphabetized Language Study Society, or NCALSS] in the Chick Char Music Club clubroom. The NCALSS drew from a movement to replace the challenging character-based Chinese writing system with romanized Chinese (Latinxua Sin Wenz) to help eradicate the widespread illiteracy impeding China's modernization. This movement had begun in 1934 and quickly gained the support of many progressives.[55] Although the movement first attracted the attention of some leaders in Hawaii's Chinese community, the NCALSS was the first organization attempting to implement the system in the Americas.

Such a radical departure from tradition in the largely conservative San Francisco Chinese community resonated like "a thunderclap in a clear sky." The controversy led the Huaqiao Wenhua Jianshe Yanjiu Hui [Overseas Chinese Cultural Construction Research Society], a newly formed organization of Chinese intellectuals, to host a public forum at the Nam Kue School to debate Sin Wenz's pros and cons and invite Chinatown cultural clubs and the Chinese press to participate.[56] Despite the NCALSS's enthusiasm for Sin Wenz, the subject did not appeal broadly in the Chinese community. Moreover, the eradication of illiteracy could only be a goal secondary to the national crisis of Japan's invasion of China.

The NCALSS established a basement clubroom at 812 Stockton Street, a few yards south of the KMT U.S. General Branch headquarters. The site continued to serve as the center for progressive Chinese youth activities for the next two decades. The NCALSS organized classes featuring Cantonese and Mandarin versions of Sin Wenz and published a monthly mimeograph, *Sin Wenz Bao,* to discuss the theory and practice of alphabetized Chinese and disseminate news of the movement. Younger members, mostly teenagers, also turned to organizing choral and harmonica groups and lectures. "Youth Nights" with music and songs, snacks, and social dancing brought together Chinese and non-Chinese youth. More young people, mostly recent immigrants, were drawn to join, and membership grew to between thirty and forty. Within three months, younger members dominated the organization, and the principal focus shifted to anti-Fascist war activities. In August 1941, society members joined the San Francisco demonstrations protesting American shipments of scrap steel to Japan.[57]

By 1942 the number of youth clubs in the San Francisco Bay area had increased. The NCALSS decided to extend its activities beyond the Sin Wenz Movement and called for the youth clubs to collaborate in the fight against fascism. Earlier the Chinese American Citizens' Alliance and Chick Char Club had mounted campaigns to send greetings and gifts to Chinese Americans in the armed services. The NCALSS decided to emulate these activities and sought out Lufeng Vernacular Drama Club and Oakland's Yehuo [Prairie Fire] Club to form the Lufeng Drama Club, Yehuo Club, and the NCALSS United National Salvation Propaganda Troupe in order to stage the five-act vernacular drama *Zhandou* [Combat] as a fund-raiser. The total membership in the three groups was around a hundred.[58]

After this event, the groups reorganized into the Chinese Youth National Salvation League of California or more simply the Chinese Youth League (CYL) in early 1943. The CYL's mission was similar to that of New York's CYC. The CYL remained one of the most active Chinatown youth groups for the rest of the war. It published a monthly mimeographed literary magazine, *Zhandou,* and a newsletter, *Qingjiu Tuanbao* [National Salvation Youth League Journal]. The CYL sponsored a number of forums on current events, social sciences, literature, and issues such as love and social relations. The club was especially active in theater and staged several dozen skits and plays with progressive themes. In January 1943, the CYL presented the large-scale drama *Xitela de jiezuo* [Hitler's Masterpiece] to fund gifts for Chinese American servicemen. It maintained friendly relations with more than a dozen Chinatown youth clubs and with progressive non-Chinese organizations. In 1944 it became a member of the mainstream progressive group American Youth for Democracy.[59]

It did not take long for political activists to try to unite clubs in the Chinese community to better channel their energy to support China's war effort. In most small- to medium-size communities, the established KMT organization or its supporters played leading roles in this cause. For example, seventeen clubs in Los Angeles, mostly of a social and nonpolitical nature, formed a Federation of Chinese Clubs in spring 1938.[60] However, in larger communities like New York and San Francisco, where the Left had a strong presence, the Left vied with the KMT to capture the leadership role. Thus in New York, the Chinese Youth Club played a prominent role in organizing thirteen clubs in December 1938 to form the New York Council of Chinese Youth Clubs.[61]

The more numerous clubs in San Francisco and the East Bay proved to be much more difficult to handle. In October 1937, thirty clubs in San Francisco and the East Bay, with a total membership of about five hundred, had formed a Federation of Chinese Clubs to work together for war refugee relief. Most of the members were American-born youth with a small minority of immigrants.[62] At that time, however, few of the youth clubs comprising principally recently immigrated members joined the federation. However, their individual active participation in support of China's war effort led community leaders to seek to recruit them.[63]

On April 1944, Jane Kwong Lee, Executive Director of the Chinatown YWCA, convened a meeting for representatives of fourteen youth clubs to discuss formation of a Federation of Chinese Youth Clubs. Almost immediately, the KMT-sponsored San Min Chu I Youth Corps and CYL locked horns and the discussions stalemated.[64] By June the youth corps and some groups had withdrawn. Lee washed her hands of the effort. The CYL continued to work with the remaining groups with liberal leanings to formally establish the Federation of Chinese Youth Organizations on March 3, 1945. The Federation had envisioned plans to expand its activities; however, the war ended in August 1945, and this Federation and its counterparts in other communities soon faded out of the picture as the youth movement declined rapidly, with many young people becoming more preoccupied with starting families, continuing their education, or establishing businesses and enterprises.[65]

Emergence of Chinese American Literature

A Chinese American literary movement also developed as a by-product of the wartime progressive cultural activities. The increasing number of young, literate Chinese people influenced by the legacy of the May Fourth Movement stimulated the flowering of literary productions using vernacular Chinese and modeled after products of the New Chinese Literature Movement. The numerous youth and a handful of literary clubs published works expressing a wide range of ideologies ranging from nationalism to critical examinations of the status quo. These writers resided throughout Chinese America, but the two principal centers of activity were New York and San Francisco.

During the 1930s, New York's *China Salvation Times* had frequently included short literary works in its pages. The arrival of many new immigrants after the outbreak of the Sino-Japanese conflict greatly enlivened the Chinese literary scene. An early literary group with several dozen members was Xi She [Daybreak Society], founded in 1939, which published two mimeographed issues of *Xi She Keyi* [Experimental Works of the Daybreak Society]. By the third issue, the group was able to publish its literary pieces under the title *Xiguang* [Light at Daybreak] on a page of the liberal newspaper *China Tribune*. However, the group had to suspend activities until after the war when key members entered the military services.

The founding of *China Daily News* was a significant event during this period. Editor Eugene Moy not only continued the policies of *Chinese Vanguard* and *China Salvation Times* in providing a forum for literary authors but also published essays on literary theory and criticism and reviewed literary works from China and other countries in its literary section.

Around 1941 or 1942, Benjamin Fee, the managing editor of *Chinese American Weekly*, had also encouraged young writers to submit manuscripts; however, Fee left the publication when the publisher turned the periodical rightward to become more pro–Chiang Kai-shek.

Some Xi She members and working-class writers organized Huaqiao Wenhua She [Overseas Chinese Cultural Society], which in December 1942 began publishing *Huaqiao Wenzhen* [Overseas Chinese Literary Front], one of the first periodicals in Chinese America devoted entirely to literary theory, criticism, and writings. Every ten days the society also published a literary page, *Qianshao* [Outpost], in the *China Tribune*. Benjamin Fee was also associated with this group and submitted poetry under the noms de plume of Muyun or Yi.[66]

On the West Coast, Gilbert and Norbert Woo, brothers and new immigrants who had landed in California in 1932 and 1934, respectively, introduced progressive Chinese literature influenced by the May Fourth Movement. Norbert Woo discussed with D. Y. Mah, editor of *Kuo Min Yat Po,* an organ of the Kuomintang left wing, about publishing a weekly literary supplement in the paper. Using the name Xin Huaqiao Xuehui [New Overseas Chinese Learned Society], the two brothers launched *Wenxue Zhoukan* [Literary Weekly], on February 3, 1935. Gilbert Woo contributed many of the articles and wrote in vernacular Chinese. However, the Marxist Left, which at the time was dominated by ultra-left attitudes, criticized the brothers for helping the KMT. Later, the KMT right also began attacking the literary supplement as leaning to the left. Finding it impossible to operate from a middle ground, the brothers gave up the literary page on May 12, 1935.[67]

Afterward, there was little in the way of progressive Chinese literature published on the West Coast until the emergence of youth clubs after 1937. Gilbert Woo became an editor of the *Chinese Times*'s literary edition and encouraged young people to submit manuscripts. Besides the newspapers, the various youth clubs' publications—the vast majority from San Francisco's Chinatown and usually mimeographed—frequently included original poetry, essays, and short stories. One of the most popular was the CYL's mimeographed monthly *Zhandou*, which appeared from 1943 to 1946 and claimed a circulation as high as three thousand.[68] The publication included essays, short stories, poetry, news items, letters from readers, and even a short English section.

By the end of the war, an emergent literary movement advocated the creation of a Chinese-language literature relevant to the social and cultural realities of the Chinese in America in both form and content. In 1945 James Lee of New York's CYC and writers from both coasts formed the Huaqiao Qingnian Wenyi She [Overseas Chinese Youth Literary Society], which published a monthly entitled *Lüzhou* [Oasis] in the literary section of *China Daily News*.[69]

In 1947 another writers' group founded New York's *Xinmiao* [The Bud], a literary monthly. In 1948 Sanfanshi Huaqiao Qingnian Qingqi Wenyi She [San Francisco Overseas Chinese Youth Light Cavalry Literary Society], which included some writers who had submitted manuscripts to *Zhandou*, also received a page in the *China Daily News* literary section to publish members' works periodically.[70]

These writers were politically progressive. Although, their output varied widely in literary merit, they often tried to reflect the reality of life in the Chinese American community and even adopted the use of local Chinese American language and idioms. This movement paralleled the progressive Chinese literary movements in Malaysia and Singapore, which had peaked during the late 1930s. However, unlike in Southeast Asia, several adverse factors hampered further developments in the United States. The relatively small Chinese American population was often preoccupied with mere survival in a hostile setting. After World War II, the rapid Americanization and loss of Chinese-language fluency among Chinese Americans were also inhibiting factors. The anti-Communist hysteria of the 1950s, which eventually overwhelmed the entire progressive movement and silenced many writers, all but ended the prospects of this movement. In the 1950s, Gilbert Woo of the liberal *Chinese Pacific Weekly* still solicited original Chinese-language submissions, but the vitality had ebbed from the movement.

Activist Students and Scholars

The emergent literary movement in the Chinese American community attracted few sojourning students and scholars, who found it difficult to enter the United States and even harder to stay longer than a specified period of time. The 1930s global depression had diminished the numbers enrolling in American schools, and in 1937, just before the outbreak of the Sino-Japanese conflict, only about 1,733 students were in the United States. Japan's occupation of China's major ports stemmed the flow of students and visiting scholars even further. During the war years, only limited numbers could exit China and reach America via an arduous route through India. However, toward the mid-1940s, with the imminent end of the war, the Chinese government eased restrictions somewhat so that profession-als and students could go abroad for work experience and advanced studies to gain additional skills needed for the anticipated postwar reconstruction of China. Although most of those going abroad were pro-government or politically neutral, there were a few dissidents. The Southern Bureau of the CCP, led by Zhou Enlai and Dong Biwu, also encouraged and sometimes even partially funded some qualified underground CCP members to go abroad, both to acquire knowledge in preparation for postwar reconstruction in China, and to build and strengthen support for the Communist political program.[71]

In June 1944, Yang Gang arrived in the United States for graduate studies. She was a well-known journalist in Chongqing who came to the country on a Radcliffe College scholarship. A special correspondent in the United States for the liberal *Ta Kung Pao,* she frequently analyzed developments in the Chinese revolution for such intellectuals and East Asian specialists as Harvard University's John K. Fairbank. She also frequently communicated with journalists such as Edgar Snow and Agnes Smedley. Yang returned to China in 1948.[72]

In 1944 the East and West Foundation invited Gong Pusheng to return to America as a lecturer, but Gong did not arrive until August 1945, just as the war had ended. When she could not get an extension on her visa to stay for graduate studies, she stayed in New York City to become a researcher in the newly founded Human Rights Department of the U.N. Secretariat in July 1946.[73]

Most activists arriving in America, however, circulated among Chinese scholars and students in academia. Huang Shaoxiang arrived in fall 1944 and enrolled in Columbia University to study U.S. history, labor history, and black history. At the same time, under the guidance of CPUSA China Bureau secretary Y. Y. Hsu, she became active among the students. In 1945 she helped Agnes Smedley translate CCP documents for her biography of Zhu De. In 1946 she worked with labor historian Philip Foner but left for China the following year.[74]

Xu Ming, underground party member, was ordered by Dong Biwu of the CCP Southern Bureau to come to the United States as a student. He arrived in late December 1944 and enrolled in Clark University to study international relations and U.S. history. He became a student activist, especially in the Chinese Students Christian Association (CSCA).[75] The same year, underground CCP members Xue Baoding and Hou Xianglin also received KMT government scholarships to come to America to gain industrial work experience and to undertake further studies in preparation for the postwar reconstruction in China.[76] They circulated mostly among students and scholars in the sciences and technology sectors.

Xue brought with him a letter written by Hou Wailu introducing Xue to Hou's brother-in-law, Y. Y. Hsu.[77]

Another KMT-sponsored arrival was Lai Yali, personal secretary to General Feng Yuxiang and also a member of the Zhongguo Minzhu Geming Tongmeng [League for Democratic Revolution in China]. He arrived as an official of China's National Resources Commission in 1945 to pursue further studies. Using the name Lai Xingzhi, he soon became chief editor at New York's *China Tribune*.[78]

With the war's end, some students and scholars returned to China to contribute to what many hoped would be its long sought-after rebirth. Most, however, remained in the United States and witnessed from afar China's deeper fall into the cataclysm of the civil war. They also later became the focus of a three-way tug-of-war among the Marxist Left, KMT agents, and the U.S. government to determine whether they should return to China, proceed to Taiwan, or stay in America.

CHAPTER 5

The Birth of a New China

Setting the Stage for Civil War

By the end of World War II, the Allies had destroyed the German and Japanese military machines, but the United States and the USSR were already poised at the brink of a new global struggle for hegemony. In Asia, weakened colonial regimes could not continue ignoring the demands of indigenous peoples for freedom and independence. In China civil war between the Kuomintang (KMT) and the Communist Party of China (CCP) rapidly beset a people already exhausted by eight years of the Sino-Japanese War and long victimized by rampant corruption and soaring inflation. In the United States, the great power least touched by the ravages of war, marginalized minorities who had served in the military to defend democracy demanded their own rights to greater equality. The American Marxist Left, including Chinese, actively participated in all these struggles.

A few months before the end of World War II, on April 12, 1945, CCP Central Committee member Dong Biwu arrived in New York on his way to serve as one of China's representatives at the founding conference of the United Nations held in San Francisco. He was the first high-ranking CCP official to openly visit America and was accompanied by Zhang Hanfu and Chen Jiakang, who handled public relations. During a brief stopover in New York, he met with Earl Browder, Communist Party of the United States of America (CPUSA) general secretary, at Philip Jaffe's home together with C. T. Chi and several other Chinese and non-Chinese progressives.

At the San Francisco Conference, Zhang and Chen were joined by Y. Y. Hsu, and the trio compiled and published in Chinese and English the pamphlet *Memorandum on China's Liberated Areas,* describing the military achievements, government, economy, education, and workers' organizations in the CCP-controlled areas of China. While Dong was in the San Francisco Bay area, he also sought out Lawrence Lowe and suggested that he look for opportunities to start a progressive newspaper on the West Coast.[1]

After the conference, Dong and his staff traveled back to New York and stayed in the area until they departed for China on November 20. In August Dong visited Agnes Smedley, whom he had first met in Xi'an in 1936, to reestablish her ties with the CCP leadership. He also visited Pearl Buck, Gen. Joseph Stillwell's daughter, John K. Fairbank, and John Carter Vincent. He discussed support for the Chinese revolution with progressives in the Chinese community and among the student population. He also persuaded C. Y. Chen, who interpreted his remarks at meetings in New York, to go to Hong Kong to head a new progressive educational institution, Dade Xueyuan [Te Teh Academy].

Earlier in 1943 the USSR had dissolved the Communist International (Comintern) as a tactical move to win greater Western support for the fight against the Axis powers. The Comintern had long been a conduit for interparty communications in the international Communist movement, and in the case of the CCP had served as a means to liaise with Chinese party members in the CPUSA and other areas on matters of concern to the CCP. In May 1944, CPUSA secretary Browder followed up by dissolving the CPUSA, changing it to a Communist Political Association (CPA) that was intended to act as an independent leftist lobbying group in American politics. Under this scheme, only U.S. citizens would be eligible to participate as association members. This situation created problems for the Chinese Marxist Left in America, which was deeply involved in the Chinese revolution and the Chinese War of Resistance against Japan.

Browder's plan aroused much opposition and was finally jettisoned in July 1945, when Browder was expelled from the party; William Z. Foster replaced him as party secretary, and the CPUSA reestablished its party organization, including the Chinese Bureau, in late summer or early fall. Actually, the Chinese Bureau had continued functioning to coordinate operations at *China Daily News* with Chu Tong, Thomas Lem Tong, Chee Fun Ho, and Y. Y. Hsu. The Chinese Bureau was reestablished under the leadership of Y. Y. Hsu. Dong Biwu arrived in New York as these events were unfolding and took steps to resolve some of them. He encouraged the leading CCP members in the East to meet regularly, mainly to provide support for the *China Daily News* by writing editorials and articles.

This group was known informally as the "Friday Club," since it met regularly at Y. Y. Hsu's apartment every Friday. Over time, the group turned to discussing contacts with the CCP and carrying out its directives, maintenance of relations with the CPUSA, the activities of the Chinese Bureau, and oversight of activities among Chinese community and student organizations. When Yang Gang returned to China and mentioned the group while reporting on the situation among Chinese in the United States, Zhou Enlai remarked that in reality it was acting as a Zhong-Gong zai Mei Gongzuo Lingdao Xiaozu [Leadership Group for CCP Activities in the United States, or LGCPUS], which became the entity's name in official references.[2]

Through Chan Shanxiang, former director at the Shanghai YWCA, Xu Ming met Y. Y. Hsu, and he, along with Yang Gang and Lai Yali, joined the LGCPUS. As the CCP stepped up its efforts to win over students and scholars from China, Gong Pusheng, Pu Shouchang, and Xue Baoding also joined. Pu was recruited to help translate selected essays by Mao Zedong, parts of which were given to Y. Y. Hsu by Dong Biwu, and an additional batch that was brought over by Chen Han-seng in 1948. However, the committee's work was often diverted by rapidly developing events in China, and it was unable to complete the project.[3]

In 1946 Y. Y. Hsu decided to return to China after an absence of two decades.[4] It so happened that Chen Han-seng was on his way to America from India to be a visiting lecturer at Washington State University. He and his wife had fled China in March 1944 upon learning that the Chongqing government had secretly issued orders for his arrest. At the time, he was associated with the International Committee for the Promotion of Chinese Industrial Cooperatives (Indusco) in Guilin. After arriving in America, Chen received secret orders from Zhou Enlai and Liao Chengzhi to liaise with the CPUSA. He also was asked to become an advisor to the LGCPUS.

After his teaching stint, Chen lectured at Johns Hopkins University and the University of Pennsylvania. He was active on many fronts: speaking to mostly non-Chinese audiences exposing the KMT government's corruption and repressive rule; advising CCP student groups; frequently conferring with Chu Tong and other key CCP members; and writing weekly reports to Qiao Guanhua in Hong Kong regarding developments in America.[5]

Throughout his American travels, Dong lectured and gave press interviews warning about the grave threat of civil war in China and calling for the formation of a democratically elected coalition government. At the same time, he decried the corruption of the KMT government.[6] His remarks quickly set the tone and direction for Chinese Marxist Left activities.

During this same period, as the war's end became certain, different political factions began maneuvering to influence politicians and public opinion regarding U.S.-China policy. On the left, the China Forum had replaced the American Friends of the Chinese People in 1944. After the war ended, this group reorganized as the Committee for a Democratic Far Eastern Policy (CDFEP) and Maud Russell, formerly connected with the YWCA in China and who had just joined the CPUSA, became its executive director in May 1946. Under Russell the CDFEP opposed U.S. support for Chiang Kai-shek and the KMT regime. Edgar Snow and Israel Epstein were among the committee's consultants. Epstein's wife, Elsie Fairfax-Cholmeley, was a committee employee and edited its publication *Far East Spotlight*.[7]

Within the Chinese American community the Left made efforts to increase community awareness of the CCP's political programs. In early July 1945, *China Daily News* published Mao's *Lun Lianhe Zhengfu* [*On Coalition Government*], along with other CCP political documents. In San Francisco in 1945–46, Hezuo [Co-operative] Publishers printed several hundred copies of Mao's *Xinminzhu-zhuyi Lun* [*On the New Democracy*] and *On Coalition Government*, along with the Chinese version of Dong Biwu's *Memorandum on China's Liberated Areas*. Hezuo Publishers had been founded by members of the Chinese Workers Mutual-Aid Association (CWMAA) after the 1941 New Fourth Army incident to combat KMT censorship by reprinting Chinese Communist documents for distribution among Chinese in America. However, the induction of key members into the armed services shelved the implementation of this plan until the war's end.[8]

During this period the Chinese Marxist Left had only one publication in Chinese America, New York's *China Daily News*. In 1945 it gained an ally when Lai Yali became chief editor at *China Tribune* and changed its editorial policy to criticize the KMT and be sympathetic toward the Communists.[9] In San Francisco, however, all the daily newspapers were pro-KMT or anti-Communist, with only the liberal *Chinese Pacific Weekly* presenting news of China fairly objectively. This publication had been founded in 1946 under the editorship of Gilbert Woo but was still struggling with limited circulation. Progressive forces controlled very few other community institutions. Through the Chinese consulates and its extensive party organization, the KMT controlled most of the Chinese media, Chinese-language schools, and Chinatown organizations, making it difficult for the Chinese American Left to make much headway within the community. Publishing CCP political essays was thus only a modest effort yielding limited results.

With the war's end, the Left organizations changed their activities to suit the new conditions. In San Francisco the Chinese Youth League reorganized as the Chinese American Democratic Youth League (CADYL, Mun Ching), which remained affiliated with the American Youth for Democracy. Members joined the activities of progressive organizations such as the California Labor School and also participated in the election campaigns of progressive candidates and movements for democratic causes such as a fair employment practice act. CADYL and the CWMAA formed the nuclei of Chinese progressive activities in the San Francisco Bay area.[10] New York's Chinese Youth Club (CYC) made similar shifts in its postwar activities and worked closely with the Chinese Hand Laundry Association (CHLA) on the *China Daily News*.

Although the Chinese Left was small in number, it was part of a much larger movement and could count on support from the Marxist Left and progressive organizations outside the Chinese community, indicating a continuing evolution of concern for domestic issues. However, the Chinese Left's effectiveness in having an impact on these areas remained limited and declined steadily beginning in the late 1940s with the mounting anti-Communist hysteria of the cold war. On the other hand, the rapidly shifting events in China attracted the Chinese Left's growing participation in support of China's revolution. This tendency was particularly marked in the East, where *China Daily News* strongly supported the Chinese revolution and many Chinese progressives were non-working-class students and intellectuals from China, or laundrymen and small shopkeepers, with little or limited involvement in American domestic issues.

Chinese Students Christian Association in North America

Toward the end of the War of Resistance, the CCP's agenda began gaining favor among many in China. Intellectuals, who had always been the social class with the keenest concern for national affairs during the Republican era, now were dismayed by China's deteriorating situation. They began to openly question and criticize KMT rule from university campuses where the Nationalists did not exert absolute control. Starting in 1942, some students and professionals went abroad— some sponsored by the government and others funded from various sources—for further study and work experience, including a number of dissidents.[11]

Students opposed to the KMT had organized in a small way even before the end of World War II. At Harvard University, the brothers Pu Shouhai, Pu Shouchang, and Pu Shoushan, together with Ding Chen and Han Depei, organized Mingzhi She [Clear Ideals Society] around 1942. The group met regularly to talk about international and China-connected issues. They also held discussion sessions on Mao's *On the New Democracy,* based on the English translation. By the mid-1940s, progressive students and scholars had formed similar *dushu hui* [reading groups], the generic name for such groups, on a number of campuses.[12] Most students, however, participated in such established student organizations as the Chinese Students Christian Association in North America (CSCA), then the oldest and most influential Chinese student group in America. Founded in 1908, the CSCA was informally connected to the YMCA's International Committee in 1917. Its membership reached a peak of approximately one thousand, and by the 1940s, it was the only national Chinese student organization. The group's declared purpose was to foster Christian morals and friendships, and to unite Chinese Christian students living in American society, but since the mid-1920s, "any Chinese student, in sympathy with the purpose of the Association" was allowed to join, vote, and hold office. Administratively, the CSCA had three district departments—Eastern, Midwest, and West Coast—with each fielding local chapters. The association provided practical services to Chinese students, such as job placement, living arrangements, or other needs.[13]

Progressive activists targeted the CSCA's eastern and midwestern departments, where large numbers of Chinese students attended Ivy League and other schools. Paul T. K. Lin, the Canadian-born son of a Protestant minister; Pu Shouchang; and Pu Shoushan were active leaders in the Eastern Department. The brothers had arrived in 1941 as students. While they were pursuing their doctorates at Harvard University, Pu Shouchang joined the CCP in 1944, and Pu Shoushan joined the

CPUSA in 1945. However, when Dong Biwu visited New York City that fall, he gave approval for Pu Shoushan to transfer his membership to the CCP. Paul Lin was also a PhD candidate at Harvard. He and the brothers probably already knew each other, since their times spent as undergraduates at the University of Michigan overlapped. As president of the CSCA in 1944, Lin became an important ally of the Pu brothers.[14]

In September 1945, Lin, the Pu brothers, and more than ninety participants, two-thirds of whom were China-born, attended the CSCA Eastern Department's summer conference in New Hampshire. Lin served as chairperson for the planning committee; his wife was secretary, while Pu Shouchang headed the debate committee. During the conference, they and progressive students Xu Ming and others criticized the KMT's one-party rule in China and advocated a popularly elected democratic coalition government that would facilitate the peaceful reconstruction of China. These remarks fell on receptive ears, and they presented for consideration a resolution that called for a coalition government. However, some attendees were concerned that the term "coalition government" might indicate CSCA sympathies toward the Communists, and this wording was revised to "transitional government" in the final version.[15]

The same summer, the Pu brothers began editing the quarterly *Chinese Students' Opinion,* which was published by the CSCA's Boston chapter. Initially, it reflected diverse opinions, but as left-wing students gained editorial control, articles about China soon reflected only progressive points of view.[16]

Meanwhile in China, the KMT government and the CCP called a fragile truce immediately after the war ended. The United States intervened in favor of the KMT by airlifting four to five hundred thousand KMT troops to key sites in northern and eastern China to receive the Japanese surrender, while U.S. Marines occupied points in North China to block the People's Liberation Army (PLA) from moving south. In an atmosphere taut with distrust and antagonism, it is not surprising that the truce began unraveling almost immediately. Such was the backdrop when Paul Lin, the Pu brothers, and other progressives attended another conference organized by the CSCA Eastern District Department in New Jersey from June 9 to 16, 1946.

Liu Liangmo was among the numerous speakers who continued their attacks on the KMT dictatorial rule. The assembly passed resolutions demanding an end to the civil war, the convening of a political consultative conference, an end to U.S. government loans to China until a coalition government could be formed, and the departure of foreign troops. This last provision originally specified "U.S. troops," but the wording was changed after lengthy debate. Compromises had to be struck to pass these resolutions, indicating that support for the progressives was highly conditional.[17]

In late June 1946, Chiang Kai-shek ordered the resumption of hostilities with the boast that KMT armies would "suppress the insurrection" within three months.

He continued to repress dissidents with determination. In July the secret police in Kunming assassinated professors Wen Yiduo and Li Gongpu, both prominent members of the China Democratic League.[18] Because treaty-port foreign concessions had been abolished during the war, a number of dissidents could only take refuge in the western colonies of Hong Kong or Macau, or in countries abroad.

Under the leadership of Zhou Enlai, key party members and sympathetic intellectuals were helped to leave China for Hong Kong and Macau, which again became centers of progressive activities. Qiao Guanhua arrived in Hong Kong in October to head the New China News Agency, the CCP's propaganda arm. He was also operating under the foreign affairs group of the CCP Central Committee, which acted as the diplomatic arm of the party before the founding of the People's Republic of China (PRC).[19] In Hong Kong and Macau, some left-wing intellectuals were placed in the Te Teh Academy and other progressive schools; others became connected with the progressive press and other sympathetic institutions. There were also some fortunate enough to possess the means and connections to go abroad as students, visiting scholars, or artists in Europe or the United States, where they became advocates of the CCP political program. Many went to university towns in the Midwest, on the eastern seaboard, or on the West Coast. Dissidents also congregated in New York City, where the Chinese Marxist Left had a strong presence.

America involved itself increasingly in the China imbroglio by signing an agreement to sell war surplus materials to the KMT government at a huge discount. America became closely identified with the KMT regime. Anti-American sentiments were further inflamed when a Peking University student claimed that a U.S. Marine had raped her on Christmas Eve. Student-led protests and demonstrations involving some five hundred thousand participants in more than ten cities raged from December 1946 to March 1947, calling for the departure of American armed forces personnel. In the meantime, the civil war continued beyond the intended three months with no end in sight, accompanied by unabated inflation, corruption, and political repression in KMT-controlled areas. On May 20, 1947, more than six thousand students from sixteen universities in northern and eastern China demonstrated in Nanjing asking for action "to resolve the crisis in education." The KMT government dispersed the students using force, injuring nineteen severely and jailing twenty-eight. Soon afterward, a million students in more than sixty cities and towns went on strike or marched in protest against "hunger, civil war, and repression." The KMT government continued its strong-arm tactics, thereby only further alienating important sectors of Chinese society. CCP underground members astutely exploited these feelings of discontent to further undermine KMT rule.[20] The deteriorating conditions in China greatly influenced the political mood among Chinese in the United States.

The 1947 Conference of the Eastern District Department of the CSCA convened in Connecticut in September with the theme "Sino-American Relations and

China's Reconstruction." By this time, Paul Lin had become the CSCA's general secretary. After he gave a bleak analysis of the political situation in China, Pu Shouchang spoke about China's economic crisis, and Pu Shoushan criticized the new Sino-American treaty with the KMT government. The conference also featured invited speakers critical of the KMT regime, such as Israel Epstein and the Canadian missionary James G. Endicott. Resolutions similar to those from previous years passed easily this time. Soon afterward, Lin spoke at the Midwest CSCA conference to a receptive audience regarding his anti–civil war, anti-hunger, anti-repression, and anti-U.S.-China policy stance.[21]

In 1948 the CSCA Eastern and Midwest district departments convened their summer conferences with the theme "Our Role in a Changing China." Before more than a hundred students at the Eastern Conference, Chen Han-seng lectured on the structure of Chinese society; Israel Epstein talked about the history and nature of the revolutionary changes in China; and Pu Shouchang analyzed the current situation in China. In a winter conference led by Xu Ming and the Columbia University students Chen Yiming and his sister Chen Xiuxia, American Friends Service's William Rehill reported on his visit to Yan'an. For recreation, conference participants learned the Yangge folk dance and sang folk songs from the liberated areas.[22]

In 1948, CSCA's Eastern Department held a retreat in Pennsylvania, where fifty-five participants pondered what attitudes Chinese students abroad should take toward the current social upheavals in China. In 1948 and 1949, New York chapter activists held regular Sunday dinner meetings to discuss such CCP documents as "On New Democracy" and "On Coalition Government" and "On the People's Democratic Dictatorship."[23]

Chinese Federation for Peace and Democracy in China

The growing antagonism toward KMT policies reflected in the CSCA's development accompanied worsening conditions for the KMT in China. In 1946 Feng Yuxiang, the famed "Christian" general, prominent veteran KMT leader, and sworn brother of Chiang Kai-shek, broke with the Chiang government. Chiang ordered him into foreign exile, and in August 1946, Feng departed China with his wife, one daughter, an English secretary, a Chinese secretary, and two water conservancy experts, ostensibly as head of a commission investigating irrigation and water conservancy facilities in the United States. The party followed the first third of a U.S. government–arranged itinerary and then abandoned the program. Instead, Feng lectured and wrote articles criticizing the Chiang Kai-shek regime. After a seventy-eight-day tour covering eight states, Feng settled with his family in Berkeley, California.[24]

On May 20, 1947, the KMT military police brutally suppressed an "anti-hunger, anti–civil war, anti-repression" student demonstration in Nanjing, leading Feng to publish "Gao quan'guo tongbao shu" [An Open Letter to Compatriots in the Entire Nation], which denounced the civil war and KMT authoritarian rule.[25] Henry Tsoi, together with other progressives, had been trying to organize an anti-KMT united front in the Bay Area and approached the general, who agreed to lead the new organization.[26]

By that fall, Feng had received an invitation from progressives Wu Maosun, Lai Yali, Wang Feng, and Chu Tong of the *China Daily News* to bring his message to the East Coast. Driven across the continent by his daughter Lida and her fiancé, Luo Yuanzheng, Feng arrived just in time to speak at a CSCA-sponsored "Double Ten" celebration of the Chinese Republic's National Day at Columbia University. The CSCA's Pu Shouchang served as interpreter, a role that he would play often at Feng's subsequent speaking engagements. The next afternoon, Feng continued to attack Chiang and the KMT regime at a press conference organized by Lai Yali and others.[27]

After meeting with Chu Tong and the five other progressives, Feng helped to found the Overseas Chinese Federation for Peace and Democracy in China (OCFPD) on November 9, 1947, with himself as chairperson. The group advocated democracy in China and opposed American interference in the Chinese civil war.[28] Soon afterward, Feng published an article in the influential liberal periodical *Nation* to explain to English-reading audiences why he broke with Chiang Kai-shek.[29]

These attacks did not sit well with the KMT government, and the party press in America began vilifying Feng. On December 20, 1947, the KMT government ordered his return to China. It abolished his official position, ended his financial stipends, voided his Chinese passport, and stripped him of his KMT membership. Through unofficial channels, the Chinese government also urged the United States to expel Feng. Despite such attempted repression, dissident KMT members in Hong Kong continued the anti–Chiang Kai-shek campaign among Chinese abroad by establishing the Revolutionary Committee of the KMT on January 1, 1948, with Feng as the committee's representative in the United States.[30]

Between the founding of the OCFPD to mid-1948, Feng traveled extensively throughout the eastern and midwestern United States, speaking to such audiences as the Chinese Hand Laundry Alliance; the Committee for a Democratic Far Eastern Policy; a conference on American policy toward China and the Far East; Methodist, Episcopal, and other church gatherings; university campuses; and even to a street corner crowd in New York's Chinatown. In one two-week period, Feng made twenty-seven speeches in the Midwest. He also appeared at five news conferences, visited government officials and politicians, and testified before a subcommittee of the House Appropriations Committee concerning aid to China. He reiterated his opposition to repression by the KMT government, the civil war in China, and U.S. aid to the Chiang regime.[31] Feng's criticism seemed to have some influence, for between 1948 and 1949 Congress reduced aid to China from

$570 million to $382 million.[32] Despite the reservations reflected in this reduction, pro-KMT, anti-Communist forces were still powerful enough to pass the China aid bill, despite widespread knowledge of KMT corruption and ineptitude.

The OCFPD's membership quickly grew to more than two hundred, mostly middle-class intellectuals. Its headquarters were in New York City, with branches in Washington, D.C., Minnesota, and San Francisco. The New York headquarters published a biweekly newsletter for its predominantly intellectual and business members. Despite this organizational growth, it was Feng who possessed the fame and charisma to attract broad audiences.

The U.S. government notified Feng and his family in early 1948 that their passports would be expiring, and they could not remain in America. By this time, the tides of battle had turned in favor of the People's Liberation Army, and a regime change appeared certain. On July 31, 1948, Feng, his wife, four children, son-in-law, and secretary Lai Yali boarded the S.S. *Pobeda,* which had been secretly chartered by the CCP to take the Feng party to China by way of the Soviet Union, where Feng expected to join the soon-to-be convened People's Political Consultative Conference.[33]

Supporting the Communist Advance

As early as fall 1947, a year into the civil war, the balance of power had shifted so much that the number of PLA regular troops approached that of the regular troops under KMT command. On September 1, the CCP Central Committee boldly announced a nationwide offensive to annihilate the enemy as its guiding principle for the civil war's second year.[34] The PLA thereby seized the tactical and strategic initiative, even though on paper the KMT forces were still more numerous and better equipped; however, afflicted with inept leadership and low morale, the KMT forces suffered a series of defeats.

Three PLA drives wrested control of large areas of eastern and central China south of the Yellow River from the KMT. By September 1948, the KMT yielded control of the Shandong Peninsula to the Communists. By November 1948, CCP forces had annihilated KMT forces in the northeastern provinces. At the beginning of 1949, the PLA captured Tianjin and then negotiated the surrender of Beijing to seize all of north China. In April the PLA easily crossed the Yangzi River to seize Nanjing, Shanghai, and other KMT strongholds in quick succession. As China awaited the imminent birth of its new government, the U.S. Department of State issued the white paper *United States Relations with China* in August 1949, which blamed the KMT government for its own downfall. On October 1, 1949, the CCP founded the People's Republic in Beijing.[35]

With the ascent of the PLA, the Chinese Left in America focused on publicizing the CCP's political program and calling for Chinese abroad to join the Communist effort to build a "New China." A growing number of news articles reported on the liberated areas, describing the CCP's restoration of law and order and control of inflation and corruption. *China Daily News* was the principal paper publishing such news. Soon after the PLA went on the offensive, an editorial in the paper challenged students and intellectuals in America, "Tongxuemen, zuguo yao nimen yonggan di qianjin!" [Fellow classmates! The ancestral land wants you to go forward courageously!].

In San Francisco, Leong Thick Hing (better known by his nom de plume Liang Xiaomai) was a young immigrant interested in literary writings who had performed his military service in China, where he made contact with Chinese progressives such as Feng Yuxiang and Guo Moruo.[36] He founded Oasis Bookstore in San Francisco in 1948, which became the largest outlet for Chinese progressive literature in the United States and a convenient place for recruiting followers for progressive activities. The backroom soon served as the meeting place for the local Overseas Chinese League for Peace and Democracy in China (OCLPDC) branch under the leadership of Henry Tsoi.

Both Chu Tong on the East Coast and Henry Tsoi on the West actively recruited cadres from the community and on campuses to help implement the growing number of activities accompanying the CCP's rise. Because CPUSA headquarters and the *China Daily News* were located in New York City and due to the presence of a sizeable community of the anti-KMT critics in the region, the East Coast played a leading role in activities of the Chinese American Left.

San Francisco on the West Coast was another center of Chinese American progressive activities. However, here the Left was operating in a community where the entrenched and well-organized KMT controlled the press and radio, the schools, and the traditionist associations. Nevertheless, the development of events in China helped Henry Tsoi recruit cadres for Left activities. In 1946 Wang Fushi and his family, after arriving in New York from India and consulting with Chu Tong, continued on to settle in San Francisco. Wang became one of the early OCLPDC members in San Francisco. Henry Tsoi also recruited Chinatown businessman Francis Leong into the OCLPDC. When he was a Peking University student, Leong had participated in the December 9, 1935, demonstrations demanding resistance against Japanese aggression. Leong in turn brought in other sympathetic businessmen in the community. Tsoi won the support of restaurateur Joe Yuey (Zhou Rui), a leader in the powerful Suey Sing Association who was disenchanted with the Chiang Kai-Shek regime. He also recruited into the CCP the graduate student Wang Jue, who had also participated in the December 9, 1935, demonstrations in Beijing. Another who joined the group was Li Chunhui, who had joined CCP in China in 1938. Party members at the University of California, Berkeley, included graduate students Jin Yinchang—another participant in the December 9, 1935, demonstrations—and Xia Xu. The group organized such events as forums for students to discuss current events in the Berkeley home of Feng Hongzhi, son of Feng Yuxiang. Thus, the influence of the CCP in the San

Francisco Bay area grew in significance even if it did not become a formidable force in the community.[37]

Beneath the surface, the Left continued to whittle away at the KMT propaganda machine. For example, through the help of OCLPDC member Kew Yuen Ja, the local Golden Star Radio program hired Paul Mar for several months to write newscast scripts with a more objective presentation of news from China. However, it was obvious that a local news organ supporting the Left was sorely needed.

The Hong Kong CCP partially filled this lack with stepped-up propaganda activities in the form of the resumption of publication of the *Far Eastern Bulletin* in June 1948 after a seven-year hiatus caused by the Pacific War. The mimeographed *Bulletin* was published by the Kuo Sin News Agency, which was backed financially by the CCP and its allies. It featured English-language news commentaries criticizing the Chiang regime and advocating the CCP's political programs. Toward the end of 1948, Oasis Bookstore became the *Bulletin*'s North American distributor, with OCFPD member Wang Fushi printing the publication locally on a mimeograph machine donated by Joe Yuey.[38]

Another new publication, the biweekly *Liu-Mei Xuesheng Tongxun* [Newsletter for Students Studying in America] targeted the student and intellectual population. Its publishing staff included Wang Heng, who had come to America as Feng Yuxiang's secretary and decided to stay after Feng departed the country. Chu Tong of the *China Daily News* had urged him to undertake the newsletter, which had a distribution of about five hundred in the United States and Canada. With the anti-Communist hysteria increasing in America, the editors and writers prudently used pseudonyms to disguise their identities from U.S. investigative agencies.[39]

China Weekly, Chung Sai Yat Po, World Theater

As the PLA continued to defeat the dispirited KMT armies in 1949, the brothers Henry Tsoi and Lawrence Lowe felt that the time was finally right to launch a newspaper in San Francisco, as Dong Biwu had suggested in 1945. *China Weekly* began publication on May 4, a date regarded by many Chinese historians as marking "the end of the old democratic revolution led by the bourgeoisie and the beginning of the new democratic revolution led by the proletariat." The Chinese name on *China Weekly*'s masthead, *Jinmen Qiaobao* [Golden Gate Overseas Chinese Newspaper], was written in calligraphy that Dong Biwu had left with Lawrence Lowe. Wang Jue and CADYL member Paul Mar were the editors.[40]

The local KMT tried to stop its publication by intimidating Chinatown printing shops, but Tsoi negotiated an agreement with the journalist Gilbert Woo for access to the *Chinese Pacific Weekly*'s antiquated printing press. The KMT then tried to prevent its distribution to news vendors. In response, Tsoi called upon Joe Yuey, the influential leader of Suey Sing Association, and the harassment ceased.[41]

China Weekly extolled the expected merits of a communist government in China and attracted readers wishing to learn more about the new regime's policies. However, its partisan and tendentious style limited audiences. Even before the emergence of *China Weekly,* another group of OCFPD members, led by Francis Leong, had started raising capital for a daily newspaper *Qiaozhong Ribao* [Overseas Chinese Daily Newspaper]. KMT opposition did manage to thwart this effort by spreading malicious rumors and issuing threats.

Mao Zedong proclaimed the founding of the PRC at Tian'anmen Square on October 1, 1949. Festivities erupted all over China and among progressive Chinese throughout the world. The CWMAA held a public celebration in conjunction with the twelfth anniversary of the association's founding on the evening of October 9 at the Chinese American Citizens' Alliance Hall. The California Labor School chorus gave San Francisco Chinatown's first performance of the *Yellow River Cantata.* In protest, KMT-hired hoodlums charged into the auditorium during a speech by William Kerner of the Committee for a Democratic Far East Policy, seized the PRC flag displayed on stage, and scattered blue dye (the color associated with the KMT) on the audience. They left after about ten to fifteen minutes, beating up Wang Fushi and an elderly white man in the audience, who were blocking their exit. The following evening, conditions remained tense in Chinatown as KMT partisans distributed a death list of fifteen Chinese progressives along the route of the parade commemorating the anniversary of the 1911 Revolution in China.[42] They even threatened the staff of the liberal *Chinese Pacific Weekly,* which had been only mildly critical of the KMT regime. With Joe Yuey taking the lead, the Suey Sing and Ying On Associations protected these individuals and prevented bloodshed. The threatened subjects were able to resume their normal activities once tensions had eased after a few days to a week.

Despite this show of naked force, the Left was still riding on the momentum of China's communist revolution. Henry Tsoi learned that the venerable *Chung Sai Yat Po* [East West Daily], then the oldest existing Chinese-language daily in the United States, was being put up for sale and alerted the *Qiaozhong Ribao* group. Francis Leong consulted with Joe Yuey, who turned to fellow clansman Sam Wah You (Zhou Sen), owner of the Centro Supermarket chain in Stockton, who successfully outbid pro-KMT investors. He became the major shareholder in the resulting Chung Wah Corporation that then leased the property to the publishing corporation formed by key OCFPD members and their associates to publish the newspaper.[43]

The rejuvenated *Chung Sai Yat Po* began publication on November 29, 1949, changing from a pro-KMT editorial policy to one favoring the newly established People's Republic.[44] The tone, however, was much more moderate than that of *China Weekly.* OCFPD member Chinatown businessman Kew Yuen Ja became manager. *China Daily News*'s Chu Tong recommended Ma Jiliang, former editor of the Hong Kong daily *Wen Wei Pao,* to be interim chief editor. After several months Ma left and was succeeded by Herbert Lee. During the first months of operation, students and OCFPD members Wang Fushi, Wang Jue, Li Chunhui, and others helped in the editorial department; however, one by one they departed for the new China.[45]

In addition to acquiring newspapers and media outlets, Communist sympathizers also ventured into the movie industry. Situ Huimin, who had come to the United States in 1946 to study filmmaking, helped local progressives establish the World Theater in San Francisco on December 23, 1949; Lawrence Lowe and Karl Fung were the registered owners.[46] The next day, the theater began screening the epic *Yijiang chunshui xiang dong liu* [The River Filled with Water in Spring Flows Eastward], a powerful condemnation of corruption in the KMT-ruled areas, the depravity of the upper classes, and their callousness toward the misery and poverty of the lower classes. The theater management sought out young people associated with CADYL to dub the Mandarin soundtrack into Cantonese. The move caused a sensation, because hitherto most Chinese films shown in Chinatown theaters usually dealt with trite and hackneyed themes.[47]

These activities dovetailed with the Communist Party's outreach to Chinese scholars, professionals, and students on American campuses. It particularly strove to persuade fence-sitting scientists and engineers to return to help build the "New China."[48] Progressives distributed information about the CCP's programs and policies, and appealed to the intellectuals' patriotism to persuade them to contribute to China's new order.

Association of Chinese Scientific Workers in America

In 1947 Xu Ming nominated Xue Baoding to be a member of the LGCPUS with the task of organizing scholars in science and technology to support the Communist revolution. During that year Xue Baoding, who had received his MS in chemical engineering at the University of Pittsburgh, went to New York to continue his studies. There he encouraged progressive scholars in science and technology to organize Jian She [Construct Society], a closed group devoted to discussions of current events and the CCP's political program and critiques of various aspects of American society. For its founding session on January 16, 1948, the group invited Chen Han-seng, whose talk was called "Zhongguo gongyehua de tujing" [Path to China's Industrialization]. In another session, journalist Israel Epstein discussed the current political situation in America. During the next few months, Xue made two cross-country trips, leading to the formation of similar groups, such as Zhao She [Morning Society], Zhi She [Chicago Society], and Ming She [Minnesota Society] on campuses in the Boston, Chicago, Minneapolis, San Francisco, and Los Angeles areas. The objective was to persuade scholars in the sciences and technology to return to serve the "New China." Xue left for China in late 1948.[49]

On January 29, 1949, more than twenty students from midwestern campuses led by Ge Tingsui, then teaching at the University of Illinois, and Hou Xianglin, then completing his doctoral work at the Carnegie Institute of Technology, founded Meizhong Zhongguo Kexue Gongzuozhe Xiehui [Association of Chinese Scientific Workers in the Midwest] in Chicago. Similar groups emerged in other regions in America. Half a year later, delegates from thirteen local groups met in Pittsburgh to establish a national body, Liu-Mei Zhongguo Kexue Gongzuozhe Xiehui [Association of Chinese Scientific Workers in America, or ACSWA] on June 18, 1949. Hou Xianglin was elected executive secretary. The association's headquarters ended up being located in Chicago, with the Philadelphia branch publishing the mimeographed monthly newsletter, which had a peak distribution of eight to nine hundred.[50]

The ACSWA grew rapidly from 410 members in nineteen branches in August 1949 to thirty-two branches with 718 members in March 1950. Association activities included scientific and technological discussions and field trips. Initially, the organization saw its principal mission as merely providing information on the CCP political program to prepare Chinese university students and visiting scholars for their return to China. However, Xu Ming, who traveled to China and reported to Zhou Enlai, returned in September with orders from Zhou that organizations such as the ACSWA and CSCA should also try to encourage students and scholars to return to China to help with national reconstruction, a task that the leftist students enthusiastically accepted.[51]

Student organizations focusing on the new China proliferated and introduced political documents, cultural activities, and news of current events. Study groups proliferated and some grew to include a large number of participants and a variety of activities. Examples included Zhongguo Xinwenhua Xuehui [New Chinese Culture Society] in New York and the Xin Zhongguo Yanjiuhui [Society for the Study of the New China].[52]

By the late 1940s, Marxist activists also introduced the study groups to activists in the community organizations CYC, CHLA, CWMAA, and CADYL to increase political consciousness by discussing current events and studying Marxist tracts. However, these efforts were not very successful, since many in community groups did not have the same strong motivations driving students and scholars to want to learn more to prepare themselves for life in the new China to which many wished to return. The community study groups were soon limited to a selected few activists meeting in closed sessions.

Because San Francisco was the major exit port for travelers to China, the local ACSWA branch, under the leadership of Jin Yinchang and Xia Xu, worked with the University of California Chinese Students Club to establish Liu-Mei Zhongguo Xuesheng Huiguo Fuwu Hui [Committee to Serve Chinese Students in America Returning to China] in early 1950 to help make travel arrangements for departing scholars and students.[53]

Exodus to the New China

As the CCP's victory became more certain, scholars and students began to leave for the Communist-controlled areas. For example, Xiao Shuzi, who was studying education technology at Columbia University, left in March 1949 and returned by way of Africa and Hong Kong. Choral music director Liu Liangmo left New York for China in March 1949. Arthur Chung, who had participated in the student demonstrations in Beijing in 1935, resigned his position at New York's Bellevue Hospital and departed with his wife, Sylvia Liang, two children, brother-in-law Liang Sili, and thirteen boxes of medical supplies. They were still on board the *S.S. President Wilson,* bound for Hong Kong, when they heard radio news of the People's Republic's founding ceremony. Yan Renying, the famous gynecologist and obstetrician, was on the same ship and recalled that excited students devised improvised Chinese flags based on the radio's description. The author Lao She, who had been invited to visit America by the U.S. State Department in 1947, departed in October 1949.[54]

The new PRC government soon made clear that its foreign policy of leaning to one side placed it firmly within the socialist camp in direct opposition to the democratic capitalist stance of the United States. The United States continued to insist that the KMT regime represented China's legitimate government, even though it only controlled Taiwan and a few offshore islands. Domestically, cold war politics imposed orthodoxy, with a Republican pro-KMT bloc blaming the Democratic administration for "losing" China.

These hardening ideological lines forced millions of Chinese to relocate as they chose sides. In America, however, anticipation of the founding of the People's Republic and participation in the building of the new China continued to attract students and scholars even as the American government was indecisive about halting the exodus. In February 1950, renowned mathematics professor Loo-keng Hua had resigned his position as professor at the University of Illinois and arrived in Hong Kong with his family of five. Zhu Guangya, a CSCA and ACSWA member and nuclear physics PhD from University of Michigan, also left in February 1950 after publishing "An Open Letter to Chinese Students in America," in which he was one of fifty-two signatories asking Chinese students in America to answer China's call to return to build the nation.[55]

Many CCP members also hastened to heed the call to return to build the new China. Gong Pusheng, who was working at the United Nations, left for China in 1948 and made her way to Xibaipo, Hebei, where the CCP Central Committee and PLA headquarters were located. In July 1949, she married Zhang Hanfu in Shanghai, which the PLA had wrested from KMT hands a little more than a month earlier. In November 1950, she returned to the UN as part of a PRC delegation to discuss the Taiwan and Korea questions. The interpreter for the delegation was CSCA activist Pu Shoushan, who had left for China in summer of 1949. Pu

Shouchang followed in November, bringing what he had translated of Chairman Mao's selected essays. Paul Lin and his family also arrived in Beijing in 1950.[56]

In October 1950, Ji Chaozhu (Chao-chu Chi), the younger half-brother of C. T. Chi, dropped out of Harvard University to travel to Hong Kong on the same ship as the physicist Zhu Guangya. Two years later, Ji Chaozhu, Pu Shoushan, Pu Shouchang, and Zhu Guangya were among those who interpreted at Kaesong, Korea, for the Chinese delegation that negotiated with the American-led coalition to reach an armistice in the Korean conflict.[57]

Others, including the majority of students and a number of sojourning intellectuals such as the author Lin Yutang, also made conscious decisions to remain in America and other countries. Many individuals also chose to leave China. Hu Shi, the philosopher and educator turned politician, left China shortly before the PLA occupied Nanjing and joined tens of thousands of intellectuals, ex-bureaucrats, entrepreneurs, and professionals beginning their exiles abroad. Many families separated, as typically parents would follow the KMT while children stayed to welcome the Communists. Often, former friends, classmates, and colleagues physically confronted each other from opposite sides of the political fence. For example, while interpreting in Korea, in one session Ji Chaozhu found himself face to face with Harvard classmate Richard Liu interpreting for the American side.[58]

There was no analogous mass exodus to the new China among revolutionary supporters and sympathizers in the Chinese American community. Walter Chee Kwon Chun, who had returned to Honolulu to marry Junnie Wong in 1947, moved with his bride to Beijing in 1950, where he was assigned to work at the Foreign Affairs Publishing House.[59] However, most Chinese American sympathizers felt that America was their home, and they lacked the sense of temporary residence that was typical of China-born students. Moreover, even those who felt disaffected with life in America often lacked the skills, training, and political connections that could smooth their paths in China. Nonetheless, a limited number of Chinese Americans did respond to the siren call of the new order. For example, during the 1950s about a dozen CADYL members departed the United States to seek their futures in the PRC.

The exodus also affected *China Daily News,* the Left's most influential voice in America. Thomas Lem Tong returned to China in 1949. Chu Tong (Tang Mingzhao) departed in 1950, followed by his wife, Constance, and American-born daughter, Wensheng (Nancy Tong), leaving the paper in the hands of Eugene Moy. Others on the staff also left, eager to find roles in the exciting task of building a new China.[60]

Ironically, just as a new political order was being imposed over China, *China Daily News* faced a staffing crisis and found it increasingly difficult to find people willing to accept the financial sacrifices and political harassment connected with working on the paper. Besides recruiting locally in the New York region, the CCP organization in San Francisco also did its part to help alleviate this shortage.

During the early 1950s, it sent Paul Mar, former editor of *China Weekly*, to work on the *China Daily News*'s editorial staff. However, Mar found that he could not support his family this way and resigned. Around 1950 and 1951, recent immigrant and CADYL member Zheng Guang became editor. Zheng wrote under the pen name Huashan. Periodically during the early 1950s, San Francisco sent CADYL members Liang Liangbin and Chen Jinfu to be New York–based correspondents providing support to *China Daily News*. As the staffing crisis worsened in the 1950s with anti-Communist hysteria continuing in high gear through intimidating investigations into Chinese immigration fraud, the West Coast sent CADYL member Liang Biao in the mid-1950s to help manage certain non-editorial functions of the paper.

The Korean War and the Embargo

Chinese people in America confronted a particularly fraught political situation as the capitalist and communist worlds squared off against each other. Although many associate the cold war with the confrontation between the United States and the USSR, the Korean War brought the PRC into direct conflict with the United States. After North Korea invaded South Korea on June 25, 1950, on June 27 the United States, under the aegis of the United Nations, went to South Korea's aid and undertook several measures to secure the western Pacific from the spread of communism. It deployed the Seventh Fleet in the Taiwan Straits to block PRC attacks on the KMT's last, beleaguered stronghold. It banned oil shipments to China and intensified military aid to the Philippines and Indochina. U.S. general MacArthur launched a successful counteroffensive in September that penetrated deeply into North Korea and threatened China's borders. The PRC sent Chinese troops to support their North Korean allies, sending UN troops reeling back to the Thirty-sixth Parallel. The United States imposed a trade embargo on China on December 16, 1950. Hostilities between the United States and the PRC led many Chinese in America to fear that they would be placed in internment camps, as had Japanese Americans during World War II. Increased surveillance by FBI agents and intensified prosecution of citizenship fraud cases by immigration officials only cowed the community further. Among left-leaning Chinese newspapers, the *China Weekly* was the first to fall, when the owners of *Chinese Pacific Weekly*, anticipating a government crackdown on the Left, refused to continue printing the paper. The venerable *Chung Sai Yat Po* was the next to go, in January 1951 when fear drove away large numbers of subscribers and advertisers. By the year's end, Henry Tsoi left for China, leaving Lawrence Lowe responsible for West Coast party affairs.[61] In 1952 the Department of Justice indicted *China Daily News* for alleged violations of the Trading with the Enemy Act.[62] Many members of the Left were deported or forced to depart "voluntarily." By the end of the 1950s, the Chinese

American Left had been so harassed and persecuted that, like the mainstream American Left, it became an inconsequential political force.[63]

The newsletter *Liu Mei Xuesheng Tongxun* ceased publication during the latter half of 1950, after most of its editorial staff departed for China. Chen Han-seng and his wife took a circuitous route from New York to Europe to reach Beijing in early 1951, where they were joined by Situ Huimin in 1952.[64]

This steady stream of departures attracted the attention of the federal government. In March 1951, the *New York Times* columnist James Reston, whom one critic described as being "a kind of advance man for U.S. government policy," wrote that many Chinese students were members of the CSCA or ACSWA and that the Department of Justice regarded their leaders as subversives.[65] Although investigated by government agencies, neither organization was included in the Department of Justice's list of subversive groups. However, growing anti-Communist hysteria in America and the departure of so many members led the ACSWA leadership to decide to dissolve on September 19, 1950.[66] In 1951 the Committee on Friendly Relations among Foreign Students of the International Committee of the YMCAs of North America also withdrew its support from the CSCA. That summer representatives from the eastern, midwestern, and western district departments agreed to disband the CSCA after four decades of activity.[67]

From early on, American authorities had felt uneasy that large numbers of Chinese students were interested in returning to their Communist-dominated homeland. Even before Chinese troops joined the Korean War, the U.S. government had tried to prevent Chinese scientists from leaving. In the most celebrated case, the jet propulsion expert Qian Xuesen (Tsien Hsue-shen) was barred from departing in August 1950. Other scholars were allowed to board the *S.S. President Wilson*, only to have U.S. authorities detain three among them, all graduates of the California Institute of Technology, upon the ship's arrival in Japan.[68] These scholars were probably targeted because they were from the same institution as Qian Xuesen and some bureaucrats suspected they might be smuggling scientific and technological secrets for him. No other Chinese scientists or technological experts on board were detained. The trio was released forty-seven days later, but only after strong international protests.[69] At this time, the U.S. Immigration and Naturalization Service (INS) had not yet formulated a definite policy regarding the departure of Chinese intellectuals, especially those in science and technology. Thus, a few scholars still managed to depart successfully. One of the late departers was Hou Xianglin, the ACSWA executive secretary, who boarded a Norwegian freighter in May 1950 and reached Qingdao on June 26, just after the outbreak of the hostilities in Korea.[70] Huang Baotong, who received an MS in chemistry at Texas Technological College and was the leader of the New York chapters of the CSCA and ACSWA, was not so fortunate. Immigration authorities arrested him on the grounds that his visa had expired and detained him on Ellis Island for 114 days before he was freed on bail. He was required to report weekly to the INS. Huang had no recourse but to return to the Brooklyn Institute of Technology to complete his doctorate, which he did in 1952, and then bided his time. Other activists were similarly detained and ruled deportable but with temporary holds on their departure.[71]

In June 1951, the U.S. Government issued orders officially restraining Chinese students and experts, especially those in the sciences and engineering, from leaving for the PRC. In September, when the *S.S. Cleveland* docked at Honolulu with nine students bound for China among the passengers, the INS detained the students, returned them to the U.S. mainland, and forbade them to leave. The Department of Justice issued restraining orders to about 120 students, mostly in the sciences, technology, and medicine, who had requested permission to depart for China.[72]

Students soon learned about these restrictions, and many did not even bother to apply for permission to leave. Instead they bided their time by immersing themselves in research, teaching in academia, or working in American industries. A rare few, like Mei Zuyan, who graduated with an MS in hydraulic engineering from the Illinois Institute of Technology in 1951, succeeded in slipping out of the country. Mei managed to obtain a visa from a careless French consulate employee in New York with a passport that had already expired. He reached Paris in 1954 and then renewed his passport at the Republic of China embassy there. He and another student from the United States then traveled to Switzerland to contact the PRC delegation that had arrived for an international conference. After reporting on the plight of Chinese students in America, the two obtained PRC passports and flew to Beijing via the Soviet Union.[73]

Mei's success, however, stemmed from a series of fortuitous circumstances. Most other students could only remain in America and fight for their right to return home. Liu Zhujin, holder of a PhD in chemistry from the University of Rochester, received a restraining order in 1952 and appealed his case to the INS repeatedly. His wife in Shanghai also wrote to Premier Zhou Enlai asking for the PRC government's help in ending the detention of the Chinese students. Liu finally received permission to depart in June 1955.[74]

Li Hengde played a leading role in these struggles. He had joined the CCP as a university student in China and edited the *ACSWA Monthly Newsletter* from summer 1949 to summer 1950. In winter 1950, the INS interrogated him for eight hours. In summer 1951, he lost his job as a researcher at the University of Pennsylvania, when the government decided that he could no longer participate in a Department of Navy research project. Without a job to pay for his education, Li sought to depart for China but was not allowed to leave. Li was interrogated again in October, after which special agents searched his home without a warrant. The INS officially warned Li not to leave the United States and that he faced a five-thousand-dollar fine, or up to five years of imprisonment, if he violated the order. The United States confiscated his passport and required him to report his whereabouts and activities every three months.[75]

In summer 1952, when the Korean War had stalemated, Li met with fourteen student friends in New Jersey. They agreed to try to return home. Each member contacted other students who shared this goal. This clandestine network soon included several dozen students in the East and Midwest. In May 1953, American progressive channels delivered to Zhou Enlai a letter signed by fifteen students, asking the Chinese government to help them leave the United States. At the end of 1953, the Indian Embassy accepted another letter with fifteen signatures addressed to Zhou Enlai. A third letter signed by sixteen students was entrusted to a Europe-bound friend for the Chinese delegation attending the Geneva International Conference on Indochina in March 1954.

In March 1954, U.S. newspapers published reports of the detention of the Chinese students, to the amazement of most Americans. Twenty-six students sent a letter to President Eisenhower, senators, organizations, and the media appealing to be allowed to be reunited with their families in China. Thirty students signed an open letter to the United Nations as well. The students also sought support from liberal groups such as the American Civil Liberties Union.

The Geneva U.S.-PRC Talks

In the meantime, the PRC and the United States met across the negotiating table for the first time at the Geneva Conference, even though U.S. Secretary of State John Foster Dulles still had not acknowledged the legitimacy of the People's Republic. The fate of the Chinese students was negotiated at the ambassadorial level. Wang Bingnan, ambassador to Poland, led the Chinese delegation, while U. Alexis Johnson, ambassador to Czechoslovakia, represented the United States. China's Foreign Ministry set up a special committee consisting of Zhang Hanfu, Qiao Guanhua, Gong Peng (sister of Gong Pusheng), Pu Shoushan, and Wang Baoliu to advise the delegation. After protracted talks, the two ambassadors announced an agreement on September 10, 1955, whereby the United States lifted the restraining order on Chinese students, while the PRC agreed to release Americans imprisoned in China. In 1956 Lai Yali became councilor at the embassy to Switzerland, and at that time he also advised Ambassador Wang as negotiations continued regarding other issues.[76]

Li Hengde finally departed in November on the *S.S. President Wilson,* and most other detainees also left eventually.[77] The rocket scientist Qian Xuesen was also "deported" in 1955. The fact that the students were already physically in the country worked to the United States' advantage. As individual students settled down into families and successful careers, an increasing number who had intended to return changed their minds and decided to stay. In the end only a minority of the Chinese students in America, some seven hundred to a thousand, chose to return to China.[78] Under the circumstances, this was perhaps the most that the PRC could have hoped for considering the obstacles.

Anti-Communist Hysteria Persecutions

During the 1950s, federal authorities stepped up surveillance and harassment of progressive individuals and organizations. Such scrutiny dated from the 1930s, when the House Special Committee on Un-American Activities had already cited Chu Tong, Benjamin Fee, C. T. Chi, Jack Chen, and others for their connections to Communist activities. During World War II, accusations of Communism flew again, when both Chi Kung-ch'uan and Chu Tong worked at the Office of War Information in New York. Tong, in particular, fell under suspicion for his connections with the CHLA, which was "reputed to be an organization affiliated with the Communist Party," and the *China Daily News* was "said to be a publication by and for the Chinese Communists." Only after lengthy discussions were Chi and Tong ruled eligible for the positions.[79] Through the late 1940s, such harassment occurred as isolated cases and did not fall into consistent patterns.

Open Season on Progressives

The coming of the cold war and its rabidly anti-Communist climate began open season on progressives. The anti-Communist bogeyman had reared its head even before the end of World War II, when Agnes Smedley had been accused of being a Communist sympathizer for objecting to Jim Crow laws in the South. The press published smear stories and innuendo that forced Smedley to move to England, where she passed away in 1950. Edgar Snow also became a target and was questioned by the FBI regarding the extent of his Communist activities. The harassment made it increasingly difficult for him to make a living, and so he moved to Geneva, Switzerland. Anna Louise Strong fared differently. Although long regarded as a Communist sympathizer, she was arrested by Soviet authorities while on her way to China in 1949 and charged with espionage. The charge was dropped in 1955, but she decided in 1958 to move permanently to China, where she edited the English-language monthly *Letter from China* for worldwide distribution.[80]

Talitha Gerlach returned to China in July 1946 to continue her work at the YWCA. Madam Sun invited her to serve on the executive committee of the China Welfare Institute, but Gerlach was recalled back to the United States in December 1947. In the changed political climate, activities that had once been praised were now regarded as treasonous. Newspapers began accusing the China Aid Council of being a Communist front, and it was added to the Attorney General's list of subversive organizations. Under mounting pressure, the council ceased operations on November 23, 1948. Some active council members decided to continue their mission and founded China Welfare Appeal in April 1949, and Talitha Gerlach became board chairperson. This new organization soon made it onto the Attorney General's list, and the YWCA decided to terminate its connection with Gerlach, despite her service of over two decades. Then approaching sixty, Gerlach decided to accept Madam Sun's invitation to return to China in 1951 to become an advisor at the China Welfare Institute. The journalist Israel Epstein, another founder of China Welfare Appeal, also investigated the possibility of returning to China when the PRC delegation came to the UN in November 1950 to discuss the Korean War. Epstein contacted delegation advisor Qiao Guanhua, whom he had known in Hong Kong. Madam Sun issued the requested invitation, and Epstein and his wife, Elsie Fairfax-Cholmeley, left separately for Europe in 1951 to meet in Poland, from whence they sailed to Tianjin. In 1952 Epstein became executive editor of *China Reconstructs,* which had been founded by Madam Sun, while Fairfax-Cholmeley supervised the publishing.[81]

The Epsteins joined a growing coterie of foreigners working alongside Chinese editors on foreign-language publications targeting readers abroad. Shortly before their arrival, Jack Chen had returned from England and subsequently worked for twenty-one years with *People's China* and *Peking Review.*[82]

Immigrant Chinese members of the left who had been in America many years also became targets. Thomas T. Y. Hu, one of the Chaotao eight, had been active in All-American Anti-Imperialist League and joined the Communist Party in 1927. Due to his opposition to the Chiang Kai-shek regime, the Nanjing government discontinued funding his education in the United States and issued orders for his arrest. Hu subsequently left the Communist Party, and during World War II, was active in the Washington, D.C., area organizing support for China's war effort working closely with the China Aid Council. After the cold war began, Hu, like many other progressives, became targets of investigation by the federal government. In 1951 he decided to return to China after an absence of more than a quarter century.[83] Frank K. M. Su, who had been active in Philadelphia doing publicity for American Friends of the Chinese People and China Aid Council during World War II, went to Beijing in 1953 with his American wife and daughter, going by way of Sweden and the Soviet Union.[84] Jack Chen's sister, the dancer Si-lan Chen, and her husband, Jay Leyda, also left Hollywood and spent the next twenty years abroad, mostly in London. The couple went to Beijing at the urging of Jack Chen and his cousin Dai Ailian, who headed the Beijing Ballet School. Si-lan Chen became an advisor there from 1959 to 1964, while her husband consulted for the China Film Archives.[85]

Federal authorities targeted leftist organizations, particularly the prominent *China Daily News.* In 1952 the Justice Department indicted the *China Daily News,* its editor Eugene Moy, business manager Albert Wong, and three CHLA members from the board of directors on fifty-three counts of violating the Trading with the Enemy Act. Until the 1950s, this had been a little-known law enacted during World War I that had never been enforced. The charges accused the newspaper of accepting payment from the PRC-owned Nanyang Bank of Hong Kong for advertisements. The other defendants had allegedly sent money to relatives and acquaintances on the Chinese mainland. In the prevailing anti-Communist climate, there was little doubt about the verdicts, and all but Albert Wong were found guilty in 1954. The court fined the paper twenty-five thousand dollars. Moy and the other defendants received jail sentences of two years and one year respectively, although after appeal the court halved the jail sentences.

These indictments and convictions sent the Chinese Marxist Left reeling. The newspaper's circulation dropped precipitously. Only financial contributions from still-loyal readers across the country enabled it to cover annual operating deficits. Nonetheless, the paper went into semiweekly publication in 1962.

Membership in left-wing Chinese organizations declined sharply during the 1950s, as apprehensive Chinese stayed away. In San Francisco, the CWMAA closed its doors permanently in 1954 with only about twenty members. In New York, the Chinese Youth Club dissolved at about the same time. The Chinese Hand Laundry Alliance nearly suffered the same fate. When Chinese armed forces entered the Korean War, the CHLA refused to join the anti-Communist campaign launched by the Chinese Consolidated Benevolent Association and was expelled for this intransigence.[86] Throughout the 1950s, FBI agents continually harassed progressive CHLA members. In conjunction with declines in the Chinese laundry business, this led to a great drop in CHLA membership. Although this organization of laundry operators stubbornly clung to existence, its influence on the New York Chinese community diminished greatly.

In San Francisco, CADYL—which had become better known as Mun Ching—survived somewhat longer with an infusion of recently immigrated teenagers during the early 1950s. The club changed its emphasis to educational, cultural, and social activities for its forty to fifty members. In 1952 it initiated counseling and tutoring programs to help members and friends pursue more education, particularly in professional and technological fields.

During this period, the KMT's control of Chinatown institutions restricted the club's cultural activities primarily to its basement clubrooms at 812 Stockton Street. Despite these limitations, Mun Ching presented what was probably the most active program of Chinese cultural events at the time, including two or three performances each year featuring vernacular and sometimes musical dramas and choral singing. The club was among the first to teach and perform Chinese folk dances learned from the new immigrants. It also published *Mun Ching*, a mimeographed Chinese-language biweekly, which became one of the first American publications to use the simplified characters introduced by the PRC in 1956. The club also pioneered the use of the Hanyu Pinyin Romanization spelling system, which is widely used today to teach Chinese language in American schools and universities. Although such activities were a retreat from the political advocacy espoused by earlier progressives, Mun Ching was forced to close in 1959 when it lost the use of its clubrooms. The members reorganized as the Haiyan [Petrel] Club, but the new group itself faded away within a few years.

During the anti-Communist hysteria of the cold war, the U.S. Attorney General had produced a list of "subversive" organizations for use in the federal employee security program. No Chinatown progressive organizations were ever officially designated as "subversive," but Chinese American progressives and their organizations nonetheless did not escape the attention of congressional fact-finding committees. For example, in 1952 the Senate Internal Security Committee subpoenaed *China Daily News* editor Eugene Moy, and the House Committee on Un-American Activities summoned World Theater manager Lawrence Lowe in 1956 and *China Daily News* editor James Lee in 1957. All refused to testify on Fifth Amendment grounds.

Despite the shrinking numbers of the Chinese Marxist Left, federal agencies zealously continued to hound them and allied progressive organizations for over two decades. Intelligence agencies spent untold hours investigating groups and individuals. Businesses owned by progressives—such as Oasis Bookstore, World Theater, and Royal Cathay (Francis Leong was a partner), all in San Francisco—found their supply sources blocked as United States Customs agents closely scrutinized and impounded any goods remotely suspected of originating in the PRC or even Hong Kong establishments connected with the PRC. Because of these supply problems, Oasis Bookstore closed down in 1957. World Theater remained in operation by rerunning existing films and occasionally purchasing new films from Hong Kong, while Royal Cathay shifted to other East Asian countries for products.

Many CADYL members inducted into the armed forces failed to receive security clearances. Even though some had served in the Korean War, the army tried to give them general discharges, and they had to seek the help of the American Civil Liberties Union to obtain honorable ones.

All this harassment undercut the effectiveness of the Chinese Marxist Left and its associated progressives, but it was the Immigration and Naturalization Service that dealt the coup de grâce through its power to deport aliens deemed to be threats to national security. The deportees included the actress Wang Ying and her husband, Xie Hegeng. The two, who had student visas, were imprisoned by immigration authorities for two months and then deported to the PRC on charges that they had written articles and editorials for the *China Daily News* and *China Tribune.* They were also accused of associating with pro-PRC journalist Agnes Smedley and helping her write a biography of Zhu De, commander-in-chief of the People's Liberation Army.[87]

America's legal exclusion of Chinese immigrants (1882–1943) had produced decades of illegal immigration by Chinese people who entered using fraudulent claims of citizenship or exempt class status, or simply by jumping ship. Authorities were well acquainted with this reality, and the Justice Department began investigating and prosecuting Chinese immigration fraud cases with extra vigor in the early 1950s to target members of the Left. In New York, immigration authorities deported or forced the "voluntary" departure of *China Daily News* staff members Zhang Manli, Yee Sun Jok, and others, along with editor Huashan and correspondent Chen Jinfu, both CADYL members sent from San Francisco. CHLA members associated with *China Daily News,* such as Chen Ke, Louie Pon, Chen Houfu and Fang Fu'er, were also expelled.[88] The continued threat of such prosecutions made it even more difficult to recruit qualified staff for the newspaper.

On the West Coast, the INS deported progressive writer and OCLPDC member Cao Fengji in 1955.[89] World Theater owners Karl Fung and Lawrence Lowe were charged with fraudulent citizenship.[90] Karl Fung chose to leave for Hong Kong in 1957 when threatened with a prison term, while the Lowe case abruptly ended when he died in an automobile accident in 1962. *Chung Sai Yat Po* major shareholder Sam Wah You faced similar charges, as did the CWMAA's Happy Lim and other active progressives. Four members of the Chinese American Youth Club—Kai G. Dere, Maurice Chuck, Jackson Chan, and Wing Joe—were indicted and tried in court. The government even forced Maurice Chuck's father to undergo the traumatic ordeal of testifying against his son in court.[91]

Numerous Chinese progressives, including more than half of the Chinese American Youth Club, lost their American citizenship because either they or their parents had entered the country using fraudulent claims of citizenship. They received permanent residence or citizenship status only after lengthy legal proceedings and thus lived with the threat of deportation hanging over their heads for extended periods.

By the mid-1950s, with the departure of most of the left-wing Chinese intellectuals and the prosecution of many leftists and progressives in the Chinese American community, Chinese American left-wing activities diminished drastically and became for all practical purposes completely irrelevant in American society.

The Civil Rights Movement and Emergence of a New Left

By the mid-1950s, the high tide of anti-Communist hysteria as exemplified by the McCarthy hearings had begun to recede somewhat. The civil rights movement was beginning under the leadership of African Americans and led ultimately to the enactment of the Civil Rights Act of 1964. The civil rights movement had little impact on Chinese Americans until the mid-1960s, when the Civil Rights Act and the accompanying War on Poverty brought government funding and service agencies into their communities. Many young Asian Americans joined the anti–Vietnam War movement that followed. These activities enabled campus and community activists, mostly American-born, to push for changes in communities heretofore dominated by the alliance between traditional associations and the KMT.

New Left organizations emerged with political philosophies that ranged from democratic liberalism to neo-Marxism. They concentrated principally on such domestic issues as discrimination, employment, equal rights, and social justice along the lines of the old Left. Internationally, they worked to foster friendship between the United States and the PRC. By this time, the older generation of Chinese American leftists did not play much of a role because many had retired or passed on. Although a few of the relatively younger older leftists played minor supporting or advisory roles, there was a distance with the new leftists, who were predominantly American-born and middle class. A number did participate in activities to improve U.S.-PRC relations and understanding such as showing films from China, joining U.S.-PRC People's Friendship Associations and celebrating China's National Day on October 1.

After the founding of the PRC, the relationship between the CCP and the Chinese Marxist Left and progressives in America changed fundamentally. The Communist-led Chinese government began playing a major role in the international Communist movement, rivaling the Soviet Union. When PRC disputes with the USSR began in the mid-1950s and split the seemingly monolithic Communist world, the CPUSA and its allies supported the Soviets, while the Chinese Marxist Left and its associated groups turned toward the CCP. By this time, however, the Chinese Marxist Left, along with the CPUSA and its associated progressive groups, had been so battered by anti-Communist repression that this schism had little effect on either the Chinese American community or the new Chinese American Left. The PRC itself had hardly any presence in the United States. With the split in the international Communist movement, the isolation of the Chinese American community was intensified by hostile relations between the PRC and the United States and the American-imposed embargo on trade and commerce. The main sign of the PRC in America were publications imported by China Books and Periodicals, which Henry and Gertrude Noyes had established in Chicago in 1959, before they moved to San Francisco in 1964.[92]

The PRC did not have an official presence on American soil until after 1971, when it assumed China's seat at the United Nations after the United States withheld its support for the KMT regime in Taiwan as representing China. PRC diplomats actively encouraged Chinese progressives to act in ways that furthered China's national interests by appealing more to their sense of nationalism than to revolutionary ideals. During the 1970s, the Left helped by urging normalization of relations between the United States and the PRC. With the exchange of full diplomatic missions in 1979 and China's open policy the same year, the PRC embarked on a proto-capitalist path of soliciting investment capital, business acumen, and technological expertise from abroad to develop the national economy. Most of the old Left often could not play major roles in such projects.

As relations between China and the United States continued to develop, the PRC sought a stronger voice in America, especially among the Chinese American community. In order to facilitate these efforts, the PRC turned often to those cadres who had spent time working with Chinese overseas or had sojourned in the United States. When China took its place at the United Nations in November 1971, Qiao Guanhua and Huang Hua were head and deputy of the PRC delegation, respectively. Chu Tong (Tang Mingzhao) returned to New York as one of the undersecretaries in 1972. He soon engineered a reorganization of the *China Daily News,* the newspaper he helped to found in the 1930s. Old Left shareowners, including CHLA activists, were shunted aside to honorary but impotent status. Liang Biao was forced out of the newspaper. The newspaper resumed daily publication in 1977 and expanded operations. Pro-PRC interests extended capital and advertising accounts, enabling the paper to purchase a building and new equipment. The corporation expanded rapidly into a multi-enterprise conglomerate by the mid-1980s. Younger intellectual activists emerged with the Protect Diaoyutai movement and took control along with the New Left.[93]

In 1973, a year after the PRC assumed China's seat at the United Nations, Ji Chaozhu came to Washington, D.C., as councilor on the PRC delegation sent to establish and operate a liaison office for laying the groundwork for resumption of normal diplomatic relations. In 1979 he was the interpreter accompanying Deng Xiaoping when the latter visited America. In 1991 he became a UN undersecretary general.[94] Between 1975 and 1981, Lai Yali returned to New York to serve as the deputy head of the permanent Chinese delegation to the United Nations.[95]

The thawing of Sino-U.S. relations, in conjunction with passage of the 1965 Immigration Act, transformed the Chinese American community. Chinese immigration surged during the 1980s, as the PRC, Taiwan, and Hong Kong all received separate quotas permitting legal entry to the United States. Immigrants and refugees came from Hong Kong, Taiwan, Indochina, and other troubled or economically disadvantaged parts of the world. The PRC relaxed its restrictive emigration policy after normalizing relations, generating great increases in the numbers immigrating directly from China, including students and workers, legal and illegal, from all over the country. The Chinese American community diversified, as the older Cantonese community became only one part of a complex mosaic.

The bloody crackdown on students at Tian'anmen Square on June 4, 1989, temporarily derailed the improving relations between the United States and China. Among Chinese Americans, this tragedy split the ranks of the Left and progressives. In New York, the *China Daily News* supported the student demonstrators and attacked the actions of the PRC government. When PRC-connected interests cut off their funding, the paper's board, headed by Wayne Tam, decided to cease publication altogether in August 1989. The CHLA, which had been shunted aside when the *China Daily News* reorganized, now denounced the newspaper's management and reaffirmed its support for the PRC government.

In January 1990, the *China Daily News* reopened as the weekly *China Press,* with Zheng Yide, a former *China Daily News* staffer, as chief editor. The paper's Chinese name, *Qiao Bao,* was a link to its historic past, for it was a term that had been extensively used as the shortened form of *Huaqiao Ribao.* By September the paper had resumed daily publication. Xiong Feiwen, from the Hong Kong office of the PRC's China News Agency, became the first head of the new newspaper, which is backed by pro-PRC capital. The paper soon became a national newspaper by expanding to San Francisco and Los Angeles.

In San Francisco, the Lowe family received infusions of new capital from pro-PRC Hong Kong investors in 1983 after suffering losses in the World Theater since the 1970s. They constructed a new four-story building on the site. The Lowe family, however, became minority partners in the newly established Golden Harbour Corporation. A representative from the majority partner assumed control in 1986 and sold the building in 1990 to another Hong Kong group. Using part of its share of the capital gains, the Lowe family established the Lawrence Choy Lowe Memorial Foundation to fund Chinese American progressive activities. The World Theater closed on December 28, 1995, because the widespread availability of feature films on videocassettes ate into attendance at the theater.[96] Thus, the last vestiges of the old Chinese Marxist Left-progressive movement in San Francisco disappeared. New York's CHLA was the only organization remaining that was still strongly pro-PRC. It no longer serves a useful function, as Chinese laundries are a dying industry; however, it still maintains a clubroom where aging members can chat and socialize.

Since the resumption of diplomatic relations, the PRC has built its own infrastructure and network in the United States, with staff who establish offices and agencies for press services, film and television, trade, travel, exchange programs, and the like. At the same time, PRC diplomats have effectively reached out to community organizations, professional and business groups, academics, and others to extend their circle of contacts. This ability to appeal to a broader range of groups stems more from China's national interests than Marxist ideology and appeals more to feelings of ethnic pride or business and professional opportunities than the idea of attaining the lofty goal of a Communist utopia.

Concluding Overview

During the nineteenth and twentieth centuries, Chinese Leftists were inspired by ideologies that promised to create better versions of society. To attain these ideals, Chinese Leftists and progressives made great personal sacrifices and waged struggles against great odds in opposition to those equally determined to maintain the status quo or follow different paths.

Chinese Americans first learned about anarchism and Marxism toward the end of the nineteenth century, mostly through Chinese-language translations and essays coming from East Asia. Around the turn-of-the-twentieth century, exiled Chinese nationalists recruited adherents among Chinese Americans. As political refugees living abroad, it is not surprising that many of the Left's activities focused on political developments in China. As local Chinese began joining the leftist movement, domestic concerns also came into play, forcing the Left to address such issues as unemployment, economic exploitation, and racial discrimination in the United States. These two orientations, sometimes complementary and sometimes conflicting, shaped the trajectory of the Chinese American Left and shifted in importance with changes in international and domestic conditions.

During the early twentieth century, Chinese Left efforts to attract support often faltered in the face of the small numbers and the isolated status of Chinese Americans, despite some initial successes. The rise of the Marxist Left and establishment of the USSR and the Communist International changed this situation. As part of an international movement, the Chinese Marxist Left in America developed under more favorable conditions from the late 1920s to the 1950s.

During these early years, Marxist Left activities in America focused almost exclusively on advancing the cause of the Chinese revolution, an unsurprising priority considering that many members were sojourning students. The 1927 split between the KMT and the CCP was a tremendous setback, from which Leftists recovered through the anti-Fascist struggle. Millions of Chinese flocked to the CCP as the main proponents of national salvation and resistance to the Japanese invasion during the 1930s. Due to the importance of China in the international scene, numerous Chinese and non-Chinese people continued to be involved in activities connected with the Communist revolution during and after the 1920s. Moreover, the fact that many were engaged in these activities in the United States and China at different times virtually guaranteed that the Communist revolution continued to be an important part of Communist activities in America.

However, during the Great Depression, the Marxist Left managed to plant roots in the Chinese communities of New York and San Francisco by addressing issues of discrimination and employment important to the working-class Chinese Americans. The international Communist movement, particularly the CPUSA, was tremendously helpful in these endeavors. However, success was limited by the preponderance of illegal immigrants in the adult population of Chinese America, who had entered the United States only by circumventing the racist exclusion laws. Their vulnerable legal status inhibited many from becoming politically active until the War of Resistance against Japan galvanized nationalist fervor. After World War II, the civil war between the Communists and the KMT absorbed the attention of the Chinese American Left. With the founding of the PRC in 1949, a mass exodus of scholars and students responded to the Communist leadership's summons to help build the new China. The outbreak of the cold war and accompanying anti-Communist hysteria in America enabled the U.S. government to use investigations of widespread illegal immigration fraud as a pretext to intimidate the Chinese American community and to harass leftists by threatening to strip them of citizenship and render them liable for deportation. These developments seriously weakened the Chinese American Left, which for all practical purposes became ineffective by the end of the 1950s. By the time U.S.-PRC relations began thawing in the 1970s, the CCP had broken with the Communist Party of the USSR in the 1960s, and the international Communist movement was no longer monolithic. The Chinese American Left organizations of the 1950s had either disappeared or were so seriously weakened that they were mostly superseded by newer groups that were more effective. *China Daily News* resumed daily publication, which was made possible only by infusion of capital and support of institutions connected with the PRC. However, the old Chinese American Left did leave legacies in the political and cultural spheres for later generation of progressives to build upon, especially in the areas of U.S.-China friendship activities and civil rights.

NOTES

Introduction

1. This description is taken from Peter Monaghan, "The Scholar Who Legitimized the Study of Chinese America," *Chronicle of Higher Education* 46, no. 19 (Jan. 14, 2000), A21.

2. William Petersen, "Success Story, Japanese-American Style," *New York Times Magazine* Jan. 8, 1966, 21–26; and "Success Story of One Minority in the U.S.," *U.S. News and World Report,* Dec. 26, 1966, 73–78.

3. "America's Super Minority," *Fortune,* Nov. 24, 1986, 148–49.

4. See the cover story of *Time,* Aug. 31, 1987, 42–51. Also see David Bell, "The Triumph of Asian Americans," *New Republic,* July 1985, 24–31; "A Formula for Success," *Newsweek,* Apr. 23, 1984, 77–78; and "Asian Americans: Are They Making the Grade?" *U.S. News and World Report,* April 1984, 4–8, 12–13.

5. See Mae Ngai, *Impossible Subjects: Illegal Aliens and the Making of Modern America* (Princeton, N.J.: Princeton University Press, 2004), 37.

6. Ngai, *Impossible Subjects,* 170.

7. See K. Scott Wong and Sucheng Chan, ed., *Claiming America: Constructing Chinese American Identities during the Exclusion Era* (Philadelphia: Temple University Press, 1998), for essays exploring this facet of Chinese American identity.

8. Christina Klein, *Cold War Orientalism: Asia in the Middlebrow Imagination, 1945–1961* (Berkeley: University of California Press, 2003), 224.

9. Klein, *Cold War Orientalism,* 226.

10. Rose Hum Lee, *The Chinese in the United States of America* (Hong Kong: Hong Kong University Press, 1960), 1.

11. Mae Ngai offers the following analysis of the evolution of the model minority exchange: "I suggest that the tortuous trajectory of Asian American citizenship during World War II–cold war period gestured ultimately toward its rehabilitation. The postwar reconstruction of Asian American citizenship, along with the end of exclusion, signaled the beginnings of a major, if costly, transformation in social and racial status of Asian Americans" (Ngai, *Impossible Subjects,* 170).

12. See Klein, *Cold War Orientalism,* 24. Klein contrasts the global imaginary of containment against the global imaginary of integration. The former "imagined the Cold War as a crusade against communism. . . . Much of the energy it generated, however, was directed inward and aimed at ferreting out enemies and subversives within the nation itself." The latter "represented the Cold War as an opportunity to forge intellectual and emotional bonds with the people of Asia and Africa. . . . When it did turn inward, the global imaginary of integration generated an inclusive rather than a policing energy" (23).

13. Klein, *Cold War Orientalism,* 25.

14. For more on Qian, see Iris Chang, *Thread of the Silkworm* (New York: Basic Books, 1995).

15. See Renqiu Yu, *To Save China, to Save Ourselves: The Chinese Hand Laundry Alliance of New York* (Philadelphia: Temple University Press, 1995), and Tung-pok Chin with Winifred C. Chin, *Paper Son: One Man's Story* (Philadelphia: Temple University Press, 2000).

16. First published in San Francisco by the Chinese Historical Society of America, 1969.

17. See *Bulletin of Concerned Asian Scholars* 4, no. 3 (Fall 1972): 10–21.

18. "Historical Survey of the Chinese Left in America," in *Counterpoint: Perspectives on Asian America,* ed. Emma Gee (Los Angeles: UCLA Asian American Studies Center, 1976), 152–59; "To Bring Forth a New China, to Build a Better America: The Chinese Marxist Left in America to the 1960s," *Chinese America: History and Perspectives* 6 (1992): 3–82; "The Chinese Marxist Left, Chinese Students and Scholars in America, and the New China: Mid-1940s to Mid-1950s," *Chinese America: History and Perspectives* 18 (2004): 7–25.

19. "Roots and Changing Identity of the Chinese in the United States," in "The Living Tree: The Changing Meaning of Being Chinese Today," ed. Tu Weiming, special issue, *Daedalus* 120 (Spring 1991): 189.

Chapter 1: China and the Chinese American Community

1. For a detailed discussion of these organizations and their interrelationships see Him Mark Lai, "Historical Development of the Chinese Consolidated Benevolent Association/ *Huiguan* System," *Chinese America: History and Perspectives* 1 (1987): 13–51.

2. Lai, "Historical Development of the *Huiguan* System"; Pei Chi Liu, *An Anecdotal History of the Chinese in the United States of America* (Taipei: Liming wenhua shiye gufen youxian gongsi, 1984), 275–80.

In 1907–8 the Dutch and Chinese governments disputed the national status of an ethnic Chinese person born in the Dutch East Indies. The Dutch claimed that all such Chinese were Dutch subjects under the *jus soli* principle and claimed that China had no code of nationality. China proclaimed its nationality law in 1909 to refute the Dutch argument and to consolidate China's claims that all ethnic Chinese regardless of place of birth or residence were Chinese subjects under the *jus sanguinis* principle. The issuing of diplomatic passports to *huiguan* presidents continued up to the 1920s, when the United States refused to recognize their diplomatic status.

3. Pei Chi Liu, *A History of the Chinese in the United States of America* (Taipei: Overseas Chinese Affairs Commission of the Legislative Yuan, 1976), 213–14, 355–59; Liu, *An Anecdotal History,* 579.

4. Liu, *An Anecdotal History,* 497. In 1882 the CCBA of San Francisco donated more than 30,000 yuan toward relief of the drought in Zhili (now Hebei). Kong Chow Association, the highest donor with 2,000 taels, received an award. In 1889 the CCBA raised more than 29,000 yuan for relief of flood victims in eastern Anhui, Jiangsu, and Henan. The Yeong Wo and Ning Yung Associations received imperial plaques for their donations. Eight persons from the Chen (Chan) clan donated more than 3,000 yuan, and Chen Zhiquan received a title. As late as 1905 and 1908, the imperial government continued to confer honors on major donors to disaster relief.

5. David T. H. Lee, *A History of Chinese in Canada* (Vancouver: Jianada ziyou chubanshe, 1967), 455–56.

6. Liu, *History of Chinese in the U.S.,* 228–30. Qing officials were completely impotent in their attempts to curb assassinations and murders by secret societies, popularly known as tong wars, which were common during this period. In 1888 all imperial minister Zhang Yinhuan could do was to issue an edict admonishing and appealing to the secret societies that fell on deaf ears.

7. Pei Chi Liu, *A History of the Chinese in the United States of America* (Taipei: Liming wenhua shiye gufen youxian gongsi, 1981), 2:469, 471–73.

8. *Chung Sai Yat Po,* Mar. 26, 30, Apr. 27, 29, June 22, 1908; *Chinese World,* Oct. 2, 1911, Sept. 3, 1912. A Chinese gunboat intercepted a Japanese ship, *Tatsu Maru,* which was smuggling a consignment of munitions into the Pearl River Delta for a Chinese merchant near Macao, and confiscated its cargo. The Japanese government demanded that the Chinese government pay for damages and issue an official apology, terms that Cantonese officials considered humiliating. Hong Kong merchants initiated a boycott of Japanese goods that lasted about eight months. San Francisco's Chinese Chamber of Commerce also passed a resolution supporting the boycott, which was not repealed until September 1912.

9. L. Eve Armentrout Ma, *Revolutionaries, Monarchists, and Chinatowns: Chinese Politics in the Americas and the 1911 Revolution* (Honolulu: University of Hawai'i Press, 1990), 33–35, 114; Silas K. C. Geneson, "Cry Not in Vain: The Boycott of 1905," *Chinese America: History and Perspectives* 11 (1997): 27–45; Eugene Anschel, *Homer Lea, Sun Yat-sen, and the Chinese Revolution* (New York: Praeger Publishers, 1984), 37–49; Kongsun Lum, ed., *Hawaii Chinese in the Foreign Language School Case: A Memorial Publication* (Honolulu: Hawaii Chinese Educational Association and Chung Wah Chung Kung Hui, 1950), 220–40.

10. H. M. Lai, "The Chinese American Press," in *The Ethnic Press in the United States: A Historical Analysis and Handbook,* ed. Sally M. Miller (New York: Greenwood Press, 1987), 27–43.

11. Betty Lee Sung, *Mountain of Gold* (New York: MacMillan Co., 1967), 269; Him Mark Lai, "The Kuomintang in Chinese American Communities before World War II," in *Entry Denied: Exclusion and the Chinese Community in America, 1882–1943,* ed. Sucheng Chan (Philadelphia: Temple University Press, 1991), 170–212.

12. Lai, "The KMT in Chinese American Communities"; Sam Ark Wong, *Hongmen geming shi* [Revolutionary History of the Triads] (San Francisco: n.p., 1936), 23–25, 31; *Chinese World,* July 25, 1914; *Young China,* Dec. 26, 1915. The five bars in the Republic's flag stood for the five principal ethnic groups in China at the time: Han, Manchu, Mongolian, Hui (Chinese Moslem), and Tibetan. After establishing the republic in 1912, CKT leader Sam Ark Wong returned to Guangzhou and sought to register the CKT as a political party. He was given the runaround by Sun Yat-sen and his lieutenant Hu Hanmin, the commander in chief in Guangdong. Sam Ark Wong was unable to complete his mission successfully. Another sore point was that the KMT did not repay funds donated for revolutionary activities that were raised by the CKT in Canada by mortgaging real estate.

13. China had declared war on Germany during World War I, hoping to recover privileges and concessions that had been forcibly seized in the Shandong Peninsula. However, the Allies at the Paris Peace Conference reassigned Germany's rights to Japan. Hearing that the Beijing government was about to sign the peace treaty, university and college students gathered at Tian'anmen and staged a demonstration on May 4, 1919, calling on

the Chinese people to fight for China's sovereignty and to punish the traitors who would sign the treaty. Protests soon erupted all over China. Yielding to popular sentiment, the Beijing government did not become a signatory.

  14. "Zhu Meiguo Zongzhibu dangwu yange gaiyao" [Outline History of Party Affairs of the U.S. General Branch], in Zhongguo Guomindang Zhongyang Weiyuanhui Disan Zu [Section 3, Central Committee of the KMT], *Zhongguo Guomindang zai haiwai* [The KMT Overseas] (Taipei, 1961), 2:12–39 (cited hereafter as Outline History of Party Affairs). Section 3 had jurisdiction over overseas Chinese party affairs.

  15. *Hu Shuying Tongzhi Aisi Lu* [Sad Memories of Comrade Hu Shuying] (New York: Mun Hay Yat Po, 1928); Liu, *History of Chinese in the U.S.,* 2:486–87.

  16. *Hawaii Chinese Annual* (Honolulu: Overseas Penman Club, 1932), 26–27.

  17. All important participants in the Los Angeles Kuomintang convention were black-listed. In another instance, derogatory information passed on to the consul general resulted in orders from the Nationalist government to arrest Li Yikong, a Chinese American aviator who had returned to China. He was accused of scattering pro–Wang Jingwei faction leaflets from an airplane over San Francisco during memorial services for Sun Yat-sen. His cause was taken to the CCBA by the Ning Yung Association. See *Chung Sai Yat Po,* Aug. 17, 20, 1929. An informant who worked at the *Kuo Min Yat Po* during this period alleged that personnel at the newspaper kept firearms ready to repulse any physical attacks. In Vancouver the struggle over the Kuomintang organ, *Canada Morning News,* resulted in the assassination of pro-Wang manager and editor Lei Mingxia, as well as reporter and typesetter Huang Youmei, on August 8. See *Chinese Times* (Vancouver), Aug. 9, 1927.

  18. *Chung Sai Yat Po,* June 8, 1929.

  19. *Young China,* Oct. 15, Dec. 3, 1927, Aug. 20, 1935; *Chung Sai Yat Po,* Nov. 18, 1927. *Young China* editor Huang Baohuan was the Yeong Wo Association delegate to a board of directors' meeting of the CCBA-operated Chung Wah School. He sat by mistake in the seat permanently assigned to the president of the Ning Yung Association and was ordered to move. Later, Huang commented on this incident in *Young China* with an article titled "Wuhu Zhonghua Huiguan zhi muqi" [Alas, the Lifeless CCBA]. Ning Yung Association leaders regarded his remarks as casting aspersions on their organization and called upon its members to boycott *Young China.* See *Chung Sai Yat Po,* Nov. 18, 1927. On December 3, 1927, the paper's editor defended Huang in an editorial, declaring that to be against *Young China* was equivalent to opposing the national revolution. Members of the association could not lightly shrug off their responsibility for the consequences, for "when fire ignites the Kunlun Mountains, both jade and stone will burn" [huo yan Kun Gang, yu shi ju fen]. Ning Yung Association leaders seized on these remarks to further inflame Taishanese anger and to intensify the boycott efforts (*Young China,* Aug. 20, 1935).

  20. *Chung Sai Yat Po,* May 14, June 8, 11, July 3, 4, 6, 17, 1928; *San Francisco Chronicle,* Oct. 23, 1929; *Chinese Times,* June 9, 1930. "Double Ten" commemorates the October 10, 1911, uprising at Wuchang that led to the overthrow of the Qing dynasty and the founding of the Republic of China.

  21. Liu, *History of Chinese in the U.S.,* 2:379–84.

  22. *Chung Sai Yat Po,* June 8, 1929. A list of banned U.S. Chinese publications was published in *Leifeng zazhi* [Thunderous Wind] (Hong Kong), Dec. 5, 1928, 49–52, and Dec. 20, 1928, 51–54. Another list (1928?) can be found among KMT documents, Special Collections, University Library, University of California at Davis. The following is compiled

from these sources. Baohuanghui publications: *Chinese World* (San Francisco), *Humorist* (San Francisco), *Sun Chung Kwock Po* (Honolulu). Chee Kung Tong publications: *Morning Sun* (San Francisco), *Chinese Republic News* (New York City), *Hon Mun Po* (Honolulu). Communist publication: *Chinese Vanguard* (San Francisco). Anarchist publication: *Equality*. KMT, pro–Wang Jingwei faction publications: *Mun Hey Yat Po* and *Kuo Min Yat Po*. Others: *Ou-Mei Tongxin* (San Francisco) and *Chung Sai Yat Po* (San Francisco).

23. *Chinese Vanguard,* Nov. 16, 1935; Him Mark Lai, "To Bring Forth a New China, to Build a Better America: The Chinese Marxist Left in America to the 1960s," *Chinese America: History and Perspectives* 6 (1992): 3–82.

24. "Wu Xianzi," in *Biographical Dictionary of Republican China,* ed. Howard L. Boorman (New York: Columbia University Press, 1970), 3:433–36; "China Wants Editor Back," *New York Times,* June 23, 1929; Cui Tongyue, *Canghai shengping* [On the Sea of Life] (Shanghai: self-published, 1935), 98–100.

25. Sun Yat-sen, *Guomin zhengfu jianguo dagang* [National Government's Outline for National Construction] (Apr. 12, 1924); see Zhongguo Guomindang Zhongyang Weiyuanhui Dangshi Weiyuanhui [Party History Committee of the Chinese Nationalist Party Central Committee], ed., *Guofu quanji* [Complete Works of the Father of the Nation] (Taipei: Zhongguo Guomindang Zhongyang Weiyuanhui Dangshi Weiyuanhui, 1973), 1:751–53; *Haiwai Huawen jiaoyu* [Chinese Language School Education Abroad] (Taipei: Qiaowu Weiyuanhui Qiaowu Yanjiushi [Overseas Chinese affairs research office, Overseas Chinese affairs commission], 1969), 31–32; *Qiaowu ershiwu nian* [Twenty-five Years of Overseas Chinese Affairs] (Taipei: Haiwai chubanshe, 1957), 15–16. Later, supervision of Chinese overseas education was transferred to the Overseas Chinese Affairs Commission. The National Government Outline for National Construction specified three stages: military rule used to unify the nation; period of tutelage when the government guides the people toward self-government; and constitutional rule with an elected government ruling in accordance with the constitution.

26. Liu, *History of Chinese in the U.S.,* 2:489–90; Lai, *The KMT in Chinese American Communities,* 170–212.

27. Liu, *History of Chinese in the U.S.,* 2:491–92.

28. "From Coolie Boy to LL.D.," *New York Times,* Sept. 24, 1922; Kuang Fuzhuo, "Liushi nian zhi huigu" [Looking Back Sixty Years], retrieved June 12, 2008, from http://www.pubhistory.com/img/text/4/1434.htm; Zhu Xia (Y. K. Chu), *Meiguo Huaqiao gaishi* [General History of the Chinese in America] (New York: China Times, 1975), 81–82 (cited hereafter as General History of the Chinese in America).

29. *Who's Who in China* (Shanghai: *The China Weekly Review,* 1931), 229; Zhu Xia, General History of the Chinese in America, 83–85.

30. Edare Carroll, "First Chinese San Francisco Medical School Graduate: Holt Cheng, M.D.," *San Francisco Medicine,* Mar. 2003, 20–21.

31. Jun Ke Choy, *My China Years, 1911–1945: Practical Politics in China after the 1911 Revolution* (San Francisco: East/West Publishing Co., 1974), xix, 22, 31.

32. Yao Manchang, "Sun Zhongshan weishidui daduizhang Yao Guanshun xiaozhuan" [Short Biography of Yao Guanshun, Leader of Sun Yat-sen's Group of Bodyguards], 95–101, in *Wenshi ziliao xuanji* [Selected Collection of Literary and Historical Materials], 16th collection (Beijing: Zhongguo Wenshi Chubanshe, 1988).

33. James. R. Ross, *Caught in a Tornado: A Chinese American Woman Survives the Cultural Revolution* (Boston: Northeastern University Press, 1994).

34. Fang Xiongpu, *Huaqiao hangkong shihua* [Historical Account of Chinese from Abroad in Aviation] (Beijing: Zhongguo Huaqiao chuban gongsi, 1991), 73–75, 93–102. A more detailed account of the role of Chinese American aviators in military aviation in China can be found in Him Mark Lai, "Sprouting Wings on the Dragon: Some Chinese Americans Who Contributed to the Development of Aviation in China," in *The Annals of the Chinese Historical Society of the Pacific Northwest,* ed. Douglas W. Lee (Bellingham, Wash.: Chinese Historical Society of the Pacific Northwest, 1984), 179–83.

35. Lin Jinzhi, Zhuang Weiji, *Jindai Huaqiao touzi guonei qiyeshi ziliao xuanji (Guangdong juan)* [Selected Edited materials on the Investment of Overseas Chinese Capital in China in Recent Times, volume on Guangdong] (Fuzhou: Fujian Renmin Chubanshe, 1989), 42, 425–28; Liu, *History of Chinese in the U.S.,* 2:265–68.

36. Liu, *History of Chinese in the U.S.,* 2:268–71.

37. Liu, *History of Chinese in the U.S.,* 2:557–62.

38. "Quanguo zuizao qiaoxiao Zhenxian xuexiao" [Zhenxian School, the Earliest School in the Nation Built by Overseas Chinese Donations], retrieved June 10, 2008, from http://www.15630.com/tour/Article_Show.asp?ArticleID=1719.

39. *Taishan xian Huaqiaozhi* [Gazetteer of Chinese Overseas from Taishan] (Taicheng: Taishan Office of Overseas Chinese Affairs, 1992), 118–31.

40. Zhu Xia, *General history of the Chinese in America,* 72–73; Zhang Guoxiong, *Kaiping diaolou* [Kaiping Watchtowers] (Guangzhou: Guangdong Renmin Chubanshe, 2005), 11; Steven Ribet, "All along the Watchtowers," *Hong Kong Standard,* Mar. 10, 2007; "Buyao ba diaolou zhi dang jing guankan" [Don't Just Regard the Watchtowers as Scenery], *China Press,* Aug. 18, 2007.

41. *Guangzhou Shi Dongshan Qu zhi* [Gazetteer of Dongshan District, City of Guangzhou] (Guangzhou: Guangdong Renmin Chubanshe, 1999), 737–38.

42. Liu, *History of Chinese in the U.S.,* 2:552–55.

43. Liu, *History of Chinese in the U.S.,* 2:669–82.

44. Him Mark Lai, "Roles Played by Chinese in America during China's Resistance to Japanese Aggression and during World War II," *Chinese America: History and Perspectives* 11 (1997): 75–123.

45. Liu, *History of Chinese in the U.S.,* 2:320–21. After the Nineteenth Route Army withdrew from Shanghai in 1932, it was ordered to Fujian to fight the Communist insurrection. In November 1933 Tsai Ting-kai, Li Jichen, Eugene Chen, and others opposed to the Chiang Kai-shek regime formed a People's Government that advocated resistance to Japanese aggression and overthrow of the Nanjing government. However, the new government fell within two months to the superior KMT forces sent against it. Tsai fled to Hong Kong, from whence he embarked on an international tour criticizing the KMT.

46. *Chinese World,* Aug. 14, 1937.

47. See Lai, "Roles Played by Chinese in America," 75–125, for a detailed discussion of Chinese American support for the War of Resistance.

48. When the Nationalists retreated from east and central China with the Japanese advance, Communist guerrillas expanded their activities into the territories once held by the KMT. Friction grew between the two forces, and beginning in mid-1939, scattered fighting broke out involving Nationalist and New Fourth Army troops. Negotiations led the New Fourth Army to agree to withdraw north of the Yangzi River. Approximately a thousand sick and wounded were sent ahead, followed in January 1941 by the remainder of the army of about eight thousand. While traveling in southern Anhui, the army was

surrounded and attacked by Nationalist troops. After a week of fighting, only somewhat more than a thousand broke through to safety, leaving almost seven thousand casualties. Their commander, Ye Ting, was captured by the Nationalists. This event shocked the Chinese abroad, who had pleaded for continued unity to face the common enemy, Japan.

49. Outline History of Party Affairs.

50. Wang Shigu, "Meizhou *Huaqiao ribao* de chuangjian he fazhan" [The Founding and Development of *China Daily News*] (unpublished manuscript, 1998); cited hereafter as Wang, Founding and Development of *China Daily News.*

51. Liu, *History of Chinese in the U.S.*, 2:391; "Jintie haiwai qiaobao banfa" [Plan for Subsidizing Overseas Chinese Newspapers], resolution by the standing committee of the Overseas Chinese Affairs Commission, Oct. 26, 1948, *Qiaowu fagui* [Overseas Chinese Affairs Regulations] (Taipei: Overseas Chinese Affairs Commission, 1956), 95.

52. Ye Hanming, "Huaqiao huidang yu Guo-Gong tongzhan: Meizhou Hongmen de lizi" [Chinese Overseas Secret Societies and the United Front Tactics of the KMT and the Chinese Communist Party: The Hongmen of the Americas as an Example], in *Zhanhou haiwai Huaren bianhua guoji xueshu yantaohui lunwenji* [Collected Essays from the International Scholarly Conference on Changes in Chinese Overseas Society after World War II], ed. Guo Liang (Beijing: Zhongguo Huaqiao Chuban Gongsi, 1990), 251–57; Liu, *History of Chinese in the U.S.*, 2:370.

53. "Li Ta-ming," in *Biographical Dictionary of Republican China*, 2:333–35; Liu, *History of Chinese in the U.S.*, 2:370; *Chinese World*, Mar. 20, Apr. 11, 1961; J. K. Choy, *The Chinese Democratic Constitutionalist Party* (San Francisco: Chinese Democratic Constitutionalist Party, 1948); Wu Xianzi, *Zhongguo Minzhu Xianzhengdang dangshi* (San Francisco: Chinese World, 1963), 144; "Chang Chia-sen," in *Biographical Dictionary of Republican China*, 1:30–35. Dai Ming Lee was a political figure active on both sides of the Pacific. Born in Kauai in 1904, Lee went with his parents to China in 1909, returned to Honolulu in 1918, and departed again for China in 1919. In 1921 Lee founded *Datong ribao* in Hong Kong and joined the Baohuanghui. He also became a noted political commentator. In 1926 Lee traveled to Hawaii, the United States, and Europe to assess the party's activities and to direct anti-KMT propaganda campaigns. In 1928 he traveled to San Francisco to assist Wu Xianzi at the *Chinese World.* Beginning in 1929 he also became principal of the newly established Confucian Chinese Language School there. Lee returned to Hong Kong in 1932 but crossed the Pacific again in 1938 to become editor of the *New China Press* of Honolulu and to teach at the Mun Lun School. It was under Lee's editorship that the paper changed from triweekly to daily publication in 1942.

The establishment of a National Socialist Party was formally announced in Tianjin by Zhang Junmai (Carsun Chang) and others in the fall of 1934. The party advocated a modified Western parliamentary system and a modified form of state socialism for China. Since the KMT banned all dissenting political parties, it was a secret underground organization until 1938, during the Sino-Japanese War. In 1941 it joined with other Chinese minority parties to form the League of Chinese Democratic Political Groups. When Wu Zhuang returned from the United States before the outbreak of the Sino-Japanese War, he had discussed with Carsun Chang a possible amalgamation of the Baohuanghui with the Chinese National Socialist Party. World War II disrupted discussions, which resumed between Chang and Dai Ming Lee in 1945, when the former attended the United Nations Conference in San Francisco. They reached agreement in August 1946 to merge as the Chinese Democratic Socialist Party with Chang as the head. The newly formed party's platform opposed civil war and one-party or one-class dictatorship, and advocated national unity under a central government and state socialism in major industries.

54. Wu Xianzi, *Zhongguo Minzhu Xianzhengdang dangshi*, 143–48; Chen Kwong Min, *The Chinese in the Americas* (New York: Overseas Chinese Culture Publishing Co., 1950), 67.

55. *Chung Sai Yat Po*, Dec. 17, 1947, Apr. 8, May 11, 28, 1948. According to the U.S. Census the Chinese population in the continental United States was 77,504 in 1940 and 117,629 in 1950, with approximately 61,080 and 90,369 respectively of age fifteen or greater. National Assembly representatives from the western United States were Yen Doon Wong, Chen Duzhou, and Cai Fengyou (Mrs. Albert Chow). Mei Youzhuo was elected from the Midwest, and Wu Tiansheng and Chen Zhonghai (Woodrew Chan) from the eastern United States; the representative from the United States, Hawaii, and Canada to the Control Yuan was Kuang Yaopu (Yue Po Fong); the two representatives from the United States to the Legislative Yuan were Chen Ruzhou (N. J. Chan) and Pan Chaoying.

56. Feng Hongda, Yu Huaxin, *Feng Yuxiang jiangjun huan gui Zhonghua* [The Soul of General Feng Yuxiang Returns to China] (Beijing: Wenshi ziliao chubanshe, 1981), 123–29; James E. Sheridan, *Chinese Warlord: The Career of Feng Yu-hsiang* (Stanford: Stanford University Press, 1966), 279–80; Wu Maosun, "Feng jiangjun zui guanghui de yi ye" [The Most Glorious Page in the Life of General Feng], in *Feng Yuxiang jiangjun jiniance* [Album in Memory of General Feng Yuxiang] (Hong Kong: n.p., 1948), 112–21.

57. *United States Relations with China, with Special Reference to the Period 1944–1949* (Washington, D.C.: Dept. of State, 1949), 303.

58. *Situ Huimin tongzhi shengping* [Obituary of Comrade Situ Huimin] (Beijing: Office of Funeral Arrangements for Comrade Situ Huimin, 1987).

59. *San Francisco Chronicle*, Oct. 10, 13, 1949. On July 24, 1948, Soviet Union occupation forces in Germany cut off all rail and highway access between West Germany and Berlin. The United States and the United Kingdom then began an airlift to bring in more than 4,500 tons of food and supplies daily for the population in Berlin. The airlift lasted until September 1949.

Whittaker Chambers, *Time* magazine senior editor and self-confessed Communist spy, testified before the House Un-American Activities Committee (HUAC) in August 1948 that Alger Hiss supplied USSR agents with classified U.S. documents while working with the U.S. State Department in the 1930s. Hiss sued Chambers for slander. Chambers subsequently produced a microfilm of documents he claimed that Hiss had given to him. A New York grand jury indicted Hiss for perjury. Representative Richard Nixon built political capital by being the HUAC member who pushed the Hiss investigation.

October 10, the anniversary of the Wuchang Uprising that led to the overthrow of the Qing dynasty, is celebrated in the Republic of China annually as National Day.

60. *Chinese American Weekly*, Sept. 8, Nov. 10, 1949; Huang Wenshan, "Zuzhi Meizhou Huaqiao fan-Gong jiuguohui jihua" [Plan for Organizing an Overseas Chinese Anti-Communist National Salvation Association in the Americas], in Huang Wenshan, *Huang Wenshan lü-Mei luncong* [Essays Published by Huang Wenshan while Sojourning in the United States] (Taipei: Zhonghua shuju, 1960), 641–42; Outline History of Party Affairs.

61. Pei Chi Liu, *Zhou Jinchao guomin waijiao jishi* [An Account of Albert Chow's Diplomatic Efforts as a Citizen] (San Francisco: n.p., 1992). Albert Chow (1902–57) was born in Fresno, California. He became an interpreter for the Immigration Service when he was

twenty-one. Later he joined the immigration law firm opened by Jack Chow, his brother, and Jack Sing Wong. He joined the KMT before World War II and was elected to the executive committee of the General Branch in 1948 and 1949. Chow was also active in the Democratic Party and attended the 1944 party convention in Chicago. There he befriended Senator Truman, who was nominated for vice-president. Chow went to Taiwan to meet with Chiang Kai-shek or other government high officials five times between 1949 and 1954. In 1956 Chow was summoned before a federal grand jury investigating Chinese immigration fraud. He was also indicted for tax evasion; however, he passed away from a heart attack in 1957 before the case could come to trial.

62. Iris Chang, *Thread of the Silkworm* (New York: Basic Books, 1995), 188–90.

63. Section 3 of the KMT, *Zhongguo Guomindang zai haiwai*, 1:242–43; Victor Nee and Brett de Bary, *Longtime Californ'* (New York: Pantheon Books, 1973), 217–22; Victor Nee and Brett de Bary, "Chiang's Last Sphere of Influence," *San Francisco Journal,* April 5, 1972. For a sampling of the state of mind of many United States Chinese, see letters to the editor in the *Chinese American Weekly,* Dec. 21, 28, 1950, Jan. 4, 1951, June 1, 1953; and editorials Nov. 30, 1950, Dec. 14, 1950.

The official public ceremony establishing the Anti-Communist League in San Francisco took place on January 14, 1951. Pei Chi Liu claimed credit for suggesting the formation of the League in San Francisco. A league was also established in the Philippines in December 1950. San Francisco was followed by New York City, Chicago, Mexico City, Mexicali (Mexico), Guadalajara (Mexico), Taegu (Korea), Tahiti, Barranquillo (Colombia), Reunion, and Rangoon (Burma). See *Huaqiao Zhi* Bianzuan Weiyuanhui [Overseas Chinese Gazetteer Editorial Committee], ed., *Huaqiao zhi* [Overseas Chinese Gazetteer] (Taipei: *Huaqiao Zhi* Bianzuan Weiyuanhui, 1964), 458–59.

Yen Doon Wong came from Portland, Maine in 1937 as Goon Dick Wong's heir apparent. He became identified with the Kuo Min Yat Po faction during World War II. Later he was variously a delegate to the Taiwan National Assembly, a member of the Overseas Chinese Affairs Committee, and a central committeeman of the KMT. See Huang Wenshan, "Huang Renjun xiansheng zhuan lüe" [Short Biography of Mr. Yen Doon Wong], in *Huang Renjun xiansheng bazhikaiyi shouqing jiniance* [Commemorative Album Celebrating the Seventy-first Birthday of Mr. Yen Doon Wong] (Taipei: n.p., 1967), 14–15.

64. Section 3 of the KMT, *Zhongguo Guomindang zai haiwai*, 1:313–26. The head of the group in the early 1970s was Chen Yuqing. In 1976 he became a member of the KMT central committee in Taiwan (*Young China,* Nov. 19, 1976) and also headed the board of directors of *Young China* (*Sun Yat-sen News,* Feb. 17, 1978). Lin Qingjiang and Zeng Guangshun then successively headed the overseas group. See *Young China,* Mar. 12, 1977; *Sun Yat-sen News,* Jan. 6, 1978.

65. Section 3 of the KMT, *Zhongguo Guomindang zai haiwai*, 1:313–26.

66. Chen Lifu, *Chengbai zhi jian: Chen Lifu huiyilu* [The Mirror of Success and Failure: Reminiscences of Chen Lifu] (Taipei: Zhengzhong shuju, 1994), 384–85; "Chen Lifu," in *Biographical Dictionary of Republican China,* 1:206–11; "P'an Kung-chan," in *Biographical Dictionary of Republican China,* 3:63–65; "Pan Gongzhan," in *Minguo renwu xiaozhuan* [Brief Biographies of Personalities of the Republic] (Taipei: Zhuanji wenxue chubanshe, 1981), 3:308–10; Paul K. T. Sih, *Kun xing yi wang* [Overcoming Difficulties in Action and Reminiscing about the Past] (Taipei: Zhuanji wenxue chubanshe, 1984), 315–16.

Chen Lifu and his brother headed the so-called C.C. Clique, which was intimately identified with the central nucleus of the KMT after establishment of the Nanjing government. He was a staunch anti-Communist who was elected to the party's powerful central committee in 1929 and held that post until 1950. When the shattered KMT met in Taiwan to form a new Central Reform Committee, Chen was left out. He left with his family to attend a Moral Rearmament Conference in Europe, from whence they went to the United States and eventually settled in New Jersey.

Pan Gongzhan edited a number of Shanghai newspapers from the 1920s to 1949. He was closely allied with Chen Bulei, Chiang Kai-shek's confidential assistant and an important member of the KMT. In 1942 he became a standing committee member of the KMT's Central Executive Committee. From 1942 to 1945 he was director of the Executive Yuan's committee concerned with censorship of books and magazines. When the Communist army reached the outskirts of Shanghai in 1949 during the civil war, Pan left for Hong Kong and reached the United States by way of Canada to settle in New York.

67. Ross Y. Koen, *The China Lobby in American Politics* (New York: Harper and Row, 1974), 35; Stanley D. Bachrack, *The Committee of One Million: "China Lobby" Politics, 1953–1971* (New York: Columbia University Press, 1976), 6; Sterling Seagrave, *The Soong Dynasty* (New York: Harper and Row, 1984), 441–48. When the Koen book was first published in 1960, elements connected with the China Lobby enjoined its distribution. More than four thousand copies were destroyed by the publisher and fewer than three hundred circulated. See R. C. Kagan, introduction to the 1974 edition, ix.

68. Mai Liqian (Him Mark Lai), *Cong Huaqiao dao Huaren* [From Overseas Chinese to Chinese American] (Hong Kong: Joint Publishing Co., 1992), 360–62 (cited hereafter as Lai, From Overseas Chinese to Chinese American).

69. The Committee to Support the *China Daily News, The Chinese Daily News Case* (New York, 1952?).

70. Chapters 2 through 5 of this anthology offer a detailed discussion of the Marxist Left from the 1920s to the 1960s.

71. Circulation figures for the 1950s were reported in the annual *N. W. Ayer and Son's Directory, Newspapers and Periodicals* (Philadelphia: N. W. Ayer and Son, Inc.) for applicable years; Jun Ke Choy, *My China Years, 1911–1945: Practical Politics in China after the 1911 Revolution* (San Francisco: East/West Publishing Co., 1974), 248; *Chinese World,* Aug. 13, 1954; *Chinese Times,* Jan. 1, 1972. Choy was identified as advisor to the Chinese Democratic Constitutionalist Party in a press release from the party dated January 18, 1948.

Choy (1892–1981) was born in Hawaii in 1892. He came back to America permanently after World War II. Still very interested in social service and in political and financial activities, he joined the One World organization for international peace shortly after landing. While visiting San Francisco in 1949, he was invited by editor Dai Ming Lee of the *Chinese World* to help organize an English edition of the paper to make it the first bilingual daily Chinese newspaper. From 1952 to 1953, he was general manager of the Wo Kee Company, then the oldest Chinese importing firm in San Francisco Chinatown, and helped to reorganize the business. At the time the United States had imposed an embargo on trade with the PRC. Choy went to Hong Kong, where he negotiated successfully with British and American trade representatives for comprehensive "certificates of origin" to indicate that his merchandise did not come from the PRC. He was also assistant vice-president at San Francisco Savings and Loan Association. Recognizing the needs of the thrifty Chinatown community, in 1956 Choy began planning the first branch of a savings and loan association in Chinatown. The branch opened in 1957 and was an instant success. By the time Choy retired, deposits at the branch had reached $60 million, the most of any Chinatown financial institution. He retired from Wo Kee at the age of sixty-five and settled with his wife in San Francisco.

72. *Chinese World,* Aug. 20, 21, 1954, June 18, 20, 1955.

73. Liu, *History of Chinese in the U.S.,* 2:371, 472.

74. Ibid., 2:357–58.

75. *Chinese World,* June 22, 1960; *San Francisco Examiner,* June 26, 1960.

76. *Chinese World,* Feb. 26, 1963; *Chinese Pacific Weekly,* Mar. 7, 1963.

77. *Chinese Times,* Oct. 12, 13, 14, 1966, Apr. 4, 1969. The Federal Home Loan Bank of San Francisco, which guaranteed the deposits, had to run advertisements in Chinatown newspapers on October 13 and 14 to reassure depositors.

78. *Chinese Times,* Sept. 25, 1970; L. Ling-chi Wang, "Six Companies Withdraw Backing for Culture Foundation," *East/West,* Sept. 30, Oct. 7, 1970.

79. *Mon War Weekly,* Aug. 13, 1971.

80. Philip A. Lum, "The Creation and Demise of the San Francisco Chinatown Freedom Schools: One Response to Desegregation," *Amerasia Journal* 5, no. 1 (1978): 57–73; *Pacific Weekly,* Sept. 16, 1971; *East/West,* Oct. 20, 1971.

81. *East/West,* Jan.19, 1972.

82. "Dabu Hongweibingdang zhengzhi shi" [A Short Political History of the Red Guards Party in San Francisco], *Getting Together,* Feb. 17, Mar. 3, 17, 1973 (cited hereafter as Short History of the Red Guards Party); Prof. Peter Kwong of Hunter College, interview with author, Dec. 22, 1985; William Wei, *The Asian American Movement* (Philadelphia: Temple University Press, 1993), 210–25; interview with Teo Ng, manager of Eastwind Bookstore, San Francisco, May 9, 1984, July 1, 1988; ACC pamphlet, ca. 1974; "Gongren Guangdian Zuzhi ye zhuangchu zhichi Zhong-Mei bangjiao zhengchanghua liao" [Even the Workers Viewpoint Organization Is Pretending It Supports the Normalization of U.S.-China Diplomatic Relations], *Getting Together,* Oct. 1977.

83. Wei, *The Asian American Movement,* 36–37, 222.

84. Short History of the Red Guards Party; Lai, From Overseas Chinese to Chinese American, 484–92.

85. Zhao Xuegong, "Luelun Nikesong zhengfude dui-Ri zhengce [A Brief Study of the Nixon Administration's Policy toward Japan], retrieved June 1, 2008, from http://www .pep.com.cn/czls/jszx/xsjl/sjsyj/2000211/t20021128_10538.htm.

86. Zhu Hongjun, "35 nian qian Huaren jingying de Bao-Diao meng" [The Protect Diaoyutai Dream of the Chinese Elite 35 Years Ago], retrieved June 2, 2008, from http:// www.fokas.com.tw/news/newslist.php?id=1869, -1870, -1871; Zhu Hongjun, "Haiwai Bao-Diao di-ling tuan" [The Overseas Protect Diaoyutai Group, no. 0], retrieved June 3, 2008, from http://www.nanfangdaily.com.cn/zm/20051006/xw/dcgc/200510090011.asp.

87. James Lee, "The Story of the Tiao Yu Tai Movement," *Bridge* 1, no. 3 (Nov./Dec. 1971): 4–16; Lai, From Overseas Chinese to Chinese American, 482–84.

88. "Meizhou *Huaqiao Ribao* chuangkan sanshiba zhounian jinian tekan" [Special Publication Celebrating the Thirty-eighth Anniversary of the Founding of *China Daily News*], *China Daily News,* July 7, 1987; Wang, Founding and Development of *China Daily News.*

89. *San Francisco Journal,* Sept. 28, Oct. 5, 1977.

90. *Centennial Celebration, United Chinese Society of Hawaii* (Honolulu: United Chinese Society, 1984), 37.

91. *China Daily News,* Feb. 12, 13, 1981.

92. *San Francisco Journal,* Nov. 22, Dec. 6, 1972; *Chinese Pacific Weekly,* Dec. 21, 1972.

93. *China Times,* Mar. 24, 1983; *Centre Daily News,* Oct. 1, 1984; *World Journal,* Oct. 18, 1984; *International Daily News,* Dec. 3, 1984; *San Francisco Journal,* Oct. 9, Dec. 1, 1984, June 28, July 25, Aug. 5, Aug. 20, Sept. 18, 21, 1985, Jan. 21, Feb. 3, Apr. 19, June 14, 1986; *Chinese Times,* Jan. 12, 1985.

94. *China Daily News,* Nov. 20, 1980; *Chinese Pacific Weekly,* Mar. 12, 1981; *San Francisco Journal,* June 13, 1985.

95. *Chinese American Association of Commerce Sixteenth Anniversary Celebration* (San Francisco: Chinese American Association of Commerce, 1996), 8; "Jiujinshan Dongwanqu Wuyi Tongxiang Lianyihui chengli xuanyan" [Declaration on the Founding of the Wuyi Fellow Villagers Friendship Association of the East San Francisco Bay] (Oakland: Jiujinshan Dongwanqu Wuyi Tongxiang Lianyihui, 1998); *Chinese Times,* Apr. 13, 1998.

96. In this essay, the term "native Taiwanese" refers to people of Chinese ancestry who migrated from mainland China before World War II. Most of these speak the Minnan dialect of southern Fujian. A minority speak Hakka and other dialects. The aboriginal Taiwanese are only a minute percentage of the Taiwan population.

97. Chen Mingcheng, *Haiwai Taidu yundong sishinian* [Forty Years of the Taiwan Independence Movement Abroad] (Taipei: Zili wanbao wenhua chubanbu, 1992), 80–87, 103 (cited hereafter as Chen, Forty Years of the Taiwan Independence Movement); Yang Yuanxun, "Qiaoxiang Feicheng Dulizhong: Lu Zhuyi yu 3F de gushi [Sounding Philadelphia's Liberty Bell: The Story of Lu Zhuyi and 3F], retrieved June 6, 2008, from http://www.wufi.org.tw/wufi/wufistory12.htm.

98. The declaration was published in 1964 by Taiwan University professor Peng Mingmin and his students Xie Congmin and Wei Tingchao in Taiwan. It advocated that all on Taiwan, regardless of provincial origin, cooperate to build a new nation, establish a new and democratic government, select a head of state by a general election in accordance with normal democratic processes, protect the legal status of opposition political parties, and allow multiparty politics. The authors were arrested and sentenced to eight years for sedition. One year later, Peng was released on parole. In 1969 he escaped to Sweden and in 1970 was given a position at the University of Michigan's Center for Chinese Studies.

99. Chen, Forty Years of the Taiwan Independence Movement, 100–102, 119–20, 139–50, 212, 215–17. In September 1979, opponents of the KMT Huang Xinjie (Huang Hsin-chieh), Xu Xinliang (Hsu Hsin-liang), and others established *Formosa Weekly* in Kaohsiung. The KMT soon began to harass and threaten the publishers. On December 10, *Formosa Weekly* organized a demonstration in Kaohsiung commemorating World Human Rights Day. The demonstrators clashed with military police and more than two hundred people were injured. The police arrested 152 opposition leaders, tried them on charges of sedition, and meted out sentences varying from one to fourteen years. By that time, Xu Xinliang had already left for the United States.

100. Chen, Forty Years of the Taiwan Independence Movement, 219.

101. *China Daily News,* July 29, 1981; Cathy Panagoulias, "Taiwan 'Informers' May Be on Campus," *Cornell Daily Sun,* May 6, 1976; Chen, Forty Years of the Taiwan Independence Movement, 96–98.

102. Donald McNeil, "Taiwanese Spies in U.S. Universities, *Daily Californian,* Mar. 15, 1976; Jueqi, "Chen Yuxi shijian: liangxin de chouren" [Prisoner of Conscience, the Chen Yuxi Affair], *Tung Feng,* Feb. 1974, 14–17.

103. Zhong Zhaoyang, "Ye Daolei an fenxi" [An Analysis of and Comments on the Rita Yeh Case], *Hsintu,* no. 27 (Feb./Mar. 1981): 28–34; Terry Caine, "Much Reason to Care: The Case of Rita Yeh," *Minnesota Daily,* Mar. 29, 1981; *China Times Weekly,* Sept. 30, 1989; *Chinese American News,* Sept. 5, 1997.

104. *China Daily News,* July 29, 1981.

105. *In Memorial of Henry Liu* (San Francisco: Jiangnan Affair Committee, 1985), 1–97; *Los Angeles Times,* Sept. 20, 1985; "Li Yaping shijian" [The Lee Ya-ping Incident], in *Tai-Gang-Ao shouce* [Taiwan, Hong Kong, Macao Handbook], ed. Chen Guoshao, Xiao Xing, and Chang Gong (Beijing: Huayi chubanshe, 1990), 1:105 (cited hereafter as Taiwan, Hong Kong, Macao Handbook).

106. *Metro Chinese Journal,* July 1987; *World Journal,* Nov. 29, 1991.

107. *U.S. News and World Report,* July 24, 1995; *New York Times,* Apr. 13, 1996.

108. "Guojianhui," in Taiwan, Hong Kong, Macao Handbook, 1:49; *USAsia News,* Feb. 28, 1986; *World Journal Weekly,* July 15, 1990, Sept. 8, 1996; *Chinese American News,* June 21, 1996.

109. *World Journal,* Apr. 29, 1988, June 30, 1989, Oct. 4, 1990, June 1, 1991, Dec. 23, 1992, Oct. 24, 1994, Feb. 6, 1996; *Chinese American News,* Apr. 13, 1991; *China Times Weekly,* Feb. 17, 1993; information from Monte Jade Web page, retrieved Aug. 28, 2009, from http://www.montejade.org/?page=about_en; *Sing Tao Daily,* Apr. 22, 1993; *China Press,* Mar. 18, 1995.

110. *Sing Tao Daily News,* July 15, 1998; Qiu Xiuwen, "Qiaojiao zhongxin 'duanchui zhen tong' you lai liao" [The Pain of Going Hungry Is Coming Again for the Culture Center], *Chinese American News,* Apr. 3, 1998; address list of culture centers, dated Aug. 2, 1996, from the Republic of China Overseas Chinese Affairs Commission Web page; *Young China,* July 2, 1987; *New Kwong Tai Press,* Aug. 5, 1988; *China Times Weekly,* Oct. 28, 1989; *International Daily News,* July 22, 1994, Mar. 9, June 6, 1995; *World Journal,* Aug. 8, 18, 19, 1998. Culture centers are located in San Francisco, Sunnyvale (Calif.), Los Angeles (two), New York, Chicago, Boston, Houston, Seattle, and Atlanta. Activity centers taken over from the KMT are located in Detroit, Dallas, and St. Louis.

111. *China Times Weekly,* June 29, 1991; *World Journal,* July 12, 1991.

112. *Ta Kung Pao* (North American Edition), Aug. 13, 1993; *World Journal,* Aug. 10, 1993, Nov. 2, Dec. 9, 1997; *International Daily News,* Nov. 27, 1995; *Sing Tao Daily,* Sept. 1, 1996.

113. *World Journal,* Aug. 19, 1996; *International Daily News,* Jan. 27, 1997.

114. Chen Li and Luwei, "Zhongguo Minzhu Tuanjie Lianmeng shinian jianshi" [A Brief History of Ten Years of the Democratic Unity Alliance of China], *China Spring* no. 117 (Feb. 1993): 97–103; no. 118 (Mar. 1993): 93–100; no. 119 (Apr. 1993): 89–96; no. 120 (May 1993): 93–98; *Beijing Spring* no. 1 (June 1993): 72–80; no. 2 (July 1993): 79–86.

115. *Sing Tao Daily,* Mar. 21, 22, 1998. Huang Yuchuan was a graduate of Zhongshan University in Guangzhou. In the late 1940s, he accepted a teaching position in Canada. Later he attended New York University. In the 1950s, Huang answered the call to return to help China's reconstruction and worked at the *Renmin huabao* [People's Pictorial] in Beijing. He was denounced in the Anti-Rightist Movement and sent to a labor camp in Heilongjiang. Huang left for Hong Kong in the mid-1960s and then immigrated to the United States in the early 1970s. He was at various times a realtor, apartment owner, travel service operator, and restaurateur.

116. *Centre Daily News,* July 5, 1989; *World Journal,* July 30, Sept. 17, 1989; *Asia Weekly,* Aug. 20, 1989; *China Times Weekly,* Sept. 23, 1989; *China Press,* May 29, 1993, June 1, 1994;

China Press, Jan. 5, 1991, Jan. 5, 1996. The loss of advertising may have provided a pretext for Fu Chaoshu to bow out, since for at least two years before the closure the paper had had serious financial problems.

117. *A Changing China* 1, no. 1 (Winter 1991): 2, 12; *World Journal,* June 21, 1989, Dec. 28, 1997.

118. *World Journal,* Sept. 24, 25, 1989; *Young China,* Feb. 20, 1990.

119. *World Journal,* Dec. 29, 1989; *China Times Weekly,* Oct. 21, Nov. 4, 1989, Jan. 6, 1990.

120. *World Journal,* Jan. 31, 1990; *China Spring* no. 118 (Mar. 1993): 6.

121. Some dissidents were permitted to go abroad as "visiting scholars," while others left to receive "medical attention." Among those who left China were such well-known dissidents as journalists Dai Qing (1991), Zhang Weiguo (1993), Wang Juntao (1994), Wu Hongda (Harry Wu; 1985), Ni Yuxian (1987), Wei Jingsheng (1997), and Wang Dan (1998).

122. "Falun Gong," retrieved Oct. 14, 2007, from http://en.wikipedia.org/wiki/Falun_Gong.

123. *International Daily News,* July 1, 1994.

124. *Committee of 100 Mission Statement and Background* (San Francisco, 2006).

125. *World Journal,* July 7, 12, Aug. 16, 1992; *China Press,* Sept. 27, 1991, Apr. 27, 1993, Mar. 10, 1994, Mar. 23, June 13, 24, 1995, Jan. 30, Mar. 4, 23, Sept. 16, 1996, Sept. 23, 1997; *International Daily News,* Nov. 12, 1996, Jan. 13, 1997; Shen Lixin, "Meiguo Huaren xinyimin zhuangkuang yanjiu" [A Study on the Condition of New Chinese Immigrants in the United States], *Overseas Chinese History of Bagui* no. 2 (1996): 26–30.

126. *China News Service,* June 26, 1984; *China Daily News,* Feb. 3, 1986; *Chinese Times,* Apr. 8, 1996; *China Press,* May 11, 1998.

127. *World Journal Weekly,* Apr. 21, May 26, 1996.

128. *China Press,* July 6, Nov. 27, 1995; *International Daily News,* Jan. 17, 1995; *Sampan,* Oct. 20, 1995.

129. Such articles were frequently published in the literary section of *International Daily News* during the late 1990s.

130. *Chinese Tribune,* Mar. 3, 1972; *Chinese Times,* Mar. 10, 1972, Sept. 22, 1994; *China Press,* Sept. 5, 1994; *World Journal,* June 10, 1995.

131. *International Daily News,* Sept. 30, 1996.

132. *International Daily News,* May 13, 2002.

133. "Meidong Sanjiang Gongsuo xiangua wuxing hongqi" [In the Eastern United States the Som Kiang Association Hoisted the Five-Starred Red Flag], retrieved Dec. 15, 2003, from http://www.chinaqw.com.

Chapter 2: Anarchism, Communism, and China's Nationalist Revolution

1. Jack London, the famous author and Socialist Party member, spared no efforts displaying his prejudice against and disdain for Asians, particularly Chinese, in many of his writings.

2. Martin Bernal, *Chinese Socialism to 1907* (Ithaca, N.Y.: Cornell University Press, 1967), 33–34; Zhang Deyi, *Sui shi Faguo ji (San shuqi)* [A Record of Events while Accompanying the Envoy in France (The Third Narrative of the Unusual)] (Changsha: Hunan renmin chubanshe, 1982), 132–33. After Germany defeated France in 1870, the French deposed

Napoleon III and set up a republic. On March 18, 1871, a popular uprising led by the National Guard of Paris, consisting mostly of workers, seized power to form a commune opposed to the Republican government. The commune was supported by Karl Marx and the International Workingmen's Association (also known as the First International). The commune instituted a number of progressive measures, such as separation of church and state and free, general education. It was soon crushed by Republican forces at the end of May in a bloodbath, and many communards fled abroad.

3. Bernal, *Chinese Socialism to 1907,* 33–48.

4. Fan Yinzheng and Li Xiongwei, eds., *Wusi Yundong qian Makesizhuyi zai Zhongguo de jieshao yu chuanbo* [Introduction and Spread of Marxism in China before the May Fourth Movement] (Changsha: Hunan renmin chubanshe, 1986), 2–3.

5. An account of the introduction of socialist doctrines into China may be found in Martin Bernal, "The Triumph of Anarchism over Marxism, 1906–1907," in *China in Revolution: The First Phase, 1900–1913,* ed. M. C. Wright (New Haven, Conn.: Yale University Press, 1968), 97–142.

6. An account of the development of anarchism in China may be found in Robert A. Scalapino and George T. Yu, *The Chinese Anarchist Movement* (Berkeley, Calif.: Center for Chinese Studies, 1961).

7. Bernal, *Chinese Socialism to 1907,* 65–67; Sun Wen (Sun Yat-sen), *"Min Bao fakanci"* [Essay on the Start of Publication of *Min Bao*], in *Guofu quanji* [Complete Works of Sun Yat-sen] (Taipei: Zhongyang wenwu gongyingshe, 1973), 2:80–81.

8. *Encyclopedia of Chinese Overseas: Volume of Media and Publication* (Beijing: Zhongguo Huaqiao chubanshe, 1999), s.v. "Xin Shiji."

9. "Xin She chuangzuo ren Liu Sifu" [Li Sifu, the Founder of Heart Society], 207–11, in Feng Ziyou, *Geming yishi* [Anecdotal History of the Revolution] 2nd collection (Chongqing: Commercial Press, 1943; repr., Taipei: Taiwan Commercial Press, 1953); *Zhongshan shi zhi* [Gazetteer of Zhongshan City] (Shaoguan: Guangdong renmin chubanshe, 1997), 1456; *Guangdong jin-xiandai renwu cidian* [Dictionary of Recent and Modern Personalities in Guangdong] (Panyu: Guangdong keji chubanshe, 1992), s.v. "Liu Sifu" (cited hereafter as Dictionary of Recent and Modern Personalities). After the founding of the Republic in 1912, Liu and his followers founded the Huiming Xueshe [Crowing in the Darkness Learned Society] in Guangzhou (Canton) in 1912 to advocate anarchism. After the Second Revolution against Yuan Shikai in 1913, he became disgruntled by his former Tongmenghui comrades, who seemed concerned only with personal advancement, and organized Xin She [Heart Society] in Guangdong to start a national anarchist movement. However, in 1914 he fled to Shanghai to avoid arrest by the warlord Long Jiguang and died there of tuberculosis in 1915. Liu had many followers in the Pearl River Delta, and several prominent anarchists in America came from his native county. Gao Jianfu, also known as Gao Lun, was the founder of the Lingnan school of Chinese painting, which combined Chinese and Western techniques. Chen Jiongming later became governor of Guangdong but lost power after a failed rebellion against Sun Yat-sen in 1922. When the American Chee Kung Tong (Chinese Freemasons or Zhigongtang) organized the Zhongguo Zhigongdang [Chee Kung Tang of China] in 1925 to play a more active role in Chinese politics, Chen was elected as titular head.

10. Philip S. Foner, *History of the Labor Movement in the United States* (New York: International Publishers, 1947), 4:82; "Kuang Zuozhi shilüe," [Biographic Sketch of George Fong], in Feng, Anecdotal History of the Revolution, 2:287–89.

11. See *Encyclopedia of Chinese Overseas: Volume of Media*, 234–35, 426; "Xinhai qian wo zai Tanxiangshan Tongmenghui he *Ziyou Xinbao* gongzuo de huiyi" [My Experiences with the Tongmenghui and as Editor at *Liberty Press* in Honolulu before the 1911 Revolution], *Xinhai geming huiyilu* [Reminiscences of the 1911 Revolution] (Beijing: Wenshi ziliao chubanshe, 1982), 8:309–43.

12. "Kuang Zuozhi shilüe," [Biographic Sketch of George Fong] in Feng, *Anecdotal History of the Revolution*, 2:287–89.

13. Kiang Kang Hu, *China and the Social Revolution* (San Francisco: Kiang Kang Hu, 1914); *Young China*, Jan. 9, 1914.

14. *Young China*, Sept. 1, 1914.

15. *Chinese Collections in the Library of Congress: Excerpts from the Annual Report(s) of the Librarian of Congress, 1898–1971*, comp. P. K. Yu (Washington, D.C.: Center for Chinese Research Materials, Association of Research Libraries, 1974), 1:69, 75–76, 87–91, 107–8.

16. *Young China*, Apr. 2, May 18, June 1, 6, 29, 1914.

17. *Young China*, Jan. 21, 22, 1919. For biographical details of Xie Yingbo (1882–1939) and his political activities in China and the United States, see *Mei Xian Zhi* [Gazetteer of Mei County] (Meizhou: Guangdong Renmin Chubanshe, 1994), 1158–59; Dictionary of Recent and Modern Personalities, 521–22; and *Tanxiangshan Zhongshan Xuexiao ershisan zhounian di-shisan jie biye jinian tekan* [Special Publication Commemorating the Twenty-third Anniversary and Thirteenth Graduating Class of Chung Shan School of Hawaii] (Honolulu: Chung Shan School, 1934), 234–35. For biographical details of Chu Su Gunn (1880–1930), see *Xinhui Xian Zhi* [Xinhui County Gazetteer](Xinhui: Guangdong Renmin Chubanshe, 1995), 1144–45.

18. Theodore Draper, *The Roots of American Communism* (1957; repr., Chicago: Ivan R. Dee, Inc., 1987), 203–4. During World War I and the years immediately following, many states passed laws against "sedition," "criminal anarchy," or "criminal syndicalism." The federal government launched a drive to round up for deportation thousands of aliens suspected of subversive affiliations or beliefs. This hysteria percolated down to local levels as zealous citizens sought out syndicalists, communists, socialists, and pacifists as threats to American society.

19. Wu Tiecheng, *Wu Tiecheng huiyilu* [Reminiscences of Wu Tiecheng] (Taipei: Sanmin shuju, 1971), 74–77.

20. *Young China*, Dec. 26, 1915. Liu Beihai passed away on Taiwan in 1967. See Qianren, "Dao Liu Beihai xiansheng" [Mourning Mr. Liu Beihai], *Wah Kiu Yat Po* [Overseas Chinese Daily], Sept. 8, 1967; T. H. Lee, *A History of Chinese in Canada* (Vancouver: Jia'nada ziyou chubanshe, 1967), 317. Wang Chang committed suicide after the killing.

21. Ma Chaojun, ed., *A History of China's Labour Movement* (Taipei: The Zhongguo Laogong fuli chubanshe, 1966), 50–51.

22. Liang Yukui, "Zhonghua Minguo Gongdang shimo" [Story of the Labor Party of the Republic of China], in *Zhongguo xiandaishi dashi jishi benmo* [Accounts of Important Events in the History of Modern China] (Harbin: Heilongjiang renmin chubanshe, 1987), 7–12; Li Xin, Li Zongyi, chief eds., *Zhonghua Minguo shi* [History of the Republic of China], part 2, *Beiyang Zhengfu tongzhi shiqi* [Period of the Rule of the Northern Government], vol. 1a, *1912–1916* (Beijing: Zhonghua shuju, 1987), 70–72; Tang Zhijun, chief ed., *Jindai Shanghai dashiji* [Chronology of Important Events in Shanghai in the Recent Period] (Shanghai: Shanghai cishu chubanshe, 1989), 754.

23. Edgar Wickberg, ed., *From China to Canada: A History of the Chinese Communi-*

ties in Canada (Toronto: McClelland and Stewart, 1982), 130, 139; Chen Jisong, "Rexin xingxue de xianqiao Chen Shuyao" [Chen Shuyao: An Early Overseas Chinese Who Enthusiastically Promoted Education], retrieved June 21, 2008, from http://www.zsnews .cn/Column/2006/02/27/545683.shtml (cited hereafter as Chen Jisong, "Chen Shuyao"); Zheng Peigang, *Xiangshan xunbao ji qi chuangbanren Zheng Anfu* [Zheng Anfu, Founder of the *Xiangshan Ten-Day Newspaper*], in *Guangdong wen-shi ziliao* [Literary and Historical Materials of Guangdong], 25th collection, ed. Zhongguo Renmin Zhengzhi Xieshang Huiyi Guangdong Sheng Weiyuanhui Wen-shi Ziliao Yanjiu Weiyuanhui [Literary and Historical Materials Research Committee, Guangdong Provincial Committee, Chinese People's Political Consultative Conference] (Guangzhou: Guangdong renmin chubanshe, Mar. 1983), 143–55 (cited hereafter as Zheng, Zheng Anfu). Although Liu Sifu's influence on the Chinese American anarchist movement was indirect, Xiangshan (now Zhongshan) immigrants were prominent in the movement before World War II. Zheng Bi'an fled to Canada in 1914 to escape the Yuan Shikai repression of the Left.

24. Ting-Chiu Fan, "Chinese Residents in Chicago" (MA diss., University of Chicago, 1926), 136–39.

25. *Kung Sing,* no. 1 (Mar. 1, 1924), and no. 2 (Apr. 1, 1924), includes a detailed account of the early history of the Unionist Guild of America up to 1924, written by editor Chen Shuyao. For more details of Chen Shuyao (1887–1944), see Chen Jisong, "Chen Shuyao."

26. The nine demands were as follows: (1) A nine-hour workday; (2) guarantees that future wages would only increase and not decrease; (3) overtime to be paid for work over nine hours; (4) double-time to be paid for work on Sundays; (5) paid vacation for American holidays; (6) employers should pay medical bills for workplace injuries; (7) apprenticeships should be limited to two months and apprentices paid weekly expenses of $1.00; (8) employers should recompense $50.00 to workers living on the premises in cases of fire; (9) workers disobeying the above regulations should be subject to discharge by the league. Factory owners eventually accepted all but the ninth demand.

27. *Chung Sai Yat Po,* July 6, 1925; Josephine Fowler, "'To Be Red and "Oriental"': The Experience of Japanese and Chinese Immigrant Communists in the American and International Communist Movements, 1919–1933" (PhD diss., University of Minnesota, 2003), 96, 116 n. cxx.

On May 30, 1925, about two thousand students and workers marched in the International Settlement in an anti-imperialist demonstration, and more than a hundred were arrested by the foreign police. When demonstrators surrounded the police station and demanded their release, the British captain in charge ordered the police to fire on the crowd, killing twelve and wounding numerous others. This incident led to a general strike and national anti-imperialist protests.

28. The name changed to Zhonghua Zonggonghui [United Chinese Labor Association] in 1931 by order of the Kuomintang government.

29. "Zhonghua Zonggonghui *Tanxiangshan Zhonghua Zonggonghui chengli ershiliu zhounian ji'nian tekan* [Special Publication Commemorating the 26th Anniversary of the United Chinese Labor Association of Hawaii] (Honolulu: United Chinese Labor Association of Hawaii, 1941), 16, 20, 66–67; Chock Lun, "Chinese Organizations in Hawaii," in *The Chinese of Hawaii,* ed. Chun Kwong Lau and Kam Pui Lai (Honolulu: Overseas Penman Club, 1936), 2:22–35.

30. Zhong Changying, "Guangzhou baoye mingren Xie Yingbo [Xie Yingbo, a Notable in Guangzhou Journalism] (July 22, 2005), retrieved Aug. 23, 2007, from http://www

.guangzhou.gov.cn/node_437/node_439/node_618/2005; Zeng Jianzhao, Chen Shanguang, "Guangdong Shehuizhuyi qingniantuan de chengli ji qi zhuyao huodong" [Founding of the Guangdong Socialist Youth League and Its Principal Activities] (1984), retrieved Aug. 23, 2007, from http://www.ccyl.org.cn/695/gqt_tuanshi/gqt_ghlc/his_study/200794/t200704_17658.htm; Dormant C. Chang, in *Tanshan Huaqiao* [The Chinese of Hawaii] (Honolulu: The Overseas Penman Club, 1929), 18, 58, 90–91; Chock Lun, "Chinese Organizations in Hawaii"; Chen Weimin, "Sun Zhongshan yu zaoqi Guangzhou gongren yundong" [Sun Yat-sen and Guangzhou's Early Labor Movement] (Shilin, Taiwan), no. 3 (1995), retrieved July 29, 2007, from cache of http://58.63.114.194:86/ssds/html/2003/08/2003081708533815.htm; Zeng Jianzhao and Chen Shanguang, "Guangdong Shehuizhuyi Qingniantuan de chengli ji qi zhuyao huodong" [The Establishment of a Young Socialist League in Guangdong and Its Principal Activities], retrieved July 29, 2007, from cache of http://cyc7.cycnet.com:8091/worksnew/content.jsp?id=666&s_code=0209.

31. The Ping Sheh advertised free copies of various pamphlets in *Chung Sai Yat Po,* Nov. 29, 1926. The first issue of *Pingdeng* appeared July 1, 1927, according to an advertisement in *Chung Sai Yat Po,* June 24, 1927. For more information about Zheng Bi'an (1875–1975), see Zheng, Zheng Anfu; and *Gazetteer of Zhongshan City,* 1453–54.

32. Pian Jiyu, "Bajin shengping ji wenxue huodong shilüe" [Short Biographical Account of the Life and Literary Activities of Bajin], Oct. 19, 2005, retrieved Nov. 13, 2005, from http://post.baidu.com/f?kz=53056213; Tang Jinhai, Zhang Xiaoyun, eds. *Bajing nianpu, 1904–1949* [Chronological Biography of Bajin] (Chengdu: Sichuan wenyi chubanshe, 1989), 140, 153–56, 167–68, 170, 173–74, 177, 179, 182; Meng Rui, "Bajin zaonian de Meiguo yuan" [Bajin's Relationship with America during His Early Years], *U.S. Week* [weekly magazine of *Sing Tao Daily,* San Francisco], Oct. 29, 2005; author's interview with Liu Zhongshi, Jan. 14, 1973. Li Feigan became an anarchist during the early 1920s. In 1927–28 he studied in France, where he took on the nom de plume of Ba Jin. "Ba" was the surname of a classmate whose suicide affected Li very deeply, and "jin" [metal] came from the accepted Chinese transliteration of the name of the anarchist Kropotkin, "Ke-lu-pao-te-jin." Ba Jin participated in the international effort to save Americans Sacco and Vanzetti from their death sentence and corresponded with numerous anarchists worldwide, including Vanzetti. After returning to China, he published the trilogy, *Jia* [Family], *Chun* [Spring], and *Qiu* [Autumn], depicting the problems of traditional families in a rapidly changing Chinese society. For correspondence between Liu Zhongshi and Ba Jin after he returned to China, see Li Cunguang, ed., *Ba Jin: Yijian xinbian* [Ba Jin: New Edition of Lost Correspondence] (Zhengzhou, He'nan: Daxiang chubanshe, 2003).

33. *Chinese World,* Mar. 22, 1928; and *Chung Sai Yat Po,* Mar. 23, 1928. Cai Xian entered the United States around 1909. He became an anarchist and did not believe in the use of family names. He identified himself as Red Jones, but later this was changed to Ray Jones. During his early years in California, Cai Xian worked variously as a sewing machine operator in San Jose, a farm laborer picking and packing fruits, and a janitor in a sheet metal shop. According to Cai, other than the arrest in 1928, he was seldom bothered by the police. During the Sino-Japanese War, however, he was beaten up at the Chinese Consolidated Benevolent Association in Chinatown for refusing to contribute to China war relief funds. Cai retired to Macao in 1973 (author's interview with Cai Xian, Jan. 14, 1973).

34. *Ping Sheh,* May Day Special Issue, May 1, 1927.

35. The first issue was published June 1, 1934. Communications to the editor were to be addressed to Ray Jones.

36. William Z. Foster, *Outline Political History of the Americas* (New York: International Publishers, 1951), 391–92.

37. *Chung Sai Yat Po,* Dec. 4, 1919. The American-born Jung was a staunch supporter of Sun Yat-sen, who had gone to China after the 1911 Revolution and later returned to the United States for further education to prepare for a career in China. For more information about Jung, see Oi-won Jung, "Zini Zhang Mingxintang Jia Zhuan" [Family History of the Zhang Mingxintang of Zini Village], manuscript, dated 1931, Ethnic Studies Library Collection, University of California, Berkeley.

38. Li Xisuo, *Jindai Zhongguo de Liuxuesheng* [Chinese Students Studying Abroad in Modern Times] (Beijing: Renmin chubanshe, 1987), 236, 256–97 (cited hereafter as Li, Students Studying Abroad). The work-study program was established in 1912 as the Liufa Jianxuehui [Association for Thrifty Education in France] and began in France in 1915 as the Liufa Qingong Jianxuehui [Association for Part-Work and Part-Study in France]. Some students became interested in Marxism and formed a Communist group in spring 1921. This group soon evolved into the European branch of the CCP and recruited members among Chinese students in France, Germany, Belgium, and other European countries. Some party members became CCP leaders in China, including Zhou Enlai, Li Lisan, Deng Xiaoping, and Chen Yi.

39. Cheng Zhongyuan, "Zhang Wentian Zhuanlüe" [A Brief Biography of Zhang Wentian], in *Zhong-Gong dangshi ziliao* [Materials on Communist Party of China History], ed. Zhong-Gong Zhongyang Dangshi Yanjiushi [Office of the Central Committee of the Communist Party of China for Research on Party History] (Beijing: Zhong Gong Dangshi Ziliao Chubanshe, 1990), 35:118–45; Jing Shengxian, *Zhang Wentian de zuji* [The Footprints of Zhang Wentian] (Shanghai: Shanghai shehui kexue chubanshe, 1995), 41–43. In 1922 members of the Shao'nian Zhongguo Xuehui [Young China Learned Society], a liberal and progressive group founded in Beijing in 1919, came to America as students. They assumed editorial responsibilities at the ailing *Chinese Republican Journal,* the Zhigongtang organ in San Francisco.

40. Howard L. Boorman, et al., eds. *Biographical Dictionary of Republican China*, vol. 1 (New York: Columbia University Press, 1967), s.v. "Ch'en Kung-po"; Wen Shaohua, "Chen Gongbo zhuan" [Biography of Chen Gongbo] (Beijing: Dongfang chubanshe, 1994), 47. Chen Gongbo joined the left-wing faction of the KMT. During the Sino-Japanese War, he was a member of the Japanese puppet government in occupied China and was convicted and executed by the KMT for treason in 1946.

41. Fowler, "To Be Red and Oriental," 94. Several underground Marxist Communist groups emerged in America after the October Revolution, but not until 1922 did they merge to form the Workers Party of America, a name that changed to Communist Party of America in 1925. In 1929 the name again changed, this time to Communist Party of the United States of America. In order to avoid confusing the reader with different names, this essay will employ Communist Party and the acronym CPUSA to refer to any of these different versions of the party's name.

42. Qinghua (Tsinghua) School was established in 1911 to prepare Chinese students to study in America. It was funded from the United States' returned portion of the Boxer indemnity and officially became a university in 1928.

43. The name Chaotao referred to the *Romance of the Three Kingdoms* in which the

heroes Liu Bei, Guan Yu, and Zhang Fei took oaths in a peach garden to become sworn brothers. Chaotao inferred that the bonds holding the group together exceeded the strength of those of the Peach Garden Oath.

Shi Huang was a member of the Bai nationality of Yunnan. According to one anecdote, he finished first in Kunming's School for Military Doctors, but instead of his winning a scholarship for advanced study in Tianjin, as had been previous practice, the son of a rich and powerful family received the award. This unfair treatment left young Shi Huang deeply resolved to fight injustice. See "Qinghuayuan zhong de juhuoren—Shi Huang" [Shi Huang—The One Who Lit a Fire on Qinghua Campus], ed. Zhonggong Dali zuzhibu [Dali Organization Department of the CCP], dated June 30, 2003, retrieved from http://dldj.ccp.org.cn/second/read.aspx?n_id=111.

44. Yang Zuntao and Zhao Liqian, "Shi Huang," in *Zhong-Gong dangshi renwu zhuan* [Personages in the Party History of the CCP], ed. Hu Hua et al. (Xi'an: Shaanxi Renmin chubanshe, 1990), 45:151–74; Shi Hui, "Shi Huang Lieshi: Qinghua Daxue liu Mei xuesheng zhong zui zao de Gongchandang yuan" [The Martyr Shi Huang: The Earliest Communist Party Member among Tsinghua School Students in America], in *Wenshi ziliao xuanbian* [Selected Historical and Literary Materials], ed. Zhongguo Renmin Zhengzhi Xieshang Huiyi Beijing Weiyuanhui, Wenshi Ziliao Weiyuanhui [Historical Materials Committee of the Beijing Committee, Chinese People's Political Consultative Conference] (Beijing: Beijing Chubanshe, 1980), 6:13–25; Shi Ji, "Qinghua Liuxuesheng zhong Zui Zao de Gongchandang Yuan zhi Yi—Shi Huang Lieshi" [One of the Earliest Communist Party Members among Tsinghua Students Abroad—The Martyr Shi Huang], in *Renwu zhi* [Accounts of personalities], ed. Qinghua Daxue Xiaoshizu [Tsinghua University School History Group] (Beijing: Qinghua Daxue chubanshe, 1983), 1:70–76.

45. On May 15, 1925, a strike by workers in a Japanese-owned cotton mill in Shanghai turned violent. Communist activists and students joined to protest foreign imperialism. British police intervened and arrested many. When Chinese demonstrated in front of the police station on May 30 to demand the prisoners' release, police fired on the crowd and killed more than a dozen, while wounding several dozen more. This violence inspired anti-imperialist demonstrations across China, involving some twelve million Chinese. The biggest strike occurred in Hong Kong and paralyzed the port. In Guangzhou on June 23, British and French police fired on demonstrators with machine guns, while foreign warships anchored on the Pearl River lobbed shells at them. Fifty-two Chinese were killed and more than 170 were wounded.

46. Fowler, "To Be Red and Oriental," 91–95.

47. Sun Dunheng, "Yi zhenxing Zhonghua wei ji ren: Qinghua xueyun xianquzhe Ji Chaoding" [One Who Regarded the Vitalizing of China as His Own Responsibility: C. T. Chi, a Pioneer in the Tsinghua Student Movement], in *Renwu zhi* [Accounts of Personalities], ed. Qinghua Daxue Xiaoshizu [Tsinghua University School History Group] (Beijing: Qinghua Daxue chubanshe, 1983), 1:77–91 (cited hereafter as Sun, "C. T. Chi"); Yang and Zhao, "Shi Huang."

48. Yang and Zhao, "Shi Huang."

49. Draper, *American Communism and Soviet Russia,* 178; Sun, "Ji Chaoding"; Yang and Zhao, "Shi Huang"; Fowler, "To Be Red and Oriental," 106, 118 n. cxl.

50. *Young China,* July 22–25, 1926, Sept. 12, 1926, Feb. 22 and 25, 1927; Zhang Bao, "Er sanshi niandai zai Meiguo de Zhongguo Gongchandang ren" [Chinese Communists in the United States during the Twenties and Thirties], in *Guoji gongyunshi yanjiu ziliao*

[Historical Research Materials on the International Communist Movement] (Beijing: 1982), 7:150–61 (cited hereafter as Zhang, Chinese Communists in the U.S.).

51. *Young China,* Dec. 13, 16, and 29, 1926; Zhang, Chinese Communists in the U.S. Luo returned to China in 1928. He and Zhang Junmai (Carsun Chang) founded the Nationalist Socialist Party of China in 1931. In the 1940s, Luo became a leader of the Chinese Democratic League, a noncommunist political group critical of KMT rule. After the founding of the PRC he was appointed to the Government Administration Council and other posts. In 1957 he was branded a "rightist member of the bourgeoisie" and was stripped of all posts. He died in 1965 in Beijing. See vol. 2 of *Biographical Dictionary of Republican China,* s.v. "Lo Lung-chi."

52. Fowler, "To Be Red and Oriental," 104–5, 118 nn. cxxxiv cxxxviii; Philip J. Jaffe, *The Amerasia Case from 1945 to the Present* (New York: Philip J. Jaffe, 1979), 1; Sun, "C. T. Chi"; vol. 1 of *Biographical Dictionary of Republican China,* s.v. "Chi Ch'ao-ting"; Wang Yongxiang, Kong Fanfeng, Liu Pinqing, *Zhongguo Gongchandang Lü-Ou Zhibu shihua* [Historical Account of the Branch of the Chinese Communist Party Sojourning in Europe] (Beijing: Zhongguo qingnian chubanshe, 1985), 246–48; *Kuo Min Yat Po,* June 20 and 24, 1927.

53. Yang and Zhao, "Shi Huang"; Yao Xiaoping, "Xian wei ren zhi de hongse gemingjia: Ji mei-Gong Zhongguoju chuangshiren he *Mao Suan* Yingyi zhuchiren Xu Yongying" [A Red Revolutionary Seldom Known to Others: Y. Y. Hsu, Founder of the Chinese Bureau, CPUSA and Director of English Translation of the Selected works of Mao Zedong], *Renwu* no. 6 (2003): 5–24 (cited hereafter as Yao, "Y. Y. Hsu").

Mei Ru'ao (1902–73), from Jiangxi, was the only member of the Chaotao eight who chose not to join the Communist Party. He went to America in 1924 and eventually received a doctorate in law. After returning to China, he taught law. After World War II, he was a judge on the military tribunal presiding over the war crimes trials in Tokyo. He turned down an appointment to head the KMT government's Ministry of Justice and in 1949 was appointed advisor to the PRC Ministry of Foreign Affairs (Ref. Note 10, Xu Suizhi, "Xu Yongying shengping nianbiao" [Chronology of the Life of Y. Y. Hsu] part 1 [Apr. 28, 2007], retrieved Aug. 21, 2007, from http://kui-shi.blog.hexun.com/9113223_d.html [cited hereafter as Xu Suizhi, Chronology of Life of Y. Y. Hsu]).

54. Yang and Zhao, "Shi Huang."

55. Fowler, "To Be Red and Oriental," 104, 401, 407–8.

56. Zhang, Chinese Communists in the U.S. For more information about Su Kaiming (1904–88), see "Su Kaiming (1904–1988)," retrieved Sept. 4, 2005, from http://www.shtong .gov.cn/node2/node2245/node69322/node69492/node69496/useobjectlai67656.html. For more information about Yu Guangsheng (1906–78), see Gao Sheng et al., eds., *Zhonghua liuxue mingren cidian* [Dictionary of Famous Chinese Who Studied Abroad] (Changchun: Dongbei Shifan Daxue Chubanshe, 1992), s.v. "Yu Guangsheng."

57. Fowler, "To Be Red and Oriental," 389.

58. Israel Epstein, *Woman in World History: Soong Ching Ling* (Beijing: New World Press, 1993), 184, 189–91; Peter Rand, *China Hands: The Adventures and Ordeals of the American Journalists Who Joined Forces with the Great Chinese Revolution* (New York: Simon and Schuster, 1995), 61; Qian Yuli, *Chen Youren zhuan* [Biography of Eugene Chen] (Baoding: Hebei Renmin Chubanshe, 1999), 175–76 (cited hereafter as Qian, Biography of Eugene Chen).

59. Anna Louise Strong had come to Wuhan in 1927 at the invitation of Madam Sun.

Her reporting on the peasant's revolution in Hunan and other observations from an earlier trip in 1925 about the Chinese revolution and the Guangzhou–Hong Kong general strike against the British appeared in her book *China's Millions* (published in 1928 and revised in 1935). Her publications' graphic descriptions shaped the impressions of many Western readers concerning life and society in China and the Soviet Union.

60. Mark J. Scher, "Anna Louise Strong," in *Salute to Smedley, Strong, and Snow,* ed. Zhongguo San-S Yanjiuhui [3S Research Society of China] (Beijing: Zhongguo Xinwen-she, 1985), 152–57; Britannica Online, "Strong, Anna Louise (1885–1970), Journalist and Author," by *Encyclopedia Britannica,* 1999, retrieved Aug. 18, 2009, from http://www.britannica.com/EBchecked/topic/569420/Anna-Louise-Strong; Epstein, *Woman in World History,* 186; Qian, Biography of Eugene Chen, 182–86; Percy Chen, *China Called Me: My Life Inside the Chinese Revolution* (Boston: Little, Brown, 1979; Chinese translation by Guo Jizu: Beijing: Commercial Press, 1983), 107–14; vol. 3 of *Biographical Dictionary of Republican China,* s.v. "Teng Yen-ta," and vol. 2, s.v. "Ho Hsiang-ning." Anna Louise Strong (1885–1970) was an advocate for child welfare who became an avowed socialist. By the 1920s, she was a journalist and supported the Soviet Union. Soviet support for the Chinese revolution led her to come to China. She spent the next two decades covering the USSR, United States, Spain, and China. In 1949 she was arrested in Moscow and expelled from the Soviet Union as a spy. Although Moscow exonerated her in 1955, she went to China in 1958, where she stayed until her death.

61. Epstein, *Woman in World History,* 200–202; Qian, Biography of Eugene Chen 187–89.

62. Epstein, *Woman in World History,* 219; Qian, Biography of Eugene Chen, 200, 204.

63. Under Deng's guidance Madam Sun improved her Chinese composition, a skill that had languished due to her mainly foreign education.

64. Epstein, *Woman in World History,* 226, 235–37, 250–55.

65. Janice R. and Stephen R. MacKinnon, *Agnes Smedley: The Life and Times of an American Radical* (Berkeley: University of California Press, 1988), 134, 140, 143–44, 150–51, 154; Rand, *China Hands,* 81–83, 85, 86, 89, 97; "Legendary Life of Chen Han-seng," Chen Han-seng, *Sige shidai de wo* [Myself during Four Time Periods] (Beijing: Zhongguo Wenshi Chubanshe, 1988), 68. Chen Han-seng was born into a family of traditional intellectuals in Wuxi but received his BA, MA, and PhD degrees in the United States and Europe. He married his lifelong companion Susie Gu (Gu Shuxing) in Seattle in 1921 then joined Beijing University as its youngest faculty member. In 1925 Li Dazhao invited him to join the Communist Party. In 1927, when the Beijing military began arresting progressives, Chen fled to the USSR, where he joined the Comintern. He returned to Shanghai in 1928, where he became deputy director of the Social Science Institute of the Academia Sinica.

66. Rand, *China Hands,* 101–2, 120, 125–31; "1930–1935 nian, Yi Luosheng: Sidalin yu Tuoluociji" [1930–1935, Harold Isaacs: Stalin and Trotsky], in Li Hui, *Zai lishi xianchang: Huan yige jiaodu de xushu* [Witnessing History: Accounts from Another Perspective] (Zhengzhou, He'nan: Daxiang Chubabshe, 2003), sections 25, 26, 27, retrieved Nov. 19, 2005, from http://lz.book.sohu.com/learning/chapter.php?id=1613&volume=6&chapter=4,5,6,7; Tang Baolin, "Yi Luosheng yu *Zhongguo Luntan,*" Harold Isaacs and the *China Forum*], retrieved Sept. 14, 2005, from http://history.xmu.edu.cn/ziliao/; Harold Isaacs, "I Break with the Chinese Stalinists (May 1934)," retrieved July 15, 2009, from http://www.marx.org/history/etol/writers/isaacs/1934/05/break.htm. After *China Forum* ceased

publication, Isaacs and his wife went to Beijing, where he worked with CCP founding member Liu Wenjing to translate CCP documents. The Isaacs left China in June 1935 after the arrest of Liu and his family. The documents taken by Isaacs formed the basis for *The Tragedy of the Chinese Revolution* (1938, rev. 1951, 1961), an authoritative analysis of developments during the Chinese revolution of the 1920s. He also wrote *Scratches in Our Minds: American Images of China and India* (1958).

67. Epstein, *Woman in World History,* 267–77; John Maxwell Hamilton, *Edgar Snow: A Biography* (Bloomington: Indiana University Press, 1988), 48–49; "The Secret Intelligence Service and the Case of Hilaire Noulens," in "The Records of the Permanent Under-Secretary's Department: Liaison between the Foreign Office and the British Secret Intelligence Service, 1873–1939," complied by FCO Historians, Mar. 2005, retrieved Nov. 11, 2005, from http://www.fco.gov.uk/Files/kFile/TheRecordofthePermanentUnder SecretaryDepartment_1.pdf; MacKinnon and MacKinnon, *Agnes Smedley,* 149, 154.

The Rueggs remained incarcerated until after the outbreak of the Sino-Japanese War. They were released August 27, 1937, and fled to Shanghai, where Madam Sun gave them sanctuary. On July 25, 1939, they left China with help from the Soviet consulate and arrived in the USSR sometime in 1940. They died there in the 1960s. Later research revealed that their names were Yakov Rudnik and Tatiana Moiseyenko.

68. Epstein, *Woman in World History,* 277–85; Yi Zhuxian, "Hu Shi zhuan," 345–48. Niu Yufeng, "Song Qingling yu Zhongguo Minquan Baozhang Tongmeng," in *Zhongguo xiandai dashi jishu benmo, 1919–1949* [Accounts of Important Events in Modern Chinese History, 1919–1949] (Harbin: Heilongjiang Renmin Chubanshe, 1987), 1:664–70; Shao Jian, "Hu Shi bei Zhongguo Minquan Baozhang Tongmeng kaichu shimo" [The Events Connected with the Expelling of Hu Shi from the China League for the Protection of Civil Rights], *Nanfang zhoumo,* Aug. 22, 2002, retrieved Dec. 31, 2005, from http://www .cddc.net/shownews.asp?newsid=2155; Zhang Yaojie, "Sanshi niandai Zhongguo Minquan Baozhang Tongmeng de jianli yu yaozhe [The Founding and Early Demise of the China League for the Protection of Civil Rights during the 1930s], abridged from essay in *Modern Chinese Studies* no. 4 (2003), retrieved Nov. 13, 2005, from http://www.cgarden.net/ stubArticle.asp?issue=030411&total=83.

69. *Kuo Min Yat Po,* Sept. 23, 1927; Zhu Guanri, "Meizhou Guomin Ribao chouban jingguo" [Course of Events in the Founding of *Kuo Min Yat Po*], in *Guomin Ribao liu zhou nian jinian tekan* [Special Publication to Commemorate the Sixth anniversary of *Kuo Min Yat Po*] (San Francisco: *Kuo Min Yat Po,* 1933), 52–57; *Kuo Min Yat Po,* Feb. 16, 1928; Xu Suizhi, Chronology of Life of Y. Y. Hsu. For more information about Huang Lingshuang (Huang Wenshan, L. S. Wong) (1897–82), see Dictionary of Recent and Modern Personalities, s.v. "Huang Lingshuang." For more information about Ma Dianru (Din Yee Ma), see Pei Chi Liu, *A History of the Chinese in the United States of America* (Taipei: Liming Wenhua Shiye Gufen Youxian Gongsi, 1981), 2:387.

70. Fowler, "To Be Red and Oriental," 414–18, 427–36; Ou Shu, "Yige bu ying bei wangji de Mei Hua zuojia, Jiang Xizeng" [H. T. Tsiang, a Chinese American Author Who Should Not Be Forgotten], *China Daily News,* Jan. 12 and 13, 1983; Floyd Cheung, introduction to H. T. Tsiang, *And China Has Hands* (repr., Forest Hills, N.Y.: Ironweed Press, 2003), 1–15; Leong Gor Yun, *Chinatown Inside Out* (New York: Barrows Mussey, 1936), 153–54. After his release from prison, H. T. Tsiang (1899–1971) left for New York to enter Columbia University in fall 1927. He submitted poems to the *Daily Worker* and *New Masses,* and in 1929 he self-published *Poems of the Chinese Revolution,* which received some good reviews.

In winter 1930, he signed on for a role in the Broadway production of Sergei M. Tretiakov's proletarian drama *Roar China*. During the 1930s, he published three novels in English with revolutionary themes: *China Red* (1931), *The Hanging on Union Square* (1931), and *And China Has Hands* (1937). Tsiang constantly faced threats of deportation throughout the 1930s, and in 1940–41 was even incarcerated at Ellis Island for eight months. After clearing his immigration status, he abandoned New York for Los Angeles to begin a new career as an actor in Hollywood films.

71. Fowler, "To Be Red and Oriental," 444–49. The Chinese term for the Chinese Bureau was "Zhongguo Ju" which indicates that support for the *Chinese* revolution was a priority to the Chinese faction.

72. Yang and Zhao, "Shi Huang"; *Zhongguo Guomindang zhu Sanfanshi zong-zhibu di'er ci daibiao dahui shi'mo ji* [Proceedings of the Second Convention of the Kuomintang San Francisco General Branch] (San Francisco: San Francisco General Branch of the KMT, 1928), 163; Y. Y. Hsu, "Xianfeng si zhounian de huigu yu qianzhan [Looking Back and Peering Forward at the Fourth Anniversary of *Chinese Vanguard*], *Chinese Vanguard*, Apr. 15, 1934; Wang Shigu, "Cong *Xianfeng* dao *Jiuguo Shibao*" [From *Chinese Vanguard* to *China Salvation Times*], in *Haiwai Huawen xinwenshi yanjiu* [Research on the History of Chinese Language Journalism Overseas] (Beijing: Xinhua chubanshe, 1998), 130–34 (cited hereafter as Wang Shigu, From *Chinese Vanguard* to *China Salvation Times*); Fowler, "To Be Red and Oriental," 445–46; Josephine Fowler, *Japanese and Chinese Immigrant Activists: Organizing in American and International Communist Movements, 1919–1933* (New Brunswick, N.J.: Rutgers University Press, 2007), 244 n. 9; Xu Suizhi, "Chronology of Life of Y. Y. Hsu."

73. Yang and Zhao, "Shi Huang." Shi Huang returned to China from the USSR in 1930. In 1933 he was captured and executed by the KMT government.

74. Li Da'nan, "Yidai waijiaojia Zhang Hanfu [Zhang Hanfu, Diplomat of a Generation], *Renwu* no. 6 (2002), retrieved Sept. 1, 2007, from http://www.renwu.com.cn/UserFiles/magazine/article/RW0160_200207101640008110.asp.

75. Zhang, Chinese Communists in the U.S.

76. Tsinghua University History Editorial Committee, "Ji Chaoding tongzhi fangwen jilu" [Record of an Interview with Comrade C. T. Chi] (Nov. 26, 1959), retrieved July 26, 2007, from http://kui-sui.blog.hexun.com/9251626_d.html (cited hereafter as Interview with Comrade C. T. Chi).

77. Interview with Comrade C. T. Chi. Zhang Youjiang became a university professor and later joined the Revolutionary Committee of the KMT.

78. Jaffe, *Amerasia Case*, 1–2; Sun, "C. T. Chi"; vol. 1 of *Biographical Dictionary of Republican China*, s.v. "Chi Ch'ao-ting"; Cao Yunding, Li Ji, "Ji Chaoding," in *Zhonggong dangshi renwuzhuan* [Biographies of Personalities in CCP History], 32nd Collection (Xi'an: Shaanxi renmin chubanshe, 1987), 312–28; Zhang, Chinese Communists in the U.S.

79. Zhang, Chinese Communists in the U.S.; Fowler, "To Be Red and Oriental," 488; vol. 1 of *Biographical Dictionary of Republican China*, s.v. "Chi Ch'ao-ting."

80. By-laws of AAACAI in *Chinese Vanguard*, Nov. 16, 1935.

81. "Su Kaming (1904–1988)," retrieved Sept. 4, 2007, from http://shtong.gov.cn/node2/node2245/node69322/node69341/node69492/node69496/userobject1ai67656.html.

82. *Chung Sat Yat Po*, July 29 and 30, Aug. 14 and 15, 1929; *New York Times*, July 29, 1929.

83. Wang Shigu, From *Chinese Vanguard* to *China Salvation Times*; Zhang, Chinese Communists in the U.S.; Peter Kwong, *Chinatown, New York: Labor and Politics, 1930–1950* (New York: Monthly Review Press, 1979), 50–52.

84. Wang Shigu, From *Chinese Vanguard* to *China Salvation Times; Chinese Vanguard,* Nov. 9, 1935, Apr. 28, 1937; Zhang, Chinese Communists in the U.S.; Leong, *Chinatown Inside Out,* 154; Kwong, *Chinatown, N.Y.,* 50–52; Fowler, "To Be Red and Oriental," 458; Fowler, *Japanese and Chinese Immigrant Activists,* 230 n. 96. Su is the CCP member best known for his efforts in organizing the Hong Kong–Guangzhou seamen's strike in 1922.

85. Xie Chuang (Xavier Dea), *Chongyang nan zu baoguoxin* [Seas and Oceans Cannot Block an Intention to Serve the Nation] (Guangzhou: Hua'nan Shifan Daxue Yinshuachang, 1993), 1–9 (cited hereafter as Xie, Seas and Oceans).

86. *Chung Sai Yat Po,* Apr. 13, 1927; author's interview with Benjamin Fee, Mar. 28, 1975; author's interview with Xavier Dea, Oct. 10, 1981; Xie, Seas and Oceans, 8; author's interview with Virginia Fee, sister of Benjamin Fee, June 24, 1990; author's interview with Roger Wong, brother-in-law of Benjamin Fee, Aug. 1, 1991; note to author from Virginia Fee, June 10, 2005. Benjamin Fee was the eldest son of the American-born Zhang Baifei (J. B. Fee), who interpreted for the Fook On Lung store. Fee was born in Guangzhou on Aug. 31, 1909. His grandfather kept him in China while his parents returned to the United States.

87. Fowler, "To Be Red and Oriental," 406–7, 478; *Chung Sai Yat Po,* Apr. 8, 13, May 30, June 13, 30, July 25, Aug. 29, Sept. 17, 19, 26, 1927.

88. *Chung Sai Yat Po,* June 11, 1928. For more information about Eva Chan, see Judy Yung, *Unbound Voices: A Documentary History of Chinese Women in San Francisco* (Berkeley: University of California Press, 1999), 365–66.

89. *Chung Sai Yat Po,* Mar. 19, May 7, 30, 1928; Benjamin Fee interview. After the KMT launched the Northern Expedition in 1925, its military successes as it proceeded northward led the foreign powers to take steps to protect their special interests. When the KMT army mined the port of Dagu (Taku), the foreign powers collectively issued an ultimatum demanding that the Beijing government keep the port open. Nationalist organizations in Beijing petitioned the KMT not to acquiesce to these demands. Guards used bayonets to disperse the crowd, wounding a number of protesters. On March 18, another mass rally by students at Tian'anmen resulted in another march of several thousand petitioning the government again. Once more, soldiers fired to break up the demonstration, killing more than forty and wounding more than two hundred.

90. *Chung Sai Yat Po,* Jan. 14, 28, and 30, 1929.

91. *Chinese Students' Monthly* 25, no. 3 (February 1930): 138; Zhang, Chinese Communists in the U.S.; Fowler, *Japanese and Chinese Immigrant Activists,* 161–62.

92. This organizational structure also enabled a number of Chinese Communists to become members of both the CPUSA and CCP, depending on where they happened to be active at any particular time. This practice apparently was discontinued by the CCP soon after the founding of the PRC.

Chapter 3: Organizing the Community

1. Situ Binghe, "Chen Qiyuan yu Situ Meitang de youyi" [The Friendship between Chen Qiyuan and Situ Meitang], Hong Kong, Nov. 24, 1996, retrieved Aug. 29, 2005, from http://wylib.jiangmen.gd.cn/jmhq/list.asp?id-4019.

2. The Left had long been active among Chinese seamen, who could be found in many ports because they jumped ship. Their murky residency status made them vulnerable in countries like the United States. This and their frequent long absences probably were the main factors preventing seamen from playing greater roles in this political movement.

3. Zhuang Jingmin, "Chongyang fengyu yi dangnian" [Reminiscing about the Wind and Rain Overseas during Those Years], 1996, retrieved Nov. 6, 2005, from http://www.rwabc .com/diqurenwu/diqudanyirenwu.asp?people_id=6246&p_name=???&category _name=??; "Xuan Rong (1893–1986)," retrieved Aug. 4, 2006, from http://wylib.Jiangmen .Gd.cn/jmhq/list.asp?id=396. Xuan Rong (Xuan Quanguang) (1893–1986) was another radical sailor. A Hong Kong–born CCP member, he became a seaman on an American ship and found his way to San Francisco in 1930, where he joined the ACWP and was associated with CPUSA member Xavier Dea. Xuan returned to Hong Kong in 1936.

4. Xie Chuang (Xavier Dea), *Chongyang nan zu baoguoxin* [Seas and Oceans Cannot Block an Intention to Serve the Nation] (Guangzhou: Hua'nan Shifan Daxue yinshuachang, 1993), 8–9 (cited hereafter as Xie, Seas and Oceans).

5. Zhang Bao, "Er, sanshi niandai zai Meiguo de Zhongguo Gongchandang ren" [Chinese Communists in the United States during the Twenties and Thirties], in *Guoji gongyunshi yanjiu ziliao* [Historical Research Materials on the International Communist Movement] (Beijing: 1982), 7:150–61 (cited hereafter as Zhang, Chinese Communists in the U.S.). Party members recruited from the Chinese community included Liu Kemian (Hartmann Liu), Zhao Yue (Chew Yoek in Cantonese), Lin Tang (Thomas Lem Tong), Ouyang Ji (Owyang Gei in Cantonese), Cen Huijian (Alice Sum), Zeng Dingyuan (Tsang Ding Yuen in Cantonese), Chen Houfu (Chan Hau Fu in Cantonese), He Huiliang (Ho Wai Leung in Cantonese), Feng Hanping (Fung Hon Ping in Cantonese), Zhou Binghun (Chow Bing Won in Cantonese), and Xu Jiyuan (Hui Gei Won), among others. For more information about some of these party members, see Xu Suizhi, "Bainian Xu Yongying zhi Xu Yongying zhuanlue" [A Short Biography of Y. Y. Hsu at His Centennial], part 3 (May 24, 2007), retrieved July 11, 2007, from http://xusuizhi.blshe.com/post/3238/55621 (cited hereafter as Xu Suizhi, Short Biography of Y. Y. Hsu); Xu Suizhi, "Chronology of the Life of Y. Y. Hsu," part 2 (Apr. 28, 2007), n. 38, retrieved Aug. 20, 2007, from http://kui-shi .blog.hexun.com/9113246_d.html; "Guangzhou Shi zhi: 4. Zao pai–Hua huiguo" [Gazetteer of Guangzhou: 4. Return to China Due to Anti-Chinese Activity], retrieved July 3, 2007, from http://www.gzsdfz.org.cn/gzsz/19/hq/sz19hq02020104.htm.

6. Bernard K. Johnpoll and Harvey Klehr, *Biographical Dictionary of the American Left* (New York: Greenwood Press, 1986), s.v. Earl Browder; Ding Jinguang, "Bai Laode yu Zhongguo geming guanxi chutan" [Preliminary Examination of Earl Browder's Relation with the Chinese Revolution] Aug. 22, 2003, retrieved Oct. 12, 2005, from http://sky .qingdao.gov.cn/department/shekeyuan.nsf/13cd2d6b6b122f6348256d52000e94d8/e2e; Philip J. Jaffe, *The Rise and Fall of American Communism* (New York:, Horizon Press, 1975), 24.

7. Josephine Fowler, "'To Be Red and "Oriental"': The Experience of Japanese and Chinese Immigrant Communists in the American and International Communist Movements, 1919–1933" (PhD diss., University of Minnesota, 2003), 445–47; Zhang, Chinese Communists in the U.S.

8. Xie, Seas and Oceans, 7–8; Josphine Fowler, *Japanese and Chinese Immigrant Activists: Organizing in American and International Communist Movements, 1919–1933* (New Brunswick, N.J.: Rutgers University Press, 2007), 161–62. Xavier Dea gave different founding dates for the Kung Yu Club. In Xie, Seas and Oceans, it was 1926, while in "The Struggle of San Francisco Chinese against Unemployment" (*Guangzhou wenshi ziliao* [Guangzhou Historical and Literary Materials], 15th collection, ed. Historical and Literary Materials Research Committee of the Guangdong Province Guangzhou Municipality Committee

of China's People Political Consultative Conference (Guanghzhou, 1965), he cited 1928. But in the "Zhonggong Kaiping Xianwei Dangshi Ban'gongshi" [Party History Office of the Kaiping County Committee of the Communist Party], "Xie Chuang," *Kaiping Wenshi*, 24th collection (Kaiping, 1990), 1–9, the date was 1927. In an interview with the newspaper *Unity* in December 1981, Xie stated 1929. Because most members of the Chaotao group appear to have joined the CPUSA in 1927, the 1926 date seems too early. On the other hand, the 1929 date seems too late, since by then Kung Yu Club was already involved in the laundrymen's dispute. However, newspaper accounts show that Dea was one of the leaders of the San Francisco Chinese Students, perhaps in 1927. This leaves 1928 as the most likely date, since it would have been logical for the activists to shift their focus from students to workers as they grew older.

9. Fowler, "To Be Red and "Oriental," 466–68.

10. Xavier Dea, interview with author, Nov. 3, 1979; Xie, Seas and Oceans, 8–9; and *Chung Sai Yat Po*, June 25, July 27, 1928. In 1929 Feng Mian joined the Communist Party, which sent him to study at Far East University in Moscow, after which he returned to China. The Kung Yu Club changed its name to Huaren Gongrenhui [Chinese Workers' Club] or Huaqiao Gonghui [Overseas Chinese Workers Club] in mid-1928. In my book *Cong Huaqiao dao Huaren* [From Overseas Chinese to Chinese American] (Hong Kong: Joint Publishing Co., 1992), I had interpreted this name change as indicating a split of moderates and conservatives from the Kung Yu Club; however, since this event occurred soon after the founding of Kung Yu Club, it seems more likely to be preparation for the group's intention to organize Chinatown workers. According to a Jan. 22, 1973, letter to the author from Benjamin Fee, Huaqiao Gonghui was a combined syndicalist-communist effort to organize Chinatown workers. Apparently, after its failure to organize Chinatown workers, the name reverted to Kung Yu Club.

11. Dea interview; *Chung Sai Yat Po*, Feb. 1, 4, 1929; *Labor Clarion*, Feb. 15, 1929. Billy Chan and Alice Sum married and later went to study in Moscow before returning to China.

12. Xavier Dea, "Struggle of San Francisco Chinese," 147–56; Xie, Seas and Oceans, 14; *Chung Sai Yat Po*, May 20, 1930.

13. Josephine Fowler, email to author, Oct. 11, 2004. See also the poem "Heihai pang" [By the Black Sea], dated July 26, 1931, in Muyun (Benjamin Fee), *Muyun shiciji* [Collected Poems of Muyun] (Hong Kong: Chih Luen Press, 1974).

14. *Chinese World*, Jan. 26, 1931.

15. *Chinese World*, Mar. 30, Apr. 4, 1931. For more information about Eva Chan, see Judy Yung, *Unbound Voices: A Documentary History of Chinese Women in San Francisco* (Berkeley: University of California Press, 1999), 367–68.

16. Xie, "Struggle of San Francisco Chinese"; "Xie Chuang," *Kaiping Wenshi*, 1–9; Xie, Seas and Oceans, 22–25; *Chinese World*, May 16, 1931.

17. "Xie Chuang," *Kaiping Wenshi*, 1–9. Immigration authorities often arrested radicals and threatened them with long prison terms, thus forcing them to depart "voluntarily." From 1931 through 1934, seventeen Japanese Communists faced the same choice and elected to take asylum in the USSR (Karl Yoneda, *Ganbatte: Sixty Year Struggle of a Kibei Worker* [Los Angeles: Asian American Studies Center, 1983], 51). During the early thirties, Wei Minghua, a Chinese student at the University of Southern California, organized an Unemployed Council and an AAACAI branch in Los Angeles. He was also arrested and deported to the Soviet Union. See *Chinese Vanguard*, Feb. 1 and 15, 1933.

Xavier Dea was in the Soviet Union until 1935, when he was sent to Shanghai. However, after failing to make contact with the party organization, Dea returned to his native Kaiping to teach school. In 1937 he finally succeeded in contacting the local Guangdong party organization and was given the task of rebuilding the party organization in Kaiping. During the Sino-Japanese War, he led the resistance in central Guangdong. Immediately after the founding of the PRC, Dea held important government posts in central Guangdong but was soon demoted to minor positions in Guangzhou for being too soft on landlords. In 1981 Dea revisited the United States. He retired in 1983, with benefits equal to that of a provincial deputy governor.

18. Benjamin Fee, interview with author, Mar. 28, 1975; Fowler, *Japanese and Chinese Immigrant Activists*, 161–62. Fowler interpreted archival documentation as indicating the existence of two youth publications: *Qunsheng* and *Resonance*. However, Fee stated in his interview that *Resonance* was the English name for *Qunsheng*. Considering the low membership in the youth association, it was unlikely to support two separate publications.

Resonance was constantly plagued by insufficient funds, according to an article dated November 15, 1933, in *Chinese Vanguard*. After producing a special edition to commemorate the October Revolution in 1934, it ceased publication and resumed only on April 27, 1935, according to a *Chinese Vanguard* announcement. On May 11, 1935, *Chinese Vanguard* published a message from *Resonance* congratulating the former on its fifth anniversary, but a similar message apparently was not sent for the *Chinese Vanguard*'s sixth anniversary.

19. *Chinese Vanguard*, Jan. 15, 1933; *Kuo Min Yat Po*, Jan. 25, 1933.

20. *Kuo Min Yat Po*, Jan. 21, 1933.

21. George Bun Low, interview with author, Mar. 17, 1971; Olden Lee and George Bun Low interview with author, Jan. 9, 1973 (cited hereafter as Lee and Low joint interview).

22. *Chinese Vanguard*, Feb. 1, 15, Apr. 1, July 15, 1934.

23. *Chinese Vanguard*, June 15, 1934; Low interview; and Lee and Low joint interview. Lawrence Lowe immigrated to the United States in November 1929 as Lowe Quai Bun, son of an American citizen, Lowe Hung Gong (see "Application and Receipt for Certificate of Identity of Lowe Quai Bun Submitted to U.S. Immigration Service," Dec. 24, 1929, Immigration and Naturalization Service file on Lowe Quai Bun). Lowe worked at his brother's restaurant in Chinatown, where he gained sympathy for the poor and often gave them food from the restaurant. He soon became involved with progressive Chinese and joined the Chinese Communist organization (Zheng Yijun, *Zhuanqi rensheng: Ji Cai Fujiu zouguo de daolu* [A Dramatic Life: The Path Traveled by Henry Tsoi] [Hong Kong: Haifeng Chubanshe, 1997], 49–50 [cited hereafter as Zheng, Tsoi biography]). However, his son Rolland Lowe stated that Lowe Quai Bun joined the Chinese Communist Party in China when he was twenty-two years old and immigrated to the United States later (Rolland Lowe, "Chinatown, My Home and My Passion," in *Chinatown: More Stories of Life and Faith*, ed. James Chuck [San Francisco: First Chinese Baptist Church, 2008], 164–66).

24. *Chinese Vanguard*, Feb. 15, 1934.

25. Fee's efforts are recorded in his letter to the author, July 29, 1973; the parallel struggle of Japanese Americans to break into the International Longshoremen and Warehousemen Union is discussed in Yoneda, *Ganbatte*, 96–98; Willie Fong, interview with author, July 31, 1971; Low interview. Olden Lee was a comrade of Xavier Dea and Benjamin Fee and was arrested and imprisoned for ninety days during the 1934 San Francisco general strike. He was the first Chinese worker to join Local 110 of the Miscellaneous Workers Union after

the strike. In 1936 he was the first Chinese to be sent as a delegate to the union's national convention (Lee and Low joint interview).

26. *Chinese Vanguard,* Jan. 19, 1935; Benjamin Fee, letter to the author, Feb. 18, 1973; Corinne Gibb, *Jennie Matyas and the ILGWU* (Berkeley: University of California Institute of Industrial Relations, Oral History Project, 1957), 171–73.

27. L. W. Cassaday, "Labor Unrest and the Labor Movement in the Salmon Industry of the Pacific Coast" (PhD diss., University of California, Berkeley, 1938), 387–97; Chris Friday, *Organizing Asian American Labor: The Pacific Coast Canned Salmon Industry, 1870–1942* (Philadelphia: Temple University Press, 1994), 152–53; "Yushi ye jian shi" [A Short History of Alaska Salmon Cannery Work], *Getting Together,* Mar. 18–21, 1972. Under the Chinese contract system, cannery owners set fixed prices with contractors for the canning of salmon. The contractor then hired workers who were under their control. Workers frequently suffered poor food, inadequate and unsanitary quarters, and exorbitant prices at company stores. The contract system was one of the most hated features of cannery work. During the nineteenth century, practically all cannery workers were Chinese. Later, other marginalized workers, such as Filipinos, Japanese, and Mexicans, were also hired.

28. Fong interview; Lin Jianfu (Happy Lim), "Huagong Hezuo Hui Huiyilu" [Reminiscences of the Chinese Workers Mutual-Aid Association], *Unity Monthly* no. 1 (Jan. 1981): 4–6.

29. According to an email from Richard Aston, May 21, 2008, marriage records in the San Francisco County Hall of Records, City-County Building, Book 380, p. 79, show that Bun Low and May Lan Chan (a.k.a. Eva Chan) were issued marriage license No. 7947 on August 28, 1937. They were married the same day by Municipal Court Judge Hugh L. Smith. However, there is no record in the San Francisco INS files of their departure for Hong Kong from San Francisco.

30. Jianfu, "Huagong Hezuo Hui de yiji jian" [One Season in the Chinese Workers Mutual-Aid Association], *Hezuo,* no. 4 (Jan. 1939): 10–14; Fee interview; Virginia Fee note to author, June 10, 2005.

After Fee left *China Salvation Times* he served a short stint editing the literary section of *Chinese American Weekly,* a news magazine founded by liberal KMT member Chin-Fu Woo. Fee quit this job after the New Fourth Army Incident tore apart the fragile KMT-Communist alliance. Fee then apparently stopped participating in Communist Party activities in the Chinese community. He became partner in a printing shop in New York for about twenty years and later worked as a business agent for ILGWU Local 23–25 in New York's Chinatown until retiring in 1977. Fee passed away in July 1978. In New York Fee used the name Zhang Mingzhi. He also wrote poetry using the nom de plume Muyun.

There are many gaps in the historical materials on the Chinese Marxist Left between 1934 and 1937. Henry Tsoi, who arrived in 1940 to coordinate party activities in the western United States, alleged that he was taking over the duties of his younger brother Lawrence Lowe, who had been asked by the CCP party organization in June 1936 to participate in party activities in Hong Kong. However, Lowe did not depart until July 1937 (Zheng, Tsoi biography, 50, 64).

31. Tet Yee, Happy Lim, Willie Fong, and Hu Jun, joint interview with author, Sept. 25, Oct. 2, 1977.

32. *New York Times,* May 23, Sept. 29, 1931; *Chinese Vanguard,* Apr. 21, 1938.

33. Zhang, Chinese Communists in the U.S.

34. For more information about Zhang Bao, see *Huaqiao Huaren baikequanshu, renwu juan* [Encyclopedia of Chinese Overseas; Volume of Who's Who] (Beijing: Chinese Overseas Publishing House, 2001), s.v. "Zhang Bao."

35. Fowler, *Japanese and Chinese Immigrant Activists,* 163; *New York Times,* May 23, Sept. 29, 1931; *Chinese Vanguard,* Apr. 21, 1938; Zhang, Chinese Communists in the U.S.; Fowler, "To Be Red and Oriental," 502–3; Xu Suizhi, "Chronology of the Life of Y. Y. Hsu." For more information about He Zhifang (1902?-1955?), see Xu Suizhi, Short Biography of Y. Y. Hsu, n. 5. For more information about Yu Guangsheng, see Gao Sheng et. al., eds., *Zhonghua liuxue mingren cidian* [Dictionary of Famous Chinese Who Studied Abroad] (Changchun: Dongbei Shifan Daxue chubanshe, 1992), s.v. "Yu Guangsheng."

36. *Chinese Vanguard,* Jan. 15, 1933.

37. *Chinese Vanguard,* Jan. 15, Feb. 1, and Mar. 1, 1933.

38. Peter Kwong, *Chinatown, New York: Labor and Politics, 1930–1950* (New York: Monthly Review Press, 1979), 57–58. The establishment of a workers center is reported in *Chinese Vanguard,* Jan. 5, 1934.

39. Kwong, *Chinatown, New York,* 121–24. By the 1920s, the Communists had organized Chinese seamen and dockworkers in ports such as Shanghai and Hong Kong. In the early 1930s, the Communist International established the International Seamen Secretariat in Hamburg, Germany. A Chinese branch was established in western Europe for the many Chinese seamen who worked on European vessels. Liao Chengzhi was one of its early organizers. This Chinese branch sent organizers to ports all over the world. See Song Chao, Shao Mingxi, and Tian Xiangdong, *Zhongguo haiyuan yundong shihua* [The Story of the Chinese Seamen] (Beijing: Renmin Jiaotong Chubanshe, 1985).

40. The Chinese Benevolent Association, or Zhonghua Gongsuo, of New York City was similar to the CCBA or Chinese Six Companies and claimed to speak for all Chinese in New York.

41. Leong Gor Yun, *Chinatown Inside Out* (New York: Burrows Mussey, 1935), chap. 5. In the Cantonese dialect, one of the meanings for "Leong Gor Yun" is "two persons." Y. K. Chu was one of the two authors collaborating on the book.

42. Kwong, *Chinatown, New York,* 76.

43. Renqiu Yu, "To Save China, To Save Ourselves: A History of the Chinese Hand Laundry Alliance of New York, 1930s-1950s" (PhD diss., New York University, 1990), 134–44; Virginia Heyer, "Patterns of Social Organization in New York City's Chinatown" (PhD diss., Columbia University, 1953), chap. 8.

44. Cen Nengrui, "Qiaojie yingcai: Tang Mingzhao he ta de nü'er Tang Wensheng" [Talent among the Chinese Overseas: Tang Mingzhao and His Daughter Tang Wensheng], *Enping Gongbao* (Enping Communiqué) no. 4 (1995): 37–38 (cited hereafter as Cen, "Tang Mingzhao"); Fee interview; Albert Lim, interview with author, Apr. 2, 1990. Tong was a 1936 graduate of the University of California at Berkeley, where he led the local CPUSA branch.

45. *China Salvation Times,* Apr. 20, 1939; *Mun Hey Yat Po,* Apr. 24–27, 1939.

46. *Chinese Vanguard,* Feb. 1, 15, 1933. Wei Minghua was a Tsinghua University student who joined the CCP in 1927 and arrived in the United States in 1928. In June 1930, he moved to Los Angeles, where he became a student at the University of Southern California. See "Qinghua di-yi ge dangzhibu de jianli" [The Founding of the First Party Branch at Tsinghua], retrieved Aug. 22, 2006, from http://news.tsinghua.edu.cn/new/news.php?id=13390.

47. Jaffe, *American Communism*, 36; Mari Jo Buhle, Paul Buhle, Dan Georgakas, eds., *Encyclopedia of the American Left* (Urbana: University of Illinois Press, 1992).

48. "The Issuing of the 'Letter to All Compatriots Regarding Resistance to Japan and National Salvation,'" No. 17 of 80 Important Events in the History of the CCP, Nov. 2, 2004, retrieved Nov. 12, 2005, from http://www.snzs.gov.cn/shownoews.asp?newsid=3495.

49. Chen Hanseng, *Sige shidai de wo* [Myself during Four Periods] (Beijing: Zhongguo Wenshi Chubanshe, 1988), 64–65; Wu Yuzhang, "Wu Yuzhang Luezhuan" [A Short Biography of Wu Yuzhang], in *Wu Yuzhang wenji* [Collected Works of Wu Yuzhang] (Chongqing: Chongqing chubanshe, 1987), 2:1295–340 (cited hereafter as Wu, Short Biography of Wu Yuzhang); Wang Shigu, "Cong Xianfeng dao *Jiuguo Shibao*" [From *Chinese Vanguard* to *China Salvation Times*], in *Haiwai Huawen xinwenshi yanjiu* [Study of the History of Chinese Language Newspapers Overseas] (Beijing: Xinhua Chubanshe, 1998), 130–34. Li Lisan was the chief editor of *Giu Guo Sh Bao*. Other editors included Liao Huanxing, Chen Tanqiu, Zhang Bao, Yu Xinchao. See "Li Lisan zai Sulian de rizi" [The Days That Li Lisan Was in the Soviet Union], retrieved Aug. 8, 2005, from http://skb.hebeidaily.com.cn/200347/ca317395.htm; Li Sishen, Liu Zikun, *Li Lisan zhi mi* [The Enigma of Li Lisan] (Beijing: Renmin chubanshe, 2005), chap. 9, retrieved Aug. 8, 2005, from http://cul.news.tom.com/1013/1014/2005223—9220.html.

Rao Shushi was the All-China Trade Union's delegate to the International Organization of Red Workers in Moscow and also part of the CCP delegation attending the 1935 Seventh Congress of the Comintern. He helped to edit *Giu Guo Sh Bao* using the pseudonym Zhao Jiansheng. Lu Cui was a prominent leader of the 1935 student demonstrations in Beijing. In October 1936 she joined the CCP. See Tan Lu, "Yi'er Jiu yundong zong de Qinghua nüjie—Lu Cui" [Loh Tsei, Heroine from Tsinghua in the December Ninth Movement], retrieved Aug. 8, 2005, from http://news.tsinghua.edu.cn. She represented Zhongguo Quanguo Xuesheng Jiuguo Lianhehui [All China Federation of Students for National Salvation] in touring North American Chinese communities with the educator Tao Xingzhi. She married Rao Shushi and became an editor at *Giu Guo Sh Bao*.

50. After the CCP issued its August 1, 1935, manifesto calling for a united front to resist Japanese aggression, the CCP established *China Salvation Times* in Paris as its mouthpiece to the Communist International. See Wu Yuzhang, *Wu Yuzhang huiyilu* [Reminiscences of Wu Yuzhang] (Beijing: Zhongguo Qingnian Chubanshe, 1978), 177–79.

51. Ni Huiru (Nancy Tsou), Zou Ningyuan (Len Tsou), *Ganlan guiguan de zhaohuan: Canjia Xibanya Neizhan de Zhongguoren* [The Call of Spain: The Chinese Volunteers in the Spanish Civil War (1936–1939)] (Taipei: Renjian Chubanshe, 2001), 211–34 (cited hereafter as Tsou, Call of Spain); *Chinese Vanguard*, June 1 and 26, Nov. 4, 1937; Zou Jingyao, "Xibanya Neizhan Guoji Zhiyuanjun Xiezhenbu [A Portrait Album of International Volunteers in the Spanish Civil War] *Renjian* (Feb. 1989), 120–37 (cited hereafter as Zou Jingyao, Portrait Album). Chen Wenrao (Dong Hong Yick) was another Chinese American who did not survive the war. The Americanized version of Chen Wenrao's name may have been Dong Hong Yick. Yick was an immigrant and restaurant worker in New York who was active in the progressive Chinese Workers Center and had joined the CPUSA in 1933. Chen reached Spain in June 1937 and served as a soldier in the Lincoln Brigade. He was killed in the Gandesa battle on April 14, 1938.

52. Tsou, Call of Spain, 165–72; Zou Jingyao, Portrait Album, 120–37. For more information about Gong Pusheng, see "Gong Pusheng," in *Yanjing Daxue renwuzhi* [Biographies of Personalities at Yenching University], 1st collection, ed. Yanjing Yanjiuyuan [Yenching Research Institute] (Beijing: Beijing Daxue chubanshe, 2001), 388–89.

53. Tsou, Call of Spain, 349–61. The following list includes names of these supporters along with their country of origin, and when available, the year each arrived in China: Dr. Norman Bethune (Canada, 1938), Dr. Menhanlal (India, 1939), Dr. Tio Oen Bik (Dutch East Indies, 1940; Chinese descent), Dr. Rolf Becker (Germany, 1939), Dr. Fritz Jensen (Austria, 1939); Dr. Frederick Kisch (Czechoslovakia, 1939), Dr. Ianto Kineti (Bulgaria, 1939), Dr. David Iancu (Romania), Dr. Walter Freudmann (Austria), Dr. Herbert Baer (Germany, 1939), Dr. Heinrich Kent (Austria), Dr. Karl Coutelle (Germany), Dr. Samuel Flato (Poland, 1939), Dr. Victor Taubenfligel (Poland), Dr. Wolf Jungermann (Poland), Dr. Leon Kamieniecki (Poland), Dr. Frantisek Kriegel (Poland), Dr. Jasul Kranzdorf (Rumania), Dr. Otto Schoen (Hungary), Dr. Alexander Volokhine (USSR), Mrs. Miriam Kamieniecka (Poland), and Ms. Edith Markus (Germany).

54. Israel Epstein, *Woman in World History: Soong Ching Ling* (Beijing: New World Press, 1993), 291–98; Zheng Canhui, Li Hongsheng, Wu Jingping, *Song Qingling yu Kang-Ri Jiuwang Yundong* [Song Qingling and the Resist Japan National Salvation Movement] (Fuzhou: Fujian renmin chubanshe, 1986), 64–67 (cited hereafter as Zheng Canhui et al., Song Qingling). The Fujian regime was established in November 1933 by political foes of Chiang Kai-shek. The 19th Route Army led by Gen. Cai Tingkai (Tsai Ting-kai) had resisted the Japanese attack on Shanghai in 1932, but they had been redeployed to Fujian to attack the Communist base in Jiangxi and formed the backbone propping up the new regime. After the Chiang government used intrigue and overwhelming force to crush it in early 1934, the Communists not only lost a potential ally, but soon found themselves forced to abandon their base and embark on the Long March in August 1934. Most of the principals in the Fujian regime later participated in the founding of the PRC in 1949.

55. Zheng Canhui et al., Song Qingling, 75–76; Shang Mingxuan, Chen Min, Liu Jiaquan, Zhao Chuyun, *Song Qingling nianpu* [Chronological Biography of Song Qingling] (Beijing: Zhongguo Shehui Kexue Chubanshe, 1986), 92–93.

56. Wang Yongqi, "Yi'er-jiu shiqi Yanda dang he geming zhuzhi de jianli" [Establishing the Party and Revolutionary Organization at Yanjing University during the December Ninth Period], retrieved Nov. 23, 2005, from http://cyc6.cycnet.com:8090/xuezhu/zishu/content.jsp?n_id=4538; Luo Ling, "Tang Mingzhao," in *Jiangmen Wuyi haiwai mingren zhuan* [Biographies of Famous Individuals abroad of Jiangmen Origin], ed. Tan Sizhe (Gulao, Heshan: Guangdong Renmin Chubanshe, 1996), 5:8–15; "Shuimu Qinghua, Part 5" in Luo Yinsheng, *Qiao Guanhua caiqing rensheng* [Qiao Guanhua's Gifted and Sentimental Life] (Beijing: Tuanjie Chubanshe, 2004), retrieved Nov. 22, 2005, from http://book.sina.com.cn/longbook/1097399113_qiaoguanhua/9.shtml. Tang was born in Enping in 1910. Both his grandfather and father had worked in America. His family moved to San Francisco in 1919. Tang returned to China and enrolled in Tianjin's Nankai Middle School in 1927 and entered Tsinghua University to study political science in 1930.

57. Zhang Ruxian, "Gu Jingsheng yu Yi'erjiu yundong" [Gu Jingshang and the December Ninth Movement], retrieved Nov. 22, 2005, from http://cyc69.cycnet.com:8090/minzu/rmhn/huigu/content.jsp?id=255524; Wang Yongqi, "Yi'erjiu shiqi Yanda dang he geming zuzhi de jianli" [The Establishing of the Party and Revolutionary Organizations at Yanjing University during the December Ninth Period], retrieved Nov. 23, 2005, from http://cyc69.cycnet.com:8090/xuezhu/zishu/content.jsp?n_id=4538.

58. John Maxwell Hamilton, *Edgar Snow: A Biography* (Bloomington: Indiana University Press, 1988), 52; Yan Chunde "Xiao Qian nianbiao" [Chronology of Xiao Qian], ed. Bao Ji, rev. Wen Jieruo, retrieved Jan. 6, 2006, from http://www.millionbook.net/xd/x/

xiaogan/; "Gong Pusheng," in *Yanjing Daxue renwuzhi,* 340, 352–54; Yan Chunde, "Yang Gang," *Ershi shiji Zhongguo zhuming nüzuojia zhuan* (Provence, France, 1985; rev., Beijing, 1995), retrieved Dec. 26, 2005, from http://www.oklink.net/a/0007/0726/essj/012.htm.

Xiao Qian (1910–99) was born into a sinicized Mongol family. He attended Furen and Yenjing universities and in 1935 edited the literary section of the liberal paper *Ta Kung Pao.* In 1938 he was sent to Hong Kong to publish the local edition. In 1939 he went to England as a special correspondent. The literary editor position went to Yang Gang, a 1932 graduate of Yenjing University. Yang Gang joined the CCP in 1928 but withdrew in 1932, only to rejoin in 1938 during the War of Resistance.

59. Chen Hanbo, "Zai Sinuo de xiao keting li: Sinuo zao Yi'erjiu yundong zhong" [In the Snows' Little Sitting Room:], retrieved Nov. 26, 2005, from http://cyc6.cycnet.com:8090/xuezhu/zishu/content.jsp?n_id=4552; Hamilton, *Edgar Snow,* 57; Gong Pusheng, "Yi'er Jiu yundong zhong de duiwai lianluo gongzuo" [The Task of External Liaisons during the December Ninth Movement], retrieved Nov. 11, 2005, from http://cyc6.cycnet.com:8090/xuezhu/zishu/content.jsp?n_id=4573. Huang Hua represented the PRC during political negotiations with the United States and its allies to end the Korean War. He also served as the PRC delegate to the United Nations in the 1970s.

60. Gong Pusheng, "Yi'erjiu yundong zhong de duiwai lianluo gongzuo"; Tan Lu: "Yi'er Jiu yundong zong de Qinghua nüjie—Lu Cui;" [Loh Tsei, Heroine from Tsinghua in the December Ninth Movement], retrieved Aug. 8, 2005, from http://news.tsinghua.edu.cn. Lu Cui (Loh Tsei) was a Qinghua University student. On December 12, 1935, she became the first student demonstrator arrested by the police and was dubbed "China's Joan of Arc" by one Western journalist.

61. "Qin du lishi shike: Fang Mao Zedong Zhou Enlai Yingyu fanyi Tang Wensheng" [One Who Personally Witnessed an Historic Moment: Interview of Nancy Tang, English Interpreter of Mao Zedong and Zhou Enlai], Oct. 11, 2002, retrieved Nov. 22, 2005, from http://gd.sohu.com/28/09/news148800928.shtml. Haiming Liu, *Transnational History of a Chinese Family: Immigrant Letters, Family Business, and Reverse Migration* (New Brunswick, N.J.: Rutgers University Press, 2005), 196, 206–8; remarks made by Frances Leong in casual conversations during various monthly meetings of the Overseas Chinese Federation for Peace and Democracy in China during 1949 when the author was present.

62. Zhou Tiandu, ed., *Jiuguo Hui* [National Salvation Association] (Beijing: Zhongguo Shehui Kexue Chubanshe, 1981), 10–14; "Zhongguo Shehui Kexueyuan zhuming xuezhe Qian Junrui" [Qian Junrui, Famous Scholar of the China Academy of Social Sciences (CASS)], retrieved Dec. 2, 2005, from http://www.cass.net.cn/y_09/y_09_01_18.htm; Zhongguo Tao Xingzhi Yanjiuhui [Chinese Tao Xingzhi Research Society], "Tao Xingzhi shengping nianbiao" [Chronology of the Life of Tao Xingzhi], Dec. 23, 2004, retrieved Dec. 25, 2005, from http://www.taoxingzhi.org; Howard L. Boorman et al., ed., *Biographical Dictionary of Republican China,* vol. 3 (New York: Columbia University Press, 1967), s.v. "T'ao Hsing-chih."

Qian Junrui (1908–85) worked with Chen Han-seng in 1929 to investigate China's rural economy. In 1935 he joined the CCP. After the founding of the PRC, he was active principally in the areas of education, culture, and economics.

Tao Xingzhi (T'ao Hsing-chih, 1891–1946) was an educator and reformer. In 1916 and 1917, he studied at Columbia University where he was influenced by John Dewey. After returning to China, he developed his own theories based on the ideas of Dewey and Wang Yangming. He started a successful mass education movement but in 1927 became a target of KMT officials and local warlords because of his left-wing associations and was forced to turn to rural education projects. His success there again drew KMT suspicion, and he fled to Japan in 1930 only to return in 1931. In 1932 he inaugurated the concept of work-study units to help students support themselves and worked with the CCP in its implementation. In 1935 he supported the student demonstrations for resistance to Japanese aggression and became a founder of the National Salvation Association. In 1936 he was a delegate to the World New Education Conference in London and also represented the National Salvation Association.

63. "Yiyongjun jinxingqu" [March of the Volunteers] was a song in the film *Fengyun ernu* [Sons and Daughters in a Storm], directed by Situ Huimin in 1935. The music was composed by Nie Er, and Tian Han wrote the lyrics. *Fangxia ni de bianzi* [*Lay Down Your Whip*] was originally written by Chen Liting soon after the Japanese invasion of the northeast in 1931. The story tells of a peasant and his daughter who had fled from the Japanese occupation after his wife was killed. As Japan expanded its occupied territory, father and daughter drifted to Shanghai. The father forced his daughter to sing on street corners for donations. One day, the daughter was so weak from hunger that she could not perform. Her angry father used a whip to force her. A young worker from the crowd knocked the father to the ground, whereupon the daughter hastened to stop the fight and recounted their sad story, inspiring the young worker, her father, and the crowd to understand that everybody should work together to defeat the Japanese imperialists. See Cheng Jihua et al., ed. *Zhongguo dianying fazhanshi* [History of the Chinese Film Industry] (Beijing: Zhongguo Dianying Chubanshe, 1963), 385–87; "Nie Er," "Cui Wei," and "Tian Han," in *Zhongguo yishujia cidian, xiandai diyi fence* [Dictionary of Artists of China, Modern Period] (Changsha: Hu'nan Renmin Chubanshe, 1981), 1:282–85, 344–47, 2:12–16.

64. Xu Shijia, *Zhongguo jin-xiandai yinyue shigang* [Outline History of Chinese Music in the Recent and Modern Periods] (Haikou, Hai'nan: Nanhai Chuban Gongsi, 1997), 184–87; "Liu Liangmo (1909–1988)," retrieved Sept. 4, 2005, from http://www.shtong.gov.cn/node2/node2245/node69322/node69341/node69492/node69496/userobject1ai67668.html.

65. "Deng Yuzhi: Zai kang-Ri jiuwang de hongliu zhong" [Cora Deng: Within the Mighty Torrent of Resisting Japan and National Salvation], retrieved Oct. 29, 2005, from http://www.unity.cn/2744/cc1.htm.

66. Reportedly, she and a fellow YWCA worker sheltered Madam Borodin, one of the Soviet advisors sent to China, from Marshal Zhang Zuolin during his purge of Communist suspects.

67. *Rewi Alley: An Autobiography* (Beijing: Foreign Language Press, 2003), 71–72, 279–81; Karen Garner, "Redefining Institutional Identity: The YWCA Challenge to Extraterritoriality in China, 1925–30," *Women's History Review* 10, no. 3 (2001): 409–40.

68. Karen Garner, *Precious Fire: Maud Russell and the Chinese Revolution* (Amherst: University of Massachusetts Press, 2003), 134–35; "Gong Pusheng: Jieyuan Lianheguo liushi nian" [Gong Pusheng: Ties to the United Nations over Sixty Years], *Jianghuai Chenbao,* Oct. 24, 2005, retrieved Nov. 6, 2005, from http://www.jhcb.com.cn/epublish/gb/paper1/20050801/class00007/hwz641669.htm; "Gong Pusheng," in *Yanjing Daxue renwuzhi,* 388–89. Gong Pusheng was the oldest daughter of Gong Zhenzhou, a supporter of Sun Yat-sen. She graduated from St. Mary's Girls' Middle School in Shanghai and then enrolled in Yenjing University in 1932 to study political science, sociology, and economics. In 1935 she was elected vice-president of the students association and became one of the organizers of the December 9 and 16 demonstrations.

69. Janice R. and Stephen R. MacKinnon, *Agnes Smedley: The Life and Times of an American Radical* (Berkeley: University of California Press, 1988), 168; Garner, *Precious Fire*, 148–49.

70. MacKinnon and MacKinnon, *Agnes Smedley*, 168–70.

71. Wu Jiliang, "Liang shi yi you sishi nian: Sinuo yu Song Qingling" [Good Teachers and Helpful Friends for Forty Years: Edgar Snow and Song Qingling], retrieved Dec. 1, 2005, from http://www.renwu.com.cn/UserFiles/magazine/srticle/RW0175_200310201009006686 .asp; Sidney Shapiro, *Ma Haide: The Saga of American Doctor George Hatem in China* (San Francisco: Cypress Press, 1993), 12, 17, 21, 27; Hamilton, *Edgar Snow*, 67–68. Hamilton notes that Snow also tried contacting Sergei Polevoy, a Beijing University Russian-language teacher who was sympathetic to the CCP. Yu Qiwei (Huang Jing) participated in student protests against Japanese aggression in Northeast China in 1931 and joined the underground CCP in 1932. He became the lover of Jiang Qing (later Madam Mao Zedong) and sponsored her to join the CCP. In 1935 he enrolled at Peking University, where he joined the local Chinese People's Committee for Armed Self-Defense. He became one of the organizers of the December Ninth student demonstration. After the founding of the PRC, he served as the mayor and party secretary of Tianjin. See "Huang Jing jianli" [Brief Biography of Huang Jing], retrieved Aug. 14, 2006, from http://www .rwabc.com/diqurenwu/diqudanyirenwu.asp?p_name=%BB%C6%BE%B4&people_ id=8239&category_name=%B9%D9%D4%B1.

72. "Dong Jianwu," retrieved Aug. 14, 2006, from http://www.shtong.gov.cn/node2/ node4/node2249/node4412/node17460/node62299/node63578/userobject1ai51461.html; Wang Guangyuan, "Hongse mushi Dong Jianwu" [The Red Pastor Dong Jianwu], *China Press*, Mar. 13, 14, 2002. Dong Jianwu became an underground CCP member in 1927. In 1930 he ran a childcare center to take care of the children of CCP leaders and orphans of CCP members. He also operated a curio shop in Shanghai as a cover. After escorting Snow and Hatem, Dong took Mao Zedong's two sons to the USSR. Dong was persecuted and passed away during the Cultural Revolution.

73. Hamilton, *Edgar Snow*, 12, 20–21, 42, 47–48, 79–80, 85–87, 90; "Sinuo" [Edgar Snow], in *Yanjing Daxue renwuzhi*, 240–241; *Giu Guo Sh Bao*, June 13, 1936; *Chinese Vanguard*, Apr. 10, 17, 24, May 1, 1937; Wang Fushi, "*Red Star over China*, The First Chinese Edition," *Beijing Review* 31, no. 41 (Oct. 10–16, 1988). Nym Wales, "Tan *Xixing manji* ji qita" [Speaking of *Red Star over China* and Other Subjects], trans. Wang Fushi, *Ta Kung Pao* (Hong Kong), Sept. 21, 22, 1979. For more details of the translation of Snow's manuscript see He Peng, "*Xixing manji* zhong de 'Xu Da' shi sui" [Who Was "Xu Da" Mentioned in *Red Star over China?*], *Renwu wangshi* [Past Activities of Personalities], in *Zhonghua Dushubao*, retrieved June 27, 2004, from http://www.sina.com.cn.

74. Zhang Xiaoding, "*Xixing manji* liushi nian: *Hongxing zhaoyao Zhongguo* jige zhongyao zhong-yiben de liuchuan he yingxiang [Sixtieth Anniversary of *Record of a Trip to the East*: The Circulation and Influence of the Several Chinese Translations of *Red Star over China*], Feb. 18, 1998, retrieved Oct. 1, 2005, from http://www.gmw.cn/01ds/1998–02/18/ GB.186^DS507.htm.

75. Israel Epstein, *My China Eye: Memoirs of a Jew and a Journalist* (South San Francisco: Long River Press, 2005), 64; MacKinnon and MacKinnon, *Agnes Smedley*, 172–81, 191.

76. Sun Dunheng, "Yi zhenxing Zhonghua wei ji ren: Qinghua xueyun xianquzhe Ji Chaoding" [One Who Regarded the Vitalizing of China as His Own Responsibility: C. T. Chi, a Pioneer in the Tsinghua Student Movement], in *Renwu zhi* [Accounts of Personali-

ties], ed. Qinghua Daxue Xiaoshizu (Tsinghua University School History Group) (Beijing: Qinghua Daxue chubanshe, 1983), 1:77–91; Zhang, Chinese Communists in the U.S.

77. Ch'iao-ting Chi, preface to *Key Economic Areas in Chinese History* (London: George Allen and Unwin, 1936).

78. Shen Qinglin, *Zhongguo kangzhan shiqi de guoji yuanzhu* [International Support during China's War of Resistance] (Shanghai: Renmin Chubanshe, 2000), 77, 92, 107, 112.

79. Advertisement, *China Today* 1, no. 5 (Feb. 1935): inside back cover; *China Today* 1, no. 6 (Mar. 1935): 112; advertisement, *China Today* 1, no. 8 (May 1935): 156; Esther Carrol, "Our Organization in Action," *China Today* 1, no. 9 (June 1935): 175; "Picket Demonstration against Japan's War Moves in China," *China Today* 1, no. 10 (July 1935): 193, 199. Fang Zhimin was a CCP Central Committee member who was captured and executed by the KMT government in 1935. See vol. 2 of *Biographical Dictionary of Republican China,* s.v. "Fang Chih-min."

80. *Liu-Mei xuesheng yuekan* [Chinese Students of North America Monthly] 1, no. 1 (Dec. 1935): 15, 17, 31; vol. 2, no. 2/3 (Jan./Feb. 1936): 21–22; vol. 1, no. 10/11 (Jan. 1937): 23–25; Jingnan, "Jinmen yiyu: Kang-Ri hongchao" [Reminiscences by the Golden Gate: The Great Tide of Resistance to Japanese Aggression], *Chinese Pacific Weekly,* Aug. 10, 1974. Qing Ruji's (1902–76) main work was *Meiguo qin-Hua shi* [History of U.S. Aggression in China], vol. 1 (1952); vol. 2 (1956). For more details of his life, see "Qing Ruji," in *Yanjing Daxue renwuzhi,* 388–89. For more information about Ma Zusheng, see "Ma Zusheng," retrieved Aug. 15, 2006, from http://218.24.233.167:8000/RESOURCE/GZ/GZHX/HXBL/HXTS0122/6604_SR.HTM.

81. Zheng Canhui et al., *Song Qingling,* 75; *Chinese Vanguard,* Feb. 1 and Aug. 15, 1934.

82. "Against Imperialist Intervention in China: 'Hands Off China' Conference in New York," *China Today* 1, no. 3 (Dec. 1934): 58–59.

83. *Chinese Vanguard,* Jan. 19, 1935.

84. *Chinese Vanguard,* Nov. 2 and 23, Dec. 7, 1935, Jan. 4, 1936. Maytong Seto (1868–1955) was a leader of the Chee Kung Tong (Triad Society of the Americas) and one of the founders of the On Leong Tong. During the 1930s, he strongly advocated resistance to Japanese aggression and criticized the KMT government. During the Chinese civil war, he represented the Triad organizations' attempts to participate in political events in China but was constantly thwarted by the KMT government. In 1948 he openly broke with the KMT to support the CCP, and after the founding of the PRC, Seto served in several minor posts in the central government. For more details see *Zhongguo Jin-xiandai renming da cidian* [Biographical Dictionary of Modern and Contemporary China], ed. Li Shengping (Beijing: Zhongguo Guoji Guangbo Chubanshe, 1989) s.v. "Situ Meitang" (cited hereafter as Li, Biographical Dictionary); Ye Hanming, "Huaqiao huidang yu Guo-Gong tongzhan—Meizhou Hongman de lizi" [Overseas Chinese Secret Societies and the United Fronts Formed by the KMT and the CCP—The Example of the Hongmen of the Americas], in *Zhanhou haiwai Huaren bianhua guoji xueshu yantao hui lunwenji* [Collection of Papers from the International Symposium on Changes among the Overseas Chinese after World War II], ed. Guo Liang et al. (Beijing: Zhongguo Huaqiao chuban gongsi, 1990), 251–57.

Wu Xianzi (1881–1959) was a member of the Chinese Empire Reform Association. He edited newspapers in Hong Kong and in China for the Reform Association and its successor, the Chinese Constitutionalist Party. In 1928 Wu became chief editor of the *Chinese World* in San Francisco. In 1935 he left for New York, where he edited *Niuyue Gong Bao*

[New York Labor Newspaper] for a year before returning to China. After World War II, he made his home in Hong Kong. See Li, Biographical Dictionary, s.v. "Wu Xianzi."

Chen Qiyuan (1887–1968), a native of Guangzhou and graduate of Beijing University, was an alternate member of the executive committee of the KMT central committee in 1926. When the KMT broke with the CCP in 1927, Chen continued to advocate Sun Yat-sen's three policies. He lost his KMT party membership and fled to the United States to avoid arrest. During the mid-1930s, he joined the *Chinese Vanguard* as an editor. After World War II, Chen left for Hong Kong. After the founding of the PRC, Chen served as deputy minister in the Ministry of Internal Affairs and other posts in the central government. See Li, Biographical Dictionary, s.v. "Chen Qiyuan."

85. Yoneda, *Ganbatte*, 63, 69.

86. *Chinese Vanguard*, Nov. 16, 1935.

87. *Chinese World*, Apr. 12, 1936. In 1933 the KMT generals Fang Zhenwu, Feng Yuxiang, and Ji Hongchang fought the Japanese invasion of Chahar Province. However, without central government support, their poorly equipped troops were quickly defeated. Fang Zhenwu fled to Hong Kong and traveled secretly to the USSR in 1935, where CCP member Wu Yuzhang let him read a draft of the CCP manifesto. Fang immediately voiced his support. See Wu, Short Biography of Wu Yuzhang, 2:1295–340.

In late 1935, Fang arrived to tour various cities in North America. While in San Francisco, he promoted the formation of a Chinese National Salvation League, which was established in April 1936. Branches soon appeared in other North American cities, except on the East Coast, where national salvation organizations were already in existence. See Pei Chi Liu, *A History of the Chinese in the United States of America II* (Taipei: Liming Wenhua Shiye Gongsi, 1981), 522–23. Fang eventually returned to Hong Kong, where he remained until 1941 when Japanese seized the city. He sought refuge in nearby Zhongshan, where he was arrested and executed by KMT agents. See Li, Biographical Dictionary, s.v. "Fang Zhenwu." Fang was the paternal grandfather of Anson Chan, Hong Kong's Chief Secretary in 1997.

88. Zhou Hongyu, "Tao Xingzhi yu Meiguo qiaojie" [Tao Xingzhi and the Chinese in the USA], Mar. 3, 2003, retrieved Aug. 29, 2005, from http://www.eicbs.com:8080/Disp .Aspx?ID=2142&ClassID=41; Liu Zuokui, "Shihai gouchen: Baiqiu'en Dafu dangnian shi zenma laidao Zhongguo de?" [Exploring Materials in the Ocean of History: How Did Dr. Bethune Come to China during That Period?], *Huanqiu Shibao*, Apr. 29, 2004, retrieved Aug. 13, 2005, from http://www.taoxingzhi.org/show.asp?id=cul.sina.com.cn/y/2000-04 -29/54618.html; Zhongguo Tao Xingzhi Yanjiuhui [Tao Xingzhi Research Society], "Tao Xingzhi shengping nianbiao" [Chronology of the Life of Tao Xingzhi], in eight parts, Dec. 23, 2004, retrieved Dec. 25, 2005, from http://www.taoxingzhi.org; Zhu Zishan, "Tao yan ziliao zhong youdai chengqing de yixie wenti" [Some Questions That Await Clarification in the Materials on the Study of Tao], Feb. 2002, retrieved from http://www.taoxingzhi .org/show.asp?id=273&1m=%BB%E1%BF%AF%B2%E9%D1%AF. When the Sino-Japanese conflict began, Tao, who had reached the West Coast, continued his speaking tour. He was credited with having met Dr. Norman Bethune at a Los Angeles banquet on July 30, 1937, honoring "Friends of the Spanish People" and describing the need for medical services in the war zone. Tao returned to China the same year after traveling to more than twenty countries recruiting help for China. He refocused his attention on the struggle for democracy in China and faced continual harassment by the KMT. In 1944 he joined the China Democratic League. Tao died of a stroke in July 1946.

Chapter 4: The War of Resistance against Japan

1. Qibing, "Kangzhan chuqi de Zhong-Gong Changjiang Ju" [The CCP's Yangzi River Bureau during the Early Part of the War of Resistance], retrieved Jan. 4, 2007, from http://bbs.tiexue.net/post_1018748_1.html; "Balu Jun" [Eighth Route Army], retrieved Jan. 5, 2007, from http://zh.wikipedia.org/wiki/%E5%85%AB%E8%B7%AF%E8%BB%8D; "Xin Si Jun" [New Fourth Army], retrieved Jan. 3, 2007 from http://zh.wikipedia.org/wiki/%E6%96%B0%E5%9B%9B%E5%86%9B.

2. Nanfang Ju Dangshi Ziliao Zhengji Xiaozu Zuzhi Zu [Organization Group of the Group to Collect Historical Materials of the Southern Bureau], "Zhong-Gong Nangfang Ju zazhi xitong kaikuang" [A Survey of the Organizational Channels of the Southern Bureau of the CCP], in *Zhong-Gong dangshi ziliao* [Materials on CCP Party History], collection 12 (Beijing: Zhong-Gong Dangshi Chubanshe, 1984), 5–45; "Balujun Chongqing banshichu jiuzhi" [Former Site of the Eighth Route Army Liaison Office in Chongqing], retrieved Jan. 3, 2007, from http://zh.wikipedia.org/wiki/%E5%85%AB%E8%B7%AF%E5%86%9B%E9%87%8D%E5%BA%86%E5%8A%9E%E4%BA%8B%E5%A4%84%E6%97%A7%E5%9D%80; "Zhong-Gong Zhongyang Nanfang Ju" [Southern Bureau of the CCP Central Committee], retrieved Dec. 27, 2006, from http://www.nsjy.com/pingbi/zp/2003kjj-te/big/2415293/hongyan/wdmd/nfj.htm.

The Yangzi River Bureau began publishing the *Xinhua Ribao* [*New China Daily*] in December 1937. After the Nationalist government abandoned Wuhan and moved to Chongqing, the Yangzi River Bureau evolved into the Eighth Route Army liaison office under the supervision of the Southern Bureau, which also managed the *New China Daily* with Zhang Hanfu as editor and *Masses Weekly* under editor Qiao Guanhua.

3. Janice R. and Stephen R. MacKinnon, *Agnes Smedley: The Life and Times of an American Radical* (Berkeley: University of California Press, 1988), 172–81, 191, 212–13.

4. John Maxwell Hamilton, *Edgar Snow: A Biography* (Bloomington: Indiana University Press, 1988), 99–101; "Bertram, James Munro," *Dictionary of New Zealand Biography,* July 7, 2005, retrieved Oct. 15, 2005, from http://www.dnzb.govt.nz/dnzb/.

5. Rewi Alley, *An Autobiography* (Beijing: Foreign Language Press, 2003), 96–97, 101, 278.

The initial CPIC in Shanghai consisted of such interested individuals as Hubert S. Liang (a Yenjing University journalism professor and social worker), Hu Yuzhi (journalist and underground CCP member since 1933), Lu Guangmian (activist in the Rural Reconstruction Movement), and Xu Xinliu (banker).

Shandong-born Ida Pruitt was the daughter of an American missionary from Georgia. After studying social work in the United States, she began working at the Peking Union Medical Center (PUMC) in 1920, heading its Department of Social Services, where she trained the first generation of professional Chinese social workers. After Japanese troops occupied Beijing, she came into contact with the CCP-led resistance through James Bertram and the Snows, and using her privileged status as a foreigner in China, she smuggled funds and medical supplies. In the summer of 1938, the Snows wrote Pruitt telling her about plans for the Chinese Industrial Cooperatives (CIC) headed by Rewi Alley. When her contract at PUMC was not renewed, she looked up Alley in Zhejiang. After visiting the industrial cooperatives, she returned to Shanghai, boarded a coastal steamer for Hong Kong, and continued on her way to America. See "Ida Pruitt (1888–1985)," retrieved Aug. 23, 2005, from http://pruitt-library.blogspot.com/; "Pruitt, Ida. Papers, 1850s-1992:

A Finding Aid—Biography," retrieved Aug. 31, 2005, from oasis.harvard.edu:10080/oasis/deliver/xs1Transform?xs1FileName-FindingAid.xsl.

6. Liang Shangwan, *Zhonggong zai Xianggang* [The CCP in Hong Kong] (Hong Kong: Guangjiaojing Chubanshe, 1989), 2 (cited hereafter as Liang Shangwan, CCP in Hong Kong).

7. Israel Epstein, *Woman in World History: Life and Times of Soong Ching Ling* (Beijing: New World Press, 1993), 323; Liang Shangwan, CCP in Hong Kong, 2, 28.

8. Zheng Yijun, *Zhuanqi rensheng: Ji Cai Fujiu zouguo de daolu* [A Dramatic Life: The Path Traveled by Henry Tsoi] (Hong Kong: Haifeng chubanshe, 1997), 49–50 (cited hereafter as Zheng, Tsoi biography); Jean Ewen, *China Nurse, 1932–1939* (Toronto: McClelland and Stewart, 1981), 46–48; Liu Zuokui, "Shihai gouchen: Baiqiu'en Dafu dangnian shi zenma laidao Zhongguo de?" [Exploring Materials in the Ocean of History: How Did Dr. Bethune Come to China during That Period?], retrieved Aug. 13, 2005, from http://cul.sina.com.cn/y/2000-04-29/54618.html; "Enping ren Xuan Quanguang: Shou ying Baiqiu'en lai Zhongguo" [Xuan Quanguang of Enping Was the First to Welcome Bethune to China], *Jiangmen Ribao*, Aug. 16, 2005, retrieved Aug. 29, 2005, from http://bg5.jmnews.com.cn/2005/08/16/08c_686293.shtml; letter dated June 24, 1941, about Low Quai Bun, citizen returning, No. 7030/8981, Law Offices of White and White (San Francisco) to District Director, Immigration and Naturalization Service (Seattle), Low Quai Bun file, INS Immigration Case Files, National Archives, Pacific Sierra Region, San Bruno, California; Shen Qinglin, *Zhongguo kangzhan shiqi de guoji yuanzhu* [International Support during China's War of Resistance] (Shanghai: Renmin Chubanshe, 2000), 247. After Xuan returned to Hong Kong from the United States in 1936, he became responsible for maintaining contact with progressives in the American labor movement and with C. Y. Chen of the CPUSA Chinese Bureau. Soon after Guangzhou fell, he was sent to Shanghai, where he worked with the CCP underground until 1949, when he transferred to Beijing to work in the Haiyuan Zong Gonghui [Federation of seamen unions]. See "Xuan Rong (1893–1986)," retrieved Aug. 4, 2006, from http://wylib.jiangmen.gd.cn/jmhq/list.asp?id=396.

Zheng, Tsoi biography, alleges that Lowe coordinated CCP activities in the western United States; however, it is puzzling as to why the CCP ordered him to leave America to come to Hong Kong, a relatively unfamiliar place. His departure may have been a personal decision caused by Benjamin Fee's divorce as he sailed for Hong Kong with Fee's former wife Eva Chan, who later became Eva Choy Lowe.

Jean Ewen had served as a nurse in China from 1933 to 1937 and had learned to speak Chinese. She served at Yan'an and with the Eighth Route and New Fourth armies before returning to Canada in spring 1939.

9. Liang Shangwan, CCP in Hong Kong, 32; Alley, *An Autobiography*, 279–80; "Geng Lishu zai kangzhan zhong [Talitha Gerlach during the War of Resistance]," retrieved Sept. 1, 2006, from http://shszx.eastday.com/node2/node22/lhsb/node2606/node2619/u1a11691.html.

10. Epstein, *Woman in World History*, 324; Israel Epstein, *My China Eye: Memoirs of a Jew and a Journalist* (San Francisco: Long River Press, 2005), 108–11. Epstein was born into a Polish Jewish family that immigrated to China. He entered journalism in 1931.

11. Liang Shangwan, CCP in Hong Kong, 40–41; Epstein, *My China Eye*, 122–23. Ye Junjian did most of the translations, but Chi Chang, a Chinese volunteer from America who survived the Spanish Civil War and had arrived to participate in the War of Resis-

tance, translated the last-named essay. Israel Epstein and CPUSA member Donald Allen smoothed out the English in translations. Donald Allen attended the founding of the Guangzhou CDL and came to Hong Kong after Guangzhou fell to the Japanese.

12. Liang Shangwan, CCP in Hong Kong, 31–35; Zheng Canhui, Ji Hongsheng, and Wu Jingping, *Song Qingling yu kang Ri jiuwang yundong* [Soong Ching-ling and the Anti-Japanese National Salvation Movement] (Fuzhou: Fujian Renmin Chubanshe, 1986), 171–72.

13. Liang Shangwan, CCP in Hong Kong, 20, 27, 31–32; Liang Honghao, "Huashang Bao shilüe" [Brief History of Hwa Shang Pao], in *Huashang Bao shihua* [History of Hwa Shang Pao] (Guangzhou: Guangdong Renmin Chubanshe, 1991), 10–24.

14. Zheng, Tsoi biography, 37–42, 50, 57–62.

15. Liang Shangwan, CCP in Hong Kong, 72; Li Jinrong, "Wo de daolu" [The Path That I Traveled], retrieved Oct. 20, 2006, from http://www.zsnews.cn/Automobile/showcontent .asp?id=545617; Lin Lin, "Chuangban Jian'guo Bao jianchi kang-Ri, jiuguo, tuanjie, minzhu, jinbu" [Launching of Jian'guo Bao: Perseverance in Resisting Japan, National Salvation, Democracy and Progress], chap. 3, part 12 of *Feilübin Huaqiao yu Kang-Ri Zhanzheng* [Philippines Chinese and the War of Resistance against Japan], retrieved Oct. 22, 2006, from http://www.gxi.gov.cn/intoguangxi/gxhq/huapiao-kangr—ml-a3–12–11.htm; Rolland Lowe, interview with author, Dec. 3, 2006; Immigration and Naturalization Service Report of Investigation, Case File 41082/14-4 "Lowe Quai Bun," Oct. 1, 1956, from Low Quai Bun file in INS Immigration Case Files, National Archives, Pacific Sierra Region, San Bruno, California.

16. Alley, *An Autobiography,* 95–101; Li Jun, Wang Xin, *Kang-Ri Zhanzheng zhong de guoji youren* [International Friends during the War of Resistance to Japan] (Beijing: Zhongyang Wenxian Chubanshe, 2005), 278, 312–13; Marjorie King, *China's American Daughter: Ida Pruitt (1888–1985)* (Hong Kong: Chinese University Press, 2006), 133; "Zhou Enlai he Hu Yuzhi de Nanyang zhi xing [Zhou Enlai and Hu Yuzhi's Trip to Nanyang], retrieved Oct. 30, 2006, from http://book.ayinfo.ha.cn/mjwj/hh/huyuzhi/zzz/008.htm.

17. Chen Han-seng, *Sige shidai de wo* [Myself during Four Time Periods] (Beijing: Zhongguo wenshi chubanshe, 1988), 68 (cited hereafter as Chen, Myself during Four Periods); Zhu Jian, *Gonghe jianshi* [Short History of the Gung Ho Movement], the following sections: part 3, "Gongye ducha de yuanwang" [Wish of an Industrial Inspector], in chap. 1, "Zhanzheng xiaoyan zhong de li'nian" [An Idea Born among Gunpowder Smoke]; part 2, "Zai Hankou de di-yi ke" [Lesson No. 1 in Hankow], in chap. 2, "Tongyi zhangxian de jiejing" [Crystallization Due to the United Front]; part 2 "Haiwai pengyou qingxin Gung Ho" [Friends Overseas Fell in Love with Indusco], in chap. 3, "Zhanzheng xiaoyan zhong de li'nian" [An Idea Born among Gunpowder Smoke]; part 1, "Gonghe Guoji Weiyuanhui de gongxian" [Contributions of the International Committee for Chinese Industrial Cooperatives], and part 2, "Haiwai youren qingxin Gunghe [Overseas Friends Admired Indusco], in chap. 7, "Yuanzhu zhi shou" [The Helping Hands], retrieved Aug. 13, from http://www.chinagungho.com; Alley, *An Autobiography,* 136; Shen Qinglin, *Zhongguo kangzhan shiqi de Guoji yuanzhu* [International Aid during the War of Resistance Period] (Shanghai: Shanghai renmin chubanshe, 2000), 214; Lü Wanru, "Chen Han-seng xiansheng yu Gonghe" [Mr. Chen Han-seng and the Chinese Industrial Cooperatives] (speech given at Conference on Chen Han-seng's Scholarship and Thoughts held in Beijing, Feb. 24, 2005), retrieved Sept. 3, 2005, from http://www.iccic.org.cn.

18. Letter, Oct. 15, 1938, Zhou Enlai to Sha Zhipei, in *Zhou Enlai shuxin xuanji* [Selected

Correspondence of Zhou Enlai], Nov. 21, 2003, retrieved Aug. 24, 2003, from http://www
.zaiting.com/bbs; Zhang Yan, "Aiguo Huaqiao Chen Zhikun Chuanqi" [The Legend of
the Patriotic Chinese Overseas Chee Kwun Chun], *China Press,* Mar. 6, 1999; Xiaoye
Xiuzi, "Chen Zhikun: Cong Jiujinshan dao Yan'an yaodong" [Chee Kwun Chun: From San
Francisco to the Cave Dwellings of Yan'an], *Yangcheng Evening News,* June 12–15, 2004,
retrieved Aug. 28, 2005, from http://www.ycwb.com; Zhu Jian, "Cong Ganzhou qibu"
[Starting from Ganzhou], part 1 in chap. 5 of "Zai dongnan kang-Ri qianxian" [In the
Southeast, Frontline of Resistance to Japan], *Gonghe Jianshi* [Short History of the Gung
Ho Movement], retrieved Aug. 13, 2006, from http://www.chinagungho.com; Alley, *An
Autobiography,* 127. Chun returned to Hawaii in 1947 to get married. He and his bride
then moved to Beijing in 1949 and were assigned to work at the Foreign Affairs Publishing
House. In 1961 he moved to Hong Kong and entered the banking business. After Nixon's
visit to China, Chun established a company to facilitate foreign corporate investment in
China and to transfer technology. He returned to Hawaii in 1987.

19. "John Jan," in *A History of the Sam Yup Benevolent Association in the United States,
1850–2000,* ed. Sam Yup Benevolent Association History Editorial Committee (San Francisco: Sam Yup Benevolent Association, 1999), 240–41.

After World War II, John Jan worked in China for the United Nations and then for the
Nationalist government to rebuild the economy. He returned to the United States in 1948
as the civil war intensified. During the 1960–70s, he became very active in the U.S.-China
People's Friendship Association, promoting better understanding. Jan passed away in
1983.

20. Chen, Myself during Four Periods, 72–73.

21. "Biographical Note," Maud Russell Papers, 1914–1990, retrieved Aug. 31, 2005, from
http://www.nypl.org/research/chss/spe/rbk/faids/russell.html; Hamilton, *Edgar Snow,*
107–9, 111, 115–17, 122; Epstein, *My China Eye,* 135, 137–40, 146, 160–61, 163, 171, 224.

22. *Chinese Vanguard,* Nov. 4, 18, 1937; *Chinese World,* Nov. 7, 1937; Esther Carroll,
"Boycott Japanese Goods; Aid China!" *China Today* 4, no. 2 (Nov. 1937): 198; Esther Carroll, "The Japanese 'Good Will' Envoys Are Rebuffed," *China Today* 4, no. 3 (Dec. 1937):
214.

23. Philip J. Jaffe, *The Amerasia Case from 1945 to the Present* (New York: Philip J. Jaffe,
1979), 9–13; Ross Y. Koen, *The China Lobby in American Politics* (New York: Harper and
Row, 1974), 61–63. Long after Chi's departure, in 1945, the magazine was implicated in
using official government documents without permission. Jaffe and a State Department
employee were let off with light fines, and a House committee concluded in 1948 that
"few, if any, of the identifiable classified documents involved in this case had any real
importance in our national defense or our war efforts."

24. "Legendary Life of Chen Han-seng," *People's Daily,* June 30, 2003; Chen, Myself
during Four Periods, 61–65; Epstein, *My China Eye,* 25–26; Wu Youwen, Tian Ye, "Chen
Han-seng shilue" [Short Biography of Chen Han-seng], in *Zhong Gong dangshi ziliao*
[Materials on Communist Party of China History], ed. Zhong Gong zhongyang dangshi
yanjiushi [Office of the Central Committee of the Communist Party of China for Research
on Party History] (Beijing: Zhong Gong Dangshi Ziliao Chubanshe, 1990), 35:188–211
(cited hereafter as Wu, "Short Biography of Chen Han-seng").

In late 1934, the Comintern sent Chen on an intelligence mission to Japan. Upon learning that his contact had been arrested in China, he fled to Shanghai, where he hid in
Agnes Smedley's and then Rewi Alley's apartments. Chen's wife also arrived from Japan

and was sheltered by a German couple. After several weeks, the Chens slipped aboard a Russian freighter bound for Vladivostok disguised as Chinese seeing off foreign friends. They made their way to Moscow, where they managed to survive on meager stipends as researchers at the Labor University of the East. At that time, CCP leaders Kang Sheng, Wang Ming, and Li Lisan were also living in Moscow.

25. Chen, Myself during Four Periods, 65–67; Wu, "Short Biography of Chen Han-seng"; Ren Xuefang, "Makesizhuyi Nongcun Jingjixue de Xianqu—Chen Han-seng Shilue" [A Pioneer in Marxist Agrarian Economics—A Short Biography of Chen Han-seng], in *Zhongguo dangdai jingjixuejia zhuanlue* [Short Biographies of Contemporary Economists in China], ed. Jingji Ribao (Shenyang: Liaoning Chubanshe, 1986), 78–115; Esther Carroll, "America in Action," *China Today* 5, no. 5 (Feb. 1939): 19.

26. Howard L. Boorman, ed., *Biographical Dictionary of Republican China,* vol. 1 (New York: Columbia University Press, 1967), s.v. "Chi Ch'ao-ting"; Cao Yunding and Li Ji, "Ji Chaoding," in *Zhonggong dangshi renwuzhuan* [Biographies of Personalities in CCP History], ed. Hu Hua, 32nd Collection (Xi'an: Shaanxi Renmin Chubanshe, 1987), 312–28; Zong Daoyi, "Jiechu de Gongchandang ren Ji Chaoding" [Ji Chaoding, an Outstanding Communist], *Fenzhou xiangqing,* 2003, retrieved Feb. 4, 2006, from http://www.isfz.com/sq/Announce/announce.asp?BoardID=-302&ID=20320&TopicSortID=20309; Zeng Junwei, "Ji Chaoding xuezhang zhuanqi de geming shengyai" [The Legendary Revolutionary Career of Leading Scholar Chao-ting Chi], Oct. 9, 2004, retrieved Feb. 4, 2006, from Tsinghua Alumni website, http://www.tsinghua.org.cn/messageshtml/6001/1097288898921.htm. Through his acquaintance with Chinese banker and entrepreneur Chen Guangfu (K. P. Chen), whom he had met through friends in the U.S. Treasury Department, C. T. Chi joined the staff of the Universal Trading Corporation, which had been established by the KMT government to procure materials from the United States. In 1941 Chi returned to China and with introductions from K. P. Chen and his father, worked for the Ministry of Finance, then headed by H. H. Kung, and rose quickly to become a key figure in government financial circles. After World War II, his wife, Harriet, and their two children came to China for the first time. They decided to divorce, because Chi did not wish to return to the United States, and she did not wish to live in China. Meanwhile, Chi remained close to H. H. Kung. After attending a meeting of the U.N. Economic Council in Australia in December 1948 as an advisor to the Chinese delegation, he was invited to Beijing to become economic advisor to General Fu Zuoyi. The city was then already under siege by the People's Liberation Army (PLA). Chi's family home was the site of several sessions at which Chi and his father persuaded General Fu to surrender the city peacefully. After the founding of the PRC, Chi served the government by handling international economic and trade issues. He also married Luo Jingyi, Shi Huang's widow. In 1963 Chi died of a massive cerebral hemorrhage, and it was not until then that his long covert membership in the Communist Party was officially acknowledged (vol. 1 of *Biographical Dictionary of Republican China,* s.v. "Ch'i Ch'ao-ting").

27. Xu Suizhi, *Xu Yongying zhuanlue* [A Short Biography of Y. Y. Hsu], part 3, 1933–1946, posted May 24, 1997, retrieved July 11, 2007, from http://xusuizhi.blshe.com/post/3238/55621 (cited hereafter as Xu Suizhi, Short Biography of Y. Y. Hsu, part 3).

28. U.S. Congress, Senate Committee on the Judiciary, Internal Security Subcommittee, "Bibliography of contributors to Institute of Pacific Relations; Far Eastern Survey and Pacific Affairs for years 1931–51," in *Institute of Pacific Relations: Hearings,* 15 pts., 82nd Cong., 2nd sess. (Washington, D.C.: Government Printing Office, 1951, 1952), 5506–633.

29. "Meiguo Yuan-Hua Hui," [China Aid Council], in *Zhongguo Fulihui zhi* [Annals of the China Welfare Institute], retrieved Jan. 19, 2006, from http://www.shtong.gov .cn/node2/node2245/node69322/node69330/node69376/node69381/userobject1ai67376. html.

30. Alley, *An Autobiography,* 277–80; Part 2, "Haiwai youren qingxin Gunghe" [Overseas Friends Admired Indusco], in Chap. 7 "Yuanzhu zhi shou" [The Helping Hands]; Zhu Jian, *Gonghe jianshi* [Short History of the Gung Ho Movement], retrieved Aug. 24, 2005, from http://www.chinagungho.com/history/jianshi/jianshi0024.htm; "Geng Lishu (Talitha Gerlach) (1896–1995)," retrieved Oct. 28, 2005, from http://www.shtong.gov.cn/node2/ node2245/node69322/node69341/node69492/node69496/userobject1ai67650.html.

31. "Historical Note," *Guide to United China Relief Records, 1928–1947,* retrieved Jan. 22, 2006, from http://www.pearlsbcn.org/c/list.asp?articleid=323; "Meiguo Yuan-Hua Lianhehui," [United China Relief], retrieved Feb. 6, 2006, from http://www.pearlsbcn .org/c/list.asp?articleid=323; T. Christopher Jespersen, *American Images of China: 1931– 1949* (Stanford: Stanford University Press, 1996), 47–48; King, *China's American Daughter,* 148–51; Peter Conn, *Pearl Buck: A Cultural Biography* (New York: Cambridge University Press, 1996), 243.

32. Advertisement in *China Today,* Jan. 1938; Si-lan Chen Leyda, *Footnote to History* (New York: Dance Horizons, 1954), 237; "Historical/Biographical Note," *Guide to the Jay and Si-lan Chen Leyda Papers 1913–1987* (bulk 1930–1980), Tamiment Library and Robert F. Wagner Labor Archives, retrieved Dec. 31, 2005, from http://dlib.nyu.edu/findingaids/ html/tamwag/leyda.html; Arthur Clegg, *Aid China, 1937–1949: A Memoir of a Forgotten Campaign* (Beijing: New World Press, 1989), 32; Jerome Klein, "Review of Modern Chinese Art," *China Today* 4, no. 5 (Feb. 1938): 17. Si-lan Chen was born in Trinidad. She learned to dance in Moscow, and after immigrating to the United States with her husband, Jay Leyda, she became one of the earliest Chinese American dancers. When she journeyed to join Leyda in the United States, being part Chinese she was subject to the Chinese exclusion law and was only permitted to remain with him for six months. Her American career was complicated by the long struggle to obtain citizenship. She performed extensively in the United States, Mexico, and the West Indies through the late 1930s and 1940s to benefit China relief. While taking ballet lessons in England, Chen would visit Trinidad during summers and organize younger relatives in dances. These activities were said to have inspired a younger cousin, Wu Ailan, to study dance in England. In 1940 Wu went to Hong Kong and contacted the CDL, which helped her to enter China, where she became known as Dai Ailian, a pioneer of China's dance movement.

Trinidad-born Jack Chen (1908–?) studied law in England but preferred art. He joined his father in China and in 1927 became one of China's first political cartoonists at the English-language newspaper *China Tribune* in Wuhan. After the Wuhan government began purging Communists, he and his older brother, Percy, left with Borodin and other Soviet advisors to the USSR, where he graduated from Moscow's Polygraphic Institute in 1930. Afterward, he joined *Moscow News* as a colleague to Anna Louise Strong. In the 1930s, he went to Shanghai and to London. During the War of Resistance, he visited Yan'an as a journalist. In 1937 and 1938, he showed his own and other artists' works worldwide in the first exhibit of Chinese revolutionary art. When the European war started, he joined the British Communist Party and wrote for the *Daily Worker* while remaining active in "aid China" campaigns. When civil war loomed in China, he returned to China and interviewed Chiang Kai-shek in Nanjing and Mao Zedong in Yan'an. He later returned to England and set up the first overseas office of the New China News Agency in 1948. He returned to China in 1950 to work at *People's China* and *Beijing Review*.

33. Huahai, "Shidai Geshou Liu Langmo" [Liu Liangmo, Songster of the Times], *Ta Kung Pao*, Aug. 1, 2, and 3, 1990; Gao Zhennong, *Shanghai zongjiaoshi* [History of Religion in Shanghai] (Shanghai: Shanghai renmin chubanshe, 1992), Chen Lian, "Huanghe Dahechang zai Haiwai" [The Yellow River Cantata Abroad]," *Renmin Ribao* (overseas ed.), Dec. 13, 1989; Epstein, *My China Eye*, 234–35; *New York Times*, Oct. 11, 1945. Liu Liangmo directed the YMCA national association. In February 1935, Liu organized a choral group in Shanghai using songs to inspire resistance to Japanese aggression. Its success led to a National Salvation Choral Movement that spread to other cities. In 1936 the authorities forced the choruses to disband. Israel Epstein worked with Ye Junjian to translate the recital and lyrics of the *Yellow River Cantana* while he and his wife were visiting in England en route to the United States in 1945. However, one source alleged that in 1941 Liu Liangmo led an English-language performance at a university near New York City. The reference did not state when the event occurred. Reference "Huanghe Dahechang de liuchuan [The Worldwide Spreading of the *Yellow River Cantata*], Oct. 13, 2005, retrieved Oct. 30. 2005, from http://www.xxcb.com.cn/show.asp?id=724838.

34. Cheng Fangwu, "Wang Ying xiaozhuan" [Short Biography of Wang Ying], in Wang Ying, *Liangzhong Meiguoren* [Two Types of Americans] (Beijing: Zhongguo qingnian chubanshe, 1980), 5–15; Li Runxin, *Jiebai de mingxing—Wang Ying* [Wang Ying, the Spotlessly White Star] (Beijing: Zhongguo qingnian chubanshe, 1987), chaps. 33, 34, 35, retrieved July 12, 2007, from http://www.shuku.net:8080/novels/zhuanji/wangying/wangying.html.

Wang Ying was born Yu Zhihua in Wuhu, Anhui. She was sold as a child bride to repay her father's debt and fled to her maternal aunt surnamed Wang in Changsha. She became acquainted with the local CCP and acted as their courier. A warrant was issued for her arrest, and in 1928 she fled to Shanghai, where she changed her name to Wang Ying and became an actress. She joined the CCP in 1930 and performed in Shanghai progressive dramatic circles. In 1936 she earned the enmity of the actress Lan Pin (later known as Jiang Qing, who married Mao Zedong), whom she beat out for the lead role in the film *Caijinhua*. For this, Wang would suffer during the Cultural Revolution. After the outbreak of the War of Resistance, Wang was principal actress in a traveling propaganda drama troupe that traveled throughout China. In 1939 the troupe performed in Southeast Asia and Hong Kong to raise funds to support China's War of Resistance. One of her best-known roles was in *Fangxia ni de bianzi*. For more information about Xie Hegeng, see "Diandian Gongchandang ren zhong zuizhuming de wodi yingxiong" [An Account of the Most Famous Communists Who Were Heroic Planted Agents], retrieved July 17, 2007, from http://www.aladding.com/view/postDetail.cfm?lv=big5&topicid=95&postid=368549.

35. "Gong Pusheng: Jieyuan Lianheguo 60 nian" [Gong Pusheng: Ties with the United Nations for 60 Years], retrieved Nov. 11, 2006, from Baidu cache of http://news.sina.com .cn/c/2005-10-24/02367247629s.shtml (cited hereafter as Gong Pusheng and the United Nations); Ding Xiaohe, ed., *Zhongguo bainian liuxue quan jilu* [Complete Record of a Century of Students from China Studying Abroad] (Zhuhai: Zhuhai chubanshe, 1998), 1049–58 (cited hereafter as Ding, Complete Record of a Century). After Gong returned to the United States in August 1945, the United Nations had just formed in San Francisco, and she frequently helped the delegation. She became friends with delegation staff member Zhang Hanfu (Xie Qitai) whom she later married in 1949 in CCP-occupied Shanghai. Ding, Complete Record of a Century, 1049–58; Gong Pusheng and the United Nations;

Gong Pusheng, "Qinli Lianheguo de suiyue" [Personal Experiences during My Years at the United Nations], in *The Chinese in the United Nations, 1945–2003*, ed. Li Tiecheng (Beijing: Renmin chubanshe, 2003), 581–88.

36. "Zhang Shuyi," in *Yanjing Daxue renwu zhi* [Gazetteer of Personalities at Yenching University], 1st collection (Beijing: Beijing Daxue chubanshe), 387–88; Xu Suizhi, Short Biography of Y. Y. Hsu, part 3.

37. "Pu Shouchang," retrieved Feb. 9, 2006, from http://www.fmprc.gov.cn/chn/gxh/zlb/zgwjrw/lrfbzjbzzl/t9085.htm.

38. Pei Chi Liu, *A History of the Chinese in North America* (Taipei: Liming Wenhua Shiye Gufen Youxian Gongsi, 1981), 2:570; Renqiu Yu, *To Save China, To Save Ourselves: The Chinese Hand Laundry Alliance of New York* (Philadelphia: Temple University Press, 1992), 90, 92.

39. Zheng et al., *Song Qingling*, 171–285.

40. Chen, Myself during Four Periods.

41. *Chinese Vanguard*, Nov. 9, 1935; Li Shengping, Ren Dakui, and Chen Youjin, *Zhongguo jin-xiandai renming dacidian* [Dictionary of Famous Chinese Modern and Contemporary Individuals] (Beijing: Zhongguo guoji guangbo chubanshe, 1989), s.v. Rao Shushi (cited hereafter as Li, Biographical dictionary); Chen, Myself during Four Periods.

42. Xu Suizhi, Short Biography of Y. Y. Hsu, part 3; Xu Ming, "He Xu Yongying jiaowang er-san shi" [Two or Three Incidents in My Contacts with Y. Y. Hsu], retrieved July 11, 2007, from http://kui-shi.blog.hexun.com/9172766_d.html (hereafter cited as Xu Ming, Two or Three Incidents).

After Zhao Jiansheng (Rao Shushi) returned to China, he became political commissar of the New Fourth Army during the Sino-Japanese War. After the founding of the PRC, he was first secretary of the East China Bureau of the Central CCP and chair of the East China Military Political Committee. In 1953 he became head of the CCP's Central Organization Department. He, along with Gao Gang, was accused of anti-party activities in 1954 and stripped of his party membership in 1955. Rao passed away in 1975 (Li, Biographical dictionary, s.v. "Rao Shushi").

43. Wang Shigu, "Cong Xianfeng dao *Jiuguo Shibao*" [From *Chinese Vanguard* to *China Salvation Times*], in *Haiwai Huawen xinwenshi yanjiu* [Research on the History of Chinese Language Journalism Overseas] (Beijing: Xinhua chubanshe, 1998); Li Runsheng and Cheng Yaoming, "Lü-Mei guiqiao, qian Meizhou Huaqiao Ribao She yewu zhuren Zhang Manli xiansheng fangwen lu" [A Record of an Interview with the Returned Overseas Chinese from America, the Former Business Manager of *China Daily News* Mr. Zhang Manli], in *Huaqiao shi lunwenji* [Collection of Papers on Overseas Chinese History] (Guangzhou: Ji'nan University Overseas Chinese Research Institute, 1981), 2:322–32 (cited hereafter as Li and Cheng, Interview with Zhang Manli); "Meizhou Huaqiao Ribao xiaoshi" [Brief History of China Daily News] in Wang Shigu, *Haiwai Huawen xinwenshi yanjiu* [Research on the History of Chinese Language Journalism Overseas] (Beijing: Xinhua Chubanshe, 1998), 135–52 (cited hereafter as Wang Shigu, Brief History of China Daily News).

Some other members of the committee were Mei Cantian (Eugene Moy), C. Y. Chen, Yan Qingrong, Liu Kemian, Tan Guangpan, Lin Tang (Thomas Lem Tong), Chee Fun Ho, Y. Y. Hsu, Tan Wei, Chen Houfu, Chen Sancai, Yu Zhimin, Huang Kang, Fang Fu'er. There are discrepancies between Zhang Manli's oral interview and Wang Shigu's accounts of the early history of *China Daily News*. I have given more weight to Zhang's account, as he was contemporaneous with the events described and managed business at the paper.

44. "Meizhou Huaqiao Ribao xiaoshi" [Brief History of *China Daily News*] in Wang Shigu, Brief History of *China Daily News,* 135–52; Li and Cheng, Interview with Zhang Manli, 2:322–32; interview with Fang Fu'er and Zhang Manli, recorded by Zhang Ting-zheng, "Jianku Fendou de Meizhou Huaqiao Ribao" [*China Daily News,* Struggling against Adversity], in *Guangzhou wenshi ziliao* [Guangzhou Historical Materials] (Guangzhou: Guangdong renmin chubanshe, 1979), 17:176–80; Zhi Xiaomin, "Ji Gungquan yu Niuyue Huaqiao Ribao [Kung-ch'uan Chi and the *China Daily News* of New York], July 1, 2005, re-trieved Feb. 5, 2006, from http://www.cc.org.cn/old/pingtai/030618300/0306183022.htm.

45. Zheng, Tsoi biography, 57–60, 64.

46. Zhang Bao, "Er sanshi niandai zai Meiguo de Zhongguo Gongchandang ren" [Chinese Communists in the United States during the Twenties and Thirties], in *Guoji gongyunshi yanjiu ziliao* [Historical Research Materials on the International Communist Movement] (Beijing: 1982), 7:150–61; Zheng, Tsoi biography, 64. Zheng alleged that Brow-der set up the Chinese Bureau after reading Zhou Enlai's letter; however, Zhang, who had left the United States several years before Tsoi arrived, described the establishment of a Chinese Bureau around the late 1920s with the same functions as that described by Zheng. See Wu Zhonghua, "Waijiao zhanxian de liangguo juxing—Tang Mingzhao he ta de nüer Tang Wensheng" [Two Big Stars on the Diplomatic Front—Chu Tong and His Daughter Nancy Tong], retrieved Aug. 25, 2005, from http://www.yanhuang.org.cn/htm/chunqiu/97_1_wu.htm. Zhang's account seems more reliable since Zhang was secretary of the Chinese Bureau and was familiar with the history of the Communist Party in America. On the other hand, the author of Tsoi's biography had apparently never been to the United States and may have misunderstood Tsoi during interviews for the biography.

47. Immigration and Naturalization Service Form SF2602 dated July 3, 1941, No. 41082/14-4 ex S.S. President Coolidge, filled out and signed by Quai Bun Low, Low Quai Bun file, INS Immigration Case Files, National Archives, Pacific Sierra Region, San Bruno, California; Zheng, Tsoi biography, 64–67.

48. Zheng, Tsoi biography, 159–60.

49. *Tanxiangshan Huaqiao Guoyuwen Xuexiao yanju chouzhu Gonghe tekan* [Special Publication of the Drama Presentation by the Chinese National Language School to Raise Funds to Support the Industrial Cooperatives] (Honolulu: Chinese National Language School, 1940), 4–5; Jingnan, "Jinmen yiyu" [Reminiscences by the Golden Gate], *Chinese Pacific Weekly,* June 29, 1975, "Leiyu de yanyuan" [The Actors for Thunder Storm], and July 3, 1975, "Leiyu yu Zhenzhu Gang" [Thunder Storm and Pearl Harbor].

A performance of *Lay Down Your Whip* took place on September 1941 in the Honolulu Chinese National Language School's program to commemorate the ninth anniversary of the Shenyang Incident and to raise funds for Indusco. It was the first Mandarin vernacular drama staged in Hawaii.

Yeyu Xiao Jutuan [Little Amateur Drama Troupe] was organized in San Francisco in 1941 to stage Cao Yu's *Thunder Storm,* which was revised into vernacular Cantonese. Performances were unfortunately scheduled for the tense days immediately following the Japanese attack on Pearl Harbor, and the attendance was very light.

50. Tan Lian'ai, "Niuyue Huaqiao Qingnian Jiuguotuan chengli yi'nian lai zhi gongzuo baogao" [Report on the Tasks of the Chinese Youth Club of New York City during the Year Since Its Founding], *Chinese Youth* no. 2 (Aug. 1939): 6–8; Li Guhong (James Lee), "Zhe yi'nian de gongzuo—Niuyue Huaqiao Qingnian Jiuguotuan: Gongzuo baogao" [This Year's Tasks—Report on the Work of the Chinese Youth Club of New York City], *Chinese Youth* no. 3 (Oct. 1940): 7–11.

51. Norbert Woo, interview with author, Aug. 10, 1974; *Chinese World,* Dec. 27, 1937; *Huayi junren ji'niance* [Commemorative Album for Chinese in Armed Forces] (San Francisco: Chick Char Musical Club, 1947).

52. *Chung Sai Yat Po,* Sept. 11, 1938; *Chinese World,* Sept. 25, 1938.

53. Yan Dichang, "Benshe zhounianlai gongzuo baogao" [Report on Activities of Our Society for the Past Year], *Lufeng zhou'nian jinian tekan* (1941), 8–13. The club name was derived from the phrase *Lugouqiao fenghuo,* or "beacon at Marco Polo Bridge"; the first shots in the Sino-Japanese conflict occurred at Marco Polo Bridge. In ancient China, beacons were used to give alarms about invaders at the border.

54. Early NCALSS member Bong Lee, interview with author, Jan. 2, 1970, Apr. 18, 1993.

55. Latinized Chinese was developed by CCP members Qu Qiubai, Lin Boqu, Xiao San, and Wu Yuzhang, who first began to research of Chinese-language reform at the end of 1929 when they were exiles in the USSR. In 1930 they devised a system of latinized Chinese (Latinxua Sin Wenz) with the assistance of Soviet experts V. S. Kolokolov and A. A. Dragunov. The system was used to educate Chinese workers in Khabarovsk and Vladivostok during the early 1930s. News of the development was first published in China in August 1933. In 1934 conservative, pro-KMT literati began campaigning to revive the use of classical Chinese and attacking the use of vernacular. During the liberal and Leftist counterattack led by the prominent writer Lu Xun, the idea that latinized Chinese might serve as a tool to eradicate illiteracy gained wide support among progressive educators. The system was much simpler to learn than the complex romanized Chinese (Gwoyeu Romatzyh) system approved by the KMT government. For more information about Sin Wenz, see "Sin Wenz," retrieved Sept. 30, 2006, from http://www.pinyin.info/romanization/sinwenz/; Ni Haishu, ed., *Ladinghua Xin Wenzi yundong de shimo he* biannian jishi [The Story of the Latinized Chinese Movement and Its Chronological History] (Shanghai: Zhishi chubanshe, 1987) (cited hereafter as Ni, Story of the Latinized Chinese Movement).

56. Ni, Story of the Latinized Chinese Movement, 159; Jianfu, "Nianyu lai de huiwu gaishu" [A Narration of Society Affairs in the Past Year or So], in *Ymen Ingau* [Language Study] (San Francisco: NCALSS, 1942), 9–10; *Sin Wenz Bao,* no. 2 (Aug. 15, 1940). *Sin Wenz Bao* was the newsletter published by NCALSS.

57. Rucong, "A Short Ten Years, Part 1," *Minqing Tuanbao,* no. 1 (Dec. 1, 1949).

58. Bochao, "Zhankai laojun yundong" [Develop the Movement to Send Greetings and Gifts to Armed Services Personnel], *Zhandou* 1, no. 8/9 (Jan. 1, 1944); Dongming, "Yidian chengxian" [A Small Contribution], *Zhandou* 1, no. 10 (Apr. 10, 1944). Later, CWMAA and the local Chinese branch of the California State Guard also joined the activity as sponsors.

59. Rucong, "A Short Ten Years, Part 2," *Minqing Tuanbao* n.s., no. 2 (Dec. 14, 1949); *Jiasheng Huaqiao Qingnian Jiuguo Tuan Tuanbao,* no. 12 (Mar. 27, 1944). The Chinese American Democratic Youth League published the newsletter *Minqing Tuanbao,* while the Chinese Youth league put out *Jiasheng Huaqiao Qingnian Tuan Tuanbao.*

60. *Chinese Digest,* April 1936; *Federation News* 1, no. 10 (Jan.–Feb. 1939). Some Chinese clubs in Los Angeles were Wah Que Boys Club, Lowa Athletic Club, Lowa Auxiliary, Chinese Students Association, Kuin Ying Club, Cathay Cultural Club, Mei Wah Club, and Los Angeles Chinese Tennis Club.

61. "Editorial: A Call to Conference!!!" in *Federation News* 1, no. 10 (Jan.–Feb. 1939); Louise Chin, "Activities of the N.Y. Council of Chinese Youth," *Chinese Youth* special issue no. 2 (Aug. 1939), 43; Pei Chi Liu, *History of the Chinese in North America,* 491–92.

In 1939 the New York Council included the following clubs: Chinese Students Forum, Edserbros Club, Ging Hawk Club, Chinese Student Club of University Heights, Young People of the Chinese First Presbyterian Church, Our Own Club, New York Ching Wah Players, Chinese Aeronautics Association, Chinese Art Club, Chinese Youth Club, Jeune Doc Club, Young Chinese Club, Chinese Boy Scouts.

62. *Chinese Digest,* October 1937. The thirty clubs were Chinese Patriotic League, Chinese Sportsmen's Club, Square and Circle, Fidelis Coterie, Philotasian Club, Cathay Club, Chitena Club, Wah Ying Club, Chinese Center, Delta Phi Sigma, Waku Auxiliary, Chinese YWCA, Chinese YMCA, UC Chinese Students Club, Sigma Omicron Pi, Yoke Choy Club, Cathayans, Chinese Youth Circle, Chinese Art Association, 307 Club, Stanford Chinese Students Club, Chinese Progressive Association, Chinatown Knights, International Workers' Order, Wah Sung Club, Tri Chi, Chinese Christian Fellowship Council, Chinese Theater Guild, Chinese Catholic Young Men's Association, and Boy Scout Troop No. 3.

63. Some clubs formed in San Francisco and Oakland between 1937 and 1945, mostly by new immigrants under thirty, are as follows: Chick Char Club (founded 1937), Yiqun [Ngai Quon; Group of Artists] Club (music; founded 1937), Zhaoyu [Chew Yu; Morning Rain] Club (music; founded 1938); Minduo Drama Society (1938), Lufeng Drama Society (founded 1940), San Min Chu I Youth Corps [1940]; Qiangyi [Keung Ngai; Strong Arts] Club (music, sports; founded 1940), New Alphabetized Chinese Language Club (1940; reorganized as Chinese Youth League, founded 1943), Feilong [Fei Loong; Flying Dragons] Club (music; founded 1942), Qiaozhi [Que Gee; Sojourner Aspirations] Club (music; founded 1942), Haifeng [Hoy Fung; Ocean Wind] Club (music, founded 1943), Qinghua [Ching Wah; Young Chinese] Club (former students of Chinese Central High School; literary, founded 1943), Xianfeng [Vanguard] Club (former students of Hip Wo School; vernacular drama, founded 1943); Yingwu [Ying Mo; Parrot] (former students from St. Mary's School; social), Chen'guang [Sun Kwong; Morning Light] Club (social), Qianjin [Chin Jun; Forge Ahead] Club (social), Kuangfeng [Violent Wind] Club (sports), Likun [Beautiful and Feminine] Club (female). In Oakland there were Yehuo [Yeh Fo; Prairie Fire] Club and Xiaojiao She [Sheau-jyue Sheh; Dawn Clarion] (literary, founded 1942).

64. Pei Chi Liu, *History of the Chinese in the United States,* 491–93; Enclosure (A) of DIO, 12ND, conf. ltr., B-7-J-1401, dated May 26, 1945: Memorandum No. A8–5/16-B-7-(9), dated Feb. 20, 1945, from H. S. Covington, District Intelligence Officer, 12th Naval District; to The Director of Naval Intelligence; Subject: Chinese Situation in the San Francisco Area, Declassified E.O. 12356, Sec. 3.3. NND Project 868156, National Archives, Pacific Sierra Region, San Bruno, Calif. The San Min Chu I Youth Corps originated in Wuhan in 1938 as an organization to prepare young people for full KMT party membership. L. S. Wong went to the United States in 1939 to establish the corps among Chinese Americans. The Eastern U.S. Corps, based in New York City, was founded in September 1940 and the Western U.S. Corps, in San Francisco, in February 1941. Corps activities included discussions of current events, Chinese and radio classes, and war support activities. The corps published a biweekly newsletter, *Meizhou Huaqiao Qingnian Shuangzhoukan* [Biweekly Publication of Chinese Youth of America]. Despite adequate funding and backing by the KMT, strict party control that discouraged corps members' initiatives made it difficult for the corps to attract recruits. The corps merged with the party in 1948.

65. Housai, "Shi'er ge yue" [Twelve Months], *Qingnian zhenxian* [Youth Front] no.1 (Mar. 3, 1945). The youth groups forming the Federation were Qianjin, Qinghua, Kuangfeng, Likun, and Xianfeng.

66. Benjamin Fee, letter to the author, Feb. 18, 1973.

67. Him Mark Lai, "A Voice of Reason: Life and Times of Gilbert Woo, Chinese American Journalist," *Chinese America: History and Perspectives* (San Francisco: Chinese Historical Society of America, 1992), 83–123. When the brothers were living in Taishan, they had participated in progressive circles. After arriving in Los Angeles, Gilbert became friends with Benjamin Fee and even submitted a manuscript to a publication edited by him. In San Francisco, Lawrence Lowe contacted Norbert and asked him about the revolutionary situation in Taishan and also recruited him for a role in a pantomime commemorating Lenin. The brothers, however, did not join the CPUSA, but instead became left-of-center liberals supporting President Franklin Roosevelt's New Deal.

68. "Ben tuan de gaizu he jinhou de renwu" [Reorganization of Our League and Our Task after That], *Zhandou*, May 1946.

69. Wenquan, "Huaqiao Wenxue Shi Nian" [Ten Years of Overseas Chinese Literature], in *Tuwei* [Breaking Out of the Encirclement] (New York: Xinmiao, 1950), 143–60.

70. Wenquan, "Huaqiao Wenxue Shi Nian."

71. Nanfang Ju Dangshi Ziliao Zhengji Xiaozu Zuzhizu [Committee on Organization of the Committee for Collection of Party Historical Materials on the Southern Bureau], *Zhong-Gong Nanfang Ju Zuzhi Xitong Gaikuang* [A Survey of the Organizational Structure of the Southern Bureau of the CCP], in *Zhonggong dangshi ziliao* [Historical Materials on the CCP], 12th collection (Beijing: Zhong-Gong Dangshi Ziliao Chubanshe, 1984), 5–45; "Chongqing da houfang kang-Ri minzhu wenhua de kongqian fanrong" [The Unprecedented Flourishing of Anti-Japanese Democratic Culture in Chongqing's Vast Rear Area], in *Chongqing Kangzhanshi* [History of the War of Resistance in Chongqing], retrieved Nov. 12, 2006, from http://www.cq.xinhuanet.com/subject/2005/2005-07/29/content_4757309.htm.

72. Wei Yuchuan, ed., *Zhongguo xian-dangdai nüzuojia zhuan* [Biographies of Modern and Contemporary Women Writers of China] (Beijing: Zhongguo Funü Chubanshe, 1990), s.v. "Yang Gang"; Yan Chunde, "Yang Gang," *Ershi shiji zhongguo chuming nüzuojia zhuan* [Biographies of Famous Twentieth-Century Female Chinese Writers] (Provence, France: 1985; revised Beijing 1995), retrieved Dec. 26, 2005, from http://www.oklink.net/a/0007/0726/essj/012.htm; MacKinnon and MacKinnon, *Agnes Smedley*, 310–11; John King Fairbank, *Chinabound: A Fifty-Year Memoir* (New York: Harper and Row, 1982), 273–76. After the fall of Hong Kong, Yang Gang continued working as a journalist in Guilin and Chongqing and was regarded highly by Zhou Enlai. After staying in the United States, she worked for *Ta Kung Pao* in Hong Kong and was responsible for the paper's switch to a pro-CCP stance. After the founding of the PRC, she became one of the best-known journalists in China. Yang was seriously injured in a car accident in 1955 and committed suicide in 1957.

73. Gong Pusheng and the United Nations; Ding, Complete Record of a Century; Gong Pusheng, "Qinli Lianheguo de suiyue," 581–91.

74. "Huang Shaoxiang xiansheng nianbiao" [Chronology of Teacher Huang Xiangsheng], retrieved Aug. 10, 2005, from http://www.cctvt.com/cgi-bin/index.dll?pageo?webid=jianwangzhan&userid=129362&columnno=25&articleid=14569. Huang Shaoxiang (1915–?) was a native of Changsha, Hunan, who studied at Qinghua University from 1934 until 1937. She was active in the 1935 Beijing student demonstrations and was one of the earliest members of the Minzu Xiangfengdui [Vanguard Group for People's Liberation]. She joined the CCP in June 1936. She became a professor at Beijing University and a member of the Academy of Social Sciences of China.

75. Xu Ming, Two or Three Incidents; Fu Zhengzheng, "Jiqi caifang duixiang de tanhua yuwang" [Stimulating the Desire of the Interviewed to Speak], retrieved Nov. 16, 2006, from http://www.zydg.net/magazine/article/1003–1286/2005/03/171649.html. After his return to China after the founding of the PRC, Xu entered the Foreign Ministry; however, in 1957 he was branded a rightist.

76. "Woguo shehui jingji xitong gongcheng de xueke daitouren zhi yi, Xue Baoding" [Xue Baoding, One of the Pioneers in Our Nation in Socioeconomic-System Engineering], retrieved Nov. 12, 2006, from http://www.chinavalue.net/wiki/showcontent .aspx?titleid=28805. Xue Baoding (1916–98) was from Wuxi, Jiangsu. He studied at Central University in Nanjing and Jinling University before becoming an underground member of the CCP in 1938. In 1944 Xue passed the qualifying examination to go to the United States for industrial work experience and advanced studies, and in 1946 he became a graduate student at University of Pittsburgh.

77. "Wo yu shiyou youyuan—Hou Xianglin zishu" [I Had a Predestined Relationship with Petroleum: Hou Xianglin's Account], part 1, retrieved Sept. 28, 2005, from http://www.agpr.net/bbs/read.php?tid=51539. Hou Xianglin (1912–?) was from Shantou, Guangdong. In 1931 he matriculated in Yenching University. After graduating in mid-1935, Hou worked at a research institute in Shanghai. In 1936 he joined a *dushu hui* [reading groups] organized by Gong Pusheng and joined the CCP in 1938. Hou passed a qualifying examination enabling him to go to the United States for industrial work experience and advanced studies, and he became a graduate student at University of Pittsburgh in 1945. Note 42, Xu Suizhi, "Chronology of the Life of Y. Y. Hsu," part 2 (Apr. 28, 2007), retrieved Aug. 20, 2007, from http://kui-shi.blog.hexun.com/9113246_d.html.

78. Chen Dunde, "Xin Zhongguo waijiao neimu" [Inside Story of the Diplomacy of the New China], part 5, retrieved Nov. 28, 2006, from http://www.xawb.com/gb/ rbpaper/2000–09/24/content_348579.htm; Wang Shigu, *Meiguo Huawen baokan jianzhi* [Brief List and Descriptions of Chinese-Language Periodicals in the USA] (1854–1997) (Beijing: Zhongguo Renmin Daxue Xinwen Xueyuan Haiwai Huawen Baokan Yanjiu Ketizu [Committee on Topics on "The Study of Chinese Overseas Periodicals" of the College of Journalism, People's University of China], 1999), 30.

Lai Yali (1910–?) was a native of Neijiang, Sichuan. He graduated from Beijing University in 1934 and became a lecturer at Gen. Feng Yuxiang's Mt. Tai retreat and also personal secretary to the general. Lai joined the CCP in 1938.

Zhongguo Minzhu Geming Tongmeng (also referred to as Xiao Min'ge) was an underground organization formed in Chongqing in May 1941 and allied to the CCP. It opposed civil war and KMT dictatorial rule and sought to win over members of the KMT left wing who were friendlier toward the CCP. Members included KMT and underground CCP members and some without any political party. CCP member Wang Bingnan was the liaison with the CCP. The group was dissolved in 1949 when the PRC was established. See Hou Wailu, "Nanfangju zai Zhongguo Minzhu Geming Tongmeng zhong de huodong" [The Activities of the Southern Bureau within the League of Democratic Revolution in China], Dangdai dangyuan [Contemporary party members], no. 2005, retrieved Dec. 22, 2006, from http://www.zydg.net/magazine/article/1007- 3566/2005/08/203851.html.

A power struggle within the local KMT led Li Xinzhi and Yu Renshan to leave New York's *Mun Hey* to form *China Tribune* in 1943. See Pei Chi Liu, *History of the Chinese in North America,* 391.

Chapter 5: The Birth of a New China

1. Yue Tao, "Mianhuai woguo waijiao zhanshi Chen Jiakang" [Cherish the Memory of Our Nation's Diplomat Warrior Chen Jiakang], retrieved Oct. 14, 2005, from http://www .people.com.cn/GB/shizeng/19/20030413/970450.html; Zheng Yijun, *Zhuanqi rensheng: Ji Cai Fujiu zouguo de daolu* [A Dramatic Life: The Path Traveled by Henry Tsoi] (Hong Kong: Haifeng chubanshe, 1997), 166 (cited hereafter as Zheng, Tsoi biography); Tet Yee, interview with author, Sept. 21, 1987.

Chen Jiakang (1913–70) joined the CCP in 1935. During the War of Resistance, he was part of the CCP's external affairs section. Chen served in the Foreign Ministry in the PRC but was persecuted and passed away during the Cultural Revolution.

2. Xu Ming, "He Xu Yongying jiaowang er san shi" [Two or Three Incidents in My Contacts with Y. Y. Hsu], retrieved July 11, 2007, from http://kui-shi.blog.hrxun.com/9172766 _d.html (cited hereafter as Xu Ming, Two or Three Incidents with Y. Y. Hsu).

3. Howard L. Boorman, eds., *Biographical Dictionary of Republican China*, vol. 3 (New York: Columbia University Press, 1967), s.v. "Tung Pi-wu"; Philip J. Jaffe, *The Rise and Fall of American Communism* (New York: Horizon Press, 1975), 56–57; Yao Xiaoping, "Xian wei ren zhi de hongse gemingjia: Ji mei-Gong Zhongguoju chuangshiren he *Mao Suan Yingyi* zhuchiren Xu Yongying" [A Red Revolutionary Seldom Known to Others: Y. Y. Hsu, Founder of the Chinese Bureau, CPUSA, and Director of English Translation of the *Selected Works of Mao Zedong*], *Renwu* no. 6 (2003): 5–24 (cited hereafter as Yao, "Y. Y. Hsu"); Xu Ming, Two or Three Incidents with Y. Y. Hsu.

4. Yao, "Y. Y. Hsu." In 1950 Xu was assigned to head the committee translating *Selected Works of Chairman Mao Zedong*. The first three volumes appeared in 1954, and the fourth in 1960.

5. Yao, "Y. Y. Hsu"; Chen Hansheng, *Sige shidai de wo* [Myself during Four Periods] (Beijing: Zhongguo Wenshi Chubanshe, 1988), 78, 80–81 (cited hereafter as Chen, Myself during Four Periods); Wu Youwen, Tian Ye, "Chen Hansheng shilue" [Short Biography of Chen Hansheng], in *Zhong-Gong dangshi ziliao* [Materials on Chinese Communist Party History], ed. Zhong Gong zhongyang dangshi yanjiushi [Office of the Central Committee of the Chinese Communist Party for Research on Party History] (Beijing: Zhong Gong dangshi ziliao chubanshe, 1990), 35:188–211; Xue Baoding, Xing Ruojun, "Chen Hansheng tongzhi zou de daolu" [The Road Traveled by Comrade Chen Hansheng], in *Shanghai Wenshi Ziliao Xuanji* [Selected Collection of Shanghai Cultural and Historical Materials] (Shanghai: Shanghai Renmin Chubanshe, 1983), 43:133–46. After his return, Hsu headed the committee translating the selected works of Mao Zedong in 1950.

6. *Biographical Dictionary of Republican China*, vol. 3, s.v. "Tung Pi-wu"; Janice R. and Stephen R. MacKinnon, *Agnes Smedley: The Life and Times of an American Radical* (Berkeley: University of California Press, 1988), 295–96; Jaffe, *American Communism*, 56–57; "Xianggang Dade Xueyuan Lishi" [History of the Ta Teh Institute of Hong Kong], retrieved Dec. 18, 2006, from http://www.guzhi.net/bbs/read.php?tid=519.

C. Y. Chen departed for Hong Kong in 1946. In July the CCP Committee of the Guang-dong Area and its allied political parties decided to establish Dade Xueyuan as a liberal arts college. The faculty consisted of progressive intellectuals taking refuge in Hong Kong. The institute was located in the home of Gen. Tsai Ting-kai and Chen became the president. It began operation on October 10, 1946, and continued until banned by the Hong Kong government on February 23, 1949.

7. Karen Garner, *Precious Fire: Maud Russell and the Chinese Revolution* (Amherst: University of Massachusetts Press, 2003), 188–89; Israel Epstein, *My China Eye: Memoirs of a Jew and a Journalist* (San Francisco: Long River Press, 2005), 230. At first, the CDFEP publication was named *Information Bulletin* (1945–46), and then changed to *Spotlight on the Far East* (1947–May 1948), before stabilizing as *Far East Spotlight* (June 1948–1952). The U.S. Attorney General placed the CDFEP on its list of subversive organizations. Beginning around 1950, Russell lectured around the country opposing American policy regarding China, but increased red-baiting ate into her support and the CDFEP faded away around 1952. Russell continued her focus on U.S.-China relations, conducting cross-country lecture tours and self-publishing *Far Eastern Reporter* (1953–89). Toward the end of her life, China embarked on economic reforms and Russell became highly critical of Deng Xiaoping's leadership of the revolution.

8. Willie Fong, interview with author, July 31, 1971; Tet Yee, Happy Lim, Willie Fong, and Hu Jun, joint interview with author, Sept. 25 and Oct. 2, 1977; Lin Jianfu (Happy Lim), "Huagong Hezuo Hui Huiyilu" [Reminiscences of the Chinese Workers Mutual-Aid Association], *Unity Monthly* no. 1 (Jan. 1981): 4–6. The CCP used the term "liberated areas" when referring to territory wrested from KMT control. This essay follows this usage without prejudice.

9. Wang Shigu, *Meiguo Huawen baokan jianzhi* [Brief List and Descriptions of Chinese Language Periodicals in the USA] (1854–1997) (Beijing: Zhongguo Renmin Daxue Xinwen Xueyuan *Haiwai Huawen Baokan Yanjiu* Ketizu [Committee on Topics on "The Study of Chinese Overseas Periodicals" of the College of Journalism, People's University of China], 1999), 30; Pei Chi Liu, *A History of the Chinese in the United States* (Taipei: Liming Wenhua Shiye Gufen Youxian Gongsi, 1981), 2:391. *China Tribune* was founded by J. S. Yu and others who had split off from the KMT organ *Mun Hey* in 1943. Lai Yali, using the name Lai Xingzhi, became acting chief editor in August 1945.

10. "Chinese American Democratic Youth League Constitution," Jan. 19, 1946; *Vanguard*, Mar. 1946.

11. According to the Chinese Students Christian Association, there were 1,733 students from China in the United States. From 1938 to 1941, only about three hundred students went abroad. After the war there were about a thousand who went to America. By 1949 the number of students in the United States, including those who had completed their studies but had not returned to China, numbered 3,916. See Pei Chi Liu, *History of the Chinese in the United States*, 423; Song Jian, "Bainian jieli liuxuechao" [A Century of Successive Tides of Studying Abroad], retrieved Dec. 9, 2006, from http://www.xingzhi.org/culture/history/26886.html.

12. For more details about Pu Shouchang (1922–?), see "Pu Shouchang," retrieved Feb. 9, 2006, from http://www.fmprc.gov.cn/chn/gxh/zlb/zgwjrw/lrfbzjbzzl/t9085.htm (cited hereafter as Pu Shouchang online biography). For more details about Pu Shoushan (1923–2003), see "Pu Shan Tongzhi shengping" [Life of Comrade Pu Shan], retrieved Feb. 9, 2006, from http://jwep.org.cn/chinese/memory/pushan/shengping.htm. For more information about Ding Chen (1919–?), see Song Jian, "Zhonghua liuxue minren cidian" [Dictionary of Chinese Studying Abroad Who Became Famous] (Changchun: Dongbei Shifan Daxue Chubanshe, 1992), s.v. "Ding Chen" (cited hereafter as Song Jian, Dictionary of Chinese Studying Abroad). For more details of Han Depei (1911–?), see Song Jian, Dictionary of Chinese Studying Abroad, s.v. "Ding Chen"; "Han Depei jianjie" [Brief Introduction to Han Depei], retrieved Feb. 5, 2005, from http://www.ntzx.net.cn/xsg/mf/HDP.htm; "Ding

Chen," retrieved Feb. 11, 2006, from http://www.shtong.gov.cn/node2/node2245/node4538/node57078/node57083/node57085/userobject1ai45585.html.

Han Depei went to Canada in 1940; he earned a master's degree in law at the University of Toronto in 1942 and then entered Harvard for advanced studies in international law. Ding Chen entered Harvard in 1941. Both Han and Ding returned to China in 1946. Han became law professor at Wuhan University. After the founding of the PRC, Ding served the Shanghai municipal government in posts regulating industries and commerce.

13. Timothy Tseng, "Religious Liberalism, International Politics, and Diasporic Realities: The Chinese Students Christian Association of North America, 1909–1951," *Journal of American–East Asian Relations* 5, no. 3–4 (1996): 305–30; overview of *Guide to the Archives of the Chinese Students' Christian Association in North America* (Record Group No. 13), Yale University Library, Divinity Library Special Collections, compiled by Martha Lund Smalley, retrieved from http://webtext.library.yale.edu/xml2html/divinity.013.con.html.

14. *Zhongguo renming dacidian, dangdai renwujuan* [Biographical Dictionary of China, Volume on Contemporary Individuals] (Shanghai: Shanghai cishu chubanshe, 1992), 1293, 1723 (cited hereafter as Biographical Dictionary of China); *Chinese Christian Student* 35, no. 1 (Nov. 1944); Pu Shouchang online biography; "Pu Shan tongzhi shengping" [Life of Comrade Pu Shan], retrieved Aug. 11, 2007, from http://www.iwep.org.cn/chinese/pushan/shengping.htm (cited hereafter as Life of Comrade Pu Shoushan).

15. *China Daily News,* Sept. 13, 15, 22, 1945.

16. Chen Yiming, Chen Xiuxia, et al., "Qingxi zuguo, xinxi renmin: Yi Beimei Jidujiao Zhongguo Xueshenghui de aiguo huodong" [Sentiments Tied to the Ancestral Land; The Heart Attached to the People: Patriotic Activities of the Chinese Students Christian Association in North America], in *Jianguo chuqi liuxuesheng guiguo jishi* [Chronicle of Events on the Return to China of Chinese Students Abroad during the Early Period of the Establishing of the Nation] (Beijing: Zhongguo Wenshi Chubanshe, 1999), 14–31 (cited hereafter respectively as Chen, Patriotic Activities of the CSCA, and Records of the Return of Students Abroad).

17. Chen, Patriotic Activities of the CSCA; *China Daily News,* July 26, 27, 28, 1946.

18. The political party China Democratic League was established in 1939 and took its present name in 1944. At its formation, it was an alliance of pro-democracy parties consisting mostly of middle-level and senior intellectuals in the fields of culture, education, science, and technology.

19. Qiao Guanhua joined the CCP in 1939 and became known as an international news analyst. After 1949 he joined the Ministry of Foreign Affairs. In 1971 Qiao headed the first PRC delegation to the UN. See *Xinzhongguo mingrenlu* [Sketches of Famous People of the New China], s.v. "Qiao Guanhua."

20. "Zhongguo Gongchandang de baiqu tongzhan gongzuo yu di-er tiao zhanxian" [The United Front Activities of the CCP in the White Areas and the Second Front], in *Zhongguo tongyi zhanxian dashi jishi-benmo* [Accounts of Important Events in United Front Activities in China], ed. Zhang Tienan, Song Chun, and Zhu Jianhua (Changchun: Jilin Daxue Chubanshe, 1990), 336–42.

21. Chen, Patriotic Activities of the CSCA; *China Daily News,* September 22, 1947. Paul T. K. Lin was the Vancouver-born son of a Chinese Protestant minister in British Columbia. He matriculated at the University of Michigan, then received an MA at Harvard University in 1945 (Prof. Edgar Wickberg, communication with the author, Aug. 5, 2002; Biographical Dictionary of China, 1293. James G. Endicott was born in Sichuan. After

returning to Canada to study, he returned to China in 1925 as a missionary in Sichuan and later served as political advisor for the KMT government's New Life Movement, but he became disillusioned by the corruption. During the War of Resistance, he met Zhou Enlai and was impressed with the Communist programs. In 1944 and 1945, he became a liaison between the U.S. military and Chinese Communist forces. After the war, he published the underground anti-KMT *Shanghai Newsletter* before returning to Canada in 1947, where he gave many pro-Communist speeches. He chaired the Soviet-dominated Canadian Peace Congress and published *Canadian Far Eastern Newsletter.* During the Sino-Soviet split, he sided with the CCP and was forced to resign from the Peace Congress but continued to publish the *Newsletter.* He then founded the Canada-China Society (see "James Gareth Endicott," *Biography,* retrieved Oct. 31, 2005, from http://www.james-gareth-endicott .biography.ms).

22. Chen, Patriotic Activities of the CSCA; Ma Daren, "Cong liuxue dao xueliu" [From Studying Abroad to Staying in America], in *Chinese Experiences Studying in America: Eighty Years of Cross Cultural Learning,* ed. Li Youning (New York: Outer Sky Press, 1999), 2:93–115; Li Hengde, "Buqu de douzheng; zhihaode shengli" [Unyielding Struggle; Proud Victory], in Records of the Return of Students Abroad, 32–92 (cited hereafter as Li, Unyielding Struggle; Proud Victory); Xu Long, "Ben xiang guangming de shike: Ji jianguo qianhou de liuxuesheng huiguo chao" [The Moment of Racing toward the Light: A Record of the Wave of Students Abroad Returning to China around the Time the Nation Was Established] in *Zhongguo liuxuesheng shicui* [Collection of Historical Essays on Chinese Students Studying Abroad] (Beijing: Zhongguo Youyi Chuban Gongsi, 1992), 98–117 (cited hereafter as Xu, "Students Returning to China"). The Yangge ("rice seedling song"; also spelled *yangko*) is a simple rural folk dance from Shaanxi that became very popular in PLA-controlled areas during the early years after liberation. Chen Yiming and Chen Xiuxia were the children of educator Chen Heqin, and both enrolled at West Michigan State University in 1946, where they received their BAs. They obtained their MAs from Columbia University Teachers' College in 1950. Chen Xiuxia returned to China in 1950 and entered the News Department of the Foreign Ministry. Chen Yiming returned to China in 1951 and served in the Shanghai Bureau of Religious Affairs.

23. Chen, Patriotic Activities of the CSCA.

24. *Biographical Dictionary of Republican China,* vol. 2, s.v. "Feng Yü-hsiang"; Feng Hongda and Yu Huaxin, *Feng Yuxiang jiangjun huan gui Zhonghua* [The Soul of General Feng Yuxiang Returned to China] (Beijing: Wenshi Ziliao Chubanshe, 1981), 48, 78–80 (cited hereafter as Feng and Yu, General Feng Yuxiang); James E. Sheridan, *Chinese Warlord: The Career of Feng Yu-hsiang* (Stanford: Stanford University Press, 1966), 277–78.

25. Feng and Yu, General Feng Yuxiang, 92–94, 301–5; *Chinese World,* May 27, 1947.

26. Zheng, Tsoi biography, 161–65; "Lü-Mei Zhongguo Heping Minzhu Lianmeng de jianshi" [Brief History of the Overseas Chinese Federation for Peace and Democracy], *Lümei Zhongguo Heping Minzhu Lianmeng Sanfanshi Zhimeng huiyuan shouce* [Handbook for Members of the San Francisco Branch of the Overseas Chinese Federation for Peace and Democracy] (San Francisco, 1949), 3. This brief history cited the founding date of the San Francisco branch of Overseas Chinese Federation for Peace and Democracy in China (OCFPD) as February 2, 1947. This predates November 9, 1947, the official founding date of the OCFPD in New York, but this may have been a typographical error, because December ("number ten-two moon" in Chinese) may have been mistakenly rendered as February ("number two moon" in Chinese).

27. Feng and Yu, General Feng Yuxiang, 112–23, 306–10; *China Daily News,* Oct. 11, 1947. For more information about Wu Maosun, see "Wu Maosun (1911–1984)," retrieved Aug. 10, 2005, from http://www.xuancheng.gov.cn/ReadNews.asp?NewsID=192. For more information about Lai Yali, see biography, retrieved Aug. 10, 2005, from http://www.pku .org.cn/data/data.jsp?id=pkuwaijiao; and Chen Dunde, "Xin Zhongguo waijiao neimu (5)" [The Inside Story of New China's diplomacy (5)], retrieved Aug. 10, 2005, from http:// www.xawb.com/gb/rbpaper/2000–09/24/content_348579.htm. For more information about Wang Feng, see Biographical Dictionary of China, s.v. "Wang Feng."

28. Feng and Yu, General Feng Yuxiang, 123–29; Wu Maosun, "Feng Xiansheng zui guanghui de yiye" [The Brightest Page in the Life of Mr. Feng], in *Feng Yuxiang jiangjun ji'niance* [Album in Memory of General Feng Yuxiang] (Hong Kong: Fuxing chubanshe, 1948), 112–21 (cited hereafter as Wu, Brightest Page in the Life of Mr. Feng). The organization's letterhead uses Overseas Chinese *Federation* for Peace and Democracy but was translated from Chinese as Overseas Chinese *League* for Peace and Democracy in China and is so described in Him Mark Lai, "To Bring Forth a New China, to Build a Better America: The Chinese Marxist Left in America to the 1960s," in *Chinese America: History and Perspectives* 6 (1992): 3–82.

29. Feng and Yu, General Feng Yuxiang, 167–69, 311–17; *Nation,* Nov. 5, 1947.

30. Feng and Yu, General Feng Yuxiang, 157–62, 173–77, 183–87. Li Jichen was governor of Guangdong Province during the Northern Expedition. In 1927 he was elected to the KMT executive central committee, and in 1933 he joined Cai Ting-kai in an anti-Chiang rebellion in Fujian Province. After its collapse, he worked with the anti-Chiang Guangxi military government, which eventually negotiated a truce with the KMT in 1936. During the Sino-Japanese War, Li directed the military field headquarters at Guilin, Guangxi. After World War II, he opposed the civil war and left for Hong Kong in 1947, where he formed the Revolutionary Committee of the KMT in 1948.

31. Feng and Yu, General Feng Yuxiang, 132, 136–57, 166, 198.

32. *United States Relations with China, with Special Reference to the Period 1944–1949, Based on the Files of the Department of State* (Washington, D.C.: Department of State, 1949), 388–89.

33. Feng and Yu, General Feng Yuxiang, 246; Sheridan, *Chinese Warlord,* 281; Wu Maosun, Brightest Page in the Life of Mr. Feng; *Biographical Dictionary of Republican China,* s.v. "Feng Yu-hsiang." While the *S.S. Pobeda* was in the Black Sea, a ship fire killed Feng and one of his daughters. His widow, Li Dequan, later became the PRC's Minister of Public Health.

In 1949 Lai Yali was on the central committee of the Revolutionary Committee of the KMT. He entered the PRC diplomatic service and was part of the 1950 PRC delegation to Moscow led by Mao Zedong and Zhou Enlai that negotiated a treaty with the USSR. See *Xiandai Zhongguo renming cidian* [Dictionary of Modern Personages of China] (Tokyo: Kazankai Foundation, 1966), s.v. "Lai Yali."

34. Mao Zedong, "Muqian xingshi he women de renwu" [The Current Situation and Our Task], issued Sept. 1, 1947, by the CCP Central Committee, retrieved Nov. 8, 2008, from http://www.mzdlib.com/mzdwk/zyzz/display.asp?Reco_ID=114.

35. Chen, Patriotic Activities of the CSCA. The September issue of *Economic Justice* published news of the protest. During the anti–civil war protests in the United States, twelve students in New Haven, Connecticut, caught the public's attention in summer 1948 by participating in a Students-in-Industry Project sponsored by CSCA and the Christian

Society of America. After assignment to the Winchester Repeating Arms Company, they discovered that the factory manufactured arms destined for KMT military aircraft and resigned en masse in protest.

36. Guo Moruo, *Nanjing yinxiang* [Impressions of Nanjing] (Shanghai: Qunyi Chubanshe, 1946), 52–60.

37. Zheng, Tsoi biography, 174–75, 178, 182; *China Press,* Oct. 16, 2004; Jin Yinchang and Tang Jixue, "Zuguo jianshe xuyao wo" [The Building of the Ancestral Land Needed Us], in Records of the Return of Students Abroad, 124–35; *Zhonghua dangdai wenhua mingren dacidian* [Dictionary of Famous Contemporary Personages in the Cultural Sector] (Beijing: Zhongguo Guangbo Dianshi Chubanshe, 1992), s.v. "Li Chunhui." Wang Jue and Jin Yinchang were both students at Yenching University. Li Chunhui studied as a graduate student in history at the University of Colorado. Jin Yinchang received his PhD in pharmacology in 1949 from the University of California, San Francisco. After Jin Yinchang returned to China, his CCP membership was not recognized by the Communist Party until 1996 ("Jin Yinchang," retrieved Sept. 20, 2008, from http://baike.baidu .com/view/307928.htm). Xia Xu was a metallurgy major at the University of California, Berkeley.

38. Handwritten testimonial to Wang Fushi by Liu Simu, Jan. 10, 1983; handwritten testimonial on *Zhongguo Ribao* stationery to Wang Fushi by Liu Zunqi, Jan. 13, 1983; Ye Yonglie "Xunfang Sinuo zhi you: Jiujinshan fang Wang Fushi" [Seeking and Finding Edgar Snow's Friend: Interviewing Wang Fushi in the San Francisco Bay Area], in *Pujiang Tongzhou* [On the Same Boat in the Pu River], no. 4 (2002). Wang Fushi (1911–?) was a native of Liaoning and son of Wang Zhuoran, president of Northeast University and advisor to the "Young Marshal" Zhang Xueliang. When the Japanese seized Northeast China, Wang Fushi was attending Dongbei University and had to move to Yanjing University in Beijing. He then attended Qinghua University from 1932 until 1935. In Beijing he met Chu Tong (Tang Mingzhao), then a student from America, and Huang Rumei (Huang Hua). Wang Fushi translated and published Edgar Snow's draft of *Red Star Over China* as *Waiguo jizhe Xibei yinxiangji* [A Foreign Journalist's Impressions of the Northwest]. During the war, Wang was variously in Malaysia, Hong Kong, and India. After the war, he and his family traveled to America. After seeing Chu Tong in New York, they settled in San Francisco but in 1950 returned to the PRC, where Wang Fushi was assigned to Guoji Shudian [International Bookstore]. He was branded a rightist in 1957, a label that stuck until 1979. Of Wang's eight children, one son died on Hainan Island during the Cultural Revolution, and the rest left China during the 1980s. He and his wife immigrated to America in the early 1990s but returned to Beijing in 2004.

39. Xu Long, "Huashuo *Liu-Mei Xuesheng Tongxun*" [Some Words Regarding *Liu-Mei Xuesheng Tongxun*], in *Zhongguo liuxue shicui* [Collection of Historical Essays on Chinese Students Studying Abroad], ed. Liuxuesheng Congshu Bianweihui [*Students Studying Abroad* Series Editorial Committee] (Beijing: Zhongguo Youyi Chuban Gongsi, 1992), 259–65 (cited hereafter respectively as Xu, Some Words Regarding *Liu-Mei Xuesheng Tongxun,* and Collection of Historical Essays on Chinese Students Studying Abroad).

40. Zheng, Tsoi biography, 177–78. Henry Tsoi recruited Wang Jue into the CCP in San Francisco around 1949.

41. Zheng, Tsoi biography, 166–68.

42. *San Francisco Chronicle,* Oct. 10, 1949. I have included a list of supporters with the locations and their principal organizational affiliations in brackets: Kew Yuen Ja [San

Francisco, OCLPDC, *Qiaozhong Ribao*]; Francis Leong [San Francisco, OCLPDC, *Qiao-zhong Ribao*]; Herbert Lee [San Francisco, OCLPDC, *Qiaozhong Ribao*]; Henry Tsoi [San Francisco, OCLPDC, *China Weekly*]; Chen Tiemin [San Francisco, OCLPDC, *Qiaozhong Ribao*]; Wang Jue [student, OCLPDC, *Qiaozhong Ribao*]; Lawrence Lee [San Francisco, OCLPDC, *Qiaozhong Ribao*]; Jen Shan Yu [New York, *China Tribune*]; Chu Tong [New York, *China Daily News*]; Olden Lee [San Francisco, CWMAA]; Wang Fushi [student, OCLPDC, *Qiaozhong Ribao*]; Happy Lim [San Francisco, CWMAA]; Li Chunhui [student, OCLPDC, *Qiaozhong Ribao*]; Paul Mar [San Francisco, OCLPDC, CADYL, *China Weekly*]; James Young [San Francisco, CADYL].

43. Zheng, Tsoi biography, 177–79.

44. *Chung Sai Yat Po,* Nov. 22, 29, 1949.

45. Zheng, Tsoi biography, 178. Henry Tsoi had recruited Li Chunhui into the CCP in San Francisco in 1949. Ma Jiliang (1914–88), also known as Tang Na, was a film actor briefly married to Jiang Qing, later Mao Zedong's wife. For more details, see Xu Zhucheng, "Tang Na juekou bu tan Jiang Qing shi" [Tang Na Kept His Mouth Shut about His Affair with Jiang Qing], *China Daily News,* Sept. 20, 1988.

46. For more information about Situ Huimin, see *Situ Huimin tongzhi shengping* [Obituary of Comrade Situ Huimin] (Beijing, 1987).

47. *Chung Sai Yat Po,* Dec. 14, 1949. Originally, the site at 649 Broadway was a burlesque theater called the Liberty. A few years later, World Theater moved into the Verdi, a movie theater across the street at 644 Broadway, when its old site was sold for construction of the Royal Pacific Motel.

48. Xu, Students Returning to China, 98–117; Zheng, Tsoi biography, 181.

49. Wang Gengjin, Zhang Xuansan, Xu Ming, "Taonian Xue Baoding Tongzhi" [Grieving Over Comrade Xue Baoding], retrieved Nov. 26, 2006, from http://web.peopledaily.com.cn/199809/16/wzb_980916001105_12.html; "Woguo shehui jingji xitong gongcheng de xueke daitouren zhi yi, Xue Baoding" [Xue Baoding, One of the Pioneers in Our Nation in Socioeconomic-System Engineering], retrieved Nov. 12, 2006, from http://www.chinavalue.net/wiki/showcontent.aspx?titleid=28805; Xue Baoding, "Han Lao guashiji de yisheng" [The Life of Han the Elder across Two Centuries], in *Chen Hansheng baosui huadan ji* [Collection Commemorating the 100th birthday of Chen Hansheng] (Beijing: Zhongguo Shehui Kexue Chubanshe, 1998), 253–59.

Xue Baoding became an underground CCP member in 1938. In 1946 the Chinese government sponsored him to go to the United States to acquire industrial work experience. The concept of Jian She was based on the organization of the same name in areas under Nationalist control. In 1939 the CCP Southern Bureau formed the Qingnian Kexue Jishu Renyuan Xiehui [Association of Young Personnel in Science and Technology] in Chongqing; however, when anti-leftist repression increased after the New Fourth Army Incident, the group went underground. After the war ended, the association resumed open activities, but to broaden its appeal and to allay the suspicion of the KMT, it was reorganized as Zhongguo Jian She [Construction Society of China]. Branches emerged in cities in North and East China when the Nationalist government moved back to Nanjing. See "Chongqing da houfang kang-Ri minzhu wenhua de kongqian fanrong" [The Unprecedented Flourishing of Anti-Japanese Democratic Culture in Chongqing's Vast Rear Area], from *Chongqing Kangzhanshi* [History of the War of Resistance in Chongqing], retrieved Nov. 12, 2006, from http://www.cq.xinhuanet.com/subject/2005/2005–07/29/content_4757309.htm (cited hereafter as Unprecedented Flourishing of Resistance). Xue returned to China to help shape policies for governing the large urban industrial centers south of the Chang River. Despite being accused of being a rightwing opportunist and persecuted during the Cultural Revolution, Xue remained a major influence in planning China's industrial economy.

50. Ding Jing and Fu Junzhao, "Huiyi 'Liumei Kexie'" [Reminiscences of the Association of Chinese Scientific Workers in America], in Records of the Return of Students Abroad, 3–13 (cited hereafter as Ding and Fu, Reminiscences of Scientific Workers); Song Jian, Dictionary of Chinese Studying Abroad, s.v. "Ge Tingsui." Ge arrived in the United States in 1941 and received a PhD in physics from Berkeley in 1943. He worked first as a research fellow at the MIT Spectroscopy and Radiation Laboratory and then at the University of Chicago Institute for the Study of Metals until 1949. After returning to China, he taught at various universities and became a member of China's Academy of Science. Another academy member was Hou Xianglin, a CCP party member since 1938 who had arrived in the United States in 1945 and received a PhD in chemical engineering from the Carnegie Institute of Technology in 1948. Hou returned to China in 1950. Ding Jing and Tu Guangchi were also scientists.

The ACSWA was patterned after Zhongguo Kexue Gongzuozhe Xiehui [Association of Scientific Workers in China, ASWC] that was founded in Chongqing in 1945 with the encouragement of the CCP. Ge Tingsui recalled that when attending a conference in the United Kingdom with the ASWC secretary in 1946, the latter urged him to organize a U.S. branch. However, since U.S. laws restricted the establishing of branches of foreign organizations, the matter was not pursued at the time. It was revived when ASWC board member Ding Zan was at the University of Chicago and worked with Ge and other activist students and scholars to finally establish ASWUS (see Unprecedented Flourishing of Resistance; Ge tingsui, "Kexue wu guojie; kexuejia you zuguo" [The Sciences Have No National Boundaries, but Scientists Have Ancestral Lands], retrieved Dec. 11, 2006, from http://chinsci.blogchina.com/viewdiary.13829751.html).

51. Feng Ji, "Yingjie xin Zhongguo de shuguang—ji jianguo qianxi de 'Liumei Kexie'" [Welcoming the Dawning of the New China—An Account of the Association of Chinese Scientific Workers in America], in Collection of Historical Essays on Chinese Students Studying Abroad, 246–58; Ding and Fu, Reminiscences of Scientific Workers; *Liu Mei Xuesheng Tongxun,* Mar. 4, 1950; Zheng, Tsoi biography, 180–83; "Wo yu shiyou youyuan—Hou Xinglin zishu" [I Have a Predestined Relationship with Petroleum—Account by Hou Xianglin in His Own Words], retrieved Feb. 8, 2006, from http://www.agpr.net/bbs/read .php?tid=51539&fpage=&toread=&page=2 (cited hereafter as Account by Hou Xianglin).

52. Zheng, Tsoi biography, 178, 180; Account by Hou Xianglin.

53. Zheng, Tsoi biography, 174–75, 180–82. Henry Tsoi recruited Jin Yinchang and Xia Xu into the CCP in 1949. In August 1949, Jin, Xu, Li Chunhui, and Wang Jue formed a CCP local branch led by Henry Tsoi.

54. "Xiao Xiansheng shengping" [The Life of Mr. Xiao], retrieved Aug. 30, 2005, from http://210.31.200.45/keyanjl/522hyjy/2.htm; Liu Liangmo, "Wo suo renshi de Meiguo" [The America That I Knew], *China Daily News,* July 6, 1950; Haiming Liu, *Transnational History of a Chinese Family: Immigrant Letters, Family Business, and Reverse Migration* (New Brunswick, N.J.: Rutgers University Press, 2005), 208; Arthur W. Chung, *Of Rats, Sparrows, and Flies: A Lifetime in China* (Stockton, Calif.: Heritage West Books, 1995), 142–43; Liang Sili, "Taiyang zui hong; zuguo zui qin" [The Sun Is the Reddest; the Ancestral Land Is the Dearest], in Records of the Return of Students Abroad, 101–7;

Yan Renying, "Jiaban shang de 'guoqing'" ["National Day" on Deck], *Guangming Daily,* Oct. 25, 1999, retrieved Jan. 9, 2006, from http://www.gmw.cn/01gmrb/1999–10/25/GB/ gm%5E18220%5E12%5EGM12–212.htm; Zhang Guixing, "Laoshe shengping dashi nian- biao" [Chronology of Important Events in the Life of Laoshe], in *Laoshe pingshuo qishinian* [Seventy years of Laoshe] (Beijing: Zhongguo Huaqiao Chubanshe, 2005), 415–37. The Chinese government sent Xiao Shuzi to the United States in 1947 to enroll in Columbia University, where he became active in the OCFPD. Xiao later became famous for pioneer- ing the use of television for instruction. Arthur Chung was associated with the Pacific Union Medical Center for many years, and from 1973 to 1976 he represented the PRC at the World Health Organization in Geneva, Switzerland. Liang Siyi became deputy director of the International Relations Department of the Chinese Red Cross. Liang Sili became an expert in rocketry and guide missiles. Yan Renying received her MD degree from Beijing's Pacific Union Medical Center in 1940, specializing in gynecology and obstetrics. In 1948 she entered Columbia University for advanced studies. After returning to China, she worked at Beijing Medical University and became a leading expert in family planning. After his return to China, Liu joined the National Political Consultative Conference in the PRC and the Three-Self Patriotic Committee of the Protestant Church of China. Lao She was known best in the United States for his novel *Rickshaw Boy.* The U.S. Department of State invited him to visit in 1946. He returned to the PRC in 1949 but struggled to fit his writings into the new order and committed suicide during the Cultural Revolution.

55. "Hua Luogeng huiguo qianhou" [Before and After L. K. Hua Returned to China], *Wenzhai Bao,* June 3, 2007, retrieved Oct. 20, 2008, from the cache of http://www.gmw .cn/01wzb/2007–06/03/content_616751.htm, as it appeared on Aug. 25, 2008; Yi feng gongkaixin yu Zhu Guangya guiguo [An Open Letter and Zhu Guangya's Return to China], Feb. 12, 2006, retrieved Sept. 19, 2008, from http://news.sohu.com/20060212/ n241783744.shtml. L. K. Hua was a famous self-taught mathematician. He arrived in the United States in 1946; he was a researcher at Princeton University and then taught at the University of Illinois. In China Zhu Guangya become a key person in the development of the PRC's nuclear weapons program.

56. "Gong Pusheng yisheng yu Lianheguo jieyuan," [Gong Pusheng Established a Re- lationship with the United Nations during Her Life], *Shijie Xinwen Bao,* Mar. 9, 2005, retrieved Sept. 28, 2005, from http://news.sina.com.cn/c/2005–03–09/11566032552.shtml; "Gong Pusheng: Jieyuan Lianheguo 60 nian" [Gong Pusheng: Ties with the United Na- tions for 60 Years], retrieved Nov. 11, 2006, from Baidu cache of http://news.sina.com .cn/c/2005–10–24/02367247629s.shtml; Biographical Dictionary of China, 1806; Life of Comrade Pu Shoushan; Pu Shouchang online biography; Yao, "Y. Y. Hsu"; "Lin Daguang," Biographical Dictionary of China, 1293,

Pu Shoushan, Pu Shouchang, and Ji Chaozhu were interpreters in the negotiations for the Korean War armistice. Both Pu Shouchang and Ji Chaozhu later interpreted for Zhou Enlai. Pu Shoushan was accused of being a rightist in 1957 and was expelled from the CCP. This decision was reversed in 1979, and from 1982 to 1988 he directed the World Economy and Politics Research Institute of the Academy of Social Sciences. Paul Lin (1920–2004) served in a news bureau and in the broadcasting sector in the PRC before returning to Canada in 1964 to teach at the University of British Columbia. In 1965 he moved to McGill University in Montreal, where he headed the Asian Studies program. See Prof. Edgar Wickberg, email to author, Aug. 5, 2002.

57. Wang Xiangtong, *Wo de zhangfu Ji Chaozhu: Sishisi nian de waijiao shengya* [My

Husband Ji Chaozhu: Forty-Four-Year Career in Foreign Affairs] (Shanxi: Shanxi jiaoyu chubanshe, 1997), 14–24, 28–33, 90–91, 103, 183 (cited hereafter as Wang Xiangtong, My Husband Ji Chaozhu).

Ji grew up in New York's Lower East Side. He entered Harvard University in 1948 and joined CPUSA in 1949. After serving from 1952 to 1954 in Korea, Ji continued to interpret for the Foreign Ministry at the Geneva and Bandung Conferences. He became Zhou Enlai's interpreter in 1956. Zhu Guangya (1924–) graduated from Xi'nan Lianda in 1945 and came to the United States, where he received his doctorate in physics from the University of Michigan in 1950. Since the mid-1950s, he has been a leading figure in research on nuclear weaponry and nuclear energy.

58. Wang Xiangtong, My Husband Ji Chaozhu, 31.

59. Zhao Xixiong, "Zuji Zhongshan de zhuming aiguo Huaqiao Chun Zhikun xian-sheng: Zai Yan'an yaodong yu Mao Zedong cu xi tanxin" [The Famous Patriotic Overseas Chinese of Zhongshan Ancestry, Mr. Chun Zhukun: He Had an Intimate Conversation with Mao Zedong in a Yan'an cave], *Zhongshan Ribao,* May 24, 2006, retrieved Aug. 11, 2007, from http://www.zsnews.cn/Column/2006/05/24/645276.shtml.

60. Thomas Lem Tong served as a member of the Overseas Chinese Affairs Commission under the Ministry of State. Later he was with the CCP Central Liaison Department. See Xu Suizhi, "Chronology of the Life Y. Y. Hsu," part 2, Apr. 28, 2007, n.22, retrieved Aug. 20, 2007, from http://kui-shi.blog.hexun.com/9113246_d.html; Luo Ling, "Tang Mingzhao," in *Jiangmen Wuyi haiwai mingren zhuan* [Biographies of Famous Individuals of Jiang-men and Wuyi], ed. Tan Sizhe (Gulao, Heshan: Guangdong Renmin Chubanshe, 1996), 5:8–15; Sam Chang, interview by Mr. And Mrs. David Wong, Laura Lai, and Him Mark Lai, Apr. 4, 1975. Tang served the PRC often in international delegations. Tang Wensheng (1943–) became well-known to Americans in 1971 when she interpreted for Zhou Enlai and Mao Zedong. Eugene Moy (1904–58) was an immigrant from Taishan, Guangdong, who arrived in America in 1921. During the late 1920s, he was editor at the New York KMT organ *Mun Hey.* He also had worked in laundries and restaurants. He became an editor at *China Daily News* when it began publishing. See Xu Suizhi, "Chronology of the Life of Y. Y. Hsu," n.28.

61. Zheng, Tsoi biography, 191. At the end of 1952, Henry Tsoi was sent to Hong Kong, where he used the name Cai Fujiu. In 1954 he became deputy manager of Hong Kong China Travel Service after the PRC government assumed control. He retired from China Travel Service in 1985. In 1994 he was invited by the San Francisco Bay Area Committee to Celebrate the 45th Anniversary of the Founding of the PRC. See Zheng, Tsoi biography, 200–205, 243, 251.

62. Lai, "To Bring Forth a New China," 47–52.

63. Lai, "To Bring Forth a New China," 51–52.

64. Biographical Dictionary of China, 352, 1127. Chen Han-seng (1897–2004) became a member of the Academy of Social Sciences, despite being imprisoned during the Cultural Revolution. Situ Huimin (1910–87) served in various posts in the state-run film industry. In 1964 he helped film the epic *East Is Red* to commemorate the fifteenth anniversary of the founding of the PRC. He was also persecuted during the Cultural Revolution. See Life of Comrade Pu Shoushan; Song Jian, Dictionary of Chinese Studying Abroad, 131, 612, 743; Biographical Dictionary of China, 1293, 1723; Prof. Edgar Wickberg, email to author, Aug. 5, 2002; Xu, Some Words Regarding *Liu-Mei Xuesheng Tongxun.*

65. Li, Unyielding Struggle; Proud Victory.

66. Zhao Weizhi, "Fuqin Zhao Zhongyao de quzhe huiguo lu" [My Father's Tortuous Road in Returning to China], in *Xiaoyou wengao ziliao, di-qi ji* [Collected Materials Written by Alumni], 7th collection (Beijing: Qinghua Daxue Chubanshe, Apr. 2000), 105–9 (cited hereafter as Zhao, My Father's Tortuous Road); Ding and Fu, Reminiscences of Scientific Workers; Chen, Patriotic activities of the CSCA.

67. Tseng, "Religious Liberalism."

68. When the ship reached Japan, U.S. Air Force personnel detained Shih-Chun Lo, San-Chuin Shen, and C. Y. Chao, and ransacked their baggage (Song Jian, Dictionary of Chinese Studying Abroad, 345, 460, 504–5).

69. Zhao, My Father's Tortuous Road, 106–9.

70. Account by Hou Xianglin.

71. Huang Baotong, "Kanke huiguo lu," in Records of the Return of Students Abroad; Li, Unyielding Struggle; Proud Victory.

72. Li, Unyielding Struggle; Proud Victory; Huang Debao, "Zhongshen nanwang dang dui haiwai youzi de guanhuai" [The Concern of the Party for Persons Wandering Abroad Cannot Be Forgotten for Life], Records of the Return of Students Abroad, 225–29.

73. Mei Zuyan, "You-Mei huiguo jingli jishi" [A Veritable Record of My Experience Returning from America to China]," Records of the Return of Students Abroad, 192–200.

74. Liu Zhujin, "Cong haiwai zhengqu huiguo de jingguo" [My Fight to Return to the Ancestral Land from Abroad], in Records of the Return of Students Abroad, 268–71.

75. Li, Unyielding Struggle; Proud Victory. Li received his MS from the Carnegie Institute of Technology in 1947 and attended the University of Pennsylvania, where he received a PhD in materials science in 1953.

76. |FCO|StrongDocument No. 130, U. Alexis Johnson to State Dept., Geneva, Jan. 13, 1956, in Lu Ning, Meiguo duiwai guanxi wenjian ji (1955–1957) [Collection of Documents on U.S. Foreign Relations (1955–1957)], |FCC|retrieved Dec.6, 2006, from http://ias.cass .cn/show/show_project_ls.asp?id=187; "Zhong-Mei dashiji huitan—zai honggou shang jiaqi yizuo qiaoliang" [The Ambassadorial-Level Meetings between the United States and China—Bridging a Chasm], retrieved Dec. 6, 2006, from http://pde.yxms.net/yule/ zs/1045.html.

77. Iris Chang, *Thread of the Silkworm* (New York: Basic Books, 1995), 189–90; Li, Unyielding Struggle; Proud Victory.

78. Out of 714 ACSWA members that returned to China, 182 were listed in *Zhongguo renming dacidian* [Dictionary of Personages in China]. See Duan Yibing, "Liu-Mei Kexie huiguo huiyuan mingkao" [Tracing the Names of ACSWA Members Who Returned to China], *Zhongguo keji shiliao* [Historical Materials on Science and Technology in China] 21, no. 1 (2000): 13–25. Chen, Patriotic Activities of the CSCA, asserted that "about twenty groups of students," with each group ranging in size from "several tens" (a Chinese term meaning 30 or more) to "a hundred and several tens" (a Chinese term meaning 130 or more) departed for China between September 1949 and June 1951. This suggests that the number should be at least six hundred (if there were twenty groups each averaging thirty persons per group). Ding and Fu, Reminiscences of Chinese Scientific Workers, mentioned that in fall of 1950, 130 ACSWA members left, followed later by about 80 others. Li Hengde recalled that more than 100 returned after the lifting of the restraining order in 1955. This roughly matched the 120 cited during Sino-U.S. negotiations in Geneva. There were probably some others unconnected with either ACSWA or CSCA who returned on their own. Based on the range of estimates from the Chens and Li, the total should be at least seven hundred and probably approaches a thousand.

79. U.S. Congress, Senate Committee on the Judiciary, *Institute of Pacific Relations: Hearings* (Washington, D.C.: U.S. Government Printing Office, 1952), 3511, 3595–97.

80. "Agnes Smedley," retrieved Aug. 31, 2005, from http://www.spartacus.schoolnet .co.uk/USAsmedleyA.htm; "Edgar Parks Snow (1905–1972)," in University of Missouri–Kansas City Archives, retrieved Sept. 9, 2005, from http://www.umkc.edu/University _Archives/INVTRY/EPS.HTM; Britannica Online, "Strong, Anna Louise (1885–1970), Journalist and Author," by *Encyclopedia Britannica*, 1999, retrieved Aug. 18, 2009, from http://www.britannica.com/EBchecked/topic/569420/Anna-Louise-Strong.

81. Li Jun, Wang Xin, *Kang-Ri Zhanzheng zhong de guoji youren* [International Friends during the War of Resistance to Japan] (Beijing: Zhongyang Wenxian Chubanshe, 2005), 312–13; Epstein, *My China Eye*, 235–46; Israel Epstein, *Woman in World History: Soong Ching Ling* (Beijing: New World Press, 1993), 666 n. 54; Chen, Myself during Four Periods, 103. Chen Hansheng led the launching of the magazine and recruited Li Boti, whom he knew in the United States as an editor and reporter. Li Boti graduated from Mount Holyoke College and had worked for *Time* magazine and the Xinhua News Agency.

82. Chen Yiwen, "Chen Yifan: Yige xinshu Zhongguo de guojiren" [Jack Chen: An International Personage Whose Heart Belongs to China], retrieved July 7, 2007, from http://news.sina.com.cn/c/2007–01–24/154412127690.shtml.

Jack Chen was sent down during the Cultural Revolution. Through the intervention of Zhou Enlai, Chen and his family were allowed to leave China for New York in 1971, just as U.S.-PRC relations were thawing. He became a consultant promoting better understanding between the two peoples. In the late 1970s, Chen moved to the San Francisco Bay area, where he researched and designed a large-scale exhibition and wrote a history, *Chinese of America, 1785–1980* (1980). His last project was *Pear Garden in the West: Chinese Theater in America*. After Chen passed away in 1995, some of his ashes were deposited in the San Francisco Bay area and some in Babao Shan in China.

83. Wang Guangze, "Jixi Longchuan liu-Mei boshi Hu Dunyuan" [Thomas D. Y. Hu from Jixi Longchuan, Who Received His Doctorate after Studying in America], Apr. 16, 2006, retrieved Aug. 19, 2007, from http://www.jixinet.com/jxwenyi/ArticleID=107. Hu was related to Hu Shi.

84. "Su Kaiming 1904–1988," retrieved Sept. 4, 2007, from http://shtong.gov.cn/node2/node2245/node69322/node69341/ node69492/node69496/userobject1ai67656.html; Language Centre Bookshop, sale announcement including Su Kaiming (Frank K. M. Su), *1840—1983 Modern China: A Topical History,* retrieved Aug. 12, 2007, from http://www .languagecentre.iinet.com.au/catalogues/asiasale.pdf.

Su translated propaganda directed toward the West but in 1963 became an editor at *China Reconstructs.* Su was imprisoned for five years during the Cultural Revolution and not released until after the fall of the Gang of Four.

85. Yu Ling, "Champion of Chinese Culture," *China Daily,* Apr. 27, 1996; "Guide to Jay and Si-lan Chen Papers, 1913–1987," *The Tamiment Library and Robert F. Wagner Labor Archives,* retrieved Dec. 31, 2005, from http://dlib.nyu.edu:8083/tamwagead/servlet/SaxonServlet?source=leyda.xml&style=saxon01t2002.xsl; Si-lan Chen Leyda, *Footnote to History* (New York: Dance Horizons, 1954), 299–310. Si-lan Chen became an advisor in Beijing from 1959 to 1964, while her husband consulted for the China Film Archives.

86. Virginia Heyer, "Patterns of Social Organization in New York's Chinatown" (PhD diss., Columbia University, 1953), 94. Jack Chen (1908–95) immigrated with his wife to the United States in 1971. From 1973 to 1978, he was a senior research associate in the

China-Japan program and Peace Studies at Cornell University. As a writer-in-residence, he published two books based on his Cultural Revolution experiences—*A Year in Upper Felicity* (1973) and *Inside the Cultural Revolution* (1976).

87. Chen Ke, "San Ci Fu Mei he Qiao Mei 25 Nian de Qinli" [Personal Experiences Going to the United States Three Times and Sojourning There Twenty-five Years], in *Guangdong wenshi ziliao* [Guangdong Cultural and Historical Materials], ed. Zhongguo Renmin Zhengzhi Xieshang Huiyi Guangdong Sheng weiyuanhui, wenshi ziliao yanjiu weiyuanhui [Historical Materials Research Committee of the Guangdong Provincial Committee, Chinese People's Political Consultative Conference] (Guangzhou: n.p., 1963), 10:182–96; Su Kaiming, "Wang Ying: Heroine in Troubled Times," in Wang Ying, *The Child Bride* (Beijing: Foreign Languages Press, 1989), i-xii; MacKinnon and MacKinnon, *Agnes Smedley,* 310. After returning to China, Wang Ying joined the Beijing Film Studio. She and her husband were imprisoned during the Cultural Revolution in China, where she died in 1974. See Xia Yan, "Bu Neng Wangque de Jinian" [An Unforgettable Commemoration], preface to *Liang zhong Meiguoren* [Beijing: Zhongguo qingnian chubanshe, 1980], 1–13.

88. Li Runsheng and Cheng Yaoming, "Interview with Chinese Returned from America, Mr. Zhang Manli, former Circulation Manager at *China Daily News,*" and Shi Yulin and Liu Kangrong, "Interview with Chinese from America Mr. Chen Ke," in *Huaqiaoshi lunwenji* [Collection of Essays of Chinese Overseas History] (Guangzhou: Ji'nan Daxue Huaqiao Yanjiusuo, 1981), 322–32, 340–48; *Guangzhou Shi zhi* [Gazetteer of Guangzhou Municipality] 19: *Huaqiao zhi* [Gazetteer of Chinese overseas], part 2, "Qiaoxiang, Guiqiao" [Emigrant Villages, Returned Overseas Chinese], chap. 2, "Guiqiao" [Returned Overseas Chinese], sec. 1, "Huaqiao guiguo" [Return of Chinese from Overseas], 4, "Zao paihua guiguo" [Returned to China Due to Anti-Chinese Actions], retrieved Aug. 29, 2005, from http://www.gzsdfz.org.cn/gzsz/19/hq/sz19hq02020104.htm (cited hereafter as Gazetteer of Guangzhou Municipality: Returned Due to Anti-Chinese Actions).

Chen Ke arrived in Boston in 1928 as a stowaway and became a laundryman. He was a founder of New York's CHLA and served on its standing committee, and he also was a shareholder in *China Daily News.* He was deported to China in 1954. Chen Houfu joined the CPUSA in Philadelphia in 1931 and was also a CHLA member. He left the United States in 1951. Fang Fu'er was a CHLA standing committee member and also served on the *China Daily News* board of directors. He joined the Committee for a Democratic Far Eastern Policy in 1943 and was deported 1952. Chen Sancai joined CPUSA in 1934 and was also a member of CHLA standing committee and board member of *China Daily News.* Zhang Manli jumped ship at New York in 1934 and became a member of ACWP. He began working for the circulation department of *China Daily News* toward the end of World War II and was deported in 1956.

89. Gazetteer of Guangzhou Municipality: Returned Due to Anti-Chinese Actions.

90. *Annual Report of the Immigration and Naturalization Service,* 1965 (Washington, D.C.: Superintendent of Documents, 1966), 11; *Annual Report of the Immigration and Naturalization Service,* 1966 (Washington, D.C.: Superintendent of Documents, 1967), 16; *Chinese Pacific Weekly,* Feb. 1, 1957, May 3, 1962.

91. For the Kai G. Dere case, see *Chinese Pacific Weekly,* Jan. 5, 1961; the cases of Maurice Chuck and Jackson Chan are reported in *Chinese Pacific Weekly,* May 25, 1961; Wing Joe's case is discussed in *Chinese Pacific Weekly,* Sept. 21, 1961. Only Dere and Chuck were found guilty.

92. Henry Noyes, *China Born: Adventures of a Maverick Bookman* (San Francisco: China

Books and Periodicals, Inc., 1989), 66–80. Henry Noyes was a grandson of the missionary Varnum Noyes, who founded Pui Ying Middle School in Guangzhou in 1879. His great aunt Harriet Newell Noyes founded True Light Seminary in Guangzhou in 1872.

93. The Diaoyutai movement of the early 1970s challenged Japanese claims of sovereignty over the Diaoyutai Islands, located between Okinawa and Taiwan. The protesters were mostly Taiwanese and Hong Kong intellectuals and students in the United States and Canada.

94. Wang, My Husband Ji Chaozhu, 90, 103, 183. Ji Chaozhu began his career as an interpreter in 1952 for the Chinese delegation at Kaesong, negotiating with the UN forces led by the United States. In the 1980s, he was variously ambassador to various islands in the South Pacific and then to the United Kingdom (Wang, My Husband Ji Chaozhu, 122–77).

95. "Changzhu Lianheguo fudaibiao (dashi xian)" [Deputy Head of the Permanent Mission to the United Nations (Ambassador Rank)], retrieved Dec. 4, 2006, from http:// www.51wm.cn/article/20050602/21611.asp.

96. *Sing Tao Daily News,* Dec. 23, 1995; *International Daily News,* Feb. 16, Aug. 31, 1996; *Chinese Times,* June 6, 1996. Between 1996 and 2000, three unsuccessful attempts were made to continue operating the theater. A group connected with the pro-PRC Chinese American Association of Commerce began operating the theater in June 1996 but turned it over to Tai Seng Video Marketing of Hong Kong in August, which was no more successful. In mid-1999, the businessman Kam Kwong rented the theater to show Chinese and English language films but gave up by mid-2000. The theater's film archive was sold to the Four Star Theater in San Francisco's Richmond District.

GLOSSARY OF CHINESE CHARACTERS

Names of Individuals and Institutions, Phrases

Advisor on National Affairs 國策顧問
All-America Alliance of Chinese Anti-
   Imperialists 美州華僑反帝大同盟
All-China Federation for National
   Salvation 全國各界救國聯合會
Alliance for a Democratic China
   中國民主聯合陣線
America Friends of the Chinese
   People 中國人民之友社
Anti-Communist National Salvation
   League 反共救國總會
Asian Americans for Equal Employment,
   Asian Americans for Equality
   亞洲人平等會
Asian Community Center 亞洲人民中心
Association of Chinese Scientists
   and Engineers (USA)
   旅美中國科學家工程師協會
Aw Boon Haw 胡文虎
Aw Sian, Sally 胡仙
Bajin 巴金
Baohuanghui 保皇會
Bei Meizhou Li Denghui Zongtong
   zhi You Lianyihui
   北美洲李登輝總統之友聯誼會
Beijiazhou Hua-mei Hangtai Xuehui
   北加洲華美航太學會
Beijing Association of the U.S.A
   旅美北京同鄉會
Beijing U.S.A. Association
   旅美北京聯誼會
Bethune, Dr. Norman 白求恩大夫
Bing Kung Tong 秉公堂
Bow, George (Yao Guanshun) 姚觀順
Bow Leong Say 保良社

Browder, Earl 白勞德
Buddhist Compassion Relief
   Tzu Chi Foundation U.S.A.
   佛教慈濟基金會美國分會
Buddhist Light International
   Association 國際佛光會
C. Q. Yee Hop. See Chun Quon
Cai Cangming. See Lowe, Lawrence
Cai Fengyou 蔡鳳有
Cai Fujiu. See Tsoi, Henry
Cai Xingzhou. See Tsoi, Henry
Cai Yuanpei 蔡元培
Cao Changqing 曹長青
Cao Fengji 曹鳳集（曹集）
Cen Huijian. See Sum, Alice
Chai Ling 柴玲
Chain, Josephine 程蕙
Chan, Calvin 陳立人
Chan, Eva (Eva Choy Lowe) 陳君綺
Chan, Jackson 溫大川
Chan, Lain (Chen Dunpu) 陳敦樸
Chan, N. J. 陳汝舟
Chan, Phillip C. 陳俊雄
Chan, Siu King 陳兆瓊
Chan, Sucheng 陳素貞
Chan, Thomas P. 陳紫培
Chan, Timothy 陳瓊漢
Chan, You Foon 陳耀垣
Chang, Carsun 張君邁
Chang, Constance 張希先
Chang, Dai Yen 鄭帝恩
Chang, H. T.. See Fee, Benjamin
Chang, T. M. 張濟民
Chang, William 張孟錚
Chang, William Y. 鄭玉安

Chang, Y. C. 章友江
Chaotao 超桃
Chee Kung Tong 致公堂
Chen, C. Y. (Chi-yuen Chen, Chen Qiyuan) 陳其瑗
Chen, Duzhou 陳篤周
Chen, Edward (Chen Yide) 陳以德
Chen, Eugene 陳友仁
Chen Gee Hee 陳宜禧
Chen Gongbo 陳公博
Chen, Han-seng (Geoffrey Chen) 陳翰笙
Chen Heqin 陳鶴琴
Chen Houfu 陳厚父
Chen, Jack 陳依範
Chen Jiongming 陳炯明
Chen Ke 陳科
Chen Kemei 陳科美
Chen, Leo 陳立鷗，陳曉六
Chen Lifu 陳立夫
Chen Liting 陳鯉庭
Chen, Percy 陳丕士
Chen, Peter 陳國坤
Chen Runqiong 陳潤瓊
Chen, Sylvia Si-lan 陳西蘭
Chen, Tao 陳韜
Chen Tianxuan 陳天璇
Chen Wencheng 陳文成
Chen Xiuxia 陳秀霞
Chen Yanni 陳燕妮
Chen Yi'an 陳宜庵
Chen Yiming 陳一鳴
Chen Ying 陳英
Chen, Yolanda Yu-lan 陳玉蘭
Chen, Yuen Ying 陳婉瑩
Chen Yu-hsi 陳玉璽
Chen Yuqing 陳裕清
Chen Zhonghai 陳中海
Cheng Shewo 成舍我
Cheung, Francis 章建國
Chi, C. T. (Chi Chao-ting) 冀朝鼎
Chi, Chao-chu 冀朝鑄
Chi, Kung-ch'uan 冀貢泉
Chiang Ching-kuo 蔣經國
Chiang Kai-shek 蔣介石
Chick Char Musical Club 叱吒音樂社
Chin, Henry (Chen Jinjian) 陳金堅

China Defense League 保衛中國同盟
China Mail Steamship Company 中國郵船公司
China News Service 中國新聞社
Chinatown Teen Post 華埠青年中心
Chinese Aeronautics Association 航空學會
Chinese American Association of Commerce 華商總會
Chinese American Associations of Chicago 芝加哥華人各界聯席會
Chinese American Citizens' Alliance 同源會
Chinese American Civic Association 華美福利會
Chinese American Democratic Youth League 三藩市華僑民主青年團
Chinese American Planning Council 華人策劃協會
Chinese Association for Resistance to Japan and National Salvation 華僑抗日救國協會
Chinese Association for Science and Technology 北美華人科技協會
Chinese Chamber of Commerce 中華總商會
Chinese Christian Herald Crusade 基督教角聲佈道團
Chinese Community Service Association of Hawaii 夏威夷華人促進會
Chinese Consolidated Benevolent Association (New York City) 紐約中華公所
Chinese Consolidated Benevolent Association (San Francisco) 舊金山中華總會舘
Chinese Constitutionalist Party 中國憲政黨
Chinese Cultural Development Center 中國文化發展中心
Chinese Culture Center 中華文化中心
Chinese Culture Foundation of San Francisco 舊金山中華文化基金會
Chinese Democratic Alliance 中國民主大同盟
Chinese Democratic Constitutionalist Party 中國民主憲政黨

Chinese Democratic Education
Foundation 中國民主教育基金會
Chinese Democratic League
中國民主同盟
Chinese Democratic Socialist Party
中國民主社會黨
Chinese Empire Reform Association
中國維新會
Chinese for Affirmative Action
(San Francisco) 華人就業協進會，
華人權益促進會
Chinese Hand Laundry Alliance
紐約華僑衣舘聯合會
Chinese Hospital 東華醫院
Chinese Hung Men Democratic
Association 中國洪門民治黨
Chinese Media Committee (San
Francisco) 華人廣播協會
Chinese National Committee
for Armed Self-Defense
中國民族武裝自衛委員會
Chinese National Salvation League
國民抗日救國會
Chinese National Socialist Party
中國國家社會黨
Chinese Newspapers Consolidated
Sales, Inc. (San Francisco)
中文報業聯營公司
Chinese Overseas Journalists
Association 海外中國新聞從業者協會
Chinese Progressive Association
華人進步會
Chinese Reform Association
中國維新會
Chinese School Association in the
United States 全美中文學校協會
Chinese Socialist Club 社會主義同志會
Chinese Students Forum 僑生討論會
Chinese Unemployment Alliance of
Greater New York 紐約華僑失業會
Chinese Welfare Society (Toronto)
華僑福利會
Chinese Workers Mutual Aid
Association 加省華工合作會
Chinese Youth Association
(Vancouver) 青年聯誼會
Chinese Youth League 紐約華僑青年團

Chinese Youth National Salvation Club
of New York 紐約華僑青年救國團
Chinese Youth National Salvation League
of California 加省華僑青年救國團
Chinn, Thomas W. 陳參盛
Chock, Lun 卓麟
Chong Kee Jan 昌記棧
Chong Wa Benevolent Association
(Seattle) 舍路中華會館
Chow, Albert 周錦潮
Chow, Ke Din 鄒克定
Chow, Robert 莫夏風
Choy, Joe Git. See Lowe, Lawrence
Choy, Jun Ke 蔡增基
Chu Su Gunn (Zhao Gongbi) 趙公璧
Chu, Louis 雷霆超
Chu, Y. K. 朱耀渠，朱夏
Chuck, Maurice (Huang Yunji)
卓忠民（黃運基）
Chun Quon (C. Q. Yee Hop)
陳滾（思喬義合）
Chun, Dick 陳德
Chun, Walter Chee Kun 陳志昆
Chung Chung Alumni Association
中山全縣中學同學會
Chung Shan School 中山學校
Chung, Arthur 張煒遜
Committee for Revival of the
Kuomintang 中國國民黨復興同志會
Coordinating Council for North
American Affairs, Headquarters
for Taipei Economic and Cultural
Representative Office in the United
States 北美事務協調委員會駐美國台
北經濟文化代表處
Crusade for Free Democratic China,
Inc. 自由中國協會
Cui Tongyue 崔東約
Cui Wei 崔嵬
Dai Ailian 戴愛蓮
Dai Qi 戴錡
Dai Qing 戴晴
Dajiang She 大江社
Dao, James 陶啓華
Dea, Xavier 謝創（謝榮創）
Democratic League 民主同盟
Democratic Progressive Party 民主進步黨

Deng Yanda 鄧演達
Deng, Cora 鄧裕志
Deng Wenzhao. See Tang, M. C.
Dere, Kai G. 謝啓基（謝榮忠）
Ding Zan 丁瓚
Dong Biwu 董必武
Dong Jianwu 董健吾
Dongping 動平
Dongsheng 動生
Dou, Bat Nau 杜不朽
Dragunov, A. A. 龍果夫
Duan Qirui 段其瑞
dushu hui 讀書會
Eastwind Bookstore 東風書店
Fairfax-Cholmeley, Elsie 丘茉莉
Falun Gong 法輪功
Fang, John 方大川
Fang Lizhi 方勵之
Fang Zhenwu 方振武
Fann, Thomas S. 范湘濤
Federation for a Democratic China
　民主中國陣線
Federation of Chinese in Europe for
　Resistance to Japan and National
　Salvation 全歐華僑抗日聯合會
Federation of Chinese in New York for
　Resistance to Japan and National
　Salvation 紐約華僑抗日救國聯合會
Federation of Overseas Hong Kong
　Chinese 華盛頓海外香港華人聯會
Fee, Benjamin (H. T. Chang, Muyun)
　張恨棠（張明之，木雲）
Feng Dongguang 馮棟光
Feng Hanping 馮漢平
Feng Lida 馮理達
Feng Yuxiang 馮玉祥
Feng Ziyou 馮自由
Flying Dragon Club 飛龍音樂社
Fong, George 鄺佐治
Fong, Yue Po 鄺瑤普
Formosan Students Club 台灣同學會
Foundation for Chinese Democracy
　民主中華基金會
Free China Political Organizations
　中國民主政團同盟
Free Formosans' Formosa
　台灣人之自由台灣

Freedom Front 自由陣線
Friends of the New Party 新黨之友
Fu, Chao-chu 傅朝樞
Gao Jianfu 高劍父
Ge Tingsui 葛庭燧
Gerlach, Talitha 耿麗淑
Ging Hawk Club 女子競學會
Glass, Frank 李福仁
Golden Harbour Corporation 金港公司
Gong Peng 龔澎（龔維航）
Gong Pusheng 龔普生
Gu Shuxing, Susie Gu 顧淑型
"Guanhuai shequ, zhencheng fuwu"
　"關懷社區，真誠服務"
Guo Hanqing. See Kuo, Larry
Guojia Jianshe Yanjiuhui
　國家建設研究會
Guojianhui 國建會
Guo Lianyin. See Kuo Lien-yin
Guomin Waijiao Xiejinhui
　國民外交協進會
Gwoyeu Romatzyh 國語羅馬字
Haass, Lily K. (Xia Xiulan) 夏秀蘭
Hahn, Henry (He Zhifen) 何植芬
Haiwai Xingzhonghui 海外興中會
Han Depei 韓德培
Han Maolin 韓茂林
Hanxiang Yinziguan 翰香印字舘
Hatem, George 馬海德
Hawaii Chinese Writers Association
　夏威夷華文作家協會
He Huiliang 何惠良
He Xiangning 何香凝
Hei She 黑社
He Zhifen. See Hahn, Henry
Ho, Charles Tsu Kwok 何杜國
Ho, James 賀鳴笙
Ho Fun 何寬
Hom, Stanley 譚樹本
Hong Wai 馮彧龍
Hongguang Primary School 洪光小學
Hongmen 洪門
Hoo Cho Chinese School 互助學校
Hoo Cho Society 青年互助社
Hosei University 法政大學
Hou Xianglin 侯祥麟
Hoy Fung Music Club 海風音樂社

Hoy, William 謝開

Hsieh, C. T. 謝啟泰

Hsieh, Francisco 謝漢屏

Hsu, Y. Y. (Hsu Yung-ying) 徐永煐

Hu Hanmin 胡漢民

Hu Lanqi 胡蘭畦

Hu Pin 胡頻

Hu Ping 胡平

Hu Shih 胡適（胡適之）

Hu Shuying 胡樹英

Hu Yuzhi 胡愈之

Hu, Thomas T. Y. (Hu Dunyuan) 胡敦元

Hu'an Houyuanhui 滬案後援會

Hua Shan 華山（鄭光，吳祖民）

Hua, Loo-keng (Hua Luogeng) 華羅庚

Huafa 化發

Huafeng Department Store
    華豐國貨公司

Huang Baotong 黃葆同

Huang Dunsheng 黃鼉盛

Huang Gongshou 黃恭壽

Huang Jing 黃敬

Huang Lingshuang. See Wong, L. S.

Huang Qiming 黃啟明

Huang San 黃三

Huang Shaoxiang 黃紹湘

Huang Shengchang 黃勝常

Huang Shijun 黃仕俊

Huang Tianji 黃天驥

Huang Wenshan 黃文山

Huang Xinjie 黃信介

Huang Ying 黃英

Huang Youmei 黃友梅

Huang Yuanyong 黃遠庸

Huang Yuchuan 黃雨川

Huang Yunji. See Chuck, Maurice

Huang Zicong 黃子聰

Huang Zunxian 黃遵憲

Huang, Garfield 黃嘉惠

Huaqiao Qingnian Wenyi She
    華僑青年文藝社

Huaqiao Wenhua Jianshe Yanjiu Hui
    華僑文化建設研究會

Huashengdun Huaren Gejie Lianhehui
    華盛頓華人各界聯合會

Hui Pei Sun 許丕新

Hung, Fei Man 熊斐文

"Huo yan Kun Gang, yu shi ju fen."
    "火炎崑岡，玉石俱焚"

Hwang, James 黃雅各

I Wor Kuen 義和拳

Isaacs, Harold 伊羅生

Ja, Kew Yuen (K. Y. Ja) 謝僑遠

Jan, John 曾紀莊

Jeune Doc Club 女子進德會

Ji Hongchang 吉鴻昌

Jian She 建社

Jiang Kanghu. See Kiang Kang Hu

Jiang Qing 江青

Jiji She 擊楫社

Jin Yinchang 金蔭昌

Jinggang Shan 井岡山

Jinyi Hang 錦衣行

Joe Yuey 周銳

Joe, Kenneth 周堅乃（關春如）

Joe, Wing 趙榮光（張毅士）

Jones, Ray (Red Jones). See
    Liu Zhongshi

Jue She 覺社

Jue Yeh Club 朝雨音樂社

Jung, Oi Won 張靄蘊

Kang Sheng 康生

Kang Youwei 康有爲

Kaohsiung 高雄

Kiang Kang Hu (Jiang Kanghu) 江亢虎

Kin Kuo School 建國學校

Kolokolov, V. S. 郭質生

Koo, V. K. Wellington 顧維鈞

Kuangfeng She 狂風社

Kung, H. H. 孔祥熙

Kung Yu Club 革命工餘俱樂部

Kuo Lien-yin (Guo Lianyin) 郭連蔭

Kuo, Larry (Guo Hanqing) 郭漢清

Kuo Sin News Agency 國新社

Kuomintang (Nationalist Party of
    China) 中國國民黨

Kwantung Army 關東軍

Kwock On Society 國安會館

Kwong, Peter 鄺治中

Lai Yali (Lai Xingzhi) 賴亞力（賴興志）

Lam, David K. 林君

Lam, Ruth Koo 古鳳英

Lan Pin 藍蘋

Laogai Research Foundation 勞改基金會

Latinized Chinese Language Study Society　中文拉丁化研究會
Latinxua Sin Wenz　拉丁化新文字
Lau, Edward　劉中原
Lau, Gordon　劉貴明
Lau, Hanson　劉恆信
League for Peace and Democracy in China　旅美中國和平民主聯盟
Lee, Catherine C.　朱勤勤
Lee, Ching Wah　李華清
Lee, Dai Ming　李大明
Lee, Frank　李華廣
Lee, Frank Ching-Lun　李錦綸
Lee, Herbert　李漢齡（李柏宏）
Lee, Jake　李鴻德
Lee, James　李顧鴻
Lee, Jane Kwong　鄺蓮真
Lee, Kan　李根
Lee, Lester　李心培
Lee, Mon Ting　李文廷
Lee, See Nam　李是男
Lee, T. Kong　李松光
Lee, Wea H.　李蔚華
Lee, William C. W.　李照華
Lee, Yan Phou　李恩富
Lee, Ya-ping　李亞蘋
Lei Mingxia　雷鳴夏
Lem Tong, Thomas　林棠
Leong, Charles　梁普禮
Leong, Francis　梁發葉
Leong Thick Hing　梁錫田
Leung, Shing Tai　梁聲泰
Lew, Gordon　劉池光（林建國）
Lew, Henry　劉宜良
Li Chunhui　李春暉
Li, David　李文中
Li Dequan　李德全
Li Fahuan　李法寰
Li Feigan　李芾甘
Li Gongpu　李公樸
Li Hengde　李恆德
Li Jichen　李濟琛
Li Lisan　李立三
Li Lu　李祿
Li Qiuguo　李求國
Li Shaoshi　李少石
Li Shengting　李聖庭

Li Tao Hsuan　李道煊
Li Teng-hui　李登輝
Li Tianfu　李天福
Li Yuan　李原
Li Zongren　李宗仁
Liang, Lucas　梁楨
Liang Qichao　梁啟超
Liang, Shing Tai　梁聲泰
Liang Sili　梁思禮
Liang, Sylvia　梁思懿
Liang Xinggui　梁慶桂
Lianhui　聯會
Liao Chengzhi　廖承志
Liao, Cynthia (Liao Mengxing)　廖夢醒
Liao Wenyi　廖文毅
Liao Zhongkai　廖仲愷
Lim, Happy　林堅夫
Lin, Anor　林太乙
Lin Boqu　林伯渠
Lin, Echo (Lin Xihu)　林錫湖
Lin Guangyuan　林廣源
Lin Guoguang　林國光
Lin, John (Lin Rongxun)　林榮勳
Lin, Paul T. K.　林達光
Lin Yinfu　林蔭溥
Lin Yun'gai　林雲陔
Lin Yutang　林語堂
Liu, Arthur　劉恕
Liu Beihai　劉北海
Liu, Bing　劉冰
Liu Binyan　劉賓雁
Liu Chengyu　劉成愚
Liu, David S. C.　劉仕誠
Liu, Hartmann (Liu Kemian)　劉克勉
Liu, Henry　劉宜良（江南）
Liu Liangmo　劉良模
Liu, Pei Chi　劉伯驥
Liu Sifu　劉思復
Liu Zhongshi (Red Jones, Ray Jones)　劉中時，蔡賢
Liu Zhujin　劉鑄晉
Liu-Mei Xuesheng Dangyuan Zuotanhui　留美學生黨員座談會
Liu-Mei Zhongguo Kexue Gongzuozhe Xiehui　留美中國科學工作者協會
Liu-Mei Zhongguo Xuesheng Huiguo Fuwu Hui　留美中國學生回國服務會

Lo, Chung-Long 羅中郎
Lo, S. S. (Luo Jingyi) 羅素抒（羅靜宜）
Long Jiguang 龍濟光
Loo, Jay (Lu Zhuyi) 盧主義
Loo Sun 盧信
Louis Wing (Lei Zhuofeng) 雷卓峰
Lowe, Eva Choy. See Chan, Eva
Lowe, Lawrence (Cai Cangming,
    Joe Git Choy, Low Quai Bun)
    蔡滄溟（蔡祖傑，劉桂斌）
Lu, George (Lu Jianhe) 盧建和
Lu Guangyan 盧廣彥
Lu Yisun 盧誼遜
Lu Zhuyi. See Loo, Jay
Lü Chaoran 呂超然
Lufeng Drama Society 蘆烽話劇社
Lum, Kalfred Dip 林疊
Lum, Walter U. 林華耀
Luo Jingyi. See Lo, S. S.
Luo Longji 羅隆基
Luo Yuanzheng 羅元錚
Luxun 魯迅
Ly, Vincent Siu-Cong 李少光
Ma Chaojun 馬超俊
Ma, Fu-chuan 馬福全
Ma, Jen Kei 馬振基
Ma, Jiliang (Tang Na) 馬季良（唐納）
Ma Senliang 馬森亮
Ma Zhanshan 馬占山
Ma Zusheng 馬祖聖
Madam Sun Yat-sen. See Soong
    Ching-ling
Mah, D. Y. 馬典如
Mah, Roy 馬國冠
Man Sang She 民生社
Mao Zedong 毛澤東
Maodun 矛盾
Mar, Cheolin 馬超林
Mei Ruao 梅汝璈
Mei Youzhuo 梅友卓
Mei Zuyan 梅祖彥
Meidong Guojian Lianyihui
    美東國建聯誼會
Meidong Huaren Xueshu Lianyuhui
    美東華人學術聯誼會
Meizhong Zhongguo Kexue Gongzuozhe
    Xiehui 美中中國科學工作者協會

Meizhou Kang-Ri Waijiao
    Houyuanhui 美洲抗日外交後援會
Meizhou Yonghu Zhongguo
    Gong-Nong Geming Datongmeng
    美洲擁護中國工農革命大同盟
Meng Shouzhuang 孟壽椿
Minduo Drama Society 民鐸戲劇研究會
Ming She 明社
Minguo Weichihui 民國維持會
Mingzhi She 明志社
Minnan 閩南
Minzhong Geyonghui 民衆歌詠會
Mo Guoshi. See Zhang Bao Zhang
    莫國史
Mo Zhendan. See Zhang Bao Zhang
    莫震旦
Mon Kee 文記
Mon Sang Association 民生社
Monte Jade Science and Technology
    Association 玉山科技協會
Morning Bell School 晨鐘學校
Moy, Eugene 梅參天
Moy, Kenneth T. C. 梅子強
Mun Ching 民青
Mun Lun School 明倫學校
Muyun. See Fee, Benjamin
Nam Kue School 南僑學校
National Association of Chinese
    Americans 全美華人協會
National Council of Associations of
    Chinese Language Schools
    全美中文學校聯合總會
National Day 國慶日
National Salvation Movement 救亡運動
Native Sons of the Golden State
    同源總局, 同源總會
New Association of Chinese Americans
    華美新社
New Chinese Alphabetized Language
    Study Society 新文字研究會
New Party 新黨
New York Chinese Hand Laundry
    Alliance 紐約華僑衣館聯合會
New York Ching Wah Players
    精華戲劇團
Ng, Assunta 吳靜雯
Ng Poon Chew 伍盤照

Southern California Foundation
for Chinese Democracy
南加州民主中華基金會
Southern Chinese Newspaper Group
(Houston) 美南報業傳播機構
Students' Society for the Advancement
of Sun Yat-senism in America
留美學生中山學會
Sue Hing Association 肇慶會館
Suey Sing Labor and Merchant
Association 萃勝工商會
Sum, Alice (Cen Huijian) 岑慧劍
Sun Yat-sen 孫逸仙，孫文，孫中山
Sung, Christina 宋秀蘭
Sunning Railroad 新寧鐵路
Tai-chi 太極拳
Tiao Yu Tai Movement. See Protect
Diaoyutai Movement
Taiping Rebellion 太平天國
Taiwan Yanjiuhui 台灣研究會
Tam, Wayne 譚華煥
Tan Pingshan 譚平山
Tan Zan (Tom Chan) 譚贊
Tang Hualong 湯化龍
Tang, M. C. (Deng Wenzhao) 鄧文釗
Tang Mingzhao. See Tong, Chu
Tang Na. See Ma Jiliang
Tao Xingzhi 陶行知
Tatsu Maru 《二辰丸》
Third Arm, The 第三臂
Tian Han 田漢
Tian'anmen Memorial Foundation
天安門紀念基金會
Tiong Hiew King 張曉卿
Tom Chan. See Tan Zan
Tom Gunn 譚根
Tong, Chu (Tang Mingzhao, Chew
Sih Tong) 唐錫朝，唐明照
Tong King Chong 唐瓊昌
Tong, Nancy (Tang Wensheng) 唐聞生
Tong, Ruddy 湯慶華
Tong, Thomas 唐憲才
Tongmenghui 中國同盟會
Toronto Association for Democracy
in China 多倫多支援中國民運會
Triad Society 三合會
Tsai, Ming-yu 蔡明裕
Tsai Ting-kai 蔡廷鍇

Tsao, Lily Yeh 葉莉莉
Tsiang, H. T. (Tsiang Hsi-Tseng, Jiang
Xizeng) 蔣希曾
Tsiang, Tingfu F. 蔣廷黻
Tsien Hsue-shen (Qian Xuesen) 錢學森
Tsoi, Henry (Cai Fujiu, Cai Xingzhou, Joe
Fook Tsoi) 蔡福就，蔡荇洲，蔡祖福
Tsung Tsin Association 崇正會
Unionist Guild 三藩市工藝同盟總會
United Federation of Chinese
Associations in New York
紐約華人社團聯合會
United Formosans for Independence
台灣獨立聯盟
United Formosans in America for
Independence 全美台灣獨立聯盟
United National Salvation Propaganda
Troupe 聯合救國宣傳團
Vancouver Society Support of
Democratic Movement
溫哥華支援民主聯合會
W. J. Bookstore, Inc. 世界書店
W. J. Cultural Center 世界日報文化廣場
Wah Mun School 華文學堂，華文學校
Wah You, Sam 周森
Wan Runnan 萬潤南
Wang Baoliu 王保流
Wang Bingzhang 王炳章
Wang Chang 王昌
Wang Dan 王丹
Wang Feng 王楓
Wang Fushi 王福時
Wang Heng 汪衡
Wang Jingwei 汪精衛
Wang Jue 王玨
Wang Juntao 王軍濤
Wang, Kenjohn 王桂榮
Wang, L. Ling-chi 王靈智
Wang Ming 王明
Wang, Tih-wu 王惕吾
Wang Xiling 王希齡
Wang Ying 王瑩
Wei Jingsheng 魏京生
Wei Minghua 魏明華
Wei Min She 為民社
Wei Tingchao 魏庭朝
Weizhen Xuehui 唯真學會
Wen Yiduo 聞一多

Wen Yuming 文毓明

Wen Zhengde (King G. Won) 溫徵德

Western Hills faction 西山派

Winam, C. 程蔚南

Wo On Society (Honolulu) 和安會館

Won Hung Fei 溫雄飛

Wong, Albert 黃文耀，余直民

Wong, Bock You 黃伯耀

Wong Buck Hung 黃北洪

Wong Ching Foo (Wong Chin Foo) 王清福

Wong, Doon (Yen Doon Wong) 黃仁俊

Wong, Ernest 黃德慶

Wong, Frank 黃毓樞，嚴斧

Wong, Goon Dick 黃君迪

Wong, L. S. (Huang Lingshuang) 黃凌霜

Wong, Larry 黃金泉

Wong Wing Tuck 黃超五

Wong, Yen Doon. See Wong, Doon

Woo, Chin-Fu, (Chin Foo Wu) 吳敬敷

Woo, Gilbert 胡景南

Woo, Norbert 胡景僑

Workers Viewpoint Organization 工人觀點組識

World Chinese Trust Group (Los Angeles) 世界華商集團

World Theater 世界戲院

World United Formosans for Independence 台灣獨立聯盟

Wu Chin Foo. See Woo, Chin-Fu

Wu Fengkun 吳豐坤

Wu, Franklin (Wu Fengyi) 吳豐義，吳育庭

Wu, Harry (Wu Hongda) 吳宏達

Wu Kejian 吳克堅

Wu, Kenneth 吳立民

Wu Maosun 吳茂蓀

Wu Shangying 吳尚鷹

Wu Siqi 吳思琦

Wu Tiansheng 伍天生

Wu Tiecheng 吳鐵城

Wu Xianzi (Wu Zhuang) 伍憲子，伍莊

Wu Yuzhang 吳玉章

Wu Zhaofa 武兆發

Wuerkaixi 吾爾開希

"Wuhu Zhonghua Huighuan zhi muqi" "嗚呼中華會館之暮氣"

Wuyi Tongxiang Lianyihui 五邑同鄉聯誼會

Wuzhengfu Gongchanzhuyizhe Lianmeng 無政府共產主義者聯盟

Xi She 曦社

Xia Xu 夏煦

Xianfeng She 先鋒社

Xianzhengdang 中國憲政黨

Xianzhenghui 帝國憲政會

Xiao San 蕭三

Xiao Shuzi 蕭樹滋

Xia Xiulan. See Haass, Lily K.

Xibaipo 西柏坡

Xie Congmin 謝聰敏

Xie Hegeng 謝和庚

Xie Qitai. See Zhang Hanfu

Xie Yingbo 謝英伯

Xigu Hua-Mei Bandaoti Xiehui 矽谷華美半導體協會

Xin Huaqiao Xuehui 新華僑學會

Xin Shehui 新社會

Xin Wenzi Yanjiuhui 新文字研究會

Xin Zhongguo Yanjiuhui 新中國研究會

Xingzhonghui 興中會

Xu Bangtai 徐邦泰

Xu Dongliang 許東亮

Xu Jiyuan 許紀雲

Xu Ming 徐鳴

Xu Qin 徐勤

Xu Qiwen 徐企文

Xuan Quanguang (Xuan Rong) 禤全光 （禤榮）

Xue Baoding 薛寶鼎

Xuehan 學涵

Yan Jiaqi 嚴家其

Yan Renying 嚴仁英

Yang, C. N. 楊振寧

Yang Gang 楊剛

Yang Hucheng 楊虎城

Yang, Kenny, Yang Jikun 楊基錕

Yang Xingfo 楊杏佛

Yang, Tom (Yang Dongjie) 楊東傑

Yao Guanshun. See Bow, George

Yap, William K. F. 葉桂芳

Yee, Dan 余進源

Yeh, Rita 葉島蕾

Yehuo She 野火社

Yen, Cecilia 延惠君

Publications, Radio and Television Programs, Authored Works

The Chinese often took much care in selecting a meaningful Chinese name for periodicals but were casual when selecting English names. The result was that the English names of many periodicals were identical. In order to help the reader distinguish among the various titles, the location where each was published is given in parentheses using the following abbreviations: Cal=Calgary, Bos=Boston, Chi=Chicago, DC=Washington, D.C., Edm=Edmonton, HK=Hong Kong, Hon=Honolulu, Hou=Houston, LA=Los Angeles (incl. Alhambra, City of Industry, El Monte, Monterey Park, Rosemead, San Gabriel), Mon=Montreal, NJ=New Jersey, NY= New York City (incl. Flushing), Phil=Philadelphia, SF=San Francisco (incl. Burlingame, Milbrae, San Mateo), SJ=San Jose (incl. Silicon Valley), Sea=Seattle (incl. Graham), Tor=Toronto, Van=Vancouver, Vic=Victoria, Win=Winnipeg.

Alberta Chinese Post (Cal) 《成功報》
Alberta Chinese Times (Edm) 《加中報》
Amasia TV 《美亞電視》
Amasian Post (SF) 《遠東報》
Amerasian Businews 《美亞商報》
America Asian News (LA) 《越柬寮報》
American Chinese News (LA)
　《美華新報》
American Chinese Times (NY)
　《美華時報》
American Chinese Times, The (Chi)
　《美中日報》
American Football Weekly (SF)
　《美式足球週刊》
American Journal of Traditional Chinese
　Medicine (LA) 《美中醫藥報》
Apple TV (NY) 《蘋果電視》
Arizona Chinese Times (Phoenix)
　《亞利桑那華報》
Asia Dragon News (Van) 《亞龍報》
Asia News (LA) 《新亞洲報》
Asia Today (Sea) 《華聲報》
Asian Gazette (Dallas) 《亞美時報》
Asian Journal (LA) 《亞美商報》
Asian-American Times (NY)
　《亞美時報》
Atlanta Chinese News 《亞特蘭大新聞》
Basic Chinese National Program for
　Fighting Japan
　《中國人民對日作戰的基本綱領》
Bay Area Chinese News (SJ)
　《北加州灣區新聞》

Bay Area Chinese Times (SF)
　《灣區時報》
Beijing Spring (NJ) 《北京之春》
Big Family Quartery (NY) 《大家雜誌》
Boston Chinese News 《波士頓新聞》
Bridge Magazine (NY) 《橋》
Buddha's Light Newsletter of Los Angeles
　《佛光世紀洛杉磯版》
Buy & Sell (Van) 《買賣報》
Calgary Chinese News 《卡城愛華報》
California China Mail and Flying Dragon
　(SF) 《飛龍》
California Daily News (LA) 《加州日報》
California Sunshine (San Mateo)
　《加州阳光》
Canada China News, The (Van)
　《中華導報》
Canada Morning News (Van)
　《加拿大晨報》
Canadian Chinese Times, The (Cal, Edm)
　《加華報》
Capital Chinese News, The (Ottawa)
　《加京華報》
Cathay Times (SF) 《光華報》
Central Daily News, International Edition
　(LA) 《中央日報，國際版》
Centre Daily News (HK, NY, LA, SF, Hou)
　《中報》
Cheng Kung News, The (Phil) 《成功報》
Chi-Am Daily News (LA) 《天天日報》
Chicago Chinese Daily News
　《芝加哥日報》

Chicago Chinese Times 《芝加哥時報》

China (HK) 《中國日報》

China Daily News (LA)
《少年中國晨報洛杉磯版》

China Daily News (NY)
《美洲華僑日報》

China Guide (LA) 《中國導報》

China Insight (*Sing Tao* magazine
supplement) 《神州》

China Journal (LA, Van) 《神州時報》

China Life (NY) 《生活》

China News Digest 《華夏文摘》

China News Group 《中國新聞組》

China News Service 《中國新聞社》

China News; China Weekly News (SF)
《中華論壇報》

China Post (LA) 《新生報》

China Post (magazine) (NY)
《大華旬刊》,《大華雜誌》

China Post, The (daily) (NY)
《紐約日報》

China Post, The (daily) (SF) 《美西日報》

China Post, The (weekly) (SF)
《中國郵報》

China Press Weekend Edition, The (NY)
《僑報周末》

China Press, The (NY, SF, LA) 《僑報》

China Reform Gazette (Van) 《日新報》

China Reform News (NY)
《中國維新報》

China Salvation Times; Giu Guo Sh Bao
(Paris, then NY) 《救國時報》

China Signature Journal (LA)
《中國鄉情報》,《鄉情週報》

China Spring (NY) 《中國之春》

China Times (semimonthly) (SF)
《華報》

China Times (U.S. edition of Taiwan
newspaper) (NY, SF) 《中國時報》

China Times Weekly (magazine) (NY)
《時報週刊》

China Times, The (NY, SF, Chi)
《中國時報》

China Tribune, The (NY) 《紐約新報》,
《《光華日報》,華美日報》at
different periods

China Voice Daily (NY) 《華聲日報》

China Weekly (LA) 《中華時報》

China Weekly (SF) 《金門僑報》

Chinatown (Tor) 《唐人街》

Chinatown, Chinatown News (Van)
《華埠雜誌》

Chinatown Commercial News (Tor)
《多倫多商報》

Chinatown Community News (NY)
《街坊報》

Chinatown News (Cleveland)
《中國城報》

Chinatown News (NY) 《華埠新聞》

Chinatown Report (NY) 《華埠導報》

Chinatown Shopper (SF) 《華商導報》

Chinavision (Tor) 《加拿大中文電視》

Chinaweek (NY) 《綜合》

Chinese American (Chi) 《華美新報》

Chinese American (NY) 《華美新報》

Chinese American Advocate (Phil)
《華美字報》

Chinese-American Digest (NY)
《光明雜誌》

Chinese American Forum (Maryland,
Missouri, Sea) 《美華論壇》

Chinese American News (Chi)
《美中新聞》

Chinese American Times (NY)
《中美時報》

Chinese American Voice (NY)
《僑聲廣播》

Chinese American Weekly (NY)
《中美週報》

Chinese-American Weekly (NY)
《中美周報》

Chinese Awareness (LA) 《覺華報》

Chinese Broadcasting Agency (Hon)
《華語播音社》

Chinese Broadcasting Bureau (Hon)
《華人播音局》

Chinese Business News, The (Hou)
《華商報》

Chinese Business Weekly (NY)
《華埠商報》

Chinese-Canadian Bulletin (Van)
《華僑經濟導報》

Chinese Canadian Daily (Tor)
《加華日報》

Chinese Canadian Magazine (Tor)
《加華雜誌》，《加華月刊》

*Chinese Canadian Newspaper Weekend
Issue* (Tor)《加華日報周末版》

Chinese Canadian Times (Tor)
《加中時報 》

Chinese Central Daily News (Chi)
《中央日報》

Chinese Commercial Journal (NY)
《美華工商報》

Chinese Commercial News (SF)《商報》

Chinese Community Magazine, The (NY)
《華僑社會雜誌》

Chinese Community News (Miami)
《邁亞密郵報》

Chinese Community News (LA)
《華興時報》

Chinese Community Tribune
(Sacramento)《天虹雜誌》

*Chinese Consumer Weekly,
Buy & Sell Classified* (LA)
《生活資訊、買賣專欄》

Chinese Daily News (LA)
《世界日報洛杉磯版》

Chinese Daily News (Sacramento)
《沙架免度新錄》

Chinese Daily Post (SF)《國民日報》

Chinese Defender, The (SF)《護公理報》

Chinese Digest (SF)《華美週刊》

Chinese Evening News (SF)《華西申報》

Chinese Express Daily Newspaper (Tor)
《快報》

Chinese Forum, The (SF)《是非》

Chinese Free Daily News (LA)
《美洲自由時報》

*Chinese Free Daily News, Eastern U.S.
Edition* (NY)《美東自由時報》

Chinese Free Press (Van)《中興日報》

Chinese Free Press; Tai Tung Po (SF)
《大同日報》，《中華民國公報》

Chinese in America (Van)
《美洲華僑月刊》

Chinese Intellectual, The (NY)
《知識份子》

Chinese Journal of *Commerce, The* (NY)
《紐約商報》

Chinese Journal (SF)《商報》

Chinese Journal, The (NY)《美洲日報》

Chinese Literature of the Americas (SF)
《紅杉林：美洲華人文藝》

Chinese Medical Report, The (NY)
《中國醫藥導報》

Chinese Monthly Magazine (Malacca)
《察世俗每月統記傳》

Chinese Monthly News, The (Bos)
《華洋新報》

*Chinese Nationalist Daily of America;
Kuo Min Yat Po* (SF)
《美洲國民日報》

*Chinese Nationalist Daily; Mun Hey Daily,
Mun Hey Yat Po* (NY)《民氣日報》

Chinese Nationalist; Mun Hey Weekly
(NY)《民氣周報》

Chinese News (Chi)《美華新報》

Chinese News (Mon, Tor)《大中報》

Chinese News (SD)
《遠東報》，《加華時報》

Chinese News (SF)《華僑生活》

Chinese News Weekly (Van)
《加拿大雲埠中華英文周報》

Chinese News, The (Sea)《眾聲報》

*Chinese News, The; Les Nouvelles
Chinoises* (Mon)《華僑新報》

Chinese Outlook (SF)《外觀報》

Chinese Overseas Broadcasting Corporation
(LA)《中華海外傳播公司》

Chinese Pacific Weekly, The (SF)
《太平洋週報》

Chinese Press; California Chinese Press
(SF)《華美週報》

Chinese Press, The; Les Presses Chinoises
(Mon)《華僑時報》

Chinese Radio Network (NY)
《中國廣播網》

Chinese Radio Program (Mon)
《華僑之聲電臺》

Chinese Record, Chinese Recorder (SF)
《華人紀錄》

Chinese Reform News (NY)
《中國維新報》

Chinese Republic News (NY)
《民國公報》,《國權報》,
《紐約公報》,《五洲公報》at
different periods
Chinese Sports Weekly (SF) 《波經》
Chinese Star (Sea) 《僑星週報》
Chinese Students Bulletin (NY)
《中國留美學生通訊》
Chinese Students Monthly (NY)
《中國留美學生月報》
Chinese Sun (NY) 《中山週報》,
《中山晨報》,《中山日報》
Chinese Television Company, Inc. (SF)
《中華電視》
Chinese Times (SF) 《金山時報》
Chinese Times; Lai Kee Bo (Hon)
《麗記報》
Chinese Times, The; Hung Chung Shih
Paa (Tor) 《洪鐘時報》
Chinese Times, The; Tai Hon Kung Po
(Van) 《大漢公報》
Chinese Tribune (NY) 《華美日報》
Chinese TV Program, La Voix de Chine
(Mon) 《中華之聲有綫電視台》
Chinese Vanguard (SF, then Phil, NY)
《先鋒報》
Chinese Voice (Hou) 《華聲導報》
Chinese Voice; Chinese Voice Daily (SF)
《華聲報》,《華聲日報》
Chinese Voice, The (Van) 《僑聲日報》
Chinese Weekend (LA) 《中國週末》
Chinese Weekly Post (LA) 《國際周報》
Chinese Weekly, The (LA) 《羅省周報》
Chinese World Television (LA)
《世華電視》
Chinese World, The; Sai Gai Yat Po (SF,
NY) 《世界日報》
Chinese Youth Magazine (SF)
《中華少年雜誌》
Chinese Youth Voice (SF)
《中國青年之聲》
Chun Phone (NY) 《春風》
Chung Hing News (LA) 《中興報》
Chung Ngoi San Po (HK) 《中外新報》
Chung Ngoi San Po (SF) 《中外新報》
Chung Sai Yat Po (SF) 《中西日報》

Chung Wah Commercial Broadcasting Co.
(NY) 《中華商業廣播電台》
Commercial News Journal (Taiwan)
《工商新聞報》
Crossroads, The (Tor) 《海上述林》
Da Zhong Bao (Van) 《大眾報》
Daily Occidental (SF) 《翰香捷報》
Dalasi Xinwen (Dallas) 《達拉斯新聞》
Dallas Times (Dallas) 《達拉斯時報》
Dalu Bao (Van) 《大陸報》
Dasheng Bao (Hon) 《大聲報》
Datongxue (China) 《大同學》
Delicacy of Life (NY) 《美味人生》
Denver Chinese News 《丹佛華報》
Detroit Chinese News 《積彩華文報》
Dezhou Shoufu Xinwen (Austin)
《德州首府新聞》
Dibao (China) 《邸報》
Dong Shan Newsletter (Sea)
《東山講堂通訊》
Dragon Post (SF) 《龍報》
Dunhuang Television (LA) 《敦煌電視》
Duolunduo Meijia Huayu Diantai (Tor)
《多倫多美加華語電台》
Duolunduo Shangye Diantai (Tor)
《多倫多商業電台》
Duowei Chinesenewsnet 《多維新聞網》
Duowei Times (NJ) 《多維時報》
Dupont Guy (SF) 《都板街》
East/West (SF) 《東西報》
East West Forum (NY) 《中外論壇》
East Wind (SF) 《東風》
Eastern Times; Chinese Community
Weekly (NY) 《美東時報》
Eastern Trends (Salt Lake City)
《東方報》
Eastweek (Sing Tao magazine
supplement) (SF) 《東周刊》
Edmonton Chinese News (Edm)
《愛華報》
Epoch Times, The (NY, DC, Phil, Bos, NJ,
Chi, Texas, Atlanta, SF, LA, SD, Tor)
《大紀元時報,美東版,美中版,
美南版,美東南版,美西版,
加拿大版》
Equality (NY) 《平等報》

Eurasian Bilingual Monthly Magazine,
The (NY) 《歐美雜誌雙語月刊》

Express (SF) 《快報》

Fairchild Broadcasting Group (Van)
《新時代廣播集團》

Fangxia ni de bianzi (China)
《放下你的鞭子》

Far East News (LA) 《遠東時報》

Far East Times (SF) 《遠東時報》

Fengyang huagu (China) 《鳳陽花鼓》

Fengyün ernü (China) 《風雲兒女》

Formosa Weekly (Kaohsiung, then LA)
《美麗島》

Four Seas Chinese Weekly News (SJ)
《四海報》

Free China Daily (SF) 《自由中國日報》

Fujian Qiaobao (NY) 《福建僑報》

Fujian Qiaosheng (NY) 《福建僑聲》

Fujian Times (Phil) 《福建時報》

Fukien Chinese Weekly (SF)
《福建僑報》

Gangfeng Bao (Hou) 《剛峰報》

Geming (SF) 《革命》

Geming Jun (SF) 《革命軍》

Getting Together (NY, SF) 《團結報》

Global Chinese Electronic Daily News
(Hou) 《環球電子日報》

Global Chinese Press (Van, Tor)
《環球華報》

Global Chinese Times (NY, NJ)
《紐約/新洲週報》，《三州新聞》

Global Forum (SF) 《環球漫畫》

Golden Hills' News (SF) 《金山日新錄》

Golden Star Radio Hour (SF)
《金星廣播電台》

Gongchan (SF) 《共產》

Guotai Zhongwen Dianshi (Van)
《國泰中文電視》

Hai Nei Wai (NY) 《海內外》

Hawai Shimpo (Hon) 《布哇新報》

Hawaii-Chinese Journal (Hon) 《檀報》

Hawaii Chinese News (Hon)
《檀山隆記新報》，《檀山新報》

Hawaii Chinese News Broadcasting Agency
(Hon) 《檀華播音新聞社》

Hawaii Chinese News, The (Hon)
《檀華新報》

Hawaii Chinese Radio News (Hon)
《檀華播音社》

Hawaii Chinese Weekly (Hon)
《夏威夷華人周報》

Health and Life Weekly (El Monte)
《醫藥生活》

Health Today (Flushing)
《健康生活》，《今日生活》

Herald (NY, Bos, Phi, LA, SF, Van, Tor)
《號角》

Hitler's Masterpiece (SF)
《希特拉的傑作》

Hon Mun Bo (Hon) 《漢民報》

Hon Sing Chinese Community Hour (SF)
《漢聲廣播電台》

Hong Kong Daily News 《新報》

Hong Kong Economic Journal 《信報》

Hong Kong Television 《香港無綫電視台》

Hong Kong Television Broadcasts (USA)
(LA) 《翡翠電視》

Hong Sheng Dianshitai (NY)
《宏聲電視台》

Hongsheng (Hon) 《洪聲》

Honolulu Chinese Chroncle; Wah Ha Bo
《華夏報》

Honolulu Chinese Monthly
《檀山華僑月報》

Honolulu Chinese Press
《夏威夷檀山日報》

Hoo Cho Monthly (Hon) 《互助月刊》

Horn Hong Bo (SF) 《翰香報》

Hsintu (NY) 《新土》

Hu Chu (Hon) 《互助》

Hua Sheng Television (SF) 《華聲電視》

Huafeng Bao (New Orleans) 《華風報》

Huanqiu Dianzi Ribao (Hou)
《環球電子日報》

Huaqiao Gongbao (Hon) 《華僑公報》

Huaqiao Tongxun (HK) 《華僑通訊》

Huaqiao Wenzhen (NY) 《華僑文陣》

Huaren Boyinju (Hon) 《華人播音局》

Huawen Zazhi (Hon) 《華文雜誌》

Huaxia Time (LA) 《華夏週報》

Huaxia Zhi Sheng (Hou) 《華夏之聲》

Huayu Boyinshe (Hon) 《華語播音社》

Huazhong Guangbo Diantai (LA)
《華鐘廣播電台》

Humorist, The (SF) 《趣怪》
Hwa Shang Pao (HK) 《華商報》
Indo Chinese News (Cal) 《僑聲報》
Indochinese News (LA) 《越棉寮報》
International Daily News (LA)
　《國際日報》
Jiahua Qiaobao (Ottawa) 《加華僑報》
Jian'guo Bao (Manila) 《建國報》
Jinmen Yinshe Shiji (SF)
　《金門吟社詩集》
Jinshan Geji (SF) 《金山歌集》
Ju-Ri Bao (Hon) 《拒日報》
Justice News (NY) 《公和報》
Kai Chee Bo (Hon) 《啓智報》
Kai Chee Shun Bo (Hon) 《啓智新報》
Kai Min Bo (Hon) 《啓明報》
Kezhou Huabao (Denver) 《科州華報》
Kiu Kwong Pao (SF) 《僑光報》
Kuangshi Yuebao (Stockton)
　《匡時月報》
Kung Shang Yat Po (Chi) 《工商日報》
Kung Yu (SF) 《工餘》
Kwong Tai Press (LA) 《光大報》
Laodong Chao (NY) 《勞動潮》
Lap Pao Weekly (LA) 《立報》
Las Vegas Chinese News 《金城華報》
Leiyu (China) 《雷雨》
Lianbang Huayu Guangbo (LA)
　《聯邦華語廣播》
Liberty News; Chee You Shin Po (Hon)
　《自由新報》
Liberty Times (Taiwan) 《自由時報》
Life Mirror (Van) 《人生漫談》
Lifestyle Magazine (Van, Tor)
　《生活雜誌》
Liming Zhi Sheng (Van) 《黎明之聲》
Literati, The (SF) 《美華文化人報》，
　《美華文學》
Liu-Mei Xuesheng Tongxun (NY)
　《留美學生通訊》
Lüzhou (NY) 《綠洲》
Macroview Weekly (Taiwan)
　《宏觀報》，《宏觀周報》
Main Stream Broadcasting Corporation
　(Van) 《匯聲廣播有限公司》
Manitoba Chinese Post (Win)
　《緬省華報》

Manitoba Indo China Chinese News (Win)
　《越棉寮華報》
Marketing News (Cleveland)
　《推廣報》
Meidong Xinwen (NJ) 《美東新聞》
Meizhou Pinglun (SF) 《美洲評論》
Mekong Tunan Vietnam (SF) 《湄江報》
Mengcheng Huayuan (Mon)
　《蒙城華苑》
Merit Times (LA) 《人間福報》
Metro Chinese Journal (DC)
　《華府新聞報》
Miami Chinese Times 《邁亞美時報》
Min Bao (Tokyo) 《民報》
Min Chih Journal (NY) 《民治日報》
Ming Pao Daily News (HK, Van, Tor,
　NY, SF) 《明報，香港版，美國版，
　加東版，加西版，美東版，美西版》
Minority Broadcasting Inc. (SF)
　《華聲電台》
Mixigen Xinwen (Michigan)
　《密西根新聞》
Modern Times Weekly (Tor, Van)
　《時代周報》
Mon Hing Bo (SF) 《文興報》
Mon Kow (SF) 《文求》
Mon War Weekly (SF) 《文華週報》
Morning Sun, The (SF) 《公論晨報》
Mott Street Journal (NY) 《華報》
Mun Hey Weekly (NY) 《民氣週報》
Mun Hey Yat Po (NY) 《民氣日報》
Mun Sang Yat Po (Hon) 《民生日報》
Neo Asian American Times (NY)
　《新亞時報》
New Asian Times, The (NY)
　《新亞時報》
*New China News; New China Daily Press,
　Sun Chung Kwock Bo* (Hon)
　《新中國報》，《新中國日報》
New Citizen (Van, then Tor)
　《新籍民報》
New Continent (Sea, then SF)
　《新大陸》
New Era, The; Kwock Won Yat Po (SF)
　《國魂日報》
New Immigrant Report (LA)
　《新僑講座》

New Immigrant Times (LA)
《新移民時報》
New Jersey China Times 《新澤西時報》
New Kwong Tai Press (LA) 《新光大報》
New Republic, The; Sun Min Kok (Vic,
   then Van) 《新民國日報》
New Tang Dynasty Television (NY)
   《新唐人電視》
New World Broadcasting Agency (Hon)
   《新大陸播音社》
New World Times (DC) 《新世界時報》
New York China Journal; China Journal
   《紐約新聞報》
New York Community Times
   《紐約社區報》
New York Jao-Pao Weekly 《紐約週報》
Newcomers News, The; Bao Trung Nam
   (SF, Hou) 《中南報》
News Digest 《新聞文摘》
Nine O'Clock News 《九點鐘新聞》
Niuyue Gongbao 《紐約公報》
North American Weekly (SF)
   《北美週報》
Northwest Asian Weekly (Sea)
   《西華報，英文版》
OCV Broadcasting (Van)
   《華僑之聲廣播電台》
One World (SF) 《天下畫報》
Oregon Chinese News (Portland)
   《中華時刊》
Orient Vancouver 《華僑雜誌》
Oriental, The; Tung-Ngai San-Luk (SF)
   《東涯新錄》
Oriental, The; War Kee (SF)
   《華記報》，《唐番公報》，
   《華番彙報》，《中西彙報》，
   《華洋新報》，《華洋日報》
Ou-Mei Tongxun 《歐美通訊》
Ours (LA) 《我們》，《我們匯報》
Overseas Chinese Communications (SF)
   《海華電視》
Overseas Chinese Economic Journal (SF)
   《信報美洲版》
Overseas Chinese Times (Hou)
   《華僑時報》，《美華報》，
   《美洲時報》

Pacific Chronicle (Tucson) 《中原報》
Pacific Journal (LA) 《太平洋時報》
Pan Pacific TV, Inc. (SF) 《太平洋電視》
Pan-American Chinese Weekly (LA)
   《美華週報》
Passion (NY) 《角聲情》
Pearl Harbor (Hon) 《珍珠港》
Peimei News, The (NY) 《北美日報》
People and Events (NY) 《人與事》
People's Daily Overseas Edition (SF, NY,
   Tor) 《人民日報海外版》
People's News (SF) 《人報》
People's Tongue (SF) 《民口雜誌》
Pingdeng 《平等》
Portland Chinese Times 《波特蘭週報》
Power News (SF) 《炮報》
Prairie Chinese News (Win)
   《中原僑報》
Press Freedom Herald (LA)
   《新聞自由導報》
Qiaosheng Xiaoshuo Yuebao (SF)
   《僑聲小說月報》
Qiaozhong Ribao (SF) 《僑眾日報》
Qihai Dianshi [Seven seas television] (LA)
   《七海電視》
Qingjiu Tuanbao (SF) 《青救團報》
Quest, The (Beijing, then NY) 《探索》
Radio Chinese (LA) 《中文廣播電台》
Renmin huabao 《人民畫報》
Resonance (SF) 《群聲》
Rōdō Shimbun 《勞動咯東新聞》
Sacramento Chinese Community
   Newsletter 《首府華人社區月刊》
Sampan (Bos) 《舢板》
San Diego Chinese Weekly News
   《聖華週報》
San Francisco China News 《正報》
San Francisco Chinese Newspaper
   《文記唐番新報》
San Francisco Journal, The 《時代報》
San Francisco Weekly 《舊金山週報》
San Min Morning Post (Chi)
   《三民晨報》
Scholar's Digest, The (Van) 《人物評論》
Sciences of Traditional Chinese Medicine
   (Alhambra) 《中醫科學》

Seattle Chinese Community *Newsletter*
《中華月刊》

Seattle Chinese News 《西雅圖新聞》

Sha Sheng Wah Po (Saskatoon)
《沙省華報》

Shanghai Hsin Pao 《上海新報》

Shangjia Bao (Hon) 《商家報》

Shaonian Zazhi (Hon) 《少年雜誌》

Shen Pao (Shanghai) 《申報》

Shengluyi Shibao (St. Louis)
《聖路易時報》

Shijie Zhongwen Dianshi (Van)
《世界中文電視》

Guotai Zhongwen Dianshi (Van)
《國泰中文電視》

Shing Wah Po, The; *Shing Wah Daily
News, The* (Tor) 《醒華週刊》，
《醒華晨報》，《醒華日報》

Silicon Valley Hi Tech (Fremont)
《矽谷科技》

Silicon Valley Journal, The (Santa Clara)
《矽谷時報》

Silicon Valley Times, The (South SF)
《矽（硅）谷時報》

Sin Wenz Bao 《新文字報》

Sing Tao Jih Pao; *Sing Tao Daily* (HK, NY,
SF, Tor, Van) 《星島日報香港版，
美洲版，美西版，美東版，加東版，
加西版》

Sing Tao Weekly (*Sing Tao* magazine
supplement) 《星島周刊》

Singtao Times Weekly (*Sing Tao* magazine
supplement) 《星時周刊》

Sino American Daily News (SF)
《新報北美洲版》

Sino Daily Express (NY) 《華語快報》

Sino Daily Express, Queens Edition
《皇后日報》

Sino Times (Rowland Heights)
《美洲文匯周刊》

Sinocast (NY) 《華語廣播》

Sinocast Radio and Television (SF)
《華語廣播電視台》

Sino-Quebec Chinese Newspaper (Mon)
《蒙城華人報》

Sino-U.S. Weekly (LA) 《美中時報》

So-Cal Community News (Monterey Park)
《南華時報》

Sound of Hope Network
《希望之聲國際廣播電台》

*Southern Chinese News, Southern Chinese
Daily News* (Hou) 《美南新聞》

Southwest Chinese Journal (Hou)
《西南時報》

*Sui Kee American and Chinese
Commercial Newspaper* (SF)
《萃記華美新報》

Sun Yat-sen News (SF) 《中山報》

Sut Yung Ying Yee (SF) 《實用英語》

Ta Kung Pao, America Edition (SF)
《大公報美洲版》

Taipei Report (SF) 《台北情報》

Taiwan and the World (NY)
《台灣與世界》

Taiwan Culture (NY) 《台灣文化》

Taiwan Daily News (Taiwan, LA)
《台灣日報》

Taiwan Review (LA) 《台灣雜誌》

Taiwan Times (LA) 《台灣民報》

Taiwan Times (Taiwan, LA)
《台灣時報》

Taiwan Tribune (NY, then LA)
《台灣公論報》

Taiwan zijiu xuanyan 《台灣自救宣言》

Taiwanese Digest (LA) 《台灣文摘》

Taiwanese New Society (LA)
《台灣新社會》

Talentvision (Van) 《城市電視》

Tanhua Boyin Xinwenshe (Hon)
《檀華播音新聞社》

Texas Chinese Television (Hou)
《美南華語電視台》

Tien Feng (NY) 《天風》

Tien Shing Pao (SF) 《天聲報》

Tomorrow Times (Taiwan, Alhambra)
《明日報》

Toronto First Radio (Tor)
《多倫多第一台》

Tribune, The (LA) 《論壇報》

True Buddha News (Van) 《真佛報》

Truth Weekly, Truth Semi-Weekly (SF)
《正言報》，《正言半週刊》

Tsun Wan Yat Po (HK) 《循環日報》

Tzu Chi World Journal (LA) 《美國慈濟世界》

U.S. China Tribune (LA) 《美中導報》

U.S. Chinese News (SJ) 《中國先驅報》

U.S. Week (*Sing Tao* magazine supplement) 《美國周刊》

United California Communications (SF) 《天祥電視》

United Chinese News (Hon) 《中華公報》

United Chinese News (Taiwan) 《聯合日報》

United Chinese Press (Hon) 《中華新報》

United Chinese TV (SF, LA, NY, Hon, DC, Chi, Hou) 《聯合華語電視》

United Daily News (Taiwan) 《聯合日報》

United Journal, The (NY) 《聯合日報》

United Times (LA) 《聯合時報》

USAsia News (Hou) 《美亞新聞》

V. C. L. Chinese Journal (Cal, Tor, Win) 《越棉寮華報》

Very Good News (Tor) 《華報》

Vietnam Post (NY) 《越南新報》

Vietnam-Chinese Newspaper (LA) 《越華報》

Voice of Chinatown (SF) 《華埠之聲》

Voice of Oakland Chinese (Oakland) 《屋崙華人之聲》

Wa Mi San Po (LA) 《華美新報》

Wa Ying Yat Bo (Van) 《華英日報》

Wah Hing Bo (Hon) 《華興報》

Wah Kiu Yat Pao (HK, NY) 《華僑日報》

Wah Kue Pao (SF) 《華僑報》

Wah Sing Po (Mon) 《華聲報》

Waiguo jizhe xibei yinxiangji (China) 《外國記者西北印象記》

Washington China Post (DC) 《華府郵報》

Washington Chinese News (DC) 《華盛頓新聞》

Weekly Occidental, The (SF) 《中外新聞》

Wei Min Pao (SF) 《為民報》

Wen Wei Pao, America Edition (SF, Monterey Park) 《文匯報美洲版》

Wenxue Zhoukan (SF) 《文學週刊》

Wenxuecity.com

Working Together (Hon) 《聯合報》

World Channel (SF) 《世界電視》

World Journal (NY, SF, Tor, Van) 《世界日報》

World Television Corporation (NY) 《世華電視》

World Wide Chinese Journal of Montreal (Mon) 《滿地可導報》

Xi She Keyi (NY) 《曦社課藝》

Xiguang (NY) 《曦光》

Xin Shiji; La Novaj Tempoj (Paris) 《新世界》

Xindalu Boyinshe (Hon) 《新大陸播音社》

Xinmiao (NY) 《新苗》

Xinmin Congbao (Japan) 《新民叢報》

Xinmin Evening News, U.S. Edition (LA) 《新民晚報，美國版》

Yada Xinwen (Atlanta) 《亞大新聞》

Yau Bo (Hon) 《友報》

Yellow Seeds (Phil) 《黃籽報》

Yi Shi Zhu Xing (NY) 《衣食住行》

Yijiang chunshui xiang dong liu (China) 《一江春水向東流》

Yiyongjun jinxingqu (China) 《義勇軍進行曲》

Young China Morning Paper, The; The Young China Daily (SF) 《少年中國晨報》

Youth, The (SF) 《美洲少年》

Youth Daily (Taiwan) 《青年日報》

Zhandou Yuekan (SF) 《戰鬥月刊》 ooo

Zhicheng Qiao Sheng (Chi) 《芝城僑聲》

Zhong Guo Daily News (LA) 《中國日報》

Zhongguo Qiaosheng (NY) 《中國僑聲》

Zhonghua Zhi Sheng Guangbo Diantai (NY, Bos) 《中華之聲廣播電台》

Zhongsheng Guangbo Diantai (LA) 《鐘聲廣播電台》

Ziwei Yuekan (SF) 《自衛月刊》

Zuang Ren Community Journal (NY) 《存仁社區導報》

BIBLIOGRAPHY OF PUBLISHED WORKS
OF HIM MARK LAI, 1967–2008

1967

"Did the Chinese Discover America before Columbus?" *East/West, The Chinese American Journal* (December 1). San Francisco.

1968

"The Cantonese—Why They Came." *East/West, The Chinese American Journal* (February 21). San Francisco.

"The Chinese and the Railroads." *East/West, The Chinese American Journal* (October 16; November 6; December 4). San Francisco.

"Chinese in the Mining Districts." *East/West, The Chinese American Journal* (May 4; June 12; July 31). San Francisco.

"Chinese Pioneers in the 19th Century." *East/West, The Chinese American Journal* (January 3). San Francisco.

"The Honeymoon—Era of Good Feeling." *East/West, The Chinese American Journal* (March 20; April 3). San Francisco.

"More on Pioneers." *East/West, The Chinese American Journal* (January 10). San Francisco.

"Pilgrimage to the Golden Hills." *East/West, The Chinese American Journal* (September 11). San Francisco.

1969

"Chinatown Garment Industry Started a Hundred Years Ago." *East/West, The Chinese American Journal* (December 3). San Francisco.

"Chinese Big Role in Reclaiming Wastelands." *East/West, The Chinese American Journal* (May 14). San Francisco.

"Chinese in the Fields." *East/West, The Chinese American Journal* (July 9). San Francisco.

"Chinese on the Land." *East/West, The Chinese American Journal* (August 14; September 10). San Francisco.

A History of the Chinese in California, A Syllabus. With Thomas W. Chinn and Philip P. Choy. San Francisco: Chinese Historical Society of America. Reprinted 1971, 1973, 1975, 1984.

1970

"Asters and Mums." *East/West, The Chinese American Journal* (June 4). San Francisco.
"Man Quong Fong: Octogenarian Pioneer, A Man of Many Enterprises." *East/West, The Chinese American Journal* (September 9). San Francisco.

1971

"Chinese in the Public Schools." *East/West, The Chinese American Journal* (August 18; September 1, 8). San Francisco.
Outlines: History of the Chinese in America. With Philip P. Choy. San Francisco: Chinese American Studies Planning Group. Reprinted 1972, 1973, 1980.
"Reminiscences of an Old Chinese Railroad Worker." *East/West, The Chinese American Journal* (May 5). San Francisco.

1972

"A Historical Survey of Organizations of the Left among the Chinese in America." *Bulletin of Concerned Asian Scholars* (Fall). San Francisco. Revised in 1976 as "Historical Survey of the Chinese Left in America."
"History of Chinese New Year (in San Francisco)." *East/West, The Chinese American Journal* (February 16). San Francisco.

1973

"The Drama Movement in San Francisco's Chinatown." *East/West, The Chinese American Journal* (April 4). San Francisco.
"The Rise and Decline of China Alley, Hanford." *East/West, The Chinese American Journal* (September 12). San Francisco.

1974

"Chinese Hospital: An Institution of, for and by the Chinese Community." *East/West, The Chinese American Journal* (January 16). San Francisco.
"Early Chinese Americans and the Right to Fight." *East/West, The Chinese American Journal* (October 30). San Francisco.
"In Unity There Is Strength: Chinese Workers' Fight for a Better Life." *East/West, The Chinese American Journal* (May 1). San Francisco.

1975

A History of the Sam Yup Benevolent Association of San Francisco. With Yuk Ow and Philip P. Choy. San Francisco: Sam Yup Association of San Francisco.

1976

"Blood and Sweat in the Golden Mountains." *East/West, The Chinese American Journal* (January 1). San Francisco.

"A Brief History of the *Chinese World.*" *Bulletin* (December). San Francisco: Chinese Historical Society of America.

"Chinese Experience at Angel Island." *East/West: The Chinese American Journal* (February 11, 18, 25). San Francisco.

"Chinese Politics and the U.S. Chinese Communities." *Counterpoint: Perspectives on Asian America.* Los Angeles: UCLA Asian American Studies Center.

"Historical Survey of the Chinese Left in America." *Counterpoint: Perspectives on Asian America.* Los Angeles: UCLA Asian American Studies Center. Revision of "A Historical Survey of Organizations of the Left among the Chinese in America" (1972).

1977

"The Angel Island Immigration Station." *Bridge Magazine* (April). New York.

Chinese Newspapers Published in North America, 1854–1975. With Karl Lo. Washington, D.C.: Center for Chinese Research Materials, Association of Research Libraries.

"Growing Wings on the Dragon." *East/West, The Chinese American Journal* (January 26). San Francisco.

1978

"The Chinese Language Sources Bibliography Project: Preliminary Findings." *Amerasia Journal* vol. 5, no. 2. Los Angeles: UCLA Asian American Studies Center.

"Island of Immortals: The Chinese and the Angel Island Immigration Station." *California Historical Quarterly* (Spring). San Francisco.

1980

Chinese of America, 1785–1980. With Joe Huang and Don Wong. San Francisco: Chinese Culture Foundation of San Francisco.

"Chinese on the Continental U.S." *Harvard Encyclopedia of American Ethnic Groups.* Cambridge, Mass.: Belknap Press.

Island: Poetry and History of Chinese Immigrants on Angel Island, 1910–1940. With Genny Lim and Judy Yung. San Francisco: Chinese Culture Foundation of San Francisco. Reprinted 1986; Seattle: University of Washington Press.

1980–81

"Roots and Linkages: A Journey through the Pearl River Delta." *East/West, The Chinese American Journal* (March 19; April 9, 16, 23; June 25; July 2; September 10; December 10, 1980; January 7; February 4, 1981). San Francisco.

1980–84

"Meiguo Huaqiao jianshi" [A short history of the Chinese in America]. *Shidaibao: San Francisco Journal* (April 2, 1980–November 13, 1984). San Francisco.

1981

"A Memorable Day 70 Years Ago." *Bulletin* (October, November). San Francisco: Chinese Historical Society of America.

1982

"The Chinese Exclusion Act: A Centennial." *East/West, The Chinese American Journal* (January 27). San Francisco.

"The Chinese Exclusion Act: Observations of a Centennial." *Amerasia Journal* vol. 9, no. 1. Los Angeles: UCLA Asian American Studies Center.

"Guangdong: The Heritage of 17.5 Million Overseas Chinese." *East/West, The Chinese American Journal* (July 7). San Francisco.

1983

"19 shiji Meiguo Huawen baoye xiaoshi" [A short history of the Chinese American press in the 19th century]. *Huaqiao lishi xuehui tongxin* no. 2 (June). Beijing. Reprinted 1989 in *Huaqiao Huaren shi yanjiuji* [Collection of essays on research into overseas Chinese history], vol. 2; Beijing. Reprinted 1984 as "19 shiji Meiguo Huawen baoye fazhan xiaoshi" [A short history of the development of the Chinese language press in America during the nineteenth century], in *Huaqiao shi yanjiu lunji* [Collection of essays on research into overseas Chinese history], vol. 1; Shanghai.

1984

"Some Notes on the Research on Overseas Chinese History in China in Recent Years." *Bulletin* (November). San Francisco: Chinese Historical Society of America.

"Sprouting Wings on the Dragon: Some Chinese Americans Who Contributed to the Development of Aviation in China." *Annals of the Chinese Historical Society of the Pacific Northwest*. Bellingham, Wash.

1985

"The Chinese Americans from Taiwan: A Rapidly Growing Community." *East/West, The Chinese American Journal* (November 20). San Francisco.

"The Overseas Chinese: Their Sun Never Sets." *East/West, The Chinese American Journal* (November 27). San Francisco.

"South of Sahara Chinese Have 1,300 Year History." *East/West, The Chinese American Journal* (October 9). San Francisco.

"Walter U. Lum: Chinese American Pioneer and Civil Rights Leader." *East/West, The Chinese American Journal* (February 27). San Francisco.

1986

"China Revisited, 1986: 'The Chinese of America Exhibit in the PRC.'" *East/West, The Chinese American Journal* (November 27). San Francisco.

"The Chinese Expulsion from Seattle in 1886." *East/West, The Chinese American Journal* (February 20). San Francisco.

"Chinese-Language TV Flourishes in Bay Area: 36 Hours Weekly in Cantonese and Mandarin." *East/West, The Chinese American Journal* (July 10). San Francisco.

"Chinese of America Exhibit in China." *Bulletin* (December). San Francisco: Chinese Historical Society of America.

"Chinese Word Processing Joins America's Computer Revolution." With Max Millard. *East/West, The Chinese American Journal* (July 31). San Francisco.

A History Reclaimed: An Annotated Bibliography of Chinese Language Materials on the Chinese of America. Los Angeles: UCLA Asian American Studies Center.

"Notes on Chinese American Historical Research in the United States." With Wei Chi Poon. *Amerasia Journal* vol. 12, no. 2. Los Angeles: UCLA Asian American Studies Center.

"Overseas Chinese Have Played Major Role in Educational Progress in Guangdong." *East/West, The Chinese American Journal* (March 6). San Francisco.

Preface to *Jinshan lu manman* [The road to the golden mountain is very long], by Cui Shuzhi and Feng Yimin. Beijing: Xinhua Publishing Company. [Translation of Diane Mark and Ginger Chih, *A Place Called Chinese America*.]

"Qianshuo zai Mei Huaren lishi de yanjiu" [Notes on Chinese American Studies]. With Wei Chi Poon. *Qiaoshi xuebao,* [Journal of Overseas Chinese History] (December). Guangzhou.

"Roots and Chinese American Heritage." *East/West, The Chinese American Journal* (April 24). San Francisco.

"Spring Festival Time in Modern Guangzhou." *East/West, The Chinese American Journal* (February 6). San Francisco.

"The Ups and Downs of the Chinese Press in the U.S." *East/West, The Chinese American Journal* (November 20). San Francisco.

1987

"The Chinese American Press." In *The Ethnic Press in the United States: A Historical Analysis and Handbook.* Edited by Sally M. Miller. Westport, Conn.: Greenwood Press.

"Historical Development of the Chinese Consolidated Benevolent Association/Huiguan System." *Chinese America: History and Perspectives.* San Francisco: Chinese Historical Society of America.

1988

"Chinese American Studies: A Historical Survey." *Chinese America: History and Perspectives.* San Francisco: Chinese Historical Society of America.

1989

"China Events Leave Some Chinese Newspapers Split and Confused." *East/West, The Chinese American Journal* (August 10). San Francisco.

"Chronology of Modern Chinese Student Protest Movements." *East/West, The Chinese American Journal* (June 15). San Francisco.

"An Historical Overview of Popular Protests in China and Repression." *East/West, The Chinese American Journal* (July 13). San Francisco.

"Yige di'er dai Huaren de zishu" [Autobiography of a second generation Chinese]. *Qiaoshi xuebao* [Journal of Overseas Chinese History], nos. 1 (June), 2 (September). Guangzhou. Reprinted 1991 as "Meiji Huaren xuezhe Mai Liqian zizhuan" [Autobiography of the Chinese American scholar Him Mark Lai], in *Haiwa Huaren shehui kexuejia zhuanji* [Biographies of social scientists among Chinese abroad]. Guangzhou: Guangdong renmin chubanshe.

1990

"The Chinese Press in the United States and Canada Since World War II: A Diversity of Voices." *Chinese America: History and Perspectives.* San Francisco: Chinese Historical Society of America.

1991

"The Guangdong Historical Background, with Emphasis on the Development of the Pearl River Delta Region." *Chinese America: History and Perspectives.* San Francisco: Chinese Historical Society of America.

Hu Jingnan wenji [Selected essays of Gilbert Woo]. Hong Kong: Heung Kong Publishing Company.

"The Kuomintang in Chinese American Communities before World War II." In *Entry Denied: Exclusion and the Chinese Community in America.* Edited by Sucheng Chan. Philadelphia: Temple University Press.

Review of L. Eve Armentrout Ma, *Revolutionaries, Monarchists, and Chinatown: Chinese Politics in the Americas and the 1911 Revolution* (Honolulu: University of Hawaii Press, 1990). *BC Studies* no. 90 (Summer). Vancouver.

1992

Cong Huaqiao dao Huaren: Ershi shiji Meiguo Huaren shehui fazhan shi [From overseas Chinese to Chinese America: A history of the development of Chinese American society during the twentieth century]. Hong Kong: Joint Publishing Company.

"Occupational Structures of Chinese Immigrants in Early Malaya and North America." With Mark Lau Fong. *Southeast Asian Journal of Social Science* 20, no. 1. Singapore.

"To Bring Forth a New China, to Build a Better America: The Chinese Marxist Left in America to the 1960s." *Chinese America: History and Perspectives.* San Francisco: Chinese Historical Society of America.

"A Voice of Reason: Life and Times of Gilbert Woo, Chinese American Journalist." *Chinese America: History and Perspectives.* San Francisco: Chinese Historical Society of America.

1993

Chinese in America: A Photographic Exhibition Catalog. With Eileen Seeto Collins. Millbrae, Calif.: Nan Hai Company, Inc.

"Meiguo de yige Huaren tongxiang shequn: Zuji Guangdong Hua Xian Huaren de fazhan shi" [A fellow villagers group in the United States: History of the development of the Chinese of Hua Xian, Guangdong ancestry]. *Zhongguo haiyang fazhanshi lunwenji: Essays in Chinese Maritime History.* Vol. 5. Nankang, Taiwan: Sun Yat-Sen Institute for Social Sciences and Philosophy, Academia Sinica.

"*Meiguo Huaqiao Shi* duanping" [Brief review of Yang Guobiao, et al., *Meiguo Huaqiao Shi* (History of the Chinese in America)]. *Qiaoshi xuebao* [Journal of Overseas Chinese History] nos. 1, 2. Guangzhou.

Review of Wu Chien-shiung, *Haiwai yimin yu Huaren shehui* [Overseas immigration and the Chinese society]. *The Continent Magazine* 87, no. 4 (October). Taipei, Taiwan.

"Zatan Zhongguo chuqi hangkongshi de yanjiu" [Miscellaneous aspects in the study of early aviation history in China]. In Liu Zhongmin, *Taishan jindai hangkong renwu lu* [Taishanese connected with aviation in modern times]. Taishan: Overseas Chinese Historical Society of Taishan.

1994

"Chinese American History: Achievements, Problems, Prospects." *Origins and Destinations: 41 Essays on Chinese America.* Los Angeles: Chinese Historical Society of Southern California and UCLA Asian American Studies Center.

"Chinese Regional Solidarity: Case Study of the Hua Xian (Fa Yuen) Community in California." *Chinese America: History and Perspectives.* San Francisco: Chinese Historical Society of America.

"Meiguo 'Yue Mian Liao' Huaren tongxiang zuzhi chutan" [A first probe into fellow townsmen organizations of Chinese in America from Vietnam, Cambodia, and Laos]. *Overseas Chinese History of Bagui,* no. 2. Nanning. Reprinted 1994 as "Zai Meiguo de Yue Mian Liao Huaren tongxiang zhuzhi" [Fellow townsmen organizations of Chinese from Vietnam, Cambodia, and Laos in America], in *The Overseas Chinese* nos. 1–2. Guangzhou.

"Unfinished Business: The Confession Program." *The Repeal and Its Legacy: Proceedings of the Conference Commemorating the 50th Anniversary of the Repeal of the Exclusion Acts.* San Francisco: Chinese Historical Society of America and San Francisco State University Asian American Studies.

1995

The Asian American Encyclopedia. Consulting editor and contributing writer. 6 vols. New York, London, and Toronto: Marshall Cavendish. [Contributed 38 articles.]

Preface to Liu Xiaoli (Lily Liu), *Da yingjia: 100 wei dingjian Huaren* [The Ultimate Winners]. Millbrae, Calif.: Think Big Publishing Company.

"A Tale of Two Brothers: Jung Oi-won and Ming S. Jung." *Chinese America: History and Perspectives.* San Francisco: Chinese Historical Society of America.

Thirty Years of the Chinese Culture Foundation and Twenty-two Years of the Chinese Culture of San Francisco. San Francisco: Chinese Culture Foundation.

1996

"Chinese Organizations in America Based on Locality of Origin and/or Dialect-Group Affiliation, 1940s–1990s." *Chinese America: History and Perspectives*. San Francisco: Chinese Historical Society of America.

1997

"Chinese in America and the War of Resistance against Japan." *Papers of the International Conference on the Fiftieth Anniversary of the War of Resistance*. Taipei: Academia Historica.

"Roles Played by Chinese in America during China's Resistance to Japanese Aggression and during World War II." *Chinese America: History and Perspectives*. San Francisco: Chinese Historical Society of America.

1998

"Chinese Communities: The United States." In *The Encyclopedia of the Chinese Overseas*. Edited by Lynn Pan. Singapore: Chinese Heritage Centre [English edition]; Chinese edition translated by Choi Kwai Keong (Hong Kong: Joint Publishing Company [traditional and simplified character editions]; Cambridge, Mass.: Harvard University Press [English edition]).

"Developments in Chinese Community Organizations in the US since World War II." In *The Chinese Diaspora: Selected Essays*. Edited by Ling-chi Wang and Wang Gungwu. Vol. 1. Singapore: Times Academic Press.

Foreword to Emma Woo Louie, *Chinese American Names*. Jefferson, N.C.: McFarland & Co.

"Potato King and Film Producer, Flower Growers, Professionals, and Activists: The Huangliang Du Community in Northern California." *Chinese America: History and Perspectives*. San Francisco: Chinese Historical Society of America.

Preface to Lani Ah Tye Farkas, *Bury My Bones in America*. Nevada City, Calif.: Carl Mautz Publishing.

1999

"China and the Chinese American Community: The Political Dimension." *Chinese America: History and Perspectives*. San Francisco: Chinese Historical Society of America.

Huaqiao Huaren baikequanshu [Encyclopedia of Chinese overseas]. Consulting editor and contributing author for articles on Chinese schools in the Americas and Hawaii, scientific and technical organizations, and educational foundations. Volume on Education, Science, and Technology. Beijing: Zhongguo Huaqiao chubanshe.

Review of Andrew Gyory, *Closing the Gate: Race, Politics, and the Chinese Exclusion Act* (Chapel Hill: University of North Carolina Press, 1998). *California History* (Winter 1999/2000). San Francisco.

2000

"A History of the Sam Yup Benevolent Association in the United States." In *A History of the Sam Yup Benevolent Association in the United States*. San Francisco: Sam Yup Benevolent Association.

"The Report Transmitting the Register of Schools of Overseas Chinese in North America to the Ministry of Education, Second Year of the Xuantong Reign Era [1910]." Translated with Ellen L. S. Yeung. *Chinese America: History and Perspectives*. San Francisco: Chinese Historical Society of America.

"Retention of the Chinese Heritage: Chinese Schools in America." In *Intercultural Relations, Cultural Transformation, and Identity: The Ethnic Chinese*. Edited by Teresita Ang See. Manila: Kaisa Para Sa Kaunlaran, Inc. Revised and divided into two parts; first part published as "Retention of the Chinese Heritage: Chinese Schools in America before World War II." *Chinese America: History and Perspectives*. San Francisco: Chinese Historical Society of America.

2001

"Aerospace to Cyberspace: Honoring Chinese Americans in Science and Technology. In the Beginning: From the Nineteenth Century through the 1960s," In *Aerospace to Cyberspace: Chinese Historical Society of America 38th Anniversary Luncheon Celebration*. San Francisco: Chinese Historical Society of America.

Foreword to *Bridging the Centuries: History of Chinese Americans in Southern California*. Los Angeles: Chinese Historical Society of Southern California, 2001.

"Mingke Meiguo Huarenshi: Mai Liqian fangtanlu" [Engraving Chinese American history in the mind: Interview with Him Mark Lai]. In Shan Dexing (Shan Te-hsing). *Duihua yu jiaoliu: Dangdai Zhongwai zuojia, pipingjia fangtanglu* [Dialogues and Interchanges: Interviews with Contemporary Writers and Critics]. Taipei: Rye Field Publications.

"Retention of the Chinese Heritage: Chinese Schools in America. Part II: From World War II to the Present." *Chinese America: History and Perspectives*. San Francisco: Chinese Historical Society of America.

Review of Ni Huiru, *Zheng Ningyuan, Ganlan Guiguan de Zhaohuan: Canjia Sibanya Neizhan de Zhongguoren (1936–1939)* [Nancy and Len Tsou, The Call of Spain: The Chinese Volunteers in the Spanish Civil War (1936–1939)] (Taipei: Renjian Chubanshe). *The Volunteer.*

Shijie Huaqiao Huaren baikequanshu: Zhuzuo xueshu juan [Encyclopedia of Chinese overseas: Volume of Academic Works]. Articles in Chinese describing Sucheng Chan's *Entry Denied,* Andrew Gyory's *Closing the Gate,* and Renqiu Yu's *To Save China, to Save Ourselves.* Beijing: Zhongguo Huaqiao Chubanshe.

2002

"Development of Chinese Schools in America after World War II." In *Essays on Ethnic Chinese Abroad, Volume III, Culture, Education and Identity.* Edited by Tsun-Wu Chang and Shi-Yeoung Tang. Taipei: Overseas Chinese Association.

Foreword to Peter H. Koehn and Xiao-Huang Yin, ed. *The Expanding Roles of Chinese Americans in U.S.-China Relations: Transnational Networks and Trans-Pacific Interactions.* Armonk, N.Y.: M. E. Sharpe.

"The 'In Search of Roots' Program: Constructing Identity through Family History Research and a Journey to the Ancestral Land." With Albert Cheng. In *The Chinese in America: A History from Gold Mountain to the New Millenium*. Edited by Susie Lan Cassel. Walnut Creek, Calif.: AltaMira Press.

Introduction to Peter H. Koehn and Xiao-Huang Yin, *Chinese Americans and U.S.-China Relations: Presence and Promise for the Pacific Century*. Armonk, N.Y.: M.E. Sharpe.

Review of Gordon H. Chang, ed. *Asian Americans and Politics: Perspectives, Experiences, and Prospects* (Washington, D.C., and Stanford, Calif.: Woodrow Wilson Center Press and Stanford University Press). *California Historical Quarterly* 81, no. 1. San Francisco.

Shijie Huaqiao Huaren baikequanshu, zonglun [Encyclopedia of Chinese overseas, Volume of General Studies]. Chinese translations of "Retention of the Chinese Heritage: Chinese Schools in America before World War II" and "Retention of the Chinese Heritage: Chinese Schools in America. Part II: From World War II to the Present." Beijing: Zhongguo Huaqiao Chubanshe.

2003

Introduction to *Bridging the Centuries: History of Chinese Americans in Southern California*. Los Angeles: Chinese Historical Society of Southern California.

Review of Adam McKeown, *Chinese Migrant Networks and Cultural Change: Peru, Chicago, Hawaii, 1900–1936* (Chicago: University of Chicago Press, 2001). *Journal of Interdisciplinary History* (Spring). Cambridge, Mass.

Translations of "Open Letter from Chinese in Tonopah, Nevada" and "Letter from Chinese Consolidated Benevolent Association Replying to Tonopah Chinese Community." *Chinese America: History and Perspectives*. San Francisco: Chinese Historical Society of America.

2004

Becoming Chinese American: A History of Communities and Institutions. New York: AltaMira Press.

2006

Chinese American Voices. With Judy Yung and Gordon Chang. Berkeley: University of California Press.

"Teaching Chinese Americans to Be Chinese: Curriculum, Teachers, and Textbooks in Chinese Schools in America during the Exclusion Era." In *Chinese American Transnationalism: The Flow of People, Resources, and Ideas between China and America during the Exclusion Era*. Edited by Sucheng Chan. Philadelphia: Temple University Press.

2008

"Chinese Guilds in the Apparel Industry of San Francisco." *Chinese America: History and Perspectives*. San Francisco: Chinese Historical Society of America.

"Guilds, Unions, and Garment Factories Notes on Chinese in the Apparel Industry." With Russell Jeung. *Chinese America: History and Perspectives.* San Francisco: Chinese Historical Society of America.

Translation and annotation of "History of Meizhou Gongyi Tongmeng Zonghui" [Unionist Guild of America]. *Chinese America: History and Perspectives.* San Francisco: Chinese Historical Society of America.

SELECTED ENGLISH-LANGUAGE
READINGS ON CHINESE AMERICAN HISTORY

Compiled by Madeline Y. Hsu

(with contributions from Roger Daniels,
Erika Lee, and Mae Ngai)

Aarim-Heriot, Najia. *Chinese Immigrants, African Americans, and Racial Anxiety in the United States, 1848–82.* Urbana: University of Illinois Press, 2003.

Armentrout-Ma, Eve. *Revolutionaries, Monarchists, and Chinatowns: Chinese Politics in the Americas and the 1911 Revolution.* Honolulu: University of Hawaii Press, 1990.

Bao, Xiaolan. *Holding Up More Than Half the Sky: Chinese Women Garment Workers in New York City, 1948–92.* Urbana: University of Illinois Press, 2001.

Brooks, Charlotte. *Alien Neighbors, Foreign Friends: Asian Americans, Housing, and the Transformation of Urban California.* Chicago: University of Chicago Press, 2009.

Chan, Sucheng. *This Bittersweet Soil: The Chinese in California Agriculture, 1860–1910.* Berkeley: University of California Press, 1986.

Chen, Shehong. *Being Chinese, Becoming Chinese American.* Urbana: University of Illinois Press, 2006.

Chen, Yong. *Chinese San Francisco, 1850–1943: A Trans-Pacific Community.* Stanford, Calif.: Stanford University Press, 2000.

Chin, Margaret M. *Sewing Women: Immigrants and the New York City Garment Industry.* New York: Columbia University Press, 2005.

Choy, Philip, Lorraine Dong, and Marlon K. Hom, eds. *The Coming Man: Nineteenth-Century American Perceptions of the Chinese.* Seattle: University of Washington Press, 1995.

Chun, Gloria Heyung. *Of Orphans and Warriors: Inventing Chinese American Culture and Identity.* New Brunswick, N.J.: Rutgers University Press, 2000.

Chung, Sue Fawn and Priscilla Wegars, ed., *Chinese American Death Rituals: Respecting the Ancestors.* Lanham, Md.: AltaMira Press, 2005.

Daniels, Roger. *Asian America: Chinese and Japanese in the United States since 1850.* Seattle: University of Washington Press, 1988.

Fong, Timothy P. *The First Suburban Chinatown: The Remaking of Monterey Park, California.* Philadelphia: Temple University Press, 1994.

Fowler, Josephine. *Japanese and Chinese Immigrant Activists: Organizing in American and International Communist Movements, 1919–1933.* New Brunswick, N.J.: Rutgers University Press, 2007.

Friday, Chris. *Organizing Asian American Labor: The Pacific Coast Canned-Salmon Industry, 1870–1942.* Philadelphia: Temple University Press, 1994.

Hom, Marlon K. *Songs of Gold Mountain: Cantonese Rhymes from San Francisco Chinatown.* Berkeley: University of California Press, 1987.

Hsu, Madeline. *Dreaming of Gold, Dreaming of Home: Transnationalism and Migration between the United States and South China, 1882–1943.* Stanford, Calif.: Stanford University Press, 2000.

Jung, Moon-Ho. *Coolies and Cane: Race, Labor, and Sugar in the Age of Emancipation.* Baltimore: Johns Hopkins University Press, 2006.

Kwong, Peter. *Chinatown, New York: Labor and Politics, 1930–1950.* New York: Monthly Review Press, 1979.

Lee, Erika. *At America's Gates: Chinese Immigration During the Exclusion Era, 1882–1943.* Chapel Hill: University of North Carolina Press, 2003.

Lee, Rose Hum. *The Chinese in the United States of America.* Hong Kong: Hong Kong University Press, 1960.

Leong, Karen J. *The China Mystique: Pearl S. Buck, Anna May Wong, Mayling Soong, and the Transformation of American Orientalism.* Berkeley: University of California Press, 2005.

Liu, Haiming. *The Transnational History of a Chinese Family: Immigrant Letters, Family Business and Reverse Migration.* New Brunswick, N.J.: Rutgers University Press, 2005.

Lui, Mary Ting-Yi. *The Chinatown Trunk Mystery: Murder, Miscegenation, and Other Dangerous Encounters in Turn-of-the-Century New York City.* Princeton, N.J.: Princeton University Press, 2005.

Lydon, Sandy. *Chinese Gold: The Chinese in the Monterey Bay Region.* Capitola, Calif.: Capitola Book Company, 1985.

Lyman, Stanford M. *Chinese Americans.* New York: Random House, Inc., 1974.

McClain, Charles J. *In Search of Equality: The Chinese Struggle against Discrimination in Nineteenth-Century America.* Berkeley: University of California Press, 1994.

McCunn, Ruthanne Lum. *Chinese American Portraits: Personal Histories, 1828–1988.* San Francisco: Chronicle Books, 1988.

McKeown, Adam. *Chinese Migrant Networks and Cultural Change: Peru, Chicago, Hawaii, 1900–1936.* Chicago: University of Chicago Press, 2001.

Miller, Stuart Creighton. *The Unwelcome Immigrant: The American Image of the Chinese, 1785–1882.* Berkeley: University of California Press, 1969.

Nee, Victor G. and Brett de Bary Nee. *Longtime Californ': A Documentary Study of an American Chinatown.* Stanford, Calif.: Stanford University Press, 1986 [1973].

Ngai, Moe M. *Impossible Subjects: Illegal Aliens and the Making of Modern America.* Princeton, N.J.: Princeton University Press, 2004.

Peffer, George Anthony. *If They Don't Bring Their Women Here: Chinese Female Immigration before Exclusion.* Urbana: University of Illinois Press, 1999.

Salyer, Lucy E. *Laws Harsh as Tigers: Chinese Immigrants and the Shaping of Modern Immigration Law.* Chapel Hill: University of North Carolina Press, 1995.

Sandmeyer, Elmer Clarence. *The Anti-Chinese Movement in California.* Urbana: University of Illinois Press, 1991 [1973].

Saxton, Alexander. *The Indispensable Enemy: Labor and the Anti-Chinese Movement in California.* Berkeley: University of California Press, 1995 [1971].

Shah, Nayan. *Contagious Divides: Epidemics and Race in San Francisco's Chinatown.* Berkeley: University of California Press, 2001.

Siu, Paul C.P. *The Chinese Laundryman: A Study of Social Isolation.* Edited by John Kuo Wei Tchen. New York: New York University Press, 1987.

Tchen, John Kuo Wei. *New York Before Chinatown: Orientalism and the Shaping of American Culture, 1776–1882*. Baltimore: Johns Hopkins University Press, 1999.

Tsai, Shih-shan Henry. *China and the Overseas Chinese in the United States, 1868–1911*. Fayetteville: University of Arkansas Press, 1983.

Wang, Guanhua. *In Search of Justice: The 1905–1906 Chinese Anti-American Boycott*. Cambridge, Mass.: Harvard University Press, 2001.

Wei, William. *The Asian American Movement*. Philadelphia: Temple University Press, 1993.

Wong, Kevin Scott. *Americans First: Chinese Americans and the Second World War*. Cambridge, Mass.: Harvard University Press, 2005.

Ye, Weili. *Seeking Modernity in China's Name: Chinese Students in the United States, 1900–1927*. Stanford, Calif.: Stanford University Press, 2001.

Yin, Xiao-huang. *Chinese American Literature since the 1850s*. Urbana: University of Illinois Press, 2000.

Yu, Henry. *Thinking Orientals: Migration, Contact, and Exclusion in Modern America*. New York: Oxford University Press, 2001.

Yu, Renqiu. *To Save China, To Save Ourselves: The Chinese Hand Laundry Alliance of New York*. Philadelphia: Temple University Press, 1992.

Yung, Judy. *Unbound Feet: A Social History of Chinese Women in San Francisco*. Berkeley: University of California Press, 1995.

Zhao, Xiaojian. *Remaking Chinese America: Immigration, Family, and Community, 1940–1965*. New Brunswick, N.J.: Rutgers University Press, 2002.

INDEX

CCP in index refers to the Chinese Communist Party. CPUSA refers to the Communist Party of the United States of America. KMT refers to the Kuomintang.

Known as "the dean of Chinese American studies," **HIM MARK LAI** (1925–2009) was an independent historian and an adjunct professor of Asian American studies at San Francisco State University. His influential works included *Becoming Chinese American: A History of Communities and Institutions*. **MADELINE Y. HSU** is an associate professor of history and the director of the Center for Asian American Studies at the University of Texas, Austin.

THE ASIAN AMERICAN EXPERIENCE

The Hood River Issei: An Oral History of Japanese Settlers in Oregon's Hood
 River Valley   *Linda Tamura*
Americanization, Acculturation, and Ethnic Identity: The Nisei Generation in Hawaii
 Eileen H. Tamura
Sui Sin Far/Edith Maude Eaton: A Literary Biography   *Annette White-Parks*
Mrs. Spring Fragrance and Other Writings   *Sui Sin Far; edited by Amy Ling and
 Annette White-Parks*
The Golden Mountain: The Autobiography of a Korean Immigrant, 1895–1960
 Easurk Emsen Charr; edited and with an introduction by Wayne Patterson
Race and Politics: Asian Americans, Latinos, and Whites in a Los Angeles Suburb
 Leland T. Saito
Achieving the Impossible Dream: How Japanese Americans Obtained Redress
 Mitchell T. Maki, Harry H. L. Kitano, and S. Megan Berthold
If They Don't Bring Their Women Here: Chinese Female Immigration before Exclusion
 George Anthony Peffer
Growing Up Nisei: Race, Generation, and Culture among Japanese Americans of
 California, 1924–49   *David K. Yoo*
Chinese American Literature since the 1850s   *Xiao-huang Yin*
Pacific Pioneers: Japanese Journeys to America and Hawaii, 1850–80
 John E. Van Sant
Holding Up More Than Half the Sky: Chinese Women Garment Workers in
 New York City, 1948–92   *Xiaolan Bao*
Onoto Watanna: The Story of Winnifred Eaton   *Diana Birchall*
Edith and Winnifred Eaton: Chinatown Missions and Japanese Romances
 Dominika Ferens
Being Chinese, Becoming Chinese American   *Shehong Chen*
"A Half Caste" and Other Writings   *Onoto Watanna; edited by Linda Trinh Moser
 and Elizabeth Rooney*
Chinese Immigrants, African Americans, and Racial Anxiety in the United States,
 1848–82   *Najia Aarim-Heriot*
Not Just Victims: Conversations with Cambodian Community Leaders in the
 United States   *Edited and with an Introduction by Sucheng Chan; interviews
 conducted by Audrey U. Kim*
The Japanese in Latin America   *Daniel M. Masterson with Sayaka Funada-Classen*
Survivors: Cambodian Refugees in the United States   *Sucheng Chan*
From Concentration Camp to Campus: Japanese American Students and
 World War II   *Allan W. Austin*
Japanese American Midwives: Culture, Community, and Health Politics
 Susan L. Smith
In Defense of Asian American Studies: The Politics of Teaching and Program Building
 Sucheng Chan
Lost and Found: Reclaiming the Japanese American Incarceration
 Karen L. Ishizuka
Religion and Spirituality in Korean America   *Edited by David Yoo and
 Ruth H. Chung*

The University of Illinois Press
is a founding member of the
Association of American University Presses.

———————————————————————

Composed in 10.5/13 Adobe Minion Pro
by Jim Proefrock
at the University of Illinois Press
Manufactured by Thomson-Shore, Inc.

University of Illinois Press
1325 South Oak Street
Champaign, IL 61820-6903
www.press.uillinois.edu